American Foreign Policy Since World War II

21st Edition

To John Spanier, whose passion for American Foreign Policy began when he escaped from Germany. His students learned for decades.

Sara Miller McCune founded SAGE Publishing in 1965 to support the dissemination of usable knowledge and educate a global community. SAGE publishes more than 1000 journals and over 800 new books each year, spanning a wide range of subject areas. Our growing selection of library products includes archives, data, case studies and video. SAGE remains majority owned by our founder and after her lifetime will become owned by a charitable trust that secures the company's continued independence.

Los Angeles | London | New Delhi | Singapore | Washington DC | Melbourne

American Foreign Policy Since World War II

21st Edition

Steven W. Hook
Kent State University, USA

John Spanier
University of Florida, USA

FOR INFORMATION:

CQ Press

An Imprint of SAGE Publications, Inc.

2455 Teller Road

Thousand Oaks, California 91320

E-mail: order@sagepub.com

SAGE Publications Ltd.

1 Oliver's Yard

55 City Road

London EC1Y 1SP

United Kingdom

SAGE Publications India Pvt. Ltd.

B 1/I 1 Mohan Cooperative Industrial Area

Mathura Road, New Delhi 110 044

India

SAGE Publications Asia-Pacific Pte. Ltd.

3 Church Street

#10-04 Samsung Hub

Singapore 049483

Printed in the United Kingdom by Ashford Colour Press Ltd.

Library of Congress Cataloging-in-Publication Data

Names: Hook, Steven W., 1959- author. | Spanier, John W.

Title: American foreign policy since World War II / Steven W. Hook, Kent State University, USA, John Spanier, University of Florida, USA.

Description: 21st edition. | Los Angeles : CQ Press, 2019. | Includes bibliographical references and index.

Identifiers: LCCN 2017042446 | ISBN **9781544326856** (pbk. : alk. paper)

Subjects: LCSH: United States—Foreign relations—1945–1989. | United States—Foreign relations—1989-

Classification: LCC E744 .H646 2018 | DDC 327.73009/04—dc23
LC record available at https://lccn.loc.gov/2017042446

This book is printed on acid-free paper.

Acquisitions Editor: Scott Greenan

Editorial Assistant: Sarah Christensen

Production Editor: Myleen Medina

Copy Editor: Diane DiMura

Typesetter: C&M Digitals (P) Ltd.

Proofreader: Talia Greenberg

Indexer: Sylvia Coates

Cover Designer: Scott Van Atta

Marketing Manager: Jennifer Jones

19 20 21 22 10 9 8 7 6 5 4

Brief Contents

Detailed Contents

Preface

This book seeks to bring about a greater understanding of America's current challenges by exploring its historical experience as the world's predominant power since World War II. As we will find, the United States has pursued its goals overseas with a distinctive national style that is deeply ingrained in the nation's political and societal culture. Both the monumental achievements of the U.S. government and its many foreign policy setbacks can be attributed to the nation's constructed identity as an exceptional world power uniquely qualified not simply to dominate but to remake the world order in its own image.

It is often argued that American primacy is unique in that, by the end of World War II, the nation found itself leading an "empire by invitation."[1] The United States had resisted the great-power politics of previous eras while playing the crucial role in the two world wars. America's success left it atop the global balance of power. Most foreign governments, which viewed the United States as a reassuring rather than menacing force, chose to *bandwagon* with Washington rather than *balance* against it.[2]

As American leaders took the lead in creating the United Nations, supporting the decolonization of Africa and other developing regions, and laying the foundations of a stable global economy, they seemed to have realized the nation's greatest ambitions. Their self-confidence was reinforced by the nation's success in the Cold War, a half-century struggle with the Soviet Union and its communist allies that, far from liberating their citizens, merely denied their economic needs and political freedoms. As we will find, the Cold War's peaceful conclusion brought little relief to the United States.

The first decades of the twenty-first century were devastating for the United States. The 9/11 terrorist attacks prompted President George W. Bush to declare a "war on terror" that would dominate American foreign policy throughout his two terms. His choice to invade Iraq in 2013 was found to be based on faulty intelligence. Taken together, the two wars exhausted the Pentagon and cost taxpayers an estimated $2 trillion. Another blow came

---

[1] Geir Lundestad, "Empire by Invitation? The United States and Western Europe, 1945–1952," *Journal of Peace Research* 23 (1986): 263–277.

[2] For two recent perspectives, see Robert Kagan, *The World America Made* (New York: Knopf, 2012), and G. John Ikenberry, *Liberal Leviathan: The Origins, Crisis, and Transformation of the American World Order* (Princeton, N.J.: Princeton University Press, 2011).

in 2008 when reckless lending by U.S. financial institutions triggered an economic crisis that spread worldwide. Barack Obama faced a country in crisis when he took office in January 2009. The 2011 "Arab Spring," which raised expectations of a democratic wave, instead unleashed political violence and the return of authoritarian thugs.

Most disabling for the United States was the erosion of the nation's moral authority, a vital asset during America's emergence as a great power. The Iraq invasion, launched without sanction by the UN Security Council, moved global public opinion against Washington. The world's attention turned instead to U.S. torture of war prisoners and the use of aerial drones to attack terrorists, a practice that often struck innocent civilians rather than the intended targets. At home, the U.S. government was found to be engaged in a massive campaign of domestic surveillance while spying on many of the nation's closest allies. All of these setbacks cast doubts about the nation's fitness as a benevolent global hegemon.

Obama made a critical decision in his second term when he refused to place "boots on the ground" in multiple war zones. This included the Syrian civil war, which left four hundred thousand dead between 2011 and beyond 2017. Also off the table were interventions by Russia. Putin's forces seized vast territories of Ukraine as they captured the Crimean Peninsula and the strategic naval bases. Obama chose not to engage directly against the ISIS fighters. Instead, he called armies in the Middle East to step up in their aggression against ISIS. To Obama, relying on U.S. forces only incites charges that America is an imperial state.

President Donald Trump, lacking foreign policy expertise, stepped directly into these conflicts relying on his generals. Beyond national security, Trump's refusal to join the Paris Treaty on global warming, his restriction of refugees from Syria, and his one-third reduction of the State Department left many other heads of state questioning the nation's values. Once again, we waver between a world of strict rationalism and realism on one side, and a world of promise, cooperation, and democracy.

It is often argued that American primacy is unique in that, by the end of World War II, the nation found itself leading an "empire by invitation." The United States had resisted the great-power politics of previous eras yet played a crucial role in the two world wars. America's success left it atop the global balance of power. As American leaders took the lead in creating the United Nations, supporting the decolonization of Africa and other developing regions, and laying the foundations of a stable global economy, they seemed to have realized the nation's greatest ambitions. Their self-confidence was reinforced by the nation's success in the Cold War, a half-century struggle with the Soviet Union and its communist allies that, far from liberating their citizens, merely denied their economic needs and political freedoms. As we will find, the Cold War's peaceful conclusion brought little relief to the United States.

In keeping with previous editions, our focus is on the *conduct* of American foreign policy rather than its *formulation*, the focal point of most textbooks.[3] Detailed knowledge of the policymaking process, including legal and institutional restraints, bureaucratic behavior, and the demands posed by civil society, is essential for all students of foreign policy. Yet only by exploring America's past actions in the global arena, and only by searching for historical precedents and patterns, can students fully grasp the dilemmas facing the United States today. Through this process of historical reflection, they become better equipped to place current problems in full context.

This search for historical lessons is a perpetual one that is fraught with conflicting judgments. Ignoring such lessons, however, tempts far greater perils. "When the past no longer illuminates the future, the spirit walks in darkness," observed Alexis de Tocqueville, the nineteenth-century French political theorist and author of *Democracy in America*. The Spanish-born American philosopher George Santayana put it a bit differently: "A country without memory is a country of madmen." Such insights inspired and sustained this volume, which was first published half a century ago and raised similar questions during the height of the Cold War. As readers will discover, past is prologue in many aspects of world politics, including American foreign policy.

A National Style Unfolding

As noted above, the United States has long approached world politics with a peculiar national style that reflects the inescapable demands posed by the interstate system along with the nation's geographical position and abundant natural resources. Historical analysis reveals how American foreign policy has been further shaped by long-standing cultural values and their impacts on the nation's identity and definitions of friends and enemies. Political culture, a "historically transmitted pattern of meanings," is commonly

---

[3]See Steven W. Hook, *U.S. Foreign Policy: The Paradox of World Power,* 5th ed. (Washington, D.C.: CQ Press, 2017).

expressed through popular conceptions of national identity.[4] These ideas have a life of their own and cannot be reduced to material interests and institutional structures.[5]

America's political culture, deeply rooted in the time and place of the nation's founding, has always shaped its approach to foreign affairs. European settlement of North America, which began early in the seventeenth century, produced leaders who espoused grand visions of a "New World" free of the political and spiritual trappings of Europe. The early development of the American colonies coincided with the Enlightenment era and its emphasis on rationality, empiricism, and individual liberty. The vast distance between the newly independent United States and the great powers of Europe and Asia further contributed to a sense of national exceptionalism that has persisted throughout the nation's history.[6]

These social forces defined the course of American foreign policy. Central to this "national style" was the tension between the anarchic and conflict-prone international system and the normative values widely held by Americans on individual liberty, representative government, free markets, and national self-determination. Driven by these values, American foreign policy evolved into a moral campaign aimed not simply at protecting the nation's interests but also at saving the self-destructive interstate system from itself. The two goals were commonly regarded as inseparable: A more democratic world, it was assumed, would be more peaceful, and only in such a world would the United States be truly secure.

America's peculiar approach to foreign policy is also expressed in alternating impulses by national leaders to detach the United States from global diplomacy and to remake the world in America's image. Detachment in this context is not synonymous with *isolation,* a term that means disengagement from the outside world and is frequently (and erroneously) used to define early American foreign policy. Rather, detachment refers to a pervasive sense that the United States should be actively engaged in global commerce but have "as little political connection as possible" with other countries—the stance recommended by President George Washington

---

[4] Clifford Geertz, *The Interpretation of Cultures: Selected Essays* (New York: Basic Books, 1973), 89.

[5] See Judith Goldstein and Robert O. Keohane, eds., *Ideas and Foreign Policy: Beliefs, Institutions, and Political Change* (Ithaca, N.Y.: Cornell University Press, 1993). See also Steven W. Hook, "Ideas and Change in U.S. Foreign Policy: Inventing the Millennium Challenge Corporation," *Foreign Policy Analysis* 4 (April 2008): 147–167.

[6] Charles Lockhart, *The Roots of American Exceptionalism: Institutions, Culture, and Policies* (New York: Palgrave Macmillan, 2003).

in his Farewell Address. Across civil society, this sense of detachment is reflected in a primary school system that neglects world history and geography, in chronic public misperceptions of global issues, and in commercial news media that reduced coverage of global issues even as the United States assumed unprecedented stature after the Cold War.

Democratic theory presumes that citizens will have a voice in foreign affairs and that they will be sufficiently informed to do so. Most Americans, however, seem unprepared to shoulder this responsibility. Public opinion surveys reveal that a minority of Americans can name their members of Congress, locate key countries on a world map, or identify major makers of foreign policy. Their misperceptions of current events are resistant to new and correct information—for example, half of Americans still believed in August 2004 that Saddam Hussein's Iraq gave "substantial support to al Qaeda," a claim officially refuted by the 9/11 Commission three months earlier.[7] The recurrent findings of these surveys attest to the sense of detachment that is deeply embedded in America's political culture.

With the current international order in a state of heightened turbulence, these are days of reckoning for the United States. It is vital, therefore, for students of American foreign policy to understand both the constraints facing Washington and its opportunities to reclaim the nation's political, economic, military, and moral leadership on the world stage. Current challenges will test the nation's geopolitical clout while revealing whether its exceptional self-image is genuine, warranted, or merely a "myth."[8] Informed students of American foreign policy, along with citizens and leaders abroad, will ultimately make this judgment.

This Edition's Outline and Refinements

The two sections of this edition of *American Foreign Policy Since World War II* are divided between coverage of the Cold War and the turbulent decades since its conclusion almost three decades ago. After introducing the book's theme in the first chapter, we review the key events of the Cold War years (1945–1991) in Chapters 2 through 7. The second half of the book (Chapters 8–14) explores American foreign policies since the Cold War. The final chapters are revised to capture the changing developments

---

[7] See Rick Shenkman, *Just How Stupid Are We? Facing the Truth about the American Voter* (New York: Basic Books, 2008), chap. 2.

[8] Ibid.

in trouble spots. We also consider choices by decision makers at critical moments. Our objective in these chapters is to provide students the information they need to grasp these ongoing foreign policy challenges and to place them in the context of America's historical approach to foreign policy.

Our narrative is complemented by features designed to engage our readers and ensure comprehensive coverage. Throughout the text, readers are introduced to important figures at home and abroad who exerted extraordinary "impact and influence" during each period described. An enhanced array of graphics is scattered within the chapters to highlight important national and global trends. The first of the five appendixes identifies the most influential makers of foreign policy in U.S. administrations since World War II. The second provides a chronology of important developments in world politics throughout the period under study. The last three appendixes provide researchers with a comprehensive listing of publications, websites, and foreign policy blogs, respectively. Not surprisingly, the turbulent developments of recent years have prompted an outburst of thoughtful books, articles, and government reports on American foreign policy. Those sources that directly informed this edition are cited in footnotes.

These features are designed to stimulate informed, critical thinking during this epochal period in American history. The immense potential of the United States to transform the world beyond its shores was recognized during its infancy. Georg W. Hegel (1770–1831), the German philosopher, described the United States of the early nineteenth century as "the land of the future, where, in the ages that lie before us, the burden of the World's History shall reveal itself." This vision of the nation's historic potential has now been realized, and the decisions made in Washington reverberate daily in all societies. With the stakes for global security never higher, informed scrutiny of American foreign policy, past and present, is itself a vital national interest.

Acknowledgments

This book is truly a group effort, and we are grateful to those who made this twenty-first a pleasure to write. First, we appreciate the help of the external reviewers who provided invaluable guidance throughout the editions of this text. Second, at CQ Press, director Charisse Kiino and acquisitions editor Scott Greenan provided continued leadership of the project. Editorial assistant Sarah Christensen managed the day-to-day details of the project and assisted in the editorial process, while Myleen Medina and Diane DiMura oversaw the book through production. Finally, we benefited greatly from the work of research assistants Joseph Kusluch and Nirjhar Mukherjee, who worked diligently and effectively in amassing bibliographic resources for this edition, collecting data, and refining the narrative. As authors, we assume the ultimate responsibility for the contents of this edition, and we welcome your comments and suggestions via shook@kent.edu.

The American Approach to Foreign Policy

These are fragile times. We confront the most dangerous and unstable period since World War II. Three fateful events took place early in 2017 that revealed the temperament of American foreign policy.

First, the new president, Donald Trump, rejected a twelve-nation trade that spanned the Western hemisphere and several European nations. This action blocked a history of multilateral cooperation in trade.

Second, while 197 heads of state pledged to reduce greenhouse gases in the next decade, newly elected president Trump rejected the Paris Climate Treaty. Only Syria and Nicaragua stayed out of the pact.

Third, German chancellor Angela Merkel declared that the United States could no longer be depended upon as an ally. "We have to know that we must fight for our future, for our destiny as Europeans."[1] Therefore, it was no surprise that American popularity fell to low levels among countries throughout the world (Figure 1-1)

---

[1] Alison Smale and Steve Erlanger, "Merkel, After Discordant G7 Meeting, Is Looking Past Trump" *New York Times* (May 28, 2017).

Figure 1-1

Views of Different Countries' Influence
Average of 18 Tracking Countries,* 2014–2017

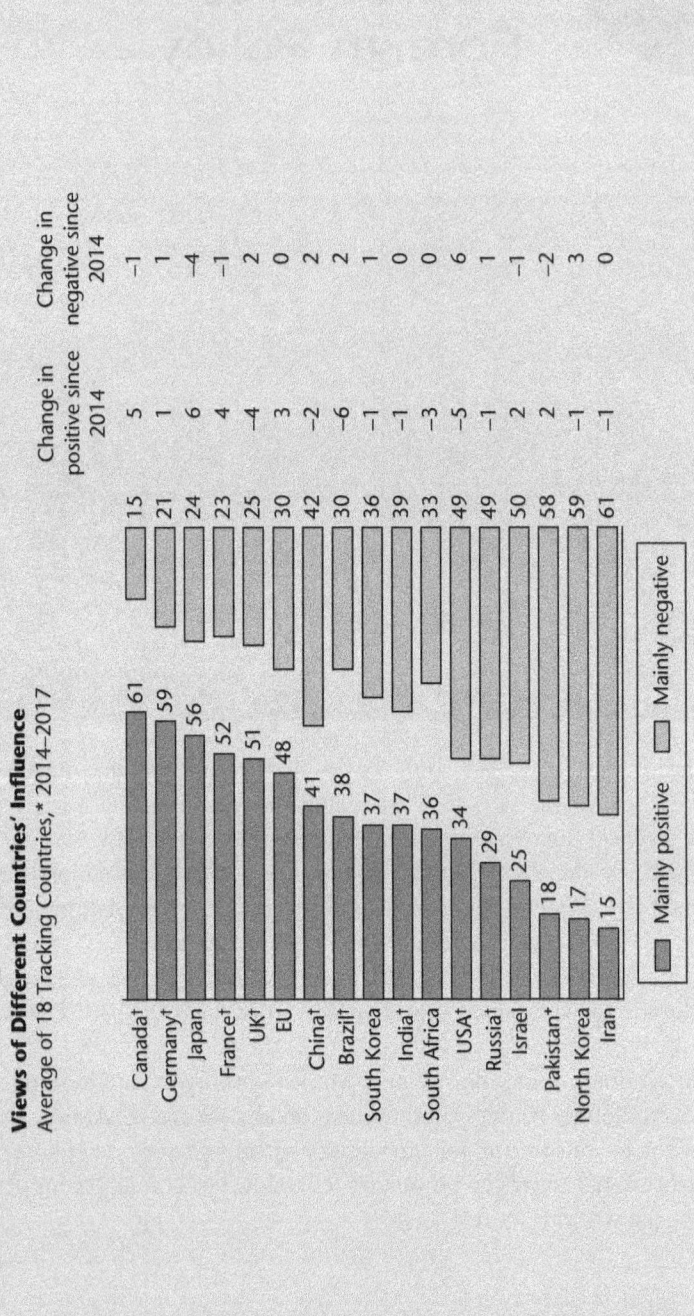

	Mainly positive	Mainly negative	Change in positive since 2014	Change in negative since 2014
Canada†	61	15	5	–1
Germany†	59	21	1	1
Japan	56	24	6	–4
France†	52	23	4	–1
UK†	51	25	–4	2
EU	48	30	3	0
China†	41	42	–2	2
Brazil†	38	30	–6	2
South Korea	37	36	–1	1
India†	37	39	–1	0
South Africa	36	33	–3	0
USA†	34	49	–5	6
Russia†	29	49	–1	1
Israel	25	50	2	–1
Pakistan*	18	58	2	–2
North Korea	17	59	–1	3
Iran	15	61	–1	0

*Tracking countries include Australia, Brazil, Canada, China, France, Germany, India, Indonesia, Kenya, Mexico, Nigeria, Pakistan, Peru, Russia, Spain, Turkey, UK, and USA.

Note: Average ratings exclude the target country's rating of itself, meaning some of the averages are based on 17 and not 18 countries. These countries are marked with a dagger symbol (†).

Peru is not a tracking country of views of India; Mexico is not a tracking country of views of Brazil.

The white space in this chart represents "Depends," "Neither/neutral," and "DK/NA."

Asked of hall of sample (except in India).

Other challenges face American foreign policy. The Arab Spring of 2011 prompted demands for democracy, but tyrants and military warlords took over with ruthless force. Three years later, the Islamic State of Iraq and Syria (ISIS) bombed its way into power and controlled much of Iraq and Syria. The civil war in Syria, which started in 2011 and continued through 2017, left more than four hundred thousand casualties and more than twelve million people uprooted. While Russia's president seized the Crimean Peninsula from southern Ukraine, China's leader staked claim to rich territorial waters held by other Asia-Pacific nations. Finally, in September 2017, North Korea tested six underground nuclear weapons and launched long-range missiles capable of reaching the United States. President Trump threatened Kim Jong Un, the Supreme Leader, that a nuclear attack would lead to the "total destroy" of the country.

At this momentous point in world history, four pivotal questions confront students of American foreign policy:

- Can the United States maintain its military primacy in the midst of threats around the world?

- Can the United States remain the locomotive of global economic growth amid growing competition?

- Can the United States uphold its political institutions, social values, and cultural appeals?

- Finally, can the United States regain the widespread respect it held during and after World War II?

As we will examine throughout this book, the world's balance of power since World War II was driven by the strength of the United States. Only this country offered its allies the military security, financial and trade institutions, supports for stable democracy and civil societies, and the foundation of global governance, including international law and the United Nations. This system functioned properly after World War II, allowing governments opportunities to pursue trade, resist corruption, and benefit from freedom. Today, many world leaders believe America's greatest years are past. If they're right, the future of world politics cannot be determined with clarity.

Learning from Experience

Our study begins with the recognition that American citizens and their leaders, like those of other countries, have a unique perspective of the world beyond their national borders. National "styles" of foreign policy vary

Impact and Influence: Woodrow Wilson

National Archives

The American style of foreign policy was personified nearly a century ago by President Woodrow Wilson (left). Wilson, the son of a Presbyterian minister, often described world politics as a struggle between good and evil. The United States, he believed, had a moral responsibility not merely to promote its own self-interests, but also to free the interstate system from its anarchic structure and warlike tendencies.

Shown here with French president Raymond Poincaré, Wilson led the United States and its allies to victory in World War I, and then chaired the U.S. commission at the Paris Peace Conference in 1919. He proposed "Fourteen Points" to reform world politics, including global disarmament, decolonization, freedom of the seas, and the abolition of secret diplomacy. Wilson also called for an "association of nations" to maintain order through a system of collective security. More than sixty foreign governments approved his plan and created the League of Nations. But Wilson, who won the Nobel Peace Prize for his efforts, could not persuade leading members of the Senate to ratify the Treaty of Versailles, and the United States never joined the League of Nations.

considerably, but all governments exhibit consistent patterns as they respond to developments around them. Many factors affect how governments conduct foreign policy, including the pressures imposed by the international system, global governance, and the constant demands of domestic politics. Taking into account such factors, including historical experiences, nations navigate their relations with allies and adversaries.

With nonthreatening neighbors to the north and south and open seas to the east and west, the United States could focus on its own economic and political development. The ability of the United States to maintain its detachment from major conflicts overseas cannot be attributed only to the nation's distance from Europe. The nature of democracy has to be considered as well. The United States saw itself as the world's "first new nation" whose government would hold its leaders accountable to the public at large.[2]

As a consequence of early America's detachment from the European powers both politically and militarily, its national style was molded by its domestic experiences and cultural traditions. Early in its history, the government had considerable freedom to put its Constitution into practice, develop an advanced market economy, and expand its territory across North America. The era of American primacy began amid the ashes of World War II, and it maintained its strength through nuclear deterrence. In 1945, the author George Orwell imagined a world with a "peace that is no peace."[3] Once the Soviet Union achieved nuclear parity in the 1950s, the Cold War was the defining reality of great-power politics. With the collapse of the Soviet Union in 1991, the United States became preeminent into the twenty-first century. Still, Americans remained anxious long after the 9/11 attacks, the costly war against Iraq, and rising threats from Russia and China.

This book explores how America's national style has influenced its conduct of foreign policy as a great power. From the aftermath of World War II into the new millennium, we consider how the ambivalent views of Americans—a fluctuating love-hate relationship with the outside world— reflects historical patterns established long before the United States joined the ranks of great powers. The first half of this book (Chapters 2–7) examines how this approach to foreign affairs both complicated and contributed to America's victory in the Cold War. The second half of the book (Chapters 8–14) describes how foreign policymakers consolidated the nation's primacy after the Cold War and confronted an array of new challenges.

The Roots of American Primacy

American foreign policy since World War II is largely the story of the tension between the world politics and the nation's political culture. Both the monumental achievements of the United States and its failures can be attributed to this uneasy relationship. In the anarchic nation-system that emerged in the seventeenth century, each nation depended on itself for maintaining its sovereignty.

---

[2] Seymour Martin Lipset, *The First New Nation: The United States in Historical and Comparative Perspective* (New York: Basic Books, 1963).

[3] George Orwell, "You and the Atomic Bomb," *British Tribune* (October 19, 1945). Two years later, the journalist Walter Lippmann made the term famous with the book *Cold War: A Study in American Foreign Policy* (New York: Harper's and Brothers).

Leaders in such a system feared potential competitors in such an unstable context. Americans, however, felt free of overseas pressures and secure in their own system of government and civil society. American foreign policy continues to reflect the cultural beliefs that prevailed long earlier. The experience of the United States today can be traced in large measure to these persistent influences.

Prior to the world wars, the United States did not maintain a global military or diplomatic presence. The nation was secure in the Western Hemisphere, which during the century after the American Revolution had witnessed the dismantling of European colonial control. Still, the great powers of Europe engaged in unending spasms of political violence that threatened to draw in the United States, a prospect that had little appeal. "Europe has a set of primary interests which to us have none or a very remote relation. Hence she must be engaged in frequent controversies, the causes of which are essentially foreign to our concerns," President George Washington observed in his 1796 Farewell Address. "Our detached and distant situation invites and enables us to pursue a different course." Washington's successors followed his advice, expanding westward without assistance and avoiding peacetime military alliances for more than 150 years.

Shifts in the Balance of Power

The United States was able to enjoy an unprecedented degree of security because a balance of power, created at the Congress of Vienna in 1815, existed on the European continent and was effectively maintained by Great Britain together with Austria, France, and Russia. The Concert of Europe, devised to implement the decisions of the Congress of Vienna, imposed a rare degree of stability on Europe. It also allowed the United States to fulfil Washington's pledge to avoid "permanent alliances." That balance was shattered, however, by Germany's unification in 1871 and the subsequent demise of several European empires. Unable to strike a new and stable balance of power, a fragile peace emerged after World War I.

The United States retreated into its hemispheric shell after World War I, but only after a failed attempt by President Woodrow Wilson to make the world "safe for democracy." Wilson proposed that a treaty be approved to prevent future wars through a system of collective security. He was so convinced of the righteousness of his cause that he personally represented the United States at the Paris Peace Conference. In 1920, Wilson persuaded European leaders to sign the Treaty of Versailles, which ended the war, and to join the League of Nations. In seeking to transform world politics, however, Wilson neglected American politics, particularly the role of Congress in ratifying treaties. Many legislators questioned whether the league would undermine the nation's sovereignty by forcing the United States to deploy troops overseas even when its own vital interests were not at stake. The Senate rejected the treaty, and the United States never joined the league.

Although the postwar U.S. economy rivaled that of all Europe, the U.S. government refused to define for the nation a political and military role consistent with its economic power. American intervention was decisive in Germany's defeat, but its leaders wanted nothing to do with great-power politics. On the contrary, the United States sought to abolish war through the 1928 Kellogg-Briand Pact, which renounced war as "an instrument of national policy." Then, as Adolf Hitler consolidated his power in Germany in the 1930s and as Benito Mussolini, the Italian dictator, moved into Africa, Congress passed two Neutrality Acts that prevented an assertive U.S. response.

The United States was forced back into the fray when Europe's balance of power was upset by the eruption of World War II in 1939 and the German defeat of France in 1940. With America again facing the possibility of Great Britain's defeat and the control of Eurasia by Germany, President Franklin D. Roosevelt undertook several measures to help London withstand any Nazi assault. Roosevelt, however, registered little concern about Japan's military expansion across East Asia. By the time Japan bombed Pearl Harbor in December 1941, a second and even bloodier world war was inevitable.

From Cold War to New World Order

The United States gained unmatched military power after World War II.[4] By the mid-1950s, however, the Soviet Union (USSR) caught up with Washington in terms of the most potent metric: nuclear weapons. At the same time, the newly established People's Republic of China (PRC) made U.S. leaders fearful that communism would spread worldwide. When the Cold War ended in 1991, American leaders turned to the United Nations, "geoeconomics," and humanitarian missions in such places as Haiti, Somalia, and the former Yugoslavia. These problems were of less concern to most citizens, who showed little interest in foreign affairs.[5]

---

[4] For a recent history of World War II, see Max Hastings, *Inferno: The World at War, 1939–1945* (New York: Knopf, 2011).

[5] When asked to identify the biggest foreign policy problems facing the United States in 1999, respondents in a national survey most often replied, "Don't know." John E. Reilly, ed., *American Public Opinion and U.S. Foreign Policy 1999* (Chicago: Council on Foreign Relations, 1999), 11.

The nation's power was tested when al Qaeda terrorists destroyed the two World Trade Centers in New York City. For the first time, American citizens could no longer consider themselves secure in their homeland. Neither could the nation devise an effective means to retaliate against terrorists. In asymmetric warfare, large armies are not required, hit-and-run attacks are common, civilians and troops mingle in urban neighborhoods, and success for terrorists is a populace that lives in constant fear. The U.S. invasion of Iraq in 2003 failed in its mission. It left more than four thousand American casualties and millions of Iraqis without a coherent government. All of this opened the door for ISIS terrorists to claim a caliphate, or an Islamic government. President George W. Bush's attack lacked the approval of the UN Security Council, offended governments around the world, and provoked further terrorist attacks on American targets. When President Obama's last year approached, he could not ignore the public's desire for "normalcy" in foreign policy.[6]

A growing number of Americans felt the United States was in decline, that American primacy was coming to an end. The apparent shift in the balance of power had two primary sources, one internal and the other external. The first stemmed from the nation's massive national debts, chronic trade deficits, record levels of income inequality, and the inability of political leaders to agree on crucial decisions. The external source came from challenges to American primacy in the global balance of power. To Russia's Vladimir Putin, Western states "continued stubborn attempts to retain their monopoly on geopolitical domination."[7] Chinese president Xi Jinping, meanwhile, created an Asian Infrastructure Investment Bank that rivaled the World Bank, based in Washington, D.C. The National Intelligence Council predicted in 2008 that China would overtake the United States in most vital categories of world power by the 2040s. According to the council, "the transfer of global wealth and economic power now under way—roughly from West to East—is without precedent in modern history."[8]

Donald Trump's rise to the presidency was a surprise to many voters. Aside from his massive wealth, he relied on a core of disenchanted citizens from rural regions who felt their standards of living were falling. These

---

[6] Dina Smeltz, *Foreign Policy in the New Millennium: Results of the 2012 Chicago Council Survey of American Public Opinion and U.S. Foreign Policy* (Chicago: Chicago Council on Global Affairs, 2012), 8.

[7] Vladimir Putin, "Meeting of Russian Federation Ambassadors and Permanent Envoys," Moscow, Russia, June 30, 2016.

[8] National Intelligence Council, "Global Trends 2025: A Transformed World" (Washington, D.C.: U.S. Government Printing Office, 2008), vi.

"populists" also believed that the United States was strongest when it was left alone, especially in world trade.[9] Trump, whose mantra was "America First," had little room for global governance, especially the United Nations. He was commited to build a wall between the United States and Mexico,[10] and he prevented citizens in six Middle Eastern countries from coming into the United States.[11] At home, populists were prone to racial anti-Semitism and racial discrimination. Meanwhile, the president confronted charges of collusion with Russia, including actions that favored Trump in his 2016 election against Hillary Clinton. Questions were raised whether the president would remain in power. [12]

Destiny and Moral Mission

The defense of the United States has always involved more than physical security. By drawing the distinction between the New and Old Worlds, Americans assumed their values to be universal, their government inspired by "special providence."[13] Still, policymakers disagreed how they would achieve their foreign policy goals. The first and more modest path—leading by example—would encourage citizens to focus on domestic development, restrain Washington from reckless foreign adventures, and prevent the rise of an expensive and potentially oppressive military establishment. The second path—intervening overseas and acting as the world's policeman— would accelerate the historical trend toward global freedom and vindicate the nation's moral mission. As the United States grew in stature, so did its appetite for enlightening citizens in faraway lands.

American primacy would not take the form of an empire or the seizure of sovereign authority. Instead, the United States would expand its sphere of influence, or *hegemony*, from its base in the Western Hemisphere to the international system as a whole. Neither the premodern empires

---

[9] Trump's populist surge came about following similar movements and complaints in Europe. Great Britain's departure from the European Union provided more evidence of rapid changes in the international system.

[10] President Trump also demanded that the Mexican government pay for the wall.

[11] These six countries are Iran, Libya, Somalia, Sudan, Syria, and Yemen.

[12] In the meantime, the President relied on three generals: H.R. McMaster, Jim Mattis Secretary of Defense, and John F. Kelly, Chief of Staff. But also the Secretary of State, Rex Tillerson played a role.

[13] Walter Russell Mead, Special Providence: American Foreign Policy and How It Changed the World (New York: Knopf, 2003).

nor the Concert of Europe of the eighteenth century came close to having such reach. American hegemony was first secured in the nineteenth century, when the Monroe Doctrine established influence spanning North and South America. The scope of U.S. hegemony extended further in the twentieth century when its economic and military supremacy was revealed in the world wars.

Going global after World War II seemed natural for American foreign policy. Such an extension of power by any other state would be distressing. While the United States benefited by its unmatched strengths, small and middle-sized nations enjoyed security and economic support, and diplomatic ties with the "benevolent hegemon."[14] American values were presumed to be universal, and American hegemony seemed natural and beneficial to all nations. The United States would underwrite the costs of global "public goods," including the promotion of human rights and the provision of the world's largest volumes of development aid to poor countries. In sum, the all-powerful "liberal leviathan" worked toward constructive ends in keeping with America's style of foreign policy.[15]

Strategic analysts though tend to be skeptical about unipolarity. First, the dominant power may be tempted to exploit its stature by taking advantage of weaker states.[16] Second, the unipolar balance of power will inevitably be short-lived as the growing costs of maintaining its control will exhaust the hegemon.[17] Finally, second-tier powers will, either alone or in hostile blocs, try to weaken the hegemon.[18] While skeptics drew upon modern history in making these claims, they failed to account for the unique nature of American power. To one observer, "The current world would be very different if it had been the U.S. and Western Europe rather than the USSR that had collapsed."[19]

Obama expressed the nation's idealism when he called for a world "where the aspirations of individual human beings really matter, where hopes and not just fears govern, and where the truths written into our founding documents can steer the currents of history in a direction of

---

[14] G. John Ikenberry. *After Victory: Strategic Restraint, and the Rebuilding of Order after Major Wars* (Princeton, N.J.: Princeton University Press, 2001).

[15] See G. John Ikenberry, *Liberal Leviathan: The Origins, Crisis, and Transformation of the American World Order* (Princeton, N.J.: Princeton University Press, 2011).

[16] Kennedy, op. cit., 184.

[17] Robert Gilpin, *War and Change in World Politics* (New York: Cambridge University Press, 1981).

[18] George Modelski, *Long Cycles in World Politics* (Seattle: University of Washington Press, 1987).

[19] Robert Jervis, "Unipolarity: A Structural Perspective," *World Politics* (January 2009), 204.

justice."[20] Resorting to the enthusiasm common among past leaders, Obama claimed in 2014 that "We are the indispensable nation. We have capacity no one else has. Our military is the best in the history of the world. And when trouble comes up anywhere in the world, they don't call Beijing. They don't call Moscow. They call us. That's the deal. That's how we roll. That's what makes us America."[21]

A Skeptical View of Power Politics

The American perception of an international harmony of interests contrasted sharply with the state system's emphasis on the inevitability of conflict and differing interests among states. Americans traditionally regarded conflict as an abnormal condition, whereas the rest of the state system perceived harmony to be an illusion. The United States, long isolated from Europe and therefore not socialized by the state system, did not accept the reality and permanence of conflicts among its members. Indeed, differences between nation-states were considered unnatural. But when they did occur, they were attributed to wicked leaders (who could be eliminated), authoritarian political systems (which could be reformed), or misunderstandings (which could be resolved through diplomacy). Once these obstacles were removed, peace, harmony, and goodwill would reign supreme.

"Power politics," the defining element of Old World statecraft, was an instrument used by selfish and autocratic rulers for whom war was a grand game. They could remain in their palatial homes and suffer none of war's hardships. The burdens fell upon the ordinary people, who had to leave their families to fight, endure higher taxes to pay for the war, and possibly see their homes and families destroyed. The conclusion was clear: Undemocratic states were inherently warlike and evil, whereas democratic nations, in which the people controlled and regularly changed their leaders, were peaceful and moral.[22]

The European countries were, by and large, three-class societies. In addition to a middle class, they contained in their bodies politic a small aristocracy, devoted to recapturing power and returning to the glorious

---

[20] Barack Obama, "Remarks by the President at the United States Military Academy," West Point, New York, May 28, 2014.

[21] President Obama interview on *60 Minutes*, September 28, 2014, www.cbsnews.com/news/president-obama-60-minutes/.

[22] These assertions form the basis of democratic-peace theory, a prominent school of thought in the study of world politics. For an elaboration and critique, see Tony Smith, *A Pact with the Devil* (New York: Routledge, 2008), chap. 4.

days of a feudal past, and a much larger proletariat consisting of low-paid farmers and industrial workers. By contrast, America was, as French political observer Alexis de Tocqueville observed in 1835, "born free" as an egalitarian, democratic society. "As a result one finds a vast multitude of people with roughly the same ideas about religion, history, science, political economy, legislation, and government."[23]

European politics was power politics, reflecting the feudal origins of European regimes. To quarantine itself from Europe's hierarchical social structures and violent conflicts, the United States had to maintain its hemispheric detachment, which was the morally correct policy. "Repudiation of Europe," novelist John Dos Passos once said, "is, after all, America's main excuse for being."

From the beginning, Americans professed a strong belief in what they considered to be their destiny—to spread *by example* freedom and social justice and to lead humankind away from its wicked ways to the New Jerusalem on Earth. Early settlers considered it their providential mission to inspire other societies to follow their lead, and the massive wave of immigration of the late nineteenth century reinforced this sense of destiny. The United States, then, would voluntarily reject power politics as unfit for its domestic or foreign policy. The Monroe Doctrine, proclaimed in 1823, first stressed this ideological difference between the New World and the Old World. President James Monroe declared that the American political system was "essentially different" from that of Europe. In this spirit, Monroe warned, "We should consider any attempt on [Europeans'] part to extend their system to any portion of this hemisphere as dangerous to our peace and safety."[24]

This view also allowed the United States to behave hypocritically by acting like other nations in its continental expansion while casting its motives in the noblest of terms.[25] In advocating U.S. expansion into Mexico in 1845, for example, journalist John O'Sullivan argued that it is "the right of our manifest destiny to overspread and to possess the whole of the continent which Providence has given us for the development of the great experiment of Liberty and federated self-government entrusted to us. Its floor shall be a hemisphere—its roof the firmament of the star-studded heavens, and its congregation a Union of many Republics, comprising

---

[23] Alexis de Tocqueville, *Democracy in America* (New York: Harper and Row, 1966), 56.

[24] Quoted in Armin Rappaport, ed., *Sources in American Diplomacy* (New York: Macmillan, 1966), 53.

[25] For a historical review of this early clash between liberalism and realism in American foreign policy, see Robert W. Merry, *A Country of Vast Designs* (New York: Simon and Schuster, 2009).

hundreds of happy millions . . . governed by God's natural and moral law of equality."[26]

Private enterprise and economic development further reinforced this disregard for power politics. John Locke, the British political theorist who inspired the American Founders, believed the role of the state should be to promote "life, liberty, and the pursuit of property." The best government, Thomas Jefferson declared, was the government that governed least. Arbitrary political interference with the economic laws of the market only upset the results—widespread prosperity and public welfare—these laws were intended to produce. The United States, therefore, would not isolate itself from the outside world in a commercial sense. Indeed, economic expansion based on foreign trade was a central element of early American foreign policy.

The key was ensuring that no political strings were attached. As George Washington proclaimed, "The great rule of conduct for us, in regard to foreign nations is, in extending our commercial relations, to have with them as little political connection as possible." This dichotomy between economics and power politics came naturally to Americans, for whom the benefits of economic freedom were as "self-evident" as the truths stated in the Declaration of Independence. Abundant natural resources, free enterprise, and supportive government policies enabled Americans to become the "people of plenty."[27]

Exceptionalism and Exceptions

One of the most telling characteristics of America's national style in conducting foreign policy has been the scrutiny and criticism applied during and after every major war to the reasons for the country's participation in the struggle. Antiwar activists organize demonstrations and encourage resistance, former government officials challenge the country's behavior on the op-ed pages, and scholars correct the historical record to rebut the conventional wisdom. Such self-criticism is common among democratic states that encourage public dissent. In the United States, however, the public discourse reveals fundamental doubts about the link between the stated goals of American foreign policy and the means chosen to achieve them.

---

[26] Quoted in Howard Jones, *The Course of American Diplomacy: From the Revolution to the Present*, 2nd ed. (Chicago: Dorsey Press, 1988), 143.

[27] David M. Potter, *People of Plenty: Economic Abundance and the American Character* (Chicago: University of Chicago Press, 1954).

The revisionist historians of the twentieth century advanced two main arguments. First, with the exception of the two world wars, the conflicts in which the United States became entangled did not in fact threaten its security interests. Therefore, the American military interventions that occurred frequently after 1800 were "wars of choice" that were unnecessary or immoral or both.[28] The enemy identified as the *provocateur* actually did not represent a direct threat to American security at all. To the contrary, the threat came from within.

Second, the United States fought wars because its leaders were manipulated by public opinion, by self-serving bureaucrats, and, above all else, by bankers and industrialists—the "merchants of death" of the 1930s, the "military-industrial complex" of the 1960s—whose economic interests benefited from the struggles. William Appleman Williams, the foremost proponent of this view, argued in 1959 that the United States was driven to global expansion by the fear of economic stagnation and social upheaval at home.[29] Similarly, Joyce and Gabriel Kolko argued in 1972 that American foreign policy after World War II was propelled "not by the containment of communism, but rather more directly [by] the extension and expansion of American capitalism."[30] Those who argued that the 2003 U.S. invasion of Iraq was "all about oil" found sufficient evidence for their argument in the president's and vice president's past associations with the oil industry. This viewpoint, originally maintained by a small group of critics, became widespread as the United States intervened repeatedly in regional conflicts during and after the Cold War.

Inspired by the revisionist historians, a new generation of political scientists argued that concepts such as liberty, national interests, and the balance of power are socially constructed by government leaders and are

---

[28] The U.S. government resorted to military force on more than three hundred occasions between 1798 and 2010, a third of these occurring since the Cold War. Formal war declarations were issued in just eleven instances, the last one for World War II. Since then, Congress has approved most military interventions through less formal authorizations. Richard F. Grimmett, *Instances of Use of United States Armed Forces Abroad* (Washington, D.C.: Congressional Research Service, March 10, 2011).

[29] William Appleman Williams, *The Tragedy of American Diplomacy* (New York: Harper and Row, 1959). See also Walter LaFeber, *The New Empire: An Interpretation of American Expansion, 1860–1898* (Ithaca, N.Y.: Cornell University Press, 1963).

[30] Joyce Kolko and Gabriel Kolko, *The Limits of Power: The World and United States Foreign Policy, 1945–1954* (New York: Harper and Row, 1972), 480.

therefore not a legitimate basis for diplomatic relations.[31] In dominating the discourse of American foreign policy, political leaders have routinely glorified the nation's values, vilified adversaries, and exaggerated overseas threats in order to preserve America's dominant position in the world. The Cold War, David Campbell observed, "was both a struggle which exceeded the military threat of the Soviet Union, and a struggle into which any number of potential candidates—regardless of their strategic capacity to be a threat—were slotted as a threat."[32]

In summary, the United States faces the world with attitudes and behavior patterns formed long ago as a result of its vast natural resources, exceptional self-image, and ambivalent relationships with foreign powers. The early success of the United States—first in detaching itself from great-power politics, and then in prevailing in two world wars—fueled the national sense of "manifest destiny." This record of accomplishment was tested during the Cold War, which dominated global relations for nearly half a century. The same lessons are being learned in the twenty-first century. As all the chapters will demonstrate, the past and present will allow students to anticipate the future of American foreign policy.

---

[31] See Alexander Wendt, "Anarchy Is What States Make of It: The Social Construction of Power Politics," *International Organization* 46 (Spring 1992): 395–424.

[32] David Campbell, *Writing Security: United States Foreign Policy and the Politics of Identity* (Minneapolis: University of Minnesota Press, 1992), 34. See also Jarrod Hayes, *Constructing National Security: U.S. Relations with India and China* (New York: Cambridge University Press, 2013).

The Cold War

From World War to Cold War

W orld War II left the European landmass in ruin. Japan and its short-lived empire were devastated. China was immersed in civil war. India remained under colonial rule, as did most of Africa. In Latin America, poverty and government repression plagued most lives.

By contrast, the United States emerged from the war physically secure, politically stable, and economically prosperous. The "arsenal of democracy" created by Franklin Roosevelt, by now the world's most potent military force, also remained intact.[1] For the second time in three decades, Americans had been drawn into world war and triumphed.

How would the United States manage its "preponderance of power"?[2] It was one thing to exploit the seemingly limitless natural resources of North America during the nation's western expansion and industrial development. It was quite another for the U.S. government to manage the transformed world order in a way that preserved its security. While many aspects of the post–World War II order remained unclear in 1945, the only thing certain was that the United States would be vital in creating and managing that order. Decisions made in Washington would reverberate worldwide; its choices of friends and enemies would determine the balance of power.

But even before the embers of World War II had cooled, the sparks of a new conflict illuminated the future of American foreign policy. The United States and the Soviet Union confronted one another with rival political systems and conflicts of interest throughout the world. As the first half of this book describes, the subsequent power struggle between the two countries would become the defining feature of world politics for decades to come. Nine American presidents would take part in managing this bipolar power balance. No foreign country would be able to escape the pressures, dangers, and consequences of the Cold War.

---

[1] See Julian E. Zelizer, *Arsenal of Democracy: The Politics of National Security from World War II to the War on Terrorism* (New York: Basic Books, 2010).

[2] Melvyn P. Leffler, *A Preponderance of Power: National Security, the Truman Administration, and the Cold War* (Stanford, Calif.: Stanford University Press, 1992).

President Franklin Roosevelt (center) confers with Soviet leader Joseph Stalin (left) and British prime minister Winston Churchill (right) in Tehran in November 1943. The three leaders, who had joined forces to defeat Germany, would meet again in Yalta in February 1945 to discuss military strategy and the structure of the postwar world.

Signs of this schism between Washington and Moscow were ignored as the final battles of World War II were fought in central Europe and East Asia.[3] Such neglect was reflected in a U.S. War Department memorandum written before a conference between British prime minister Winston Churchill and President Franklin Roosevelt. "With Germany crushed, there is no power in Europe to oppose her [the Soviet Union's] tremendous military forces," the report stated. "The conclusions from the foregoing are obvious. Since Russia is the decisive factor in the war, she must be given every assistance, and every effort must be made to obtain her friendship. Likewise, since without question she will dominate Europe on the defeat of the Axis, it is even more essential to develop and maintain the most friendly relations with Russia."[4] The importance of this assessment lies less

---

[3] For an elaboration of this critical "hinge" period from several perspectives, see Arnold A. Offner and Theodore A. Wilson, eds., *Victory in Europe, 1945: From World War to Cold War* (Lawrence: University Press of Kansas, 2000).

[4] Quoted in Robert E. Sherwood, *Roosevelt and Hopkins: An Intimate History,* vol. 2 (New York: Bantam Books, 1950), 363–364.

in its prediction of the Soviet Union's postwar position, which was fairly obvious, than in its statement of American expectations about future U.S.-Soviet relations. Military leaders apparently accepted without any major misgivings the prospect of the Soviet Union as the new dominant power in Europe. They did not imagine that it might replace Nazi Germany as a grave threat to the European and global balance of power. Although twice in the twentieth century, the United States had been propelled into Europe's wars at exactly those moments when Germany became so powerful that it almost destroyed this balance, the lessons of history—specifically, the impact of any nation's domination of Europe on American security—had not yet been absorbed. Roosevelt and the U.S. government did not attempt to reestablish a balance of power in Europe to safeguard the United States; they expected this security to stem from mutual U.S.-Soviet goodwill, unsupported by considerations of power. This reliance on goodwill and mutual esteem was to prove foolish at best—and fatal at worst.

American Wartime Illusions

Postwar expectations of an "era of good feelings" between the Soviet Union and the United States epitomized the idealistic nature of American foreign policy, which perceived war as a disruption of the normal harmony among nations. Once the war was finished, this thinking presumed natural harmony would be restored, and the struggle for power would end. In Washington, government leaders celebrated the triumph of America's moral vision and its rejection of old-style power politics. As World War II wound down, Secretary of State Cordell Hull anticipated the day in which "there will no longer be need for spheres of influence, for alliances, for balance of power, or any other of the special arrangements through which, in the unhappy past, the nations strove to safeguard their security or to promote their interests."[5]

Such optimism about the future of U.S.-Soviet relations made it necessary to explain away continuing signs of Soviet distrust during World War II. When the Allies postponed the launching of their western front against Germany from 1942 to 1944, Soviet leader Joseph Stalin rejected Allied explanations that they were not yet properly equipped for such an enormous undertaking. Stalin especially denounced Churchill for refusing

---

[5] Quoted in Herbert Feis, *Churchill, Roosevelt, Stalin: The War They Waged and the Peace They Sought* (Princeton, N.J.: Princeton University Press, 1957), 238.

to intervene until the Germans were so weakened that Allied forces would not have to suffer massive losses.

It is no wonder, then, that the Soviets adopted their own interpretation of American and British behavior. From the Marxist viewpoint, the Allies were doing exactly what a rational observer would expect: postponing the second front until the Soviet Union and Germany, the communist and fascist superpowers in Europe, respectively, had exhausted each other. Then the United States and Britain could land in France, march into Germany without heavy losses, and dictate the peace to both countries. The Western delay was seen in Moscow as a deliberate attempt by the world's leading capitalist powers to destroy their two major ideological opponents at one and the same time.

For their part, American leaders found a ready explanation for the Soviets' suspicions. Roosevelt placed Soviet distrust squarely in the context of the West's previous anti-Sovietism: The Allied intervention in Russia at the end of World War I aimed at overthrowing the Soviet regime and, after the failure of that attempt, the establishment of a *cordon sanitaire* in Eastern Europe to keep Soviet influence from spreading; the West's rejection of Soviet offers in the mid- to late 1930s to build an alliance against Adolf Hitler; and, especially, the effects of the Munich agreement of 1938, when Britain and France stood by while the Nazi dictator destroyed Czechoslovakia, opening his gateway to the East. These efforts by the West to weaken and ultimately destroy the Soviet Union, as well as its attempts to turn Hitler's threat away from Western Europe and toward Russia, were considered the primary reasons for Soviet hostility. To overcome this attitude, American leaders thought they had only to demonstrate good intentions.

Roosevelt's efforts to gain this cooperation focused on Stalin. In that respect, Roosevelt's instincts were correct: If he could gain Stalin's trust, postwar U.S.-Soviet cooperation would be possible. But in another respect, his instincts were poor. Roosevelt's political experience was in the domestic arena. He had dealt successfully with all sorts of politicians and had managed to resolve differences by finding compromise solutions. As a result, he had great confidence in his ability to win Stalin's favor. He would talk to Stalin as "one politician to another." In short, Roosevelt saw Stalin as a Russian version of himself—a fellow politician who could be won over by a mixture of concessions and goodwill. It did not occur to Roosevelt that all of his considerable skill and charm might not suffice with the man he referred to as "Uncle Joe." At home, these qualities were enough because he and his opponents agreed on ultimate goals; differences were largely over the means to achieve them. But the differences between the United States and the Soviet Union were over the ends, the kind of world each expected to see when the war was over.

In February 1945 at the Yalta Conference of the Big Three—Roosevelt, Stalin, and Churchill—Roosevelt and his advisers believed they had firmly established amicable and lasting relations with the Soviet Union.[6] Stalin had made concessions on a number of vital issues and had pledged cooperation in the future. In the Declaration on Liberated Europe, he promised to support self-government and allow free elections in Eastern Europe. He also responded to the wishes of the American military and promised to enter the war against Japan after Hitler was finally subdued. Stalin sought repeatedly to reassure the Allies by expressing hope for fifty years of peace and great-power cooperation.

Upon his return from Yalta, Roosevelt told Congress and the American people that his recent conference with Stalin and Churchill "ought to spell the end of the system of unilateral action, the exclusive alliances, the spheres of influence, the balances of power, and all the other expedients that have been tried for centuries—and have always failed." Instead, "We propose to substitute for all these, a universal organization in which all peace-loving nations will fully have a chance to join."[7]

The new era of goodwill was to be embodied in the United Nations (UN), the symbol of democracy working on a global scale. Through the UN, power politics would be replaced by reliance on sound universal principles and cooperation. Roosevelt hosted the UN's organizing conference, which was held in San Francisco early in 1945. Under the plan approved by fifty governments at the conference, the UN's General Assembly would provide a forum for all countries to meet and discuss their concerns. The most pressing and immediate problems would come before the UN Security Council, composed of fifteen countries. Ten of these seats would rotate among all UN members, and the United States and four other great powers—Britain, China, France, and the Soviet Union—would have permanent seats and would be able to veto any proposed actions they opposed. These measures were a bow to the realism that was lacking in Woodrow Wilson's League of Nations, and assured passage of the UN Charter and construction of the UN headquarters in New York City.

---

[6] Susan Butler, *Roosevelt and Stalin: Portrait of a Partnership* (New York: Knopf, 2015).

[7] Quoted in James MacGregor Burns, *Roosevelt: The Soldier of Freedom* (New York: Harcourt Brace Jovanovich, 1970), 582.

The Russo-Soviet
Approach to Foreign Policy

In Chapter 1 it was argued that before World War II, American foreign policy was shaped by a cultural tradition that reflected the nation's detachment from the great powers of Europe and its pursuit of regional security in the Western Hemisphere. It is thus useful to contrast the American tradition with that of its Cold War rival, the Soviet Union, whose leaders also inherited a distinct style of foreign policy, the product of centuries of fragile coexistence with a menacing external environment. These leaders then integrated the lessons of Russian history with the maxims of Marxist-Leninist ideology to fashion an assertive and confrontational approach to postwar foreign affairs. The emergence of the Soviet Union as a global superpower, and the American response to this shift in the balance of power, would dominate world politics for nearly half a century.

The Russian Background

Understanding the source of the Russo-Soviet foreign policy begins by simply analyzing a globe. Unlike the United States and other maritime powers, Russia was not blessed by geography. Unprotected by natural barriers such as oceans or mountains, its people were vulnerable to invasions from several directions. And the enormous size of its territory rendered internal cohesion, communication, and transportation very difficult—a situation exacerbated by the diverse ethnic backgrounds, languages, and religious identities of the Russian people.

Russian leaders viewed their history as a succession of external attacks on their territory. During the thirteenth and fourteenth centuries, Mongols from the East ruled Russia. By the 1460s, their domination had been repelled, and a Russian state had emerged with Muscovy (Moscow) as its capital. In more modern times, Napoleon Bonaparte's armies invaded and captured Moscow in 1812. British and French armies, backed by their allies in the Ottoman Empire, sought to occupy the Crimean Peninsula from 1854 to 1856, capturing several cities in bloody battles. Half a century later, Japan attacked and claimed territories in eastern Russia in 1904–1905. Most notably, Germany invaded Russia twice during the twentieth century. Its first attack prompted the final collapse of the Russian monarchy, civil war, and the rise of the communists to power; its second cost the Soviet Union millions of lives and untold destruction of property. The United States under Woodrow Wilson also deployed troops to Russia, launching an expedition in 1918 to support anti-Bolshevik forces that tried, unsuccessfully, to prevent the creation of a communist government in Moscow.

Historically, then, Russia could not take its security for granted or give priority to domestic affairs. In these circumstances, power became centralized. All the political leaders, under both the czarist and communist governments, firmly held their far-flung regions together. Such efforts, however, required large standing military forces, and much of the Russian population was mobilized in their service. Indeed, the Russian armed forces were consistently larger than the armies of the other European great powers, a fact not lost on political leaders in Warsaw, Budapest, Paris, and London.

This militarization of Russian society, purportedly for defensive purposes, also carried with it the potential for outward aggression. The same lack of natural frontiers that failed to protect Russia from invasion also allowed its power to extend beyond its frontiers. To the historian Richard Pipes, Russia no more became the world's largest territorial state by repelling repeated invasions than a man becomes rich by being robbed.[8] Indeed, sustained territorial expansion became known as the "Russian way." According to Zbigniew Brzezinski, President Jimmy Carter's national security adviser, any list of aggressions against Russia in the last two centuries would be dwarfed by a list of Russia's expansionist moves against its neighbors.[9]

Whether Russian motives were defensive or offensive, the result was a pattern of expansion. To the degree that Russian rulers feared attacks, they pushed outward to keep the enemy as far away as possible. Territorial extension became a partial substitute for the lack of wide rivers or mountains that might have afforded a degree of natural protection. Individual rulers' ambitions, such as Peter the Great's determination to have access to the sea, also resulted in territorial conquest and defeat of the power blocking that aim (in this case, Sweden). Even before the communist revolutionaries, or Bolsheviks, seized power and established a one-party state, authoritarianism, militarism, and expansionism characterized the Russian government. The basic "rules" of power politics—the emphasis on national interests, distrust of other states, expectation of conflict, self-reliance, and the possession of sufficient power, especially military power—were deeply ingrained in Russia's leaders.

---

[8] Richard Pipes, as quoted by Zbigniew Brzezinski, *Game Plan: A Geostrategic Framework for the Conduct of the U.S.-Soviet Contest* (Boston: Atlantic Monthly Press, 1986), 19–20.

[9] Zbigniew Brzezinski, "The Soviet Union: The Aims, Problems, and Challenges to the West," in *The Conduct of East-West Relations in the 1980s, Adelphi Paper No. 189, Part I* (London: International Institute for Strategic Studies, 1984).

The Soviet Ingredient

These attitudes, deeply embedded in Russian history, were modified and strengthened by the outlook of the new regime after 1917. Vladimir Lenin, the founder and first premier of the Soviet Union, fused Russian political culture with Marxist ideology. His all-encompassing *weltanschauung* (worldview) did not dictate action in specific situations. Instead, Lenin's perspective provided the new regime with a broad framework for understanding and relating to the outside world.

For Lenin and his fellow Bolsheviks, history centered on the class struggle between the rich and privileged who owned the means of production and the greater numbers of propertyless citizens who worked for them. Why were most human beings poor, illiterate, and unhealthy? Why did states fight wars? The answer was that a small minority of capitalists, monopolizing the industrialized world's wealth and power, exploited the men and women who worked in their factories to maximize profits. To keep wages down, they kept food prices low, with the result that agricultural labor also lived in destitution. Domestically as well as internationally, wars were one product of the ongoing search by these capitalists for profits.

The predictable result was the conflict waged over dividing up the non-European colonial world. For Lenin, global imperialism represented the "highest stage of capitalism." As he summed up his argument in 1917, "Imperialism is capitalism in that stage of development in which the dominance of monopolies and finance capital has established itself; in which the export of capital has acquired pronounced importance; in which the division of the world among the international trusts has begun; in which the division of all territories of the globe among the great capitalist powers has been completed."[10] Lenin viewed World War I as a climactic showdown among capitalist empires, a fight for the spoils of the developing world now that their own frontiers were settled. Like a shark, the capitalist economy could not be still. Capitalists had to expand their firms and markets constantly lest they be swallowed up in the competition for economic markets. If human beings were ever to live in freedom and enjoy a decent standard of living, capitalism must be replaced by communism—by revolution if necessary.

As Lenin was aware, the application of Marxism to Russia suffered from one glaring deficiency. In Karl Marx's dialectic view, communism stemmed directly from the failures of capitalism. Thus, a communist society must first experience industrialization, urbanization, and the enlistment of its

---

[10]Vladimir I. Lenin, *Imperialism: The Highest Stage of Capitalism* (New York: International Publishers, 1939), 89.

working classes into an organized "proletariat," none of which occurred in Russia to the extent necessary to spark revolution. Lenin attempted to resolve this problem by centralizing power in a "vanguard" of enlightened Marxists, who would bring communism to the Russian people without first exposing them to the contradictions and inequalities of capitalism. Once firmly in place within the Kremlin, this vanguard would then disseminate Lenin's ideological vision through a pervasive propaganda campaign.

Soviet leaders believed the state system, increasingly composed of capitalist states with close economic ties, was a very hostile environment. They rejected the latter's professions of goodwill and peaceful intentions and committed their country to the "inevitable and irreconcilable struggle" against these states. Stalin fostered a strong emphasis on self-reliance and an equally intense emphasis on Soviet power. Tactically, he was convinced that when an enemy made concessions in negotiations or became more accommodating, it was not because the enemy wanted a friendlier relationship; rather, it was because the enemy was *compelled* to do so by the Soviet Union's growing strength, a rationale used by Stalin to amass ever more military power. In short, Stalin and his successors imposed constant pressure on the United States and its allies while managing their communist system at home with an iron fist.[11]

Russian history served as a warning to Soviet leaders that peace was but preparation for the next war. The Soviet worldview, in short, reinforced the historically repetitive cycles that had resulted in further expansion of Soviet power. Even if insecurity, rather than any historical mission, drove this expansion, the result for neighboring states remained the same—they were vulnerable. They were perceived as inherent threats to Soviet interests, and they represented possible additions to the Soviet Union's own frontiers. Such a drive to achieve absolute security in a system that rendered such security utterly impossible left other governments insecure in the early Cold War. The contrast between the American culture, which emphasized peace as normal and conflict as abnormal, and the culture of the Soviet Union, which stressed the pervasiveness of war, could not have been more striking. Both societies felt a sense of historical mission, and yet their principles, goals, and tactics were worlds apart. These clashing approaches to foreign policy were to confront one another as the Soviet and Western armies, led by the United States, advanced from the opposite sides of Europe.

---

[11] For a recent history and critique of the Soviet leadership, see Vladislav M. Zubok, *A Failed Empire: The Soviet Union in the Cold War from Stalin to Gorbachev* (Chapel Hill: University of North Carolina Press, 2007).

Soviet Expansion after World War II

The American dream of postwar peace was shattered when the Soviet (Red) Army, having finally halted the Nazi armies and decisively defeated the Germans at Stalingrad in late 1942, began to pursue the retreating Germans westward toward Berlin. Even before the war ended, the Soviet Union expanded into eastern and central Europe and began to impose its control on Poland, Hungary, Bulgaria, Romania, and Albania. In these nations, the Soviets unilaterally established "puppet" governments. With key posts in communist hands, the Soviets found it easy to extend their domination further. It became clear that the Yalta Declaration, in which the Soviets had pledged to allow democratic governments in Eastern Europe, meant something different to the Soviets than to the Americans. After suffering two German invasions in less than thirty years, it was not surprising that the Soviet Union would try to establish "friendly" governments throughout the area. For the Soviets, democratic governments were communist regimes, and free elections were elections only among members of the Communist Party. Western peace treaties with the former German satellite states (Hungary, Bulgaria, Romania), painfully negotiated by the victors in 1945 and 1946, could not loosen the Kremlin's grip on what were by now Soviet satellites.

In terms of the state system, the Soviet behavior was understandable. Each state had to act as its own guardian against potential adversaries in a system characterized by conflict among states and a sense of insecurity and fear on the part of its members. As the alliance against the common enemy came to an end, the Soviet Union predictably would strengthen itself against the power most likely to be its new opponent. As czarist Russia, with a long history of invasions from the east and the west, it had learned the basic rules of the international game through bitter experience. As the Soviet Union, its sense of peril and mistrust had been intensified by an ideology that posited capitalist states as implacable enemies. In the war, it had suffered more than twenty million casualties, soldiers and civilians. Thus, the establishment of noncommunist regimes in Eastern Europe was unacceptable, and the American insistence on free elections was viewed as an attempt to push the Soviet Union out of Europe.

U.S.-Soviet Differences

The question of elections vividly illustrated the differences between the United States and the Soviet Union. During the war, Roosevelt worried that Soviet and U.S. interests might clash in the period of flux after Germany's defeat. He therefore single-mindedly pursued a policy of friendship toward the Soviet Union. Roosevelt, however, did not view free elections in Eastern Europe in terms of the creation of a new anti-Soviet belt. For him, free elections and a friendly attitude between East and West were quite compatible.

The model he had in mind was Czechoslovakia. As the only democracy in that area, Czechoslovakia had maintained close ties with the West since its birth after World War I. But because France and Britain had failed to defend Czechoslovakia at Munich in 1938 and betrayed it by appeasing Hitler, it also had become friendly with the Soviet Union. After 1945, Czechoslovakia, like the other Eastern European states, knew that it lay in the Soviet sphere of influence and that its security depended on getting along with, not irritating, its powerful neighbor. Thus, Czech leaders expressed amicable feelings for the Soviet Union and signed a security treaty with Moscow. Later, in one of the rare free elections the Soviets allowed in Eastern Europe, the Communist Party received the largest vote of any party and therefore the key posts in the government.

During World War II, the heroic Soviet war effort and sacrifices had created a reservoir of goodwill in the West. Had the Soviets acted with greater restraint after the war and accepted states that, regardless of their governments' composition, would have adjusted to their Soviet neighbor, Stalin could have had the security he was seeking. But Stalin did not trust the American government. No matter how personable Roosevelt was, Stalin saw him as the leader of a capitalist nation. As a "tool of Wall Street," Roosevelt could not be sincere in his peaceful professions.

From London, Winston Churchill voiced concerns about Soviet expansion and urged the United States to send forces to take control of Berlin and to advance further east into Czechoslovakia. He also suggested that, until Stalin observed his agreements in Eastern Europe, U.S. forces not pull back to their agreed-upon occupation zones in Germany and the United States not shift its military power to the Far East for the final offensive against Japan. Roosevelt rejected all of these suggestions. He had assured Stalin that all American troops would be withdrawn within two years after the war. Why then should Stalin worry about U.S. opposition to his efforts to control Eastern Europe? Carefully waiting to see what the United States would do, Stalin allowed free elections in Czechoslovakia and Hungary, the two states closest to American power. But elsewhere, he solidified Soviet control.

In the absence of Western protests about Stalin's actions, Hungary's freedom was soon squashed by the Soviets.[12] Then in 1948, the Czech government was overthrown by the Soviets in a coup d'état, even though the

---

[12] For elaboration, see Charles Gati, *Hungary and the Soviet Bloc* (Durham, N.C.: Duke University Press, 1986).

Communist Party had the largest plurality. Contrary to Roosevelt's expectations, not even a communist-controlled coalition government was acceptable to Stalin. The Soviet leader's conception of Soviet security left little, if any, security for his neighbors. The limits of Moscow's power had to be defined by the United States.

The Soviet Push to the South

Just as in the two world wars when Britain had led the effort to contain Germany, London—not Washington—took the first step toward opposing the Soviet Union after 1945. Indeed, the United States at first tried to play the role of mediator between the Soviet Union and Britain. Only when British power proved to be insufficient did the United States take over the task of balancing Soviet power. America's initiative, discussed in greater detail later in this chapter, evolved gradually over 1946–1947 and was precipitated by Stalin's attempt to consolidate his power beyond Eastern Europe. The Soviets began moving even before the smoke from World War II had cleared. Turkey, Greece, and Iran were the first to feel their pressure. If Soviet behavior in Eastern Europe could be explained in defensive terms, this was less true for the area south of the Soviet Union, the line from Turkey to India. Long before Stalin, the czars sought to establish a warm-water port on the Mediterranean Sea and to establish a presence in the Middle East, goals that Stalin later shared.

The Soviet Union first sought to gain influence in Turkey in June 1945, when it made several demands: the cession of several Turkish districts lying on the Turkish-Soviet frontier; a revision of the Montreux Convention governing the Dardanelles Strait in favor of a joint Soviet-Turkish administration; the severance of Turkey's ties with Britain and the conclusion of a treaty with the Soviet Union; and, finally, an opportunity to lease bases in the Dardanelles for Soviet naval and land forces, to be used for "joint defense." These demands aroused great concern in the United States, which sent a naval task force into the Mediterranean Sea. Twelve days later, the United States formally replied to the Soviets by rejecting their demand to share responsibility for the defense of the straits with Turkey. Britain sent a similar reply.

In Greece, communist pressure was exerted on the government through widespread guerrilla warfare, which began in the fall of 1946. Civil war in Greece was nothing new. During World War II, communist and anticommunist guerrillas had spent much of their energy battling each other instead of the Germans. When the British landed in Greece and the Germans withdrew, the communists attempted to take over Athens. Only after several weeks of bitter street fighting and the landing of British reinforcements was

Map 2-1   Soviet Expansion in Europe, 1939–1948

Soviet gains in Western territory 1939–1947

States under Soviet control by 1948

Independent communist state

– – – – –   Soviet border 1939

————   Soviet border 1947–1991

the communist control of Athens dislodged; a truce was signed in January 1945. Just over a year later, the Greeks held a general election in which right-wing forces captured the majority of votes. In August 1946, the communist forces renewed the war in the north, where the Soviet satellites in Eastern Europe could keep the guerrillas well supplied.

Meanwhile, the Soviet Union intensified pressure on Iran by refusing to withdraw its troops from that country. The troops had been there since late 1941, when the Soviet Union and Britain had invaded Iran to forestall the spread of Nazi influence and to use the nation as a corridor through which the West could ship military aid to the Soviet Union. The Soviets had occupied northern Iran, the British the central and southern sections. When the British withdrew, the Soviets sought to convert Iran into a Soviet satellite. The Iranian prime minister's offer of oil concessions to convince the Soviets to withdraw was rebuffed. Moscow's goal was nothing less than detaching the northern area of Azerbaijan and then by various means pressuring Iran into servile status. The U.S. government was once more confronted by the need to support London. After the United States and Britain delivered firm statements that they would use force to defend Iran, Stalin finally relented.

Although American foreign policies in these areas were largely effective, actions taken by President Harry S. Truman, Roosevelt's successor, were merely swift reactions to immediate crises.[13] The policies were not the product of an overall American strategy toward waging and winning the Cold War. Such a coherent strategy came only after a reassessment of Soviet foreign policy that placed Moscow's behavior after World War II in historical perspective.

The Strategy of Containment

Eighteen months passed before the United States undertook that review—from the surrender of Japan on September 2, 1945, until the announcement of the Truman Doctrine on March 12, 1947. Perhaps such a reevaluation could not have been made any more quickly. Public opinion in a democratic country does not normally shift drastically overnight. It would have been too much to expect Americans to suddenly abandon their friendly attitude toward the Soviet Union, inspired largely by the images of Soviet wartime bravery and endurance and by hopes for peaceful postwar cooperation. Moreover, war-weary citizens of the United States wished to be left alone to occupy themselves once more with domestic affairs.

Military leaders urged Truman to reduce the armed forces gradually in order to safeguard the enhanced strategic position of the United States. But the president and Congress, sensing the national desire for detachment from

[13] Joseph Lelyveld, *His Final Battle: The Last Months of Franklin Roosevelt* (New York: Knopf, 2016).

foreign concerns, ordered the "most rapid demobilization in the history of the world."[14] Total active-duty troop levels fell from more than 12 million in 1945 to fewer than 1.5 million in 1948 (see Figure 2-1). This reduction in military strength, a symptom of America's psychological demobilization, no doubt encouraged the Soviet Union's intransigence in Europe and its attempts to extend its influence elsewhere. Even with the steep reductions in military personnel, the United States continued to possess the largest navy in the world and a nuclear monopoly. But after U.S. commitments to occupied territories were taken into account, "the United States lacked the ground forces required to intervene in anything greater than a minor conflict."[15]

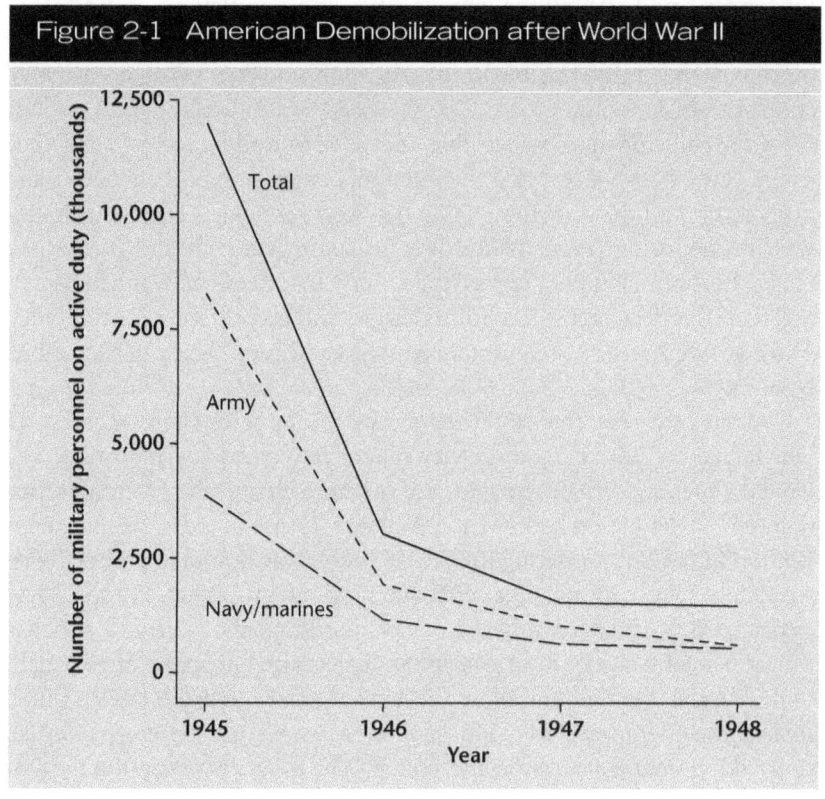

Figure 2-1 American Demobilization after World War II

---

[14] Stephen E. Ambrose, *Rise to Globalism: American Foreign Policy since 1938*, 5th rev. ed. (New York: Penguin, 1988), 79.

[15] Robert A. Pollard, *Economic Security and the Origins of the Cold War, 1945–1950* (New York: Columbia University Press, 1985).

When Soviet expansion finally led to a reevaluation of American policy, three strategic positions became clear. At one extreme stood that old realist Winston Churchill, who had long counseled against the withdrawal of American troops from Europe. He insisted that the presence of British and American troops would force the Soviet Union to live up to its Yalta obligations to allow free elections in Eastern Europe and to withdraw the Red Army from eastern Germany. After the United States rejected his plea, Churchill took his case directly to the American public in a March 1946 speech at Fulton, Missouri: "From Stettin in the Baltic to Trieste in the Adriatic, an iron curtain has descended across the continent. Behind that line lie all the capitals of the ancient states of Central and Eastern Europe. Warsaw, Berlin, Prague, Vienna, Budapest, Belgrade, Bucharest, and Sofia, all the famous cities and populations around them lie in the Soviet sphere and all are subject in one form or another, not only to Soviet influence but to a very high and increasing measure of control from Moscow."[16]

Churchill did not believe that the Soviets wanted war: "What they desire is the fruits of war and the indefinite expansion of their power and doctrines." And the only thing lying between the Soviets and their desires was the opposing power of the British Commonwealth and the United States. In short, Churchill was saying bluntly that the Cold War had begun, and that Americans must recognize this fact and give up their dreams of Big Three (United States, Great Britain, and Soviet Union) unity in the United Nations.

At the other extreme stood Secretary of Commerce Henry A. Wallace, who felt Churchill's antagonistic views merely inflamed Soviet hostility. The United States and Britain, he said, had no more business in Eastern Europe than the Soviet Union had in Latin America. Consequently, Western intervention in nations bordering the Soviet Union was bound to arouse Soviet suspicion. "We may not like what Russia does in Eastern Europe," said Wallace. "But whether we like it or not, the Russians will try to socialize their sphere of influence just as we try to democratize our sphere of influence." Only mutual trust would allow the United States and the Soviet Union to live together peacefully, and such trust could not be created by an unfriendly American attitude and policy. "The tougher we get, the tougher the Russians will get," Wallace predicted.[17]

---

[16] The entire speech can be found in Thomas G. Paterson, ed., *The Origins of the Cold War*, 2nd ed. (Lexington, Mass.: D. C. Heath, 1974), 11–17.

[17] Henry Wallace, "The Way to Peace," September 12, 1946, http://newdeal.feri.org/wallace/haw28.htm.

George Kennan and the New Grand Strategy

The task of devising a comprehensive U.S. response to the Soviet Union was assigned to George F. Kennan, the State Department's foremost expert on the Soviet Union. In a detailed telegram sent from the U.S. embassy in Moscow, Kennan in 1946 analyzed the Soviets' outlook on world affairs and mapped out a counterstrategy that would form the basis of American foreign policy for nearly half a century.[18] More generally, Kennan devised a plan for "political warfare [that]? sought the integration of every possible method, short of war, to achieve U.S. objectives."[19]

Kennan's report began with a summary of Russia's long history of insecurity with vast, largely unprotected frontiers. This cultural trait was then combined with communist ideology, which claimed that it was the communists' duty to overthrow the capitalist states throughout the world. This assertion of Soviet military power, guided by "the powerful hands of Russian history and tradition," sustained Moscow in its pledge to destroy the capitalist system.[20] From the U.S. government's standpoint, this hostility was visible daily in Soviet foreign policy: "the secretiveness, the lack of frankness, the duplicity, the war suspiciousness, and the basic unfriendliness of purpose." Kennan explained that "these characteristics of the Soviet policy, like the postulates from which they flow, are basic to the *internal* nature of Soviet power, and will be with us . . . until the nature of Soviet power is changed."[21] Until that moment, he said, Soviet strategy and objectives would remain the same.

The U.S.-Soviet struggle would thus be a long one, but Kennan stressed that Soviet hostility did not mean the Soviets would embark on a do-or-die program to overthrow capitalism by a fixed date. Given their sense of historical inevitability, they had no timetable for conquest. In a brilliant passage, Kennan outlined the Soviet concept of the struggle:

---

[18] This "long telegram" was later reprinted in the famous "X article" titled "The Sources of Soviet Conduct," which appeared in the July 1947 issue of *Foreign Affairs*. It is also reproduced in George F. Kennan, *American Diplomacy, 1900–1950* (Chicago: University of Chicago Press, 1951), 107–128.

[19] Scott Lucas and Kaeten Mistry, "Illusions of Coherence: George F. Kennan, U.S. Strategy and Political Warfare in the Early Cold War, 1946–1950," *Diplomatic History* 33 (January 2009), 40. See also Robert Frazier, "Kennan, 'Universalism,' and the Truman Doctrine," *Journal of Cold War Studies* 11 (Spring 2009), 3–34.

[20] Kennan, *American Diplomacy*, 111–112.

[21] Ibid., 115, emphasis added.

The Kremlin is under no ideological compulsion to accomplish its purposes in a hurry. Like the Church, it is dealing in ideological concepts which are of a long-term validity, and it can afford to be patient. It has no right to risk the existing achievements of the revolution for the sake of vain baubles of the future. The very teachings of Lenin himself require great caution and flexibility in the pursuit of communist purposes. Again, these precepts are fortified by the lessons of Russian history: of centuries of obscure battles between nomadic forces over the stretches of a vast unfortified plain. Here caution, circumspection, flexibility, and deception are the valuable qualities. . . . The main thing is that there should always be pressure, increasing constant pressure, toward the desired goal. There is no trace of any feeling in Soviet psychology that the goal must be reached at any given time.[22]

How could the United States counter such a policy? Kennan's answer was that American policy would have to be one of "long-term, patient, but firm and vigilant containment." He viewed containment as a test of American democracy to conduct an intelligent, long-range foreign policy *and* simultaneously contribute to changes within the Soviet Union that ultimately would bring about a moderation of its revolutionary aims. The United States, he emphasized in a passage that was to take on great meaning four decades later,

has it in its power to increase enormously the strains under which Soviet policy must operate, to force upon the Kremlin a far greater degree of moderation and circumspection than it has had to observe in recent years, and in this way to promote tendencies which must eventually find their outlet in either the breakup or the gradual mellowing of Soviet power. For no mystical, messianic movement—and particularly not that of the Kremlin—can face frustration indefinitely without eventually adjusting itself in one way or another to the logic of that state of affairs.[23]

And why was the United States so favorably positioned for a long-term struggle with the Soviet Union? The reason, Kennan argued, was that industry was the key ingredient of power and the United States controlled

---

[22] Ibid., 118.

[23] Ibid., 127–128.

most of the centers of industry. There were five such centers in the world: the United States, Britain, West Germany, Japan, and the Soviet Union. The United States and its allies constituted four of these centers, the Soviet Union just one. Containment meant confining the Soviet Union to that one. The question, Kennan said, was not whether the United States had sufficient power to contain the Soviet Union, but whether it had the patience and wisdom to do so.[24]

Alternatives to Containment

Kennan's containment strategy was generally well received in Washington, which then embarked on the complex task of translating the strategy's generalities into specific initiatives. These initiatives would, in turn, entail new strategies for the military services, a greater emphasis on economic statecraft and foreign assistance, and an ongoing effort to enlist foreign countries into bilateral and multilateral alliance networks (see Chapter 3).

In adopting containment, the Truman administration implicitly rejected two other courses of action that had substantial support. The first was a retreat into the traditional pattern of U.S. isolation from European diplomacy. This alternative was rejected when, on the afternoon of February 21, 1947, the first secretary of the British embassy in Washington visited the State Department and handed American officials two notes from His Majesty's government. One concerned Greece, the other Turkey, but in effect they said the same thing: Britain could no longer meet its traditional responsibilities to those two countries. Because both countries were on the verge of collapse, the meaning of the British notes was clear: A Soviet breakthrough could be prevented only by an American commitment to stopping it.

February 21 was a turning point for the West. Britain, the only remaining power in Western Europe, was acknowledging its exhaustion. It had fought Philip II of Spain, Louis XIV and Napoleon Bonaparte of France, and Kaiser Wilhelm II and Adolf Hitler of Germany. It had long preserved the balance of power that had protected the United States, but its ability to protect that balance had declined steadily in the twentieth century, and twice it had needed American help. Each time, however, Britain had

---

[24]For recent profiles of Kennan, who died in March 2005, see John Lewis Gaddis, *George F. Kennan: An American Life* (New York: Penguin Press, 2011); John Lukacs, *George Kennan: A Study of Character* (New Haven, Conn.: Yale University Press, 2008); and T. Christopher Jesperson, ed., *Interviews with George Kennan* (Jackson: University of Mississippi Press, 2002).

Impact and Influence: George Kennan

AP Photo/John Roone

The euphoria surrounding the end of World War II quickly gave way in the United States to concerns about the emerging Cold War. The U.S. government turned to George Kennan, a State Department officer based in the Soviet Union during and after World War II, to devise an appropriate response to the Soviet challenge in central Europe. U.S. presidents would follow Kennan's "containment" strategy, described in this chapter, until the collapse of the Soviet Union in 1991.

Although Kennan profoundly influenced American foreign policy after World War II, he spent most of the postwar era out of government. In 1950, he joined Princeton University's Institute for Advanced Study, from where he continued to inform the foreign policy debate, often deflecting criticism that his containment policy had led directly to U.S. interventions in Korea, Vietnam, and Latin America. Defending his record, Kennan charged that American leaders had strayed from the strategy he proposed. More generally, he criticized the "legalistic-moralistic" approach to American foreign policy and claimed it had prevented the nation from focusing on its national interests in the late twentieth century. In this respect, Kennan is considered one of the key postwar realists whose views ran counter to the American style of foreign policy.

fought the longer battle; the United States had entered the wars only when it was clear that Germany and its allies were too strong for Britain and that America would have to help safeguard its own security.

The second course rejected in adopting the strategy of containment was a direct military assault on the Soviet Union, which was physically ravaged after World War II. While U.S. conventional forces were far stronger than Moscow's, such an attack had little support as war-weary American troops returned home. Although the United States possessed a nuclear monopoly in the late 1940s and the potential to cripple the Soviet Union, this option was also discarded. Quite clearly, launching a preemptive nuclear attack on the Kremlin would violate universal standards of morality.

Still, American leaders sought to maintain their nuclear monopoly as long as possible. Their proposal—first drafted in the 1946 Acheson-Lilienthal Report and then delivered, in modified form, to the United Nations as the Baruch Plan—called for international control of nuclear weapons material along with pledges by all world leaders not to develop such weapons. The United States would only destroy its own nuclear stockpiles after these pledges were made and, particularly in the case of the Soviet Union, backed up by rigorous UN inspections. Not surprisingly, Stalin did not trust Truman's motives and rejected the Baruch Plan. In the words of his UN ambassador, Andrei Gromyko, "America had established a monopoly on the manufacture of nuclear weapons and wanted to retain that monopoly."[25] It also came as little surprise when, on August 29, 1949, the Soviet Union successfully tested its own nuclear weapon, thus launching a long, complex, and perilous nuclear arms race.

For centuries, the principal task of military armaments had been to win wars. From now on, their main purpose for the superpowers would be to *deter* wars. Nuclear weapons could have no other rationale. The United States now had to wage a protracted, low-intensity conflict that was contrary to its traditional style of foreign policy. The term frequently given to this conflict—Cold War—was apt indeed. *War* signified that the U.S.-Soviet rivalry was serious; *Cold* referred to the fact that nuclear weapons were so utterly destructive that, even with conventional weapons, a war between the two nuclear powers could not be waged.

Even though communist containment was adopted as the linchpin of U.S. strategy, it drew criticism from many quarters. Some felt it did not go far enough, that it failed to exploit U.S. military and economic supremacy and provided the Soviets with the initiative to set the time and place of superpower confrontations.[26] Others felt it went too far. Located as it was between the two extremes, however, containment attracted support among moderates both in the United States and abroad. It thus heralded an auspicious new era in U.S. foreign policy, perhaps best reflected in the title of Secretary of State Dean Acheson's memoir, *Present at the Creation*. For Acheson, the late 1940s "saw the entry of our nation, already one of the superpowers, into the near chaos of a war-torn and disintegrating world society. To the responsibilities and needs of that time the nation summoned an imaginative effort unique in history and even greater than that made in

---

[25] Quoted in Michael Gordin, *Red Cloud at Dawn* (New York: Farrar, Straus, and Giroux, 2009), 53.

[26] For a prominent critique, see Walter Lippmann, *The Cold War: A Study in U.S. Foreign Policy* (New York: Harper, 1947).

the preceding years of fighting. All who served in those years had an opportunity to give more than a sample of their best."[27]

The Cold War that followed was characterized by long-term hostility and by a mutual determination to avoid a cataclysmic military showdown. As it took over Britain's role as the keeper of the balance of power, the United States had to learn power politics. In protecting itself, it also had to learn how to manage a protracted conflict in peacetime, a new experience and one at odds with its historical ways of dealing with foreign enemies and the international system.

Declaring Cold War: The Truman Doctrine

On March 12, 1947, President Harry Truman went before a joint session of Congress to deliver one of the most important speeches in American history. After outlining the situation in Greece, he spelled out what would become known as the Truman Doctrine. The United States, he said, could survive only in a world in which freedom flourished. And it would not realize this objective unless it was

> willing to help free peoples to maintain their institutions and their national integrity against aggressive movements that seek to impose upon them totalitarian regimes. This is no more than a frank recognition that totalitarian regimes imposed on free peoples, by direct or indirect aggression, undermine the foundations of international peace and hence the security of the United States. . . .
>
> At the present moment in world history nearly every nation must choose between alternative ways of life. The choice is often not a free one. . . . I believe that we must assist free peoples to work out their own destinies in their own way.[28]

The president asked Congress to appropriate $400 million for economic aid and military supplies for Greece and Turkey and to authorize the dispatch of American personnel to assist with reconstruction and to provide

---

[27] Dean Acheson, *Present at the Creation: My Years in the State Department* (New York: Norton, 1969), 725.

[28] The drama of this period and Truman's speech to Congress are still best captured in Joseph M. Jones, *The Fifteen Weeks* (New York: Viking Press, 1955), 17–23.

their armies with appropriate instruction and training. And he implicitly offered U.S. assistance to "free peoples," a largely rhetorical pledge aimed to demonstrate his benevolent motives.[29] One of his most critical tactical victories in winning approval for these measures was gaining the support of Michigan senator Arthur Vandenberg, a prominent Republican isolationist and chair of the Senate Foreign Relations Committee. With Vandenberg's endorsement, Congress embraced the spirit and financial requirements of the Truman Doctrine.[30]

The United States thus launched its policy of containment. The emerging clash between the postwar superpowers, anticipated by the Truman administration in the late 1940s, was evident in the hostile actions being taken on both sides. To many, the defining moment occurred on July 2, 1947, when the Russian delegation walked out of a meeting organized by Western leaders in Paris to discuss the distribution of Marshall Plan aid (see Chapter 3). From then on, the two antagonists would not even put forward the appearance of great-power cooperation.

In this volatile atmosphere, Soviet behavior left the United States with little choice but to adopt a countervailing policy. During World War II, the United States had sought to overcome the Kremlin's suspicions of the West, to be sensitive to Soviet security concerns in Eastern Europe, and to lay the foundation for postwar cooperation. At the end of the war, the principal concern of American policymakers was not to eliminate the Soviet Union, the self-proclaimed bastion of world revolution and enemy of Western capitalism, nor did they seek to push the Soviet Union out of Eastern Europe. After all, American policy was not the product of a virulent and preexisting anticommunist ideology. Rather, it was animated by its desire to prevent a major nation from achieving dominance in Europe, an occurrence that twice in the twentieth century had led the United States into war.

In this respect, American military strategy toward Europe at the dawn of the Cold War was consistent with that in the early stages of the two world wars, which were fought first against a conservative monarchy in Germany and then against the fascist states of Germany and Italy. In the Cold War, the adversary was the Soviet Union, a repressive communist regime. American strategy and subsequent action remained the same regardless of the

---

[29] See Denise M. Bosterdoff, *Proclaiming the Truman Doctrine: The Cold War Call to Arms* (College Station: Texas A&M Press, 2008).

[30] For recent elaborations of the Truman Doctrine, see Jan S. Prybyla, *The American Way of Peace: An Interpretation* (Columbia: University of Missouri Press, 2005), chap. 7; and Arnold A. Offner, *Another Such Victory: President Truman and the Cold War, 1945–1953* (Stanford, Calif.: Stanford University Press, 2002), chap. 8.

opponent's ideology. This does not mean, however, that ideology was irrelevant to these conflicts. On the contrary, all these adversaries maintained systems of government and state-society relations that offended American democratic ideals and seemed threatening to those ideals. Thus, the fascist and "godless" communist regimes, located at both ends of the ideological spectrum, also inflamed the moral passions of the American government and provided a further rationale for Cold War. The strategy fit neatly into the traditional American dichotomy of seeing the world as either good or evil, thereby arousing the nation for yet another moral crusade.

The contrasting nature of U.S. and Soviet conduct after World War II reinforced these normative tensions. The Soviet Union, which already had annexed the Baltic states of Estonia, Latvia, and Lithuania, imposed communist regimes on its neighbors and stationed Soviet forces there to ensure the loyalty of these states. In fact, none of these governments could have survived without the presence of Soviet troops. By contrast, Iran, Turkey, and Greece invited American assistance because they feared Soviet pressure and intimidation. Soviet expansion meant their loss of independence; American assistance was designed to preserve it. All shared the U.S. perception of the Soviet Union as a threat to their political independence and territorial integrity, and they urged Washington to redress the post-1945 imbalance. Their concern was not U.S. expansion and hegemony, but abandonment.

The Truman Doctrine in its immediate application was intended to be specific and limited, not global. American policymakers were well aware that the United States, although a great power, was not omnipotent; national priorities had to be decided carefully and power applied discriminately. American responses, then, would depend both on where the external challenges occurred and on how Washington defined the relation of such challenges to the nation's security. Containment was to be implemented only where the Soviet state appeared to be expanding its power. The priority given to balance-of-power considerations was evident from the very beginning.

Despite the democratic values expressed in the Truman Doctrine, it was first applied to Greece and Turkey, neither of which was democratic. Their strategic locations were considered more important than the character of their governments. In Western Europe, however, America's strategic and power considerations were compatible with its democratic values; containment of the Soviet Union could be equated with the defense of democracy. The United States thus confronted a classic dilemma: Protecting strategically located but undemocratic nations such as Iran, Turkey, and Greece might make the containment of Soviet power possible, but it also risked America's reputation and weakened the credibility of its policy. Yet alignment only with democratic states, of which there were all too few, might make U.S. implementation of its containment policy impossible. The purity of the cause might be preserved, but the security of democracy would be weakened. This dilemma was to plague U.S. policy throughout the Cold War, and the same dilemma persists today in the war against terrorism.

In summary, the emerging bipolar state system and the behavior of the Soviet Union were fundamental factors precipitating the Cold War. What, if any, was America's contribution to its onset? Perhaps at the time, the United States could not have done more than simply protest Soviet expansion and hegemony in Eastern Europe. It was true that the American people, like the British, admired the heroic efforts of the Red Army in stopping and driving back the Nazi forces. Moreover, the staggering Soviet losses, compared with the relatively light losses of the Allies, were recognized in the West. In these circumstances, the hope for good postwar relations with the Soviet Union was understandable. These optimistic projections, however, were quickly dispelled by events in Eastern Europe. As the United States proceeded with its withdrawal and military demobilization, Soviet leaders made it clear that their control over the region would be anything but temporary. Thus, the threatened states bordering the Soviet bloc looked to Washington for help. Having abandoned its hopes for a harmonious world order after World War II, the United States finally took the necessary measures to stand up to Stalin.

Containment: From Theory to Practice

Twenty-one years (1918–1939) separated the two world wars, providing their combatants with time to recover from their losses, restore some semblance of domestic order, redefine their national interests, and prepare for future challenges. But that was not true after World War II. Even before the conflict was over, both the Soviet Union and the Western Allies were posturing for spheres of influence in central Europe. And it was only six months after the Japanese surrender that Winston Churchill gloomily proclaimed that an "iron curtain" had descended across central Europe, defining the battle lines of the next global confrontation. If there was an "interwar" period in this case, it was hardly perceptible. Fortunately for the United States, the late 1940s were among the most imaginative years in U.S. diplomatic history. With the guidance of an unusually cohesive team of advisers, President Harry Truman transformed the nation's foreign policy so the United States could compete indefinitely as a political, economic, and military superpower. The "wise men" of the Truman administration established the basis of the Western strategy that ultimately prevailed in the Cold War.[1]

The global scope of the challenge guaranteed that putting containment into practice would be a monumental task. The obstacles were especially great because of the traditional American penchant for withdrawal and isolation from great-power politics in peacetime. Further hampering the United States was the lack of an institutional basis for dealing with a worldwide threat that was not likely to disappear or be defeated militarily within a few years. The U.S. government had maintained a sizable diplomatic corps only since the end of World War I, and Americans had long viewed a standing army with apprehension. But as this chapter describes, America's leaders overcame these obstacles and created a web of national security structures and multilateral organizations that resisted the Soviet Union from all sides.

---

[1] Walter Isaacson and Evan Thomas, *The Wise Men: Six Friends and the World They Made* (New York: Simon and Schuster, 1986).

The citizens of West Berlin, Germany, watch the arrival of a U.S. Air Force transport plane in 1948. The Soviet Union had blocked all water and land access to the city in June 1948, leaving the residents of West Berlin dependent on the United States for their survival until late 1949. The Berlin airlift became one of the U.S. foreign policy success stories of the early Cold War.

These arrangements extended beyond the struggle against communism. The central role of the United States in creating and managing the postwar order gave American leaders added leverage with their European allies, along with developing countries from East Asia to Africa and Latin America. Further, the "constitutional" order designed by the United States, which favored international law and political freedoms in participating states, served as a means to advance American values while benefiting the peoples of weaker countries through foreign aid, military protection, and other forms of support.[2] The enduring value of this order would be evident decades later, because the network of domestic and global institutions established in the late 1940s remained intact long after the Cold War. But for those in power at the time, the immediate concern was resisting the threat posed by Moscow.

In its first step, the Truman administration sought to revive its war-ravaged allies in Western Europe, which, from Washington's point of view, urgently needed to form a united front against Moscow. Such a task would be impossible, however, if the historic internal rivalries among the European states were allowed to persist. The United States thus encouraged close cooperation among the European governments in rebuilding their economies, settling their political disputes, and protecting the region

---

[2] See G. John Ikenberry, *After Victory* (Princeton, N.J.: Princeton University Press, 2001).

from external aggression. Such cooperation would be supported not only rhetorically but also financially by the United States, which covered much of the costs of Western Europe's recovery.

But the United States would not stop with Europe. To contain communism, it also would have to become actively engaged elsewhere. In the late 1940s and early 1950s, the Asian perimeter of the Soviet Union and China became the second target of U.S. containment. In contrast to Western Europe, many Asian states had only recently emerged from colonialism, and their nationalistic and anti-Western feelings were strong. The coming to power of a communist Chinese government in 1949 particularly weakened the U.S. position in Asia. The United States then confronted two militarily powerful communist states, one (the Soviet Union) covering the world's largest land-mass, the other (China) governing the world's largest population. As George Kennan warned, the Cold War would be vast in scope and long in duration (see Chapter 2).

New Economic and Military Structures

Unlike the situation confronting other great powers, U.S. military strength was greater *after* World War II than before. The United States maintained undiminished industrial capacity, a monopoly on nuclear weapons, and a global deployment of troops. The U.S. economy had been strengthened by the war, especially when compared with the battered industrial economies of Europe and East Asia. Americans produced one-quarter of global output even after the recovery of its economic competitors, giving it unprecedented wealth to match its military muscle (see Figure 3-1).

The foreign policy of a great power requires more than a widely accepted grand strategy, no matter how widely supported that strategy is. Foreign policymakers also must pay attention to the brick and mortar of the political institutions, both domestic and international, that will carry out the strategy. In addition to leading the effort to create the United Nations, which came into being just three months after World War II, American officials focused on two areas. First, they created an international economic system to support commerce among the capitalist states. Second, they rebuilt the country's military structures and created an elaborate web of alliances. Taken together, these reforms established the institutional blueprint that remained in place throughout the Cold War and has endured in its aftermath.

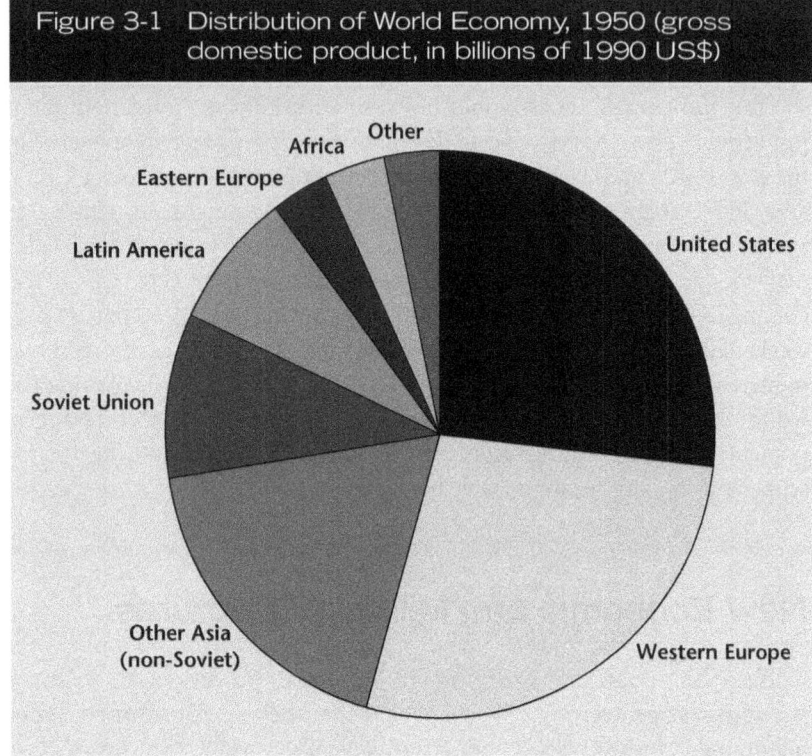

Figure 3-1 Distribution of World Economy, 1950 (gross domestic product, in billions of 1990 US$)

Source: Angus Maddison, *The World Economy: A Millennial Perspective* (Paris: Organisation for Economic Co-operation and Development, 2001), 261.

The Bretton Woods System

Western governments agreed during World War II that a new system was needed to manage global economic relations. They recognized that trade restrictions, subsidies for national industries, and other forms of mercantilism had contributed to the Great Depression of the 1930s, which, in turn, had aroused nationalist passions and led to the birth of Nazi Germany. It was widely believed that a liberal international economic order, based on open markets and leading to the recuperation of the European industrial states, could prevent a recurrence of this calamity.[3] The market-based economic order also would reduce the appeal of communism by creating prosperous capitalist societies. But this latter goal was secondary. Since the

---

[3] An influential argument at the time was made by theorist Nicholas Spykman in *America's Strategy in the World* (New York: Harcourt, Brace, 1942).

nation's founding, America's leaders had agreed that the country's economic prosperity, and global stability in general, depended on an integrated global economy that encouraged trade and investments across national borders.

Although they often breached their own commitment to free trade, these leaders clung to the notion that the "invisible hand" of open markets would lead the way to global prosperity.[4] Along with European leaders, they devised a plan for international economic, fiscal, and monetary cooperation to be underwritten by the vast economic resources of the United States. In 1944, representatives of forty-four countries met at Bretton Woods, New Hampshire, to approve this plan, which already had been devised by American and British officials. The Bretton Woods system played a critical role in hastening the recovery of the industrialized states. Along the way, the new system strengthened the market economies against their communist rivals.

The Bretton Woods accords created two institutions to promote economic growth among the market economies.[5] The first, the International Bank for Reconstruction and Development (IBRD), or World Bank, would lend the funds member states needed to rebuild their industries. The United States provided much of the World Bank's funding in the institution's early days, which the bank then lent to member states on generous terms. European governments were the first to receive support from the World Bank, which later shifted its aid programs to developing countries that were becoming free of colonial rule. The second, the International Monetary Fund (IMF), would govern currency exchanges and provide credits for member states facing short-term currency crises. Members were prevented from simply printing more money to cover their deficits, a practice that had led to rampant inflation and the collapse of central banks in many countries during the 1930s.

The major economic powers tried, but failed, to create a third institution that would govern international trade. The International Trade Organization (ITO), proposed in the 1948 Havana Charter, called for sweeping controls over global commerce, including foreign investment, employment policies, and prices for commodities. But several governments, including the United States, felt the ITO would violate their economic sovereignty as well as the principles of free enterprise. Instead, the United States joined twenty-two

---

[4] See Robert A. Pollard, *Economic Security and the Origins of the Cold War, 1945–1950* (New York:Columbia University Press, 1985).

[5] For a comprehensive historical review, see Harold James, *International Monetary Cooperation since Bretton Woods* (New York: Oxford University Press, 1996).

other countries in approving the General Agreement on Tariffs and Trade (GATT), which established rules for "nondiscrimination" in world markets. Subsequent GATT negotiations would further restrict the ability of states to violate the rules of free trade. These GATT "rounds" ultimately led to the creation of the World Trade Organization in 1995.

The Bretton Woods system laid the foundation for a more integrated world economy. The stability of the market economies was maintained by a system of fixed currency exchange rates based on the U.S. dollar, which was based, in turn, on the value of U.S. gold reserves at $35 an ounce.[6] The dollar thus became a world currency that provided reassurance to financial markets and a simple framework for trade and foreign investment. Once they had benefited from the Bretton Woods reforms, the Marshall Plan (described later in this chapter), and other assistance programs from Washington, U.S. allies in Western Europe and Japan were able to rebound quickly from World War II and enjoy unprecedented economic growth. Meanwhile, the Soviet Union continued to isolate itself, along with its client states in Eastern Europe, from the market-based global economy, a move that had ominous implications for the outcome of the Cold War.

The National Security Act

As the Cold War set in, Truman received strong congressional support to reshape the nation's military structures so they would be able to meet the demands of containing communism. Under the National Security Act of 1947, the formerly separate Departments of the Army and Navy were brought together in the new Department of Defense (DOD), a successor to the Department of War. Now the United States would have a *permanent* military establishment based on the general principle of national defense rather than war fighting. As part of the reorganization, the air force, a third branch of the military formerly controlled by the army, became an independent service. It soon overshadowed the two older services because its principal task was to organize the growing U.S. nuclear arsenal.

The National Security Act also created the Central Intelligence Agency (CIA), an offspring of the Office of Strategic Services (OSS), which had gathered foreign intelligence and conducted spy operations during World War II. The OSS, widely considered a "rogue" operation that undertook

---

[6]The United States held about 75 percent of the world's gold reserves at the time, amounting to about $25 billion.

secret missions around the world with little oversight, was disbanded immediately after the war. A larger intelligence operation than the OSS, the CIA quickly became an essential, albeit controversial, part of America's containment effort. The agency was essential because it collected and analyzed information that became the basis of American foreign policy. It was controversial because, in the tradition of the OSS, CIA officers often carried out secret operations overseas and sought to subvert governments believed hostile to the United States.

Finally, the act established the National Security Council (NSC) to help the president coordinate foreign policy. Located in the White House, the NSC was composed of the president (its chair), the vice president, and the secretaries of state and defense. The head of the Joint Chiefs of Staff and the CIA director also often attended NSC meetings, along with other government officials whose advice the president sought. A small NSC staff was created to provide information to these leaders, and the national security adviser, a new position, was to serve as a "gatekeeper" and close confidant of the president. Through the NSC, the president gained greater control over U.S. foreign policy, in part by reining in departments such as State and Defense, whose leaders were widely suspected of being captives to their respective bureaucracies. And, no less important, the NSC became the primary crisis management agency for the president, a function that took on increasing urgency in the nuclear age.[7]

The concentration of foreign policy powers within the executive branch and the creation of a large, permanent military force ran counter to the nation's traditional style of foreign policy. As noted earlier, the Founders had deliberately constrained presidential powers and avoided standing armies in order to prevent the United States from behaving recklessly in foreign affairs. Thomas Jefferson and other early leaders further feared the creation of a "garrison state" and a "warrior class" that could someday threaten individual liberties.[8] Despite the recurrence of these fears during the Cold War, the president's growing control over national security was widely accepted as the price of world power.

---

[7] See John Prados, Keeper of the Keys: A History of the National Security Council from Truman to Bush (New York: Morrow, 1991). For more recent analyses, see David J. Rothkopf, Running the World: The Inside Story of the National Security Council and the Architects of American Power (New York: Public Affairs, 2005); and Karl F. Inderfurth and Loch K. Johnson, eds., Fateful Decisions: Inside the National Security Council (New York: Oxford University Press, 2004).

[8] For an elaboration, see Aaron L. Friedberg, In the Shadow of the Garrison State: America's Antistatism and Its Cold War Grand Strategy (Princeton, N.J.: Princeton University Press, 2000).

Reviving the Western European Allies

Europe's collapse after World War II raised anew a fundamental question that had bedeviled U.S. leaders since the nation's founding: was European stability vital to U.S. security? America's interventions in the two world wars suggested the answer was obvious. But both times the United States had been drawn into the conflicts only after prolonged periods of hesitation and by threats of German domination of the continent. At the end of each conflict, the United States had tried to detach itself politically from Europe, the almost pathological instinct of Americans dating back more than two centuries. After World War II, however, the United States was forced, for the first time, to establish an *ongoing*, multifaceted relationship with Western Europe, because, in the precarious postwar order, America alone had the resources to take the initiative.

Europe's vital importance became especially clear in the emerging bipolar world. The region ranked second only to the United States in its collective economic power—in industry, productivity, skilled workers, scientists, and engineers. Moreover, trading networks and cultural ties between the United States and Western Europe were long-standing and strong. And, not least, Western Europe represented a "buffer zone" between the two superpowers, and thus it occupied a crucial strategic position in the emerging Cold War. Because of Western Europe's enormous potential and its geographic position, its stability was inseparable from U.S. security.

The devastation of World War II in Europe, however, left the continent highly unstable. The war had penetrated its heartland, and few cities or towns had escaped Allied bombing, street fighting, or willful destruction by the Nazis as they retreated. Millions of people had no food or shelter. By January 1947, production had fallen to 31 percent of the 1936 level. These difficult conditions forced American officials to respond immediately. It was obvious they could not limit their actions to a single area such as economic development, military defense, or political reform. Their response must be comprehensive and dedicated to preserving Western Europe as the front line of Cold War defense.

The Marshall Plan

With Western Europe on the verge of not only economic ruin but also political and social upheaval, the region's weary governments were forced into dependence on the United States. Most of the items needed for reconstruction and economic vitality—wheat, cotton, sulfur, sugar, machinery, trucks, and coal—could be obtained in sufficient quantities only from American suppliers. But short of food and fuel, with its cities and factories destroyed, Europe could not earn the dollars to pay for these products. Moreover, the United States was so well supplied with everything that it did not have to buy much from abroad. The result was a *dollar gap*, a term that denoted Europe's dependence on the United States for recovery.

Because the United States could not permit the Soviet Union to extend its influence into Western Europe, U.S. policymakers had to find a way to help the region recover. Secretary of State George Marshall called on the European states to devise a plan for their common needs and common recovery. The United States would furnish the funds through the European Recovery Program (later known as the Marshall Plan), but the Europeans had to assume the initiative and do the planning. The result was the Organisation for European Economic Co-operation (OEEC), which estimated the cost of Europe's recovery over a four-year period to be $33 billion. Truman asked Congress for $17 billion, but lawmakers cut the sum to $13 billion. The amount actually spent between 1948 and the end of 1951, when the program ended, was just over $12 billion. Britain, France, and West Germany received more than half of this amount.

The original offer by the United States was deliberately extended to all European countries, including the Soviet Union and the nations of Eastern Europe. If the United States had invited only the nations of Western Europe, it would have been blamed for the division of Europe and the intensification of the Cold War. It had to be the Soviets who, by their rejection of Marshall Plan aid, would be responsible for the division of Europe. If the Soviets agreed to participate, however, Congress probably would not have supported the Marshall Plan, as its cost would have risen astronomically because of the heavy damage suffered by the Soviet Union during the war. Fortunately, Joseph Stalin failed to call the Americans' bluff. He refused the offer of assistance and ordered his clients in Eastern Europe to do likewise.[9]

Was the Marshall Plan a success? The results tell their own story. By 1950, Europe already was exceeding its prewar production by 25 percent; two years later, this figure was 200 percent higher. British exports were doing well, French inflation was slowing, and German production had reached its 1936 peak. The dollar gap had been reduced from $12 billion

---

[9] In place of the Marshall Plan, the Soviet Union created the Council for Mutual Economic Assistance (CMEA) to provide economic assistance to the Eastern European governments. The actual aid extended by Moscow, however, was modest compared with that of the Marshall Plan.

to $2 billion. Europe's cities were being rebuilt, and its factories were busy, its stores restocked, and its farmers productive. The Marshall Plan was a huge success, and at a cost that represented only a tiny fraction of the U.S. national income over the same four-year period. The Europeans themselves, of course, were primarily responsible for their achievements, but such a rapid turnaround would not have been possible without the Marshall Plan, which Winston Churchill called "the most unsordid act in history."[10]

Roots of the European Union

In making American aid to Western Europe conditional on economic cooperation among the European states, the United States clearly was holding itself up as a model. The Economic Cooperation Act of 1948 called specifically for the creation of an integrated European market—in much the same way that the then forty-eight American states were organized economically. America, it stated, was "mindful of the advantage which the United States has enjoyed through the existence of a large-scale domestic market with no internal trade barriers and [believed] that similar advantages can accrue to the countries of Europe." The official American opinion was that economic integration was essential for Europe's recovery and long-range prosperity.

Renewed fears of Germany's rising strength further stimulated efforts toward European integration. The specter of a fully revived Germany struck fear into most of its neighbors. The French, with their memories of the Franco-Prussian War (1870–1871) and both world wars, were particularly alarmed by the prospect. Germany's recovery, stimulated by America's response to the Cold War, posed a serious problem for Germany's partners: how could they hold Germany in check when it was potentially the strongest nation in Europe outside of the Soviet Union?

Aware of the failure of the traditional balance-of-power strategy in which a weaker power seeks to balance against a stronger one, France sought a new way to exert some control over Germany's growing power. Through the creation of a *supranational* community to which Germany and other European states would transfer certain sovereign rights, German power could be controlled. Instead of serving national purposes, Germany's strength would serve Europe's collective purposes, while its government regained some measure of regional credibility.

---

[10]The Marshall Plan remains the subject of current policy debates regarding the use of American financial assistance. For a recent assessment, see Eliot Sorel and Pier Carol Padoan, eds., *The Marshall Plan: Lessons Learned for the 21st Century* (Paris: Organisation for Economic Co-operation and Development, 2008).

France made a bold move in the direction of a united Europe in May 1950, when Foreign Minister Robert Schuman proposed the formation of the European Coal and Steel Community (ECSC) composed of "Little Europe" (France, West Germany, Italy, and the Benelux countries of Belgium, the Netherlands, and Luxembourg). The aim of the Schuman Plan was to interweave German and French heavy industry to such an extent that it would be impossible to separate them. Germany never again would be able to use its coal and steel industries for nationalistic and militaristic purposes. War between Germany and France would become not only unthinkable but also impossible.

As the benefits of pooling heavy industry became clear, European leaders expected that other sectors of the economy would follow suit, possibly leading to the creation of a "United States of Europe."[11] They took a major step in this direction in 1957 when the six governments of "Little Europe" established the European Economic Community (EEC), more commonly known as the Common Market. Members of the EEC agreed to eliminate the tariffs and quota systems that hampered trade among them and to abolish restrictions on the regional movement of goods, services, labor, and capital. In addition, they created a variety of governing bodies, including a European Parliament, to pave the way toward political unification.

Not surprisingly, the Soviet Union voiced strong opposition to the Common Market. A thriving Western Europe, economically prosperous and politically stable, not only would prove a powerful barrier to Soviet expansion, but also might threaten the status quo in Eastern Europe. The Western European societies were a magnetic attraction for Soviet clients, especially when the gaps in living standards between the two blocs became evident. After Stalin's protests fell on deaf ears in the West, the Soviet leader redoubled his efforts to isolate Eastern Europeans and subject them entirely to Moscow's control.

European Security and the NATO Alliance

Soon after the Marshall Plan was launched, it became clear that economic measures alone would not adequately counter Soviet expansion. In February 1948, the Soviets engineered a coup d'état in Prague, and—ten years after the Munich agreement and Adolf Hitler's subsequent seizure of

---

[11] For an early elaboration of this "functionalist" approach to regional integration, see David Mitrany, *A Working Peace System* (Chicago: Quadrangle Books, 1966). Also see Ernst Haas, *The Uniting of Europe: Political, Social, and Economic Forces, 1950–1957* (Stanford, Calif.: Stanford University Press, 1968).

that betrayed nation—Czechoslovakia disappeared behind the iron curtain. A few months later, in June, the Soviets challenged the postwar division of Germany that had left West Germany occupied by the Western powers, East Germany in Soviet hands, and the city of Berlin similarly divided. The challenge took the form of a Soviet blockade of West Berlin in an effort to dislodge the occupying Allied powers. It is not surprising that Western Europeans were alarmed by these overt acts of Soviet hostility. It suddenly became clear that a second requirement for Europe's continued economic recovery, along with regional integration, was greater military security.

The Europeans already had taken modest steps in this direction. In March 1947, France and Britain had signed the Treaty of Dunkirk to provide for their mutual defense against a threat to their security. A year later, Britain, France, the Netherlands, Belgium, and Luxembourg signed the Brussels Pact for their collective self-defense. Its members expected the system of collective defense, officially proclaimed the Western European Union, to attract American military support. They were not disappointed. In April 1949, these countries—along with the United States, Canada, Denmark, Iceland, Italy, Norway, and Portugal—created the North Atlantic Treaty Organization. The NATO treaty called for "continuous and effective self-help and mutual aid" among its signatories; an invasion of one "shall be considered an attack against them all." Former isolationist Arthur Vandenberg, chair of the Senate Foreign Relations Committee, hailed the agreement as "the most important step in American foreign policy since the promulgation of the Monroe Doctrine."

The creation of NATO set a precedent for the United States. Long wary of "entangling alliances," especially with the European powers, the United States committed itself to an alliance in peacetime. It would not allow another gap in the balance of power, nor would it allow itself to become drawn into a war after it had begun. It would commit itself indefinitely to preserving the European balance. From Washington's perspective, NATO would serve two vital functions. First, in countering the Soviet threat, the alliance would enhance the *collective defense* of its members against Soviet provocations. Second, by subordinating their military forces to the U.S.-led alliance, the Western European governments would defuse their internal rivalries, which had sparked both world wars. This function of regional *collective security*, though rarely emphasized by European and American leaders, played a vital role in their calculations. When West Germany joined NATO in May 1955, the alliance's role in dampening internal tensions became even greater.

Like the Marshall Plan, the birth of NATO provoked the Soviet Union to respond in kind. Just after West Germany's entry into NATO, the Soviets established the Warsaw Treaty Organization, comprising the Soviet Union and its seven satellite states in Eastern Europe: Albania, Bulgaria, Czechoslovakia, East Germany, Hungary, Poland, and Romania. The Warsaw Pact, as it became known, was modeled on NATO, although the Soviet satellites played a relatively minor role in managing the alliance. Indeed, Eastern Europeans had little choice in the matter because their governments were controlled by Moscow.

The creation and expansion of NATO were closely linked to the future of Germany, which bordered on the Soviet bloc. Germany had held the key to the European balance of power since at least 1870 when Prussia defeated France, Europe's preeminent land power, and established a united Germany. And Germany continued in that role even after its defeat in 1945. It was inevitable, then, that the Soviet Union and the United States would clash over the future of Germany. As noted, Soviet troops occupied eastern Germany, and the Allies controlled the western region. Late in the war, the leaders of Great Britain, France, and the United States had chosen to merge their territories and govern them as a single unit. The Soviet Union would be alone in controlling the eastern frontier.

This stalemate produced the division of Germany along Cold War lines. The Allies sought to create an independent, democratic, and economically viable West Germany based in Bonn. Meanwhile, the Soviet Union consolidated its hold over East Germany and installed a pro-Soviet government that would become part of the communist bloc in Eastern Europe. The Allies, which had decided to assist rather than punish their former enemy, benefited most from this arrangement. West Germany contained the majority of Germany's population and much of its industrial power. East Germany possessed far fewer resources, and what little it retained after World War II was hauled away in boxcars to the Soviet Union.

Recurring Conflicts over Berlin

The Soviets reacted to the creation of a potentially strong West Germany by blockading West Berlin in 1948. Berlin, like Germany, was supposed to be administered by the four occupying powers, but the growing Cold War had divided the city just as it had Germany. Lying deep in East German territory, surrounded by Soviet divisions, the western half of the city was a vulnerable spot where the Soviets could apply pressure on the Western powers. But the issue at stake was more than the Western presence in Berlin: it was Germany itself. Berlin, as the old capital of Germany, was the symbol of the ongoing conflict between the Soviet Union and

West. If the Allies could be forced out of Berlin, German confidence in the United States would be undermined.

The Soviet attempt to drive the United States out of Western Europe left Washington with little choice but to defend its position in West Berlin. To that end, Truman launched a continuous airlift of supplies to Berlin instead of attempting to puncture the blockade on the ground, which might have sparked armed conflict between the superpowers. The Soviets waited to see if the Western powers could take care of West Berlin's 2.5 million citizens indefinitely. It would require a minimum of four thousand tons of food and fuel daily—an enormous amount to ship in by air. But after 324 days, the Soviets were convinced that the Americans and British were more than equal to the task. Although the total supplies did not immediately reach the four-thousand-ton target, Western planes, landing at three-minute intervals, eventually flew in as much as thirteen thousand tons a day, or 60 percent more than the eight thousand tons previously sent in each day by ground transport. Faced with this colossal Allied achievement, the Soviets called off the blockade in May 1949.

The United States had plainly demonstrated to the Soviet Union that it was determined to hold Western Europe and not allow further Soviet expansion and to the West Germans that they could count on America to protect them. Economically, the United States hastened Germany's recovery through Marshall Plan funds. Militarily, through NATO, West Germany would enjoy a greater sense of national security without becoming a threat to its neighbors.

Later attempts by the Soviet Union to evict the Western Allies from Berlin only strengthened West Germany's resolve. Joseph Stalin's successor, Nikita Khrushchev, was left with an almost impossible task. His attempted reforms, designed to soften the hard edges of Stalinism, only encouraged dissent and threats to Soviet control over Eastern Europe. The Soviet Union's credibility as the regional hegemon depended on maintaining a presence in West Berlin. Khrushchev pursued this objective by issuing an ultimatum to the Allies in 1958 to end the four-power occupation of the in six months. His threats, however, fell on deaf ears. Finally, in 1961, hchev ordered the construction of a wall through Berlin to separate rn and western parts of the city and eliminate the escape hatch rmans. The Berlin Wall became the most vivid symbol of the ld War in Europe.

merica's postwar strategy in Western Europe during of the Cold War accomplished its many objectives. ne discouraged Soviet meddling in the domestic

d War

politics of America's allies. The Bretton Woods accords and Marshall Plan set Western Europe on the path to economic recovery, democracy, and social stability. Through NATO, the United States established a formidable military presence that further enhanced European security. Most of all, by drawing a clear line between the American and Soviet spheres of influence, the United States demonstrated that it was in Europe to stay.

Confronting Revolution in East Asia

Whereas Europe held strategic priority in the U.S. defense strategy of the early Cold War years, Asia continued to be of secondary interest. In fact, the United States found Western Europe so vital to American security that it vowed that any Soviet move into the region would provoke an all-out clash with the United States and NATO. Moreover, it explicitly delivered this promise to Soviet leaders throughout this period. By contrast, no single area in Asia was thought to be worth the cost of total war. The region was too distant, its economies too modest, and its political and social systems too distinct from those in the West.

Yet, as American leaders revived Western Europe, they soon recognized that, to contain communism, they would have to channel their economic and military resources to other parts of the world, including the Asian perimeter of the Soviet Union and China. But whereas pressure on Europe united the Western powers, developments in Asia divided Europe and the United States. In Washington, upheavals in Asia inspired a prolonged and heated debate between "Asia firsters" and those seeking to limit U.S. containment efforts to Western Europe. Events would propel the United States into action on both fronts.

The collapse in 1949 of Nationalist China, on which the United States was counting in the emerging Cold War, led to the establishment of the People's Republic of China (PRC) under the leadership of communist Mao Zedong. The communists' victory was quickly followed by China's annexation of neighboring Tibet, a treaty of friendship between China and the Soviet Union, and the invasion of South Korea by communist North Korea. The logic of George Kennan's containment strategy would be put to the test far from the iron curtain, as would the leadership of the United States in the emerging anticommunist coalition. American resolve required more than words. Concrete action was essential to sustain containment on a global scale.

The Chinese Revolution

During World War II, the United States had two goals in the western Pacific region: to defeat Japan and to help sustain the government of China so it could play a leading role in protecting the postwar peace in East Asia.[12] At a meeting in Cairo in 1943, President Roosevelt and British prime minister Winston Churchill promised Chinese premier Chiang Kaishek that all Chinese territories conquered by Japan would be returned after the war. In typically American fashion, Roosevelt thought that the mere pronouncement of China as a great power could actually convert it into one: one need only believe strongly enough in the desirability of an event for it to happen. But American faith without a viable Chinese government was not enough to accomplish the task. In their desire to create stability in East Asia based on a U.S.-Sino alliance, the Roosevelt and Truman administrations ignored the depth of hostilities between the ruling Chinese Nationalists and communists, who at the time were engaged in a protracted civil war.

Already in control of large segments of China before World War II, the communists had extended their sphere during the war. Meanwhile, the pro-American Nationalist regime was losing popular support and disintegrating. Chiang's failure to satisfy the peasants, the vast majority of China's population, as well as rampant corruption among government officials, paralyzed his efforts to gain control of the country. A government whose principal supporters were the landlords was unlikely to carry out the reforms the peasants sought. As Chiang continued to lose popularity, he turned to repressive measures that further alienated the people, ensuring a communist victory in the civil war. Recognizing his defeat, Chiang withdrew to Taiwan (then called Formosa), an island lying one hundred miles off China's coast. In the fall of 1949, the leader of the communist forces, Mao Zedong, proclaimed victory and established the People's Republic of China.

In Washington, policymakers debated the question of whether the United States could have prevented the PRC's victory. The answer was "perhaps"—*if* American officers had taken over the command of the Nationalist armies; *if* the United States had been willing to commit large-scale land, air, and sea forces; and *if* the United States had been willing to commit even more financial aid than the some $2 billion it had contributed since its victory over Japan. But these conditions could not have been met. America's rapid demobilization had left it with too few forces either to

---

[12] See Herbert Feis, *The China Tangle: The American Effort in China from Pearl Harbor to the Marshall Mission* (New York: Atheneum, 1967).

Impact and Influence: Mao Zedong

Bettmann / Contributor

Today's People's Republic of China (PRC), one of the world's major superpowers, still stands in the shadow of its founding father, Mao Zedong. Born in 1893, Mao had childhood memories of the Chinese government struggling to break free from foreign interference at the turn of the century. After receiving a modern education, Mao struck out as a social reformer, organizing peasant and industrial unions in the 1920s. He then moved into the countryside and established rural "soviets," or revolutionary groups bent on creating a communist system. In the 1930s, Mao's attention shifted to military struggle and civil war, and, as chairman of the breakaway Soviet Republic of China, he led the "long march" in 1934 and 1935 of antigovernment revolutionaries across the country. During World War II, he led his armies against two enemies at once: the Japanese occupying forces and the forces of China's Nationalist regime, led by Chiang Kai-shek.

As the first leader of the PRC in 1949, Mao soon amassed unrivaled control over the world's largest population. At the age of fiftysix, he placed himself at the center of government and society, forcing all citizens to adopt the Chinese Communist Party's "mass line." After several years, Mao briefly softened his rigid posture, declaring in 1956 that Beijing would "let a hundred flowers bloom, let all the schools of thought contend." But he quickly reversed this move toward liberal reform after watching anticommunist rebels nearly topple the Soviet Union's client state in Hungary. He announced that dissent would not be tolerated in China, and that he personally would distinguish between "fragrant flowers and poisonous weeds." Mao then ruled China ruthlessly for the rest of his life, through such societal upheavals as the "Great Leap Forward" and the Cultural Revolution. His death in 1976 left the Communist Party still firmly in control, but it also left the Chinese economy paralyzed by more than a quarter-century of central planning and social engineering that left tens of millions of citizens dead or dislocated. Mao's break with the Soviet Union in the 1960s, and his opening of diplomatic relations with the United States in 1972, made him less threatening to the United States in his final years in power.

supply the officers needed to direct the Nationalist forces or to intervene in China. The United States had only a modest standing army at home, even after the signing of the National Security Act. Nor were the American people in any mood to rearm and remobilize in the late 1940s. There was little sentiment in favor of "rescuing" Eastern Europe from Soviet domination—and far less for fighting a war in China.

Looking beyond the communist victory in China, American officials were optimistic. Secretary of State Dean Acheson expressed his belief that, despite the common ideological points of view of the Chinese and Soviet regimes, they eventually would clash. Acheson predicted that Russia's traditional appetite for a sphere of influence in Manchuria and northern China would arouse Chinese nationalism. Thus Acheson warned President Truman and members of Congress that the United States "should not deflect from the Russians to ourselves the righteous anger and hatred of the Chinese people."[13]

The implications of Acheson's point of view were clear. If the Chinese communists were genuinely concerned about the preservation of China's national interest, they would resist Soviet advances. Mao might become an independent communist leader like Yugoslavia's Marshal Josip Broz Tito, who refused to join the Soviet bloc in Eastern Europe. But if Mao proved subservient to the Soviet Union, he would lose the support of the Chinese people. His regime would be identified with foreign rule because he would appear to serve the interests of another power, even a fellow communist regime. In the end, despite their ideological affinities, Stalin and Mao distrusted one another, and each viewed himself as the true leader of international communism. Even as the two leaders signed a treaty of friendship in 1950, their mutual antagonism was apparent. But before the U.S. divide-and-conquer strategy could be tested, war broke out in another part of East Asia. The conflict on the Korean peninsula created a bitter gulf between the United States and the PRC that lasted for a generation.

Hot War in Korea

Mounting concerns within the Truman administration led to the release in April 1950 of the report known as NSC-68, a dire warning by the National Security Council about communist expansion beyond Europe. "The issues that face us are momentous, involving the fulfillment or destruction not only of this Republic but of civilization itself," wrote Paul Nitze,

---

[13]Dean Acheson, Present at the Creation: My Years in the State Department (New York: Norton, 1969), 356.

the primary author of the government report.[14] The report was designed to gain congressional approval for a major increase in U.S. defense spending. More important, the authors of NSC-68 deliberately sought to alarm the general public, whose support would be required for the escalation of the Cold War.[15]

Events in East Asia quickly affirmed NSC-68's dire forecasts. The invasion of South Korea by North Korea in June 1950 provoked a military response by the United States, under the aegis of the United Nations, and represented the first test of George Kennan's containment strategy. More broadly, the Korean War demonstrated that the Cold War would occasionally become "hot," thrusting the superpowers into active hostilities all along the containment frontier.

Korea had been a divided country since the end of World War II. Under the terms of the postwar settlement, the Soviets would disarm the Japanese in occupied Korea above the thirty-eighth parallel, and the United States would take on the task below, thereby dividing the country until a new government could be established. With the beginning of the Cold War, however, this division became permanent. All American attempts to negotiate an end to the division and establish a united Korea failed.[16] The United States had taken the problem to the United Nations in 1947, calling on it to sponsor free elections throughout the Korean peninsula. The Soviets, however, refused to allow elections in North Korea, which had been transformed into a dictatorship, and thus only the South Koreans cast ballots. The United States quickly recognized South Korea as its newest ally.

Both the South and North Korean governments regarded themselves as the legitimate representatives of the Korean people, and each was dedicated to the reunification of the peninsula under its control. In that sense, the war that broke out when North Korea attacked South Korea on June 25, 1950, was a civil war between two regimes determined to eliminate each other. But it also was an international war because events in Korea after 1945

---

[14]Quoted from the report in Ernest R. May, ed., *American Cold War Strategy: Interpreting NSC-68* (New York: Bedford, 1993), 26.

[15]The NSC-68 report had deep economic roots, as American corporations aggressively lobbied members of Congress, as well as Pentagon officials, for strong action against communist states. See Curt Caldwell, *NSC and the Political Economy of the Early Cold War* (New York: Cambridge University Press, 2011).

[16]See William W. Stueck, *The Korean War: An International History* (Princeton, N.J.: Princeton University Press, 1995). Also see Bruce Cumings, *The Origins of the Korean War* (Princeton, N.J.: Princeton University Press, 1981).

served as a micro-cosm of the Cold War rivalry. North Korea's invasion could not have occurred without Stalin's approval, which, according to evidence revealed later, was given in March 1949.[17]

The survival of South Korea became immediately identified with the containment doctrine. If the principal purpose of containment was to prevent further Soviet expansion, American inaction in the face of such overt provocation would only encourage future aggressive acts. And if the United States stood by while South Korea fell, it would demonstrate to the world that the United States was either afraid of Soviet power or unconcerned about the safety of its allies. American guarantees to help preserve other nations' political independence would be regarded as valueless, leaving them with no alternative but to turn to neutralism for protection and to seek some form of accommodation with the Soviet Union.

At first, the United States tried to stem the North Korean advance using air and sea forces alone. But after a few days, Gen. Douglas MacArthur, the U.S. military commander in the Far East, reported that Korea would be lost unless ground forces were deployed to halt the advancing enemy army. In response, Washington ordered its occupation troops from Japan to Korea to participate officially in a United Nations peacekeeping force. The UN's involvement in the conflict suited the United States because one of the aims of American foreign policy was to associate its Cold War policies with the humanitarian values and peace-making functions of the UN. Although many countries justified their policies in moral terms, American leaders were especially motivated to do so. The nation's power had to be "righteous" power, used not for purposes of power politics and selfish national advantage but for the peace and welfare of all people.

North Korea's offensive extended far beyond Seoul, and by September 1950, the UN coalition had retreated to the southeastern corner of the peninsula. On September 15, in a daring operation, MacArthur, now UN supreme commander, landed troops at the west coast port of Inchon and launched a counteroffensive that was intended to divide and conquer the North Korean forces. This strategy succeeded as the UN coalition regained control of the peninsula's center while North Korean troops in the region retreated northward. Those left in the southern region were trapped without reinforcements and supplies.

---

[17]Zhihua Shen, *Mao, Stalin and the Korean War: Trilateral Communist Relations in the 1950s*, trans. Neil Silver (New York: Routledge, 2012), 114–125. See Kathryn Weathersby, "The Soviet Role in the Early Phase of the Korean War: New Documentary Evidence," *Journal of American–East Asian Relations* (Winter 1993): 425–458.

When the UN forces reached the thirty-eighth parallel, the question confronting U.S. leaders was whether to cross it. The political aims of the war were compatible with the restoration of South Korea; they did not require a total war and the elimination of the North Korean government or the unconditional surrender of its troops. But the military situation favored the fulfillment of an American goal of several years' standing: the unification of the Korean peninsula. Thus the U.S. government shifted its emphasis from containing the expansion of Soviet power to the forceful elimination of a communist state. The result— North Korean retrenchment, Chinese intervention, and ultimate stalemate—was to teach the United States the foolishness of changing limited political goals in the middle of a war in response to battlefield successes.

The new objective of a militarily united Korea was sanctioned by a UN resolution on October 7. The Chinese viewed the resulting march to their border as threatening, just as Washington had felt threatened by North Korea's march southward toward Japan. So Beijing sent its armies into North Korea under the guise of "volunteers," and in late November it launched a major offensive that drove the UN forces south of the thirty-eighth parallel. Throughout December 1950 and early January 1951, it was far from clear that UN troops could hold the peninsula, but they rallied and turned back the Chinese offensive. By March, they had once more advanced to the thirty-eighth parallel. The United States was again faced with the decision of whether to seek a militarily unified Korea or accept the status quo, a divided Korea.[18]

There was no doubt about what MacArthur, articulating the traditional American approach to war, wanted to do. War, he said, indicated that "you have exhausted all other potentialities of bringing the disagreements to an end," and, once engaged, "there is no alternative than to apply every available means to bring it to a swift end. War's very objective is victory—not prolonged indecision. In war there is no substitute for victory."[19] MacArthur recommended a naval blockade of the Chinese coast; air bombardment of China's industrial complex, communications network, and military bases; and "diversionary action possibly leading to counter-invasion" by Chiang Kai-shek against the mainland.

---

[18] See Rosemary Foot, A Substitute for Victory: The Politics of Peacemaking at the Korean Armistice Talks (Ithaca, N.Y.: Cornell University Press, 1990).

[19] Quoted in John Spanier, The Truman-MacArthur Controversy and the Korean War (Cambridge, Mass.: Belknap Press, 1959), 222.

But Truman rejected MacArthur's proposals as too risky, because such actions could spark a full-scale war between the superpowers. Unable to persuade his military commander, the president was forced to fire MacArthur rather than endure a prolonged internal struggle between the White House and the Pentagon. Such infighting was very costly in view of the stakes involved. The Sino-Soviet treaty bound the Soviet Union to come to the aid of China if it were attacked by Japan "or any other state which should unite with Japan" (an obvious reference to the United States). The Soviets' need to maintain their prestige in the communist world made it impossible for them to ignore a direct attack on China.

The truce talks begun in the summer of 1951 produced nothing but deadlock. The war was a drain on the United States and had to be ended. When Dwight D. Eisenhower took office in January 1953, he decided that if his efforts to gain an armistice failed, the United States would bomb Chinese bases and supply sources, blockade the mainland coast, and possibly use atomic weapons. It is doubtful, however, that the administration's threats were responsible for ending the war in July. Other factors appeared more critical. Chief among these was Stalin's death in March. His successors called for "peaceful coexistence" with the West and tried to convince the noncommunist world that they wanted to relax international tensions. Agreement on an armistice would provide evidence of their goodwill.

The Korean War thus ended just where it had begun—at the thirty-eighth parallel—and on basically the same terms the Truman administration had been unable to reach. As a result, the Korean partition became part of the global dividing line between the communist and noncommunist blocs. In August 1953, the United States signed a mutual security pact with South Korea designed to deter another attack from the north, a pact that remained in place throughout—and beyond—the Cold War.

The line of containment also was drawn in the Taiwan Strait, where U.S.-Sino relations had turned increasingly bitter after China's revolution and subsequent intervention in Korea. To Mao, Taiwan was an "outlaw province" that must be brought under Beijing's control; to American leaders, Taiwan was the legitimate seat of China's government. Eisenhower requested and received from Congress in January 1955 the authority to deploy American forces to protect Taiwan and "such related positions and territories" as the president judged necessary. As in Korea, the United States established its commitment to defend a line of containment in East Asia, this time just off the PRC's coast. The struggle over Taiwan defined the Cold War in East Asia in much the same way the Berlin Wall epitomized the conflict in Europe.

Domestic Pressures for a Global Crusade

The Chinese revolution and the Korean War dramatically altered American foreign policy less than a decade after its conception. Whereas U.S. policy had been limited to containing Soviet power in Western Europe and the Mediterranean, it now spilled over into a broader anticommunist crusade. Americans were shocked by the collapse in 1949 of Nationalist China, the establishment of a communist PRC, and the hot war in Korea. Suddenly, the security achieved by the containment policies in Europe—the Truman Doctrine, the Marshall Plan, the Berlin airlift, and NATO—seemed to have disintegrated. It appeared that the United States had stemmed communism in Europe only to see it break out in Asia.

The resulting insecurity and anxiety were heightened by other developments. The first was the explosion in 1949 of the Soviet Union's first atomic bomb, which shattered the American monopoly on the weapon widely regarded as the principal deterrent against a Soviet attack. The creation of a communist regime in China and the subsequent outbreak of the Korean War added to American insecurities. At home, bipartisan support for Truman's foreign policy had steadily eroded. The conservative wing of the Republican Party was especially restless. Led by Wisconsin senator Joseph R. McCarthy, these critics argued that the reason China fell was that the "pro-communist" administrations of Franklin Roosevelt and Harry Truman had either deliberately or unwittingly "sold China down the river." Therefore, the U.S. government must be filled with communist sympathizers who "tailored" American policy to advance the global aims of the Soviet Union. Low morale among the Chinese Nationalists, the Nationalist government's corruption and military ineptitude, and Chiang's repressive policies had nothing to do with it; nor did the communists' superior organization, direction, morale, and ability to identify with popular aspirations.

The State Department bore the brunt of this rhetorical onslaught. McCarthy verbally attacked Foreign Service officers and Secretary of State Dean Acheson on a daily basis. But his accusations, which continued as he chaired the Government Operations Committee in the Eisenhower administration, were not directed only toward government officials. Academics and others also were charged with being security risks or were accused of being "un-American." Many of the accused were fired, and others—especially stage actors and Hollywood figures—were blacklisted. Nationally, the political atmosphere during the early 1950s bordered on hysteria. Although McCarthy was censured by the Senate in December 1954 for

Map 3-1 The Korean War, 1950–1953

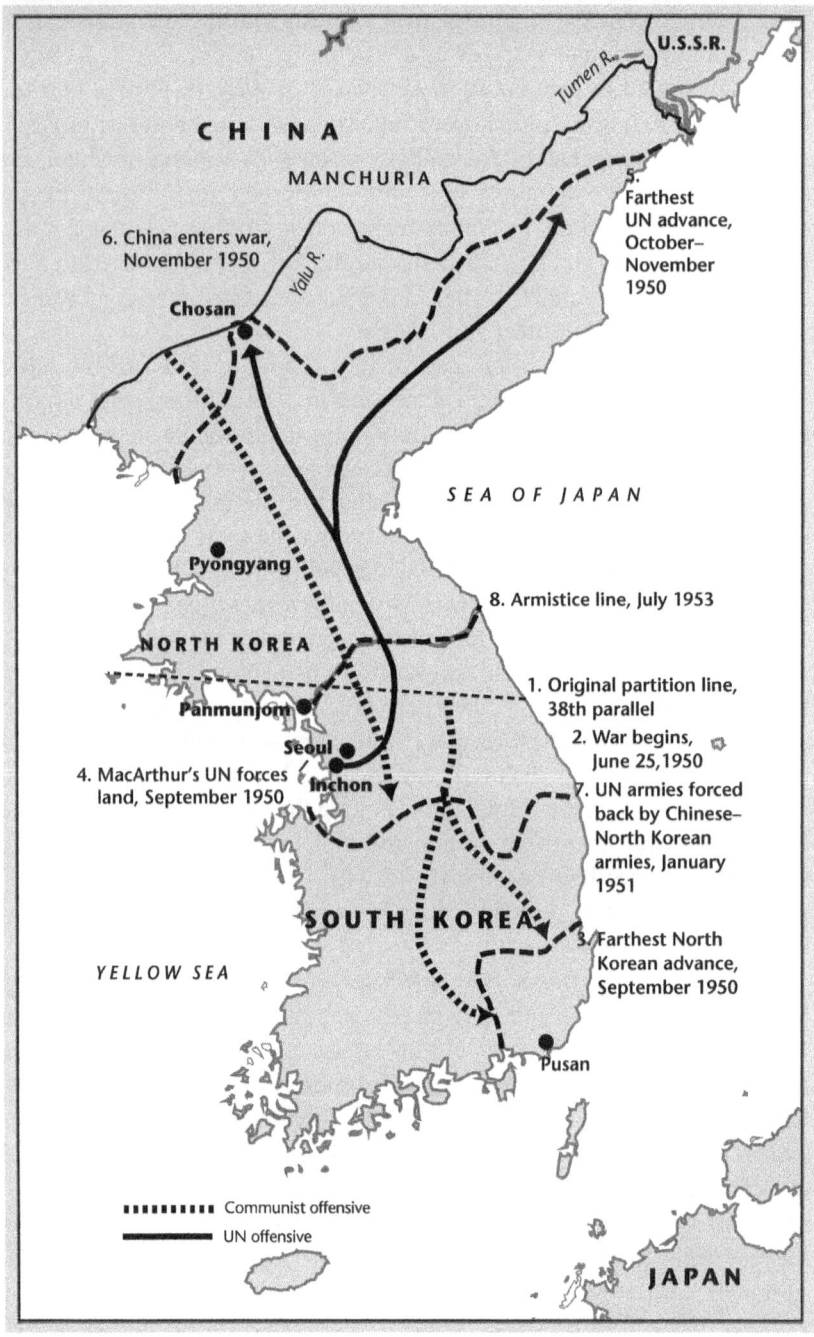

5. Farthest UN advance, October–November 1950

6. China enters war, November 1950

8. Armistice line, July 1953

1. Original partition line, 38th parallel

2. War begins, June 25, 1950

7. UN armies forced back by Chinese–North Korean armies, January 1951

3. Farthest North Korean advance, September 1950

4. MacArthur's UN forces land, September 1950

CHINA

MANCHURIA

U.S.S.R.

Tumen R.

Yalu R.

Chosan

Pyongyang

NORTH KOREA

Panmunjom

Seoul

Inchon

SOUTH KOREA

YELLOW SEA

Pusan

SEA OF JAPAN

JAPAN

▪▪▪▪▪▪▪▪▪ Communist offensive
━━━━━ UN offensive

his excessive claims and vicious tactics, his contribution to the frenzied national mood was irreversible.

The most significant result of all these developments was the transformation of American foreign policy from a limited anti-Soviet orientation to a broader anticommunist crusade. The primary goal was now to prevent territorial expansion by any member of the Sino-Soviet bloc. All communist states were considered enemies, regardless of size, location, or status. Lost in the crusading spirit were critical distinctions between America's vital and secondary interests. In the Cold War, all interests were vital, all states were either allies or enemies, and all citizens were expected to fall in line.

Eisenhower's "New Look" in Foreign Policy

Eisenhower maintained his popular national image even as public fears regarding the Cold War continued to fester. He sought to allay these fears in several ways—primarily by bolstering U.S. conventional and nuclear forces, creating new security alliances, and approving a variety of covert operations by the CIA. In 1953, U.S. defense spending consumed 60 percent of the federal budget as 3.5 million men and women served in the armed forces. The State Department, meanwhile, quadrupled its staff and greatly expanded its diplomatic presence overseas. The "arsenal of democracy" created by Franklin Roosevelt during World War II had become a permanent fixture in the United States—one that would outlast the Cold War.[20]

As described in the previous chapter, nuclear weapons played a key role in the globalized struggle against communism. The fear of nuclear annihilation was expected to discourage the superpowers from upsetting the status quo. In short, nuclear weapons were designed not so much to be used, but to serve the vital function of mutual *deterrence*. Nuclear weapons also made possible a reduction in military expenditures. In addition to his credentials as a war hero,

President Eisenhower was a fiscal conservative who was impressed by the ability of nuclear weapons to give the United States "more bang for the buck."[21]

---

[20] On Eisenhower's efforts to centralize the armed forces, see David Jablonsky, *War by Land, Sea, and Air: Dwight Eisenhower and the Concept of Unified Command* (New Haven, Conn.: Yale University Press, 2010).

[21] Eisenhower's nuclear strategy faced strong resistance from the Pentagon, which claimed the president was trying to maintain American security "on the cheap." See Dale R. Herspring, *The Pentagon and the Presidency: Civil–Military Relations from FDR to George W. Bush* (Lawrence: University Press of Kansas, 2005), chap. 4.

For this and other reasons, Eisenhower assigned nuclear weapons a prominent role in his restructuring of U.S. security policy, labeled the "New Look." In the future, U.S. military forces would rely less on conventional forces—which cost a great deal to train, equip, and maintain—and more on nuclear deterrence. At the same time, Eisenhower and his secretary of state, John Foster Dulles, believed that the only effective means of preserving the "balance of terror" (a term coined by Winston Churchill) was to make clear that challenges to the status quo would be met with "massive retaliation." In their view, the communists would not have invaded South Korea had they known their attack would be met with retaliatory air strikes on Moscow. Their expectation was that by going to the brink of war, the United States would be able to deter future Koreas.[22]

In this environment, the survival of U.S. nuclear forces became central not only to the nation's security, but also to the security of its allies, which were protected by the "extended" deterrent of U.S. and NATO nuclear forces. In recognition of this situation, the Eisenhower administration sought to disperse the nation's nuclear forces in a "triad"—ground-based launchers, aircraft, and submarines—so that the weapons were less vulnerable to a surprise attack. The goal of protecting nuclear forces became as crucial as their production. Preserving deterrence was a continuing, never-ending task, not simply because some change in the balance might precipitate war, but because shifting strategic balances might affect the risks each side was willing to take.[23]

Eisenhower's "New Look" took on other dimensions as well. Even before his election, American leaders had departed further from their traditional aversion to "entangling alliances." In addition to NATO, the United States pledged in 1947 to defend the countries of the Western Hemisphere through the Inter-American Treaty of Reciprocal Assistance. The Rio Treaty, as it became known, was followed a year later by the creation of the Organization of American States, in which twenty-one countries in the region extended their cooperation beyond collective security. In 1951, the United States joined Australia and New Zealand in creating the ANZUS alliance in the Pacific. Individual security guarantees also were extended to Japan, the Philippines, Taiwan, and South Korea as "pactomania" took hold among American military planners.

---

[22] See Richard H. Immermann, *John Foster Dulles and the Diplomacy of the Cold War* (Princeton, N.J.:Princeton University Press, 1990).

[23] For an elaboration, see Lawrence Freedman, *Deterrence* (Cambridge, UK: Polity Press, 2004). Also see Freedman, *The Evolution of Nuclear Strategy*, 3rd ed. (New York: Palgrave Macmillan, 2003).

This process of alliance building escalated under the Eisenhower administration, which in 1954 created the Southeast Asia Treaty Organization (SEATO). The new alliance, designed to "contain" the Soviet Union beyond the European front, included the United States, Australia, Great Britain, France, New Zealand, the Philippines, Pakistan, and Thailand. Five years later, Eisenhower presided over the creation of the Central Treaty Organization (CENTO), which brought together the United States, Great Britain, Iran, Pakistan, and Turkey. Both of these alliances, however, proved less durable than NATO given their lack of popular support. When these states sought to maintain the containment walls, they were often unable, despite American help, to mobilize their citizens, many of whom viewed the alliances as attempts to preserve Western influence and prop up authoritarian regimes. America's containment strategy thus encountered greater difficulties as its geographic scope widened, a pattern that became painfully evident in the developing world during the 1960s and 1970s.

Finally, Eisenhower greatly expanded the mission of the CIA, which launched a variety of "covert" operations that sought to tip the balance of power in favor of the United States without the use of large-scale (and public) military force. Among other such operations, the CIA in 1953 helped organize the overthrow of Iran's prime minister, Mohammad Mossadegh, after he attempted to nationalize his nation's oil fields. A year later, Eisenhower approved a CIA covert operation in Guatemala (described in the next chapter), whose elected leader was suspected of being a communist sympathizer. Such covert operations, which were hardly mentioned when the CIA was created just a few years earlier, became highly controversial once they became known to the American people and foreign governments. To many Americans, such actions contradicted the democratic values of the United States and threatened its self-image as an "exceptional" world power.

Also apparent was the fact that most CIA covert operations took place in the developing world, far from the front lines of the Cold War in central Europe. The use of such tactics demonstrated how complex American foreign policy became when North-South tensions overlapped with the tensions between the Cold War superpowers. Africa and Latin America emerged as bloody "theaters" of the Cold War, and the conflict in Vietnam paralyzed the U.S. containment effort. As the following chapter describes, managing these conflicts consumed the energies of American foreign policymakers, even as they sought new ways to resolve the festering East-West tensions between Washington and Moscow.

Map 3-2 U.S. Cold War Alliances

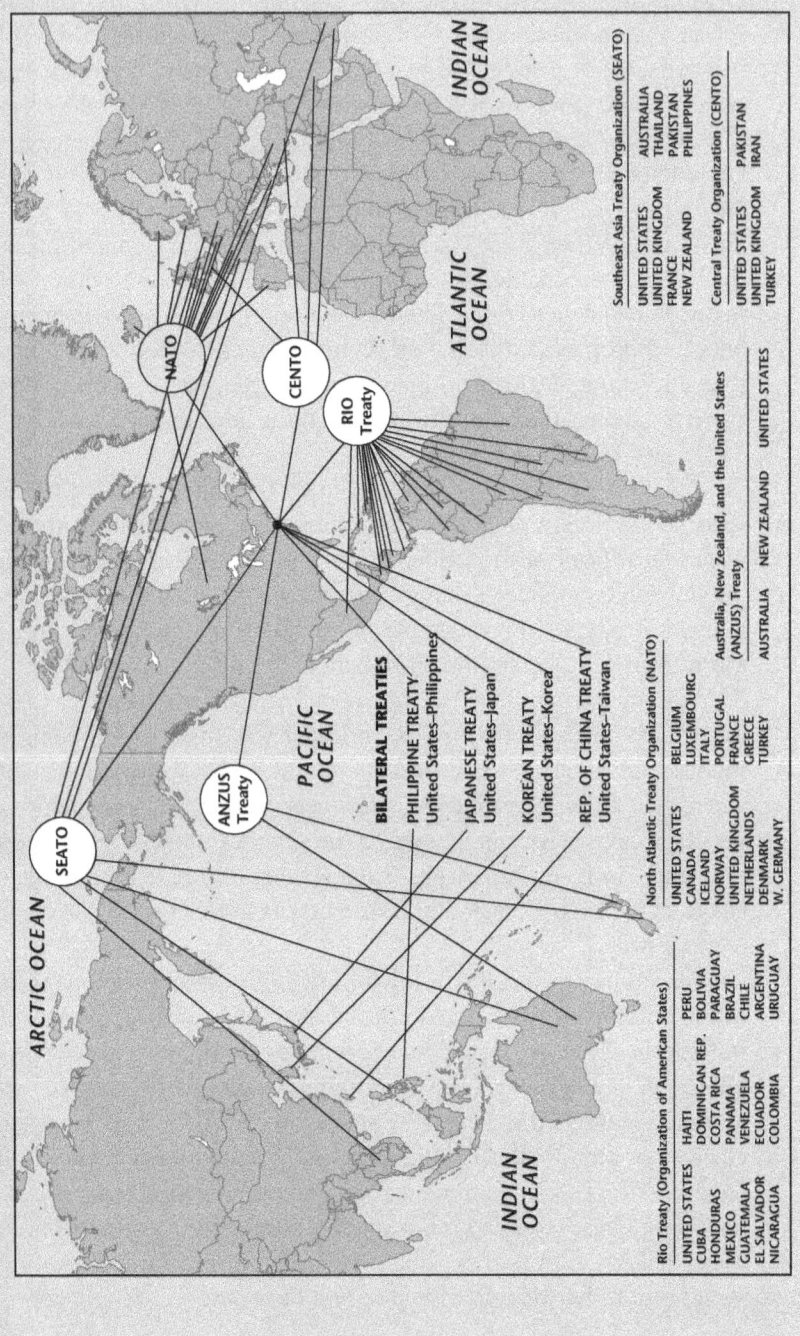

4

North-South Tensions and the Vietnam War

The Cold War was generally viewed as a struggle between "East" (the Soviet bloc) and "West" (the American bloc). The same period, however, featured a vital North-South dimension. From this perspective, the world was functionally, if crudely, divided into industrialized countries and those that were primarily agricultural in nature—the so-called *developing* countries. The importance of this North-South dimension increased during the two decades after World War II as the European powers relinquished their colonies in Africa, southern Asia, and other areas. Although this was clearly a step forward in terms of global democracy, American leaders worried about the unstable political and economic conditions that accompanied the emergence of the "Third World."[1]

The evolving membership of the United Nations (UN) confirmed the importance of these countries. The UN had 55 members in 1946; 76 members in 1955; 127 members in 1970; and 154 members in 1980. By 2009, UN membership stood at 192. With each increment of growth, the proportion of states located in developing regions increased. Aside from the former colonies, the established countries of Latin America, East Asia, and other areas became part of the "South" in the economic balance of world power. With its principle of one country–one vote in the UN General Assembly, these member-states could—and would—dominate the agenda.

Developing Countries in the Crossfire

In the bipolar context of the Cold War, the developing countries did not represent independent centers of power but rather represented objects of competition for the two superpowers. During their early years of independence, however, most former colonies refused to align themselves with

---

[1] Although the term *Third World* obscures the regional diversity among developing countries, for political leaders and most scholars of the period, the term served to differentiate these largely impoverished states from northern capitalist countries—the *First World*—and communist countries—the *Second World*.

U.S. Army helicopters provide air cover for South Vietnamese ground troops as they attack a Vietcong camp near Saigon in March 1965. Although American troop levels soared to more than five hundred thousand during this period, the United States was unable to wrest control of the conflict and prevent the creation of a communist government in Vietnam.

Washington or Moscow. Instead, they created a "nonaligned movement" that, despite their best efforts, proved futile.

Communist leaders saw decolonization as proof that the international capitalist order was disintegrating. The colonial powers such as Great Britain and France had maintained capitalist economies that, according to Marxist-Leninist theory, depended on captive overseas territories for raw materials and export markets. This theory offered a ready explanation for World War I and the Great Depression: a predictable consequence of capitalist states exhausting their opportunities for colonial expansion. Steeped in this perspective, Soviet and Chinese leaders embraced and supported the new states. Their overtures appealed to the hostility within many developing countries toward their former colonial rulers.

From Washington's very different perspective, worries about the introduction of Soviet and Chinese communism into developing areas stemmed not from fears of conspiracy or military control, but from the repressive model of development that communism offered. The Soviet Union held itself up as a model of a primitive feudal society that had been transformed into a modern industrial state in one generation. Overlooked, however, were the coercion, massive terror, and staggering human costs associated with that accomplishment. Joseph Stalin's forced collectivization of Soviet agriculture resulted in the deaths of more than ten million peasants (*kulaks*), either through the purges and mass murders of Stalin's opponents or through the crushing famine of the early 1930s.[2] The Soviet leader waged an undeclared war throughout the period against non-Russian minorities in the Soviet Union, particularly Muslims, and his security forces brutally suppressed leaders of the once-flourishing Christian churches.

An even greater number of Chinese peasants died under Mao Zedong's reform efforts, particularly the "Great Leap Forward" initiated in 1958. In the years that followed, the Chinese leader forced the huge population of peasants into massive agricultural collectives and then ordered them to produce steel and manufactured goods as well as commodities. In the end, though, his grandiose experiment produced mainly chaos and a massive famine, bringing China's agricultural and industrial production to a crashing halt.[3] Then, in the mid-1960s, Mao launched a "Cultural Revolution" against his enemies and dispatched thousands of Red Guards to harass, torture, and kill those who strayed from his "mass line." Teachers, artisans, and intellectuals were the primary targets, but the crackdown included anyone who was suspected of having sympathy for Western values. The social upheaval that resulted further isolated China from most foreign countries and produced a sullen, resentful popular mood that persisted long after Mao's death in 1976. An estimated seventy million Chinese citizens died from Mao's social engineering and executions of "counter-revolutionaries."[4] The casualties also included natives of Tibet, a formerly independent region in western China whose Buddhist customs and monasteries were destroyed in Mao's reign of terror.[5]

Despite these calamities and atrocities committed by the Soviet Union and China, U.S. leaders worried that the heads of poor countries might decide that the potential benefits of communism outweighed its social costs. Compounding their anxiety, the atrocities being committed under Stalin and Mao were generally unknown outside those closed societies; all that was conveyed publicly was the promise of mass

---

[2] See Robert Conquest, *The Great Terror: A Reassessment* (New York: Oxford University Press, 1990).

[3] See Frederick C. Teiwes, *China's Road to Disaster: Mao, Central Politicians, and Provincial Leaders in the Unfolding of the Great Leap Forward, 1955–1959* (Armonk, N.Y.: M. E. Sharpe, 1999).

[4] Jung Chang and Jon Halliday, *Mao: The Unknown Story* (New York: Knopf, 2005), 83.

[5] For an elaboration, see Mary Craig, *Tears of Blood: A Cry for Tibet* (New York: HarperCollins, 1992).

liberation. In this context, U.S. policymakers believed that the economic model developing countries chose to adopt was critical to U.S. security and, more broadly, to an international environment safe for open and democratic societies.

Once the countries of the Third World became independent, they confronted a legacy of poverty, illiteracy, and disease. In the 1950s, for example, the annual per capita income of these states rarely reached $100, and life expectancies seldom exceeded fifty years. To remedy their distress and to narrow the enormous gap between poor and rich nations, many new countries sought to transform their traditional agrarian societies into modern industrial states. This transformation also had great political significance, for it demanded that citizens transfer their allegiance from the ethnic and religious groups that had held their loyalty to their newly constructed nation-states. The fact that the concept of national loyalty was largely unfamiliar to the citizens of the newly independent countries intensified the need to satisfy the popular "revolution of rising expectations." American state builders believed the former colonies must be "modernized and then integrated into a broader, liberal capitalist system. . . . Economic development became the watchword of economists and others concerned with issues of global raw materials production, finance and trade, technical aid, trade discrimination, labor, and general poverty."[6]

In considering their prospects for economic development, leaders of the new countries realized their success depended on whether their economic growth would advance faster than their population growth. In 1830, the world population was one billion; by 1930, it had doubled to two billion, and by 1975—just forty-five years later—it had doubled again to four billion. In October 1999, the global population surpassed six billion. Just as developing countries represented a majority of nation-states by 1970, their share of the world's population also grew dramatically so that, in 2014, 83 percent of the world's population of 7.2 billion lived in the developing world.[7] By contrast, birthrates in the industrialized countries declined after 1850. With industrialization and the growth of cities came the spread of literacy and birth-control techniques. Developing states, however, did not reach a comparable level of economic development.

---

[6] James M. Carter, *Inventing Vietnam: The United States and State Building, 1954–1968* (New York: Cambridge University Press, 2008), 28–29.

[7] Population Reference Bureau, "2014 World Population Data Sheet," http://www.prb.org/pdf14/2014-world-population-data-sheet_eng.pdf.

The poorer the populations were in developing countries, the higher their rates of population growth.[8]

Conflicts abounded in the developing countries, whose citizens often had no common culture upon which national unity could be based. Citizens also had no natural loyalty to their newly created states, whose boundaries were frequently drawn crudely along colonial frontiers. Once the struggle for independence ended, power tended to fragment. India, for example, split violently into Hindu and Islamic regions after independence, and the latter dissolved further into Pakistan and Bangladesh. Cyprus divided into Turkish and Greek factions, which resulted in partition and an endless UN peacekeeping presence. In 1972, the Tutsi tribe in the African nation of Burundi slaughtered more than one hundred thousand Hutus, initiating a cycle of violence that reached a more horrifying scale in 1994, when some eight hundred thousand Tutsis were slain in Burundi and neighboring Rwanda. The same period witnessed almost constant bloodshed between the Sinhalese and Tamil ethnic communities in Sri Lanka, a large island lying just off the coast of India.

The absence of a strong sense of state identity was soon reflected in the way many leaders of the new countries built themselves up as symbols of nationhood. They did not find this essential task difficult because, as leaders of the movements for independence, their prestige was usually high. One-party rule or military governments existed almost everywhere in the developing world. For example, in Africa, the world's last continent to be freed from colonialism, three-fourths of its 345 million people in 1970 lived under single-party or military rule ten years after independence. Such regimes were highly repressive, but political leaders believed them to be justified and necessary. In their view, an American-style democracy would have led not just to a change of government but also to mass chaos and anarchy.

To many in the developing countries, communism offered a disciplined means of bringing about rapid political, social, economic, and cultural change. Supposedly, the beneficiaries of this system were not the rulers, but the mass populations who had labored for centuries without receiving a significant share of the wealth they produced. Communism, in

---

[8] Whereas the population growth rates of industrialized countries averaged 0.2 percent in 1995, the growth rates of developing countries averaged nearly 2 percent, with many of the world's poorest countries in sub-Saharan Africa recording growth rates well over 3 percent. For an elaboration of this trend, see Richard J. Tobin, "Environment, Population, and the Developing World," in *Environmental Policy in the 1990s: Reform or Reaction?* ed. Norman J. Vig and Michael E. Kraft (Washington, D.C.: CQ Press, 1997), 321–344.

either the Soviet (Leninist) or the Chinese (Maoist) form, thus promised an egalitarian form of economic growth with the benefits of development redistributed fairly among all segments of the population. The emphasis was to be on internal development and the detachment of the developing countries from a global market that, according to neo-Marxist thought, benefited the "core" Western capitalist states and perpetuated the dependency of "peripheral" developing countries.[9]

These arguments appealed to the leaders of many developing countries, who sought in the early 1970s to create a "New International Economic Order" that would be less dependent on the wealthy industrialized states. In the UN, the developing countries formed the Group of 77 to serve as a vehicle for promoting their economic interests. Given their numerical superiority in the UN General Assembly, the developing countries expected to control the UN's agenda, dictate the structure and goals of UN agencies, and, through their strength in numbers, force the industrialized states to meet their demands. Yet such accomplishments would not be easy. Western economists insisted that the economic development of developing countries would stem from their integration into, not isolation from, the market-based economic order established by the Bretton Woods system. Although authoritarian rule might be necessary in the short term to ensure stability, economic growth would pave the way for political reform.[10] American and European leaders optimistically predicted that, with the assistance of industrialized states, the developing countries would evolve through predictable "stages of growth" into modern, industrialized, and democratic societies.[11]

To make this happen, the industrialized countries agreed to contribute a fixed share of their gross national product (GNP) for development aid. In 1969, the World Bank's Pearson Commission endorsed a minimum contribution of 1 percent of GNP, a figure that was lowered to 0.7 percent by the

---

[9] Influential works during this period included Immanuel Wallerstein, *The Modern World-System: Capitalist Agriculture and the Origins of the European World-Economy in the Sixteenth Century* (New York: Academic Press, 1974); Gunner Myrdal, *Economic Theory and Underdeveloped Regions* (New York: Harper and Row, 1971); and Andre Gunder Frank, *Capitalism and Underdevelopment in Latin America: Historical Studies of Chile and Brazil* (New York: Monthly Review Press, 1969). For a more recent assessment, see Wallerstein, "The Inter-state Structure of the Modern World-System," in *International Theory: Positivism and Beyond*, ed. Steve Smith et al. (Cambridge, UK: Cambridge University Press, 1996), 87–107.

[10] See Samuel Huntington, *Political Order in Changing Societies* (New Haven, Conn.: Yale University Press, 1968).

[11] See W. W. Rostow, *Politics and the Stages of Growth* (New York: Cambridge University Press, 1971).

UN and widely accepted by the governments of industrialized states. But, in practice, these aid flows generally fell far below their targets, while benefiting the donors themselves as much as the recipients. After the eruption of the Korean War in 1950, most U.S. aid took the form of military support for authoritarian governments that sided with the United States in the Cold War. Meanwhile, Britain and France disbursed foreign aid primarily to their former colonies, prompting charges of "neocolonialism," and Japan offered large-scale "tied" aid only to its neighbors in East Asia so they could pay for Japanese exports. Only the small nations of Scandinavia, which provided the least volume of aid on an absolute level, consistently reached the World Bank's targets for aid as a percentage of national output.[12]

Many Americans found the plight of the developing world difficult to understand. With its middle-class society, America had managed to avoid the kinds of class conflicts and disputes over basic values that had afflicted European countries and many developing countries. The United States had not experienced a genuine social revolution at its birth—a social revolution seeks to destroy the institutions and social fabric of the old society and create a new society with new institutions and social classes. America, then, was not particularly sympathetic to revolutions and tended to equate them with communism. As a result, Washington's reaction to the communist threat was to support almost any regime, no matter how repressive, if it claimed to be anticommunist. The United States allied itself with many dictators whose days were numbered. Chiang Kai-shek in China, Bao Dai in Indochina, and Ferdinand Marcos in the Philippines are but three of many examples.

This attitude was typical of America's self-righteousness and its inability to understand the deeper social struggles of the Third World. In its attempt to suffocate the communist menace, the United States became committed to the domestic, social, and political status quo in these regions. In trying to preserve freedom, the United States was paradoxically supporting despots who ignored their peoples' aspirations. This internal contradiction within the U.S. alliance system eventually had to be resolved. American support for "strategic allies" only bottled up the social and political resentment and ferment even more, thereby adding to the explosive forces that would burst forth during the Cold War and in its aftermath. When the internal difficulties of the developing countries spilled over into neighboring states, or when they resulted in political disintegration and civil war, they attracted the Soviet Union or the United States, leading to confrontation and, often, military conflict.

---

[12] Steven W. Hook, *National Interest and Foreign Aid* (Boulder, Colo.: Lynne Rienner, 1995).

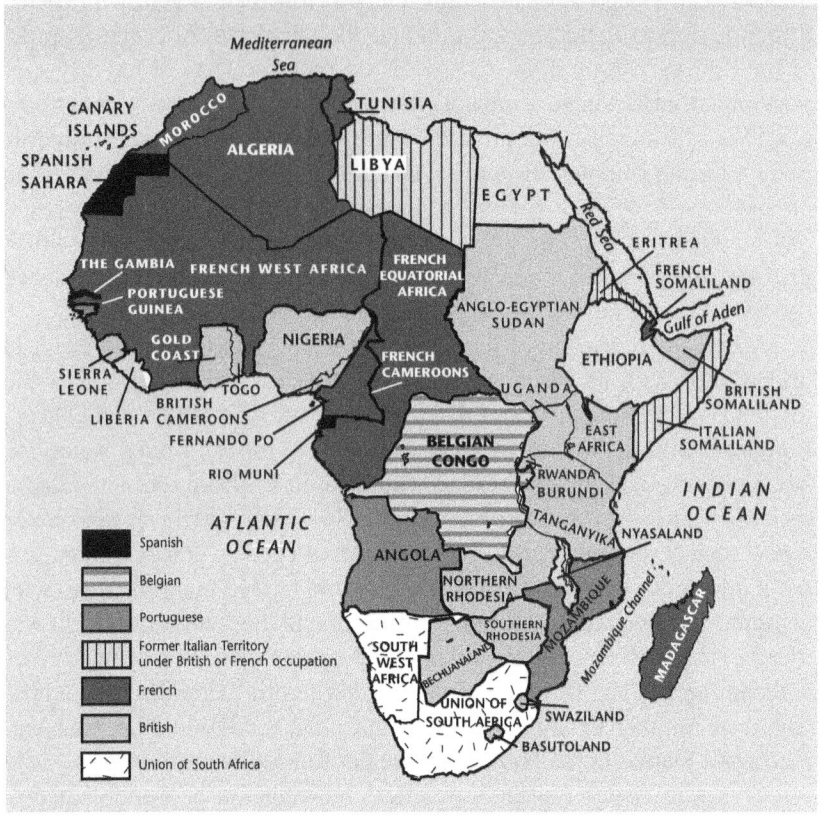

Map 4-1 Africa in 1945

Sub-Saharan Africa proved especially vulnerable to such "failed states," as they became known in the 1990s. Decolonization led to the creation of dozens of countries whose boundaries were drawn, often arbitrarily, by the departing European powers. Meanwhile, the region experienced rapid population growth and urbanization, which increased demands on the new states for expanded utilities, roads, housing, and public services. Lacking the resources to cover these expenses, African leaders often had no choice but to turn to Washington or Moscow for help. Social instability and turmoil were further propelled by the intellectual and cultural changes that accompanied modernization. Many of the customs and religious values that provided some measure of social stability collapsed as people were torn from their age-old moorings. Robbed of their precolonial traditions, they became marginalized in the rapidly changing world. The result too often was a descent into civil war or revolution.

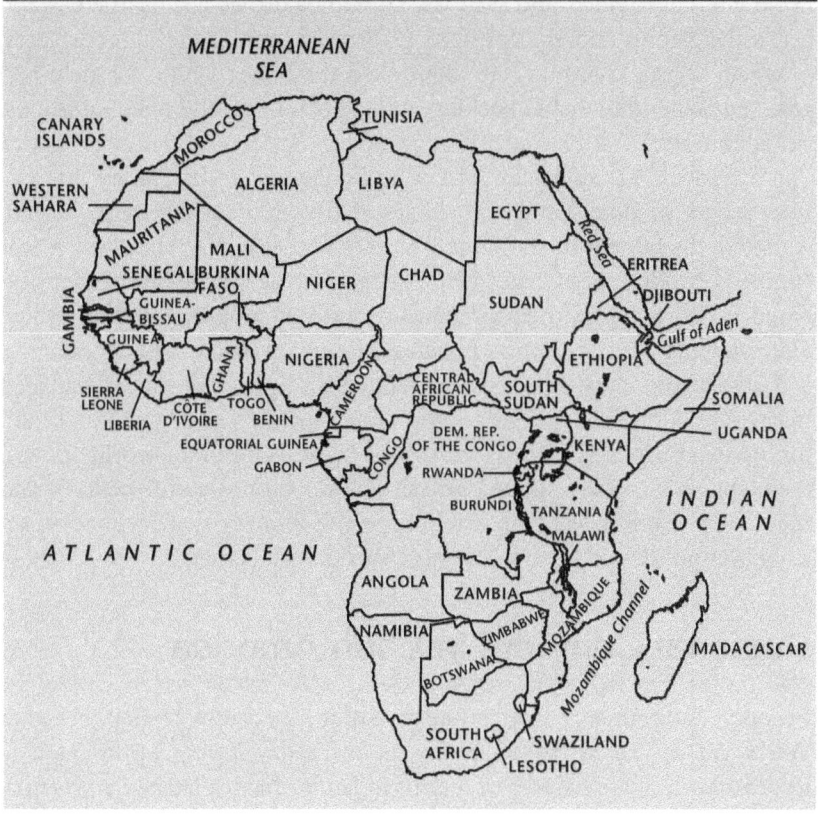

Map 4-2 Africa Today

A dramatic example of Africa's struggle after independence was the Belgian Congo, which became independent in 1960 and almost immediately fell into chaos. The political deterioration began when the rich mining province of Katanga split off into a separate state. Then the Congolese army revolted against the Belgian officials who had remained in the new government to provide technical assistance. In a wild spree, Congolese soldiers began to attack Belgian women and children, which prompted families to flee. Meanwhile, all public services collapsed, because the Congo lacked a well-trained civil service.

When the Belgian government flew in paratroopers to protect its citizens, Congolese premier Patrice Lumumba appealed to the UN to resist the former colonial rulers. It was at this point that the Cold War was injected into the Congo. The UN troops did not compel the Belgians to leave because Secretary-General Dag Hammarskjöld had ordered them to avoid internal conflicts and rivalries. Lumumba turned against the UN and accused Belgium and the Western powers, especially the United States, of conspiring against him. He then asked the Soviet Union for help and received Soviet diplomatic backing, military supplies, and offers of troops, or "volunteers."

In early 1962, after all efforts to unify the Congo had failed, the UN reversed its original stand and deployed troops to quash the civil war. Although the UN efforts took many months and cost lives, the country was "unified." Mobutu Sese Seko, who emerged as the Congo's leader for several decades, renamed the country Zaire and was supported by the United States for his anticommunist policies. Mobutu received vast amounts of U.S. foreign aid, most of which he used to solidify his rule rather than feed his people. Along the way, he expropriated much of Zaire's mineral wealth for his own purposes, to the point that he became one of the world's richest men while his country slipped further into poverty. Mobutu's actions, and the case of Zaire in general, symbolized the disarray that resulted when Cold War politics collided with Third World development.

Regional Conflicts in Latin America

Events in Latin America further illustrate how American foreign policy after World War II was propelled by events in the developing world. As U.S. leaders saw it, mass-based revolutions in Latin America created a potential foothold for communism in the Western Hemisphere and thus constituted a threat to the United States. They responded to the growing unrest in their "backyard" by intervening throughout the region, indirectly in most cases, but directly when a communist victory appeared imminent.

Latin Americans shared two aspirations that were sweeping through developing areas in the decades following World War II: a better life for their masses and self-determination of their national destinies. Since the departure of Spain and Portugal from Latin America in the early 1800s, the United States had dominated its hemispheric neighbors, usually through alliances with the wealthy, landowning governing class. Americans may have believed Latin Americans were free of colonialism, but most inhabitants of the region disagreed. The Monroe Doctrine of 1823 had turned the entire Western Hemisphere into a U.S. sphere of influence; the United States did not have to resort to direct colonial rule. Invested American capital spoke louder than guns, and the U.S. government did not have to give political orders when a nation was a "banana republic."

Map 4-3 Latin America

UNITED STATES

BAHAMA ISLANDS

MEXICO

CUBA

PUERTO RICO

CAYMAN ISLANDS

BELIZE
HONDURAS
JAMAICA

DOMINICAN REPUBLIC
HAITI

GUATEMALA
EL SALVADOR

NICARAGUA

VENEZUELA

CENTRAL AMERICA AND THE CARIBBEAN

COSTA RICA
PANAMA
COLOMBIA

TRINIDAD & TOBAGO

ATLANTIC OCEAN

VENEZUELA
GUYANA
SURINAME
FRENCH GUIANA

COLOMBIA

ECUADOR

PERU

BRAZIL

BOLIVIA

PACIFIC OCEAN

PARAGUAY

CHILE

ATLANTIC OCEAN

ARGENTINA
URUGUAY

FALKLAND ISLANDS

SOUTH AMERICA
Cape Horn

In contrast to their rhetorical calls for democratic rule, U.S. leaders actively supported military rulers throughout Latin America, and the United States exercised its self-appointed "international police powers" in the region.[13] The United States intervened frequently in Central America and the Caribbean early in the twentieth century to maintain *stability*, a word that was synonymous with U.S. control. When American troops withdrew, they left behind handpicked military leaders to protect U.S. economic and military interests. The Good Neighbor Policy, launched by President Franklin Roosevelt in 1933, was designed primarily to cement close relations with pro-American dictators, including Fulgencio Batista of Cuba, Rafael Trujillo of the Dominican Republic, and Anastasio Somoza García of Nicaragua, all of whom enjoyed lavish state visits to Washington. Of Somoza, whose family ruled the impoverished and repressed nation until 1979, Roosevelt remarked, "He's a son of a bitch, but at least he's our son of a bitch."[14]

The U.S. attitude toward Latin America took on an especially hard edge during the Cold War, when the perceived threat was defined no longer generally as internal unrest, but very specifically as a communist revolution. As in Africa and southern Asia, the vast majority of Latin Americans possessed little wealth and even less political power. Their plight strengthened the appeal of Marxist ideology, which not only sought to explain their difficulties but also promised the peasants a way out. Consequently, the long-standing U.S. interest in dominating Latin American affairs became even stronger. Through the Organization of American States (OAS), created in 1948, the United States effectively guaranteed the security of its neighbors throughout the hemisphere. In so doing, the U.S. government also guaranteed that communism would not take hold in the region without a fight.

Guatemala's Military Coup

No single event more epitomized Washington's approach than the U.S. intervention in Guatemala, one of the poorest states in Latin America. For

---

[13] This term was coined by President Theodore Roosevelt, whose 1905 "corollary" to the Monroe Doctrine legitimized the recurring series of U.S. interventions and occupations in Latin America and the Caribbean. For a critical view, see Walter LaFeber, *Inevitable Revolutions: The United States in Central America*, 3rd ed. (New York: Norton, 1993).

[14] Quoted in Peter H. Smith, *Democracy in Latin America: Political Change in Comparative Perspective* (New York: Oxford University Press, 2005), 111. Also see Smith, *Talons of the Eagle: Dynamics of U.S.–Latin American Relations*, 2nd ed. (New York: Oxford University Press, 2000), chap. 3.

decades, the country's large plantations had been controlled by a small elite that maintained closer contacts with U.S. banks and corporations than with the landless *campesinos* who made up more than 90 percent of Guatemala's population. Thus it should have come as no surprise in 1950 when democratic reforms in the country produced opposition leaders who sought to abolish this system. Jacobo Arbenz Guzmán, who received support from a growing Communist Party in Guatemala, gained power and promised sweeping reforms. He attempted to take over many of the plantations and give the land, including 225,000 acres owned by the U.S.-based United Fruit Company, to the peasants.

Fearing that such drastic land reform would provoke further uprisings elsewhere in Central America and threaten U.S. control of the Panama Canal, President Dwight Eisenhower supported a plan to overthrow Arbenz. In 1954, Arbenz provided the pretext needed by the United States—the importation of weapons from Czechoslovakia—and the Central Intelligence Agency (CIA) executed its military coup. Within days, Arbenz was removed from power, his reforms were abolished, the military regained control of the *campesinos*, and the United States reinforced its image as an enemy of revolution in Latin America.[15]

In the face of the widespread resentment against the United States, American leaders declared their intention to use foreign assistance to improve the living standards of Latin Americans. Their stated goal was to help the Latin American economies foster a self-sustaining rate of economic growth and develop conditions in which enterprises other than the extraction of raw materials or agriculture directed at single exportable crops would attract private capital. Because of projections of a rapid increase in Latin America's population, the efforts to achieve these goals became all the more urgent. To meet this challenge, President John F. Kennedy, soon after assuming office in 1961, established the Alliance for Progress. He pledged $20 billion in aid over the next decade to Latin America, and, even more significantly, he emphasized the need for social change. Through the Peace Corps and other innovations, Kennedy hoped to revitalize Roosevelt's aspiration to make the United States a "good neighbor" of Latin America. Kennedy realized that, in the absence of such an effort, the possibilities of economic development were slight, and the prospect of new insurgencies was strong.

Kennedy's Alliance for Progress, however, never lived up to the president's stated objectives. The political atmosphere throughout Latin America

---

[15] For an elaboration, see Stephen Schlesinger and Stephen Kinzer, *Bitter Fruit: The Untold Story of the American Coup in Guatemala* (Garden City, N.Y.: Anchor Press, 1982).

had become so polarized that any attempt by the United States to support moderates proved futile. And in the economic sphere, any discussion of reducing the disparity of wealth and creating a middle class was thwarted by the elites, who clung to their wealth and their close ties to the military. On the home front, Kennedy was unable to gain support for his initiative; congressional leaders stubbornly identified reform with revolution, and revolution with communism. As a result, the president was forced to maintain the status quo in Latin America, which during the Cold War meant widespread economic distress, political repression, and social unrest.

The Cuban Missile Crisis

The intrusion of superpower tensions into U.S. relations with Latin America was most sharply demonstrated in Cuba, where, in 1962, American and Soviet leaders came as close to direct—and potentially apocalyptic— conflict as during any other phase of the Cold War. Cuba's revolutionary government dated from January 1, 1959, when armed rebels overthrew the U.S.-backed dictatorship of Fulgencio Batista. Among the rebels, Fidel Castro identified himself with social justice and gained widespread support from the Cuban people. This public support ensured the victory of his guerrilla army against the larger government forces. The new government moved to improve living conditions by instituting land reform and building low-cost housing, schools, and clinics. Castro's social revolution, however, was bound to clash with the more conservative political ideology of the United States.

American leaders were instrumental in freeing Cuba from Spain in the Spanish-American War at the turn of the century. In keeping with the nation's moralistic approach to foreign policy, they alternately described Cuba as a victim of European imperialism, a "child" deserving of protection, and a "piece of fruit" that would inevitably fall into the arms of its caretakers in Washington. From this perspective, the United States had demonstrated its virtue as an "exceptional" world power by liberating its neighbor from colonial rule.[16] In 1902, Congress added an amendment to the Cuban constitution that granted Americans the right to intervene at any time in Cuba to preserve Cuban independence and uphold stability on the island. While this action was also justified on moral grounds, American

---

[16] For an elaboration on these and other metaphors used to justify American intervention in Cuba, see Louis A. Pérez, *Cuba in the American Imagination: Metaphor and the Imperial Ethos* (Chapel Hill: University of North Carolina Press, 2008).

leaders imposed the heavy hand of power politics on Cuba, located less than one hundred miles from Florida.

By 1934, when the so-called Platt Amendment was repealed, the United States had directly intervened militarily in Cuba once (1906–1909) and had established a naval base at Guantánamo Bay. American capital controlled 80 percent of Cuba's utilities, 90 percent of its mines and cattle ranches, nearly all of its oil, and 40 percent of its sugar production (about 25 percent of the American market was reserved for Cuban sugar). It was not surprising, then, that the Cuban revolution directed its long pent-up nationalism and social resentment against "*Yanqui* imperialism." Once firmly in power, Castro's government increasingly gravitated toward communism. If he was going to break with Washington, then he had to look to Moscow, its rival. In so doing, the Cuban leader betrayed the revolution's original democratic promises, and Cuba became a dictatorship. All political parties were abolished except for one—the Communist Party. Castro then aligned Cuba with the Soviet Union, which supplied Cuba with vast amounts of military aid. To Nikita Khrushchev, the Soviet leader, Cuba's revolution served as a role model for other developing countries. "Our era," Khrushchev proclaimed in January 1961, is "an era of socialist revolutions and national liberation revolutions; an era of the collapse of capitalism and the liquidation of the colonial system; an era of the change to the road of socialism by more and more nations; and of the triumph over capitalism on a world scale."[17]

As Cuban-Soviet relations worsened, American leaders began to plan for Castro's overthrow. To this end, in April 1961, the new Kennedy administration launched an attempt by Cuban exiles to take over the island. The CIA, which had planned the operation under Eisenhower, assumed that Castro's army and much of Cuba's population would welcome the invaders as liberators. But the CIA predictions proved wrong, and Castro's forces easily repelled the attack on the shores of the Bay of Pigs. American prestige, already damaged by the Guatemala coup, sank to a new low.[18] The results of the fiasco were predictable. Castro's elevation to superhero status revived Latin American defiance of Washington and stoked U.S. allies' loss

---

[17] Quoted in John Lewis Gaddis, *We Now Know: Rethinking Cold War History* (New York: Oxford University Press, 1997), 183.

[18] According to historian Howard Jones, "not only did the Bay of Pigs fiasco expose [Kennedy] to the charge of imperialism; worse, it showed he wasn't even good at it." Jones, *The Bay of Pigs* (New York: Oxford University Press, 2008), 131. For a more recent account, see Jim Rasenberger, *The Brilliant Disaster: JFK, Castro, and America's Doomed Invasion of Cuba's Bay of Pigs* (New York: Scribner, 2011).

Impact and Influence: Fidel Castro

AP Photo

Both during and after the Cold War, no developing country leader played a more visible role in denouncing the United States than Fidel Castro. In 1959, the Cuban leader directed a successful revolution against the U.S.-backed regime of Gen. Fulgencio Batista. He then took control of Cuba's new communist government, the first of its kind in the Western Hemisphere, and became a close ally of the Soviet Union.

Castro, along with his brother Raúl and Ernesto "Che" Guevara, hoped to make Cuba an inspiration for other revolutionary movements. After the revolution, Castro extended social services such as education and health care to all Cubans. His dictatorial rule, however, prompted many to flee the island for the United States, and the Cuban economy deteriorated under communist control. But Castro remained popular as a symbol of defiance as the feud between the United States and Cuba continued into the twenty-first century. Castro retired as president in 2008 after years of illness. His brother Raúl was unanimously chosen by the National Assembly to lead the government.

of confidence in America's leadership. As for Cuba, it became a communist base from which the Soviet Union could threaten the United States and elicit support from other developing nations in the Western Hemisphere. The United States could no longer fulfill the stated intention of the Monroe Doctrine.

Kennedy could, however, harass the new Cuban government, and he did so through campaigns of propaganda, sabotage, and attempts to assassinate Castro. But these provocations, little known to the American public, merely heightened the Kremlin's commitment to protecting Cuba at all costs.[19] In October 1962, a U-2 spy plane discovered, to the great surprise and consternation of American policymakers, that the Soviets were building launch sites in Cuba for dozens of short- and intermediate-range ballistic

---

[19] See Sheldon M. Stern, *The Cuban Missile Crisis in American Memory: Myths versus Reality* (Stanford, Calif.: Stanford University Press, 2012).

missiles that could carry nuclear warheads. That Khrushchev had dared to move his missiles so close to the United States, and that he apparently expected no reaction beyond diplomatic protests, was a dangerous sign. Washington's failure to respond would prove to its North Atlantic Treaty Organization allies what they already feared: the United States had become vulnerable to attack and could no longer be relied upon to protect Europe.

But the Soviet Union pressured the United States in the wrong place. If the stakes were high for the Soviet Union, they were even higher for the United States, and Kennedy felt that under no circumstances could he afford to lose.

Indeed, because he had explicitly warned the Soviet leader against placing offensive missiles in Cuba, Kennedy had to compel their withdrawal to preserve his credibility. Kennedy met night and day with his political and military advisers for nearly two weeks in late October. Some recommended a diplomatic compromise; others pushed for massive air strikes or even a full-scale invasion of Cuba.[20] The first option was rejected because Kennedy knew that compromising with Moscow would result in further loss of prestige for the United States. The second and third options were dismissed as too dangerous.

Thus Kennedy chose a fourth option and ordered a blockade of Cuba to prevent further missile shipments. On October 22, he demanded the removal of the missiles already in place. To demonstrate his resolve, Kennedy placed the Strategic Air Command on its highest alert status and ordered the deployment of more than five hundred B-52 bombers armed with nuclear warheads. Meanwhile, American submarines and surface ships patrolled the Caribbean Sea, under orders to attack Soviet naval vessels that violated the blockade. Much to everyone's relief, the Kremlin backed down; Khrushchev called back his ships and ordered deactivation of the missile sites. As Secretary of State Dean Rusk vividly described it, "We were eyeball to eyeball, and the other fellow just blinked."

While Kennedy's act of brinkmanship produced its desired outcome, Castro survived the Cuban missile crisis and remained a menace to the United States. His continuing influence was illustrated in April 1965 by the U.S. intervention in the Dominican Republic, a poor nation in the Caribbean Sea that shared the island of Hispaniola with Haiti. The crisis was sparked in 1961 by the over throw of Rafael Trujillo, a dictator who had oppressed the Dominican people while enriching himself for thirty-one years. He was replaced two years later by Juan Bosch, a popular author and

---

[20] See Graham T. Allison and Philip Zelikow, *Essence of Decision*, 2nd ed. (New York: Longman, 1999).

fierce critic of Trujillo, who came to power in the nation's first free elections. Appealing to the majority of Dominicans living in extreme poverty, Bosch enacted sweeping social and economic reforms designed to improve living standards beyond the small elite. But the military, closely tied to wealthy landowners and the Catholic Church, accused Bosch of being "another Castro." A military coup ended Bosch's short reign in September 1963.

American leaders, still fixated on Cuba's influence in Latin America, watched these developments with relief. In 1965, however, President Lyndon Johnson chose military action when Bosch's supporters staged their own overthrow of the Dominican Republic's government. Johnson, whose top priority was enacting Kennedy's domestic programs, accepted U.S. embassy and CIA reports that "grossly exaggerated the extent of communist influence in the rebellion."[21] The U.S. invasion force of more than twenty-three thousand soldiers quickly crushed the effort to restore Bosch to power. With the return of the authoritarian status quo, Latin America's ruling classes could relax. Washington could be counted on to save them from the consequences of clinging to an unjust way of life. Far from shifting the regional power balance toward Washington, however, Johnson's actions in the Dominican Republic only solidified Castro's popularity across the region and his hold on power at home.

Strong-Arming Chile

As in the case of Central America and the Caribbean Sea, Washington had long regarded South America as within its sphere of influence. During the Cold War, U.S. leaders feared the rise of communist regimes across the continent might bring Soviet influence close to America's shores. Among other flashpoints in South America, Chile gained worldwide attention in 1973 when the United States opposed its democratically elected president and engineered his overthrow.

Three years earlier, Chilean citizens elected the reformist Salvador Allende to the presidency. In the United States, President Richard Nixon sought first to prevent Allende from taking office and then, when that failed, to make life difficult for him. Of particular concern to Nixon was Allende's effort to nationalize many of Chile's industries and to displace U.S.-owned copper mines, banks, and utilities. When Allende refused to bend to American pressure, Nixon oversaw his removal from power in

---

[21] Michael Grew, *U.S. Presidents and Latin American Interventions: Pursuing Regime Change in the Cold War* (Lawrence: University of Kansas Press, 2008), 81. As Bosch (ibid., p. 82) later said, "There were not enough communists in my country to run a good hotel, let alone the country."

1973 through a military coup d'état that was carried out by disgruntled Chilean military forces. Chile then fell under the control of a four-man junta led by Gen. Augusto Pinochet, who emerged as a ruthless leader determined to prevent a communist takeover of his country. In return for Washington's patronage, Pinochet served as a loyal U.S. ally through the end of the Cold War. But his reign produced criticism that Washington was "coddling" a foreign dictator in the name of containment, a practice that extended to other countries as well.[22]

Such charges were largely valid. As in other developing countries during the Cold War, the United States had allied itself with a military dictatorship in Chile rather than run the risk that the nation would become a beachhead of Marxist revolution. Moral absolutism in these cases gave way to moral relativism. Authoritarian governments routinely fell short of Jeffersonian democracy, especially when private citizens were deprived of political power and punished for speaking out against the state. But from the American perspective, anything was better than a totalitarian Marxist regime, which was unlikely to modify its behavior or end its hostility toward the capitalist world.[23]

As we have seen, the globalization of containment had profound implications for Latin America. As many critics of the policy feared, far from its shores, the United States gradually became immersed in civil wars and regional conflicts, many of which were grounded less in communist subversion than in the masses' aspirations for the same freedoms enjoyed by most Americans. In escalating containment into a boundless anticommunist crusade, American leaders violated the democratic values they supposedly were promoting, and they turned the presumed beneficiaries of U.S. largesse—the mass populations of developing countries—against the United States. To make matters worse, interventions by the United States frequently backfired, leading to the establishment of new regimes that were openly hostile to Washington. But the White House continued to intervene throughout the developing world. Its strategy led to the calamitous war in Vietnam, where the containment strategy was put to the ultimate test.

---

[22] Pinochet remained in power until 1990, when Chilean citizens voted to restore civilian rule. In 1998, a Spanish judge exercising "universal jurisdiction" indicted Pinochet on charges of human rights violations, and the former dictator was held in a London jail until he was allowed to return to Chile in 2000. He faced multiple trials upon his return but died in December 2006 without having been convicted of any crimes.

[23] For an elaboration of this view by a former U.S. ambassador to the United Nations, see Jeane J. Kirkpatrick, "Dictatorships and Double Standards," Commentary (November 1979): 34–45.

Vietnam: The Limits of Containment

Of the many developing nations that found themselves trapped in the rivalry between the United States and the communist bloc, no country suffered more than Vietnam, a somewhat obscure province in the region of Southeast Asia known as Indochina. Beginning in the 1860s, Indochina became an important part of France's colonial empire; it provided the French with vast quantities of rubber and other raw materials. As a result, French officials refused to grant independence to Indochina after World War II, even though Japanese forces had displaced the French presence during the conflict. While the United States prepared the Philippines for independence in July 1946, and as Great Britain followed suit the following year in India, French leaders reimposed colonial rule over Indochina. Their decision proved disastrous not only for France but also for the United States, which could not resist the temptation to view the conflict in Indochina as a microcosm of the larger East-West struggle.[24]

Even though the turmoil in the region after France's return transformed Vietnam into a "vital interest" to the U.S. government, Americans generally knew little about the history, cultural traditions, or politics of Indochina. This ignorance extended to the U.S. military, which "lacked the time and opportunity to see and understand Vietnam as anything other than a hot, humid, dangerous, and often hostile place."[25] American leaders turned to universities, private foundations, and religious groups to generate public support for a wholesale reconstruction of Vietnam. "From the outset the project involved transforming, or inventing, Vietnam to produce a modern state that could be integrated into a much larger regional, and even global, capitalist system."[26]

France initially recognized the Democratic Republic of Vietnam in 1946 as a "free state" within the newly formed French Union, which also included Laos and Cambodia. But this arrangement was opposed by the Revolutionary League for the Independence of Vietnam, otherwise known as the Vietminh. The fighting soon escalated into the "first" Vietnam War, which lasted from 1946 until 1954. Ho Chi Minh, the revolutionary leader

---

[24] For a comprehensive review, see Stanley Karnow, *Vietnam: A History* (New York: Penguin, 1983).

[25] Robert E. Vadas, *Cultures in Conflict: The Vietnam War* (Westport, Conn.: Greenwood Press, 2002), 58. For a detailed account of American misperceptions about Vietnam, see Jeffrey Record, *The Wrong War: Why We Lost Vietnam* (Annapolis, Md.: Naval Institute Press, 1998).

[26] Carter, *Inventing Vietnam*, 44.

who organized the Vietminh, had embraced communism in the 1920s after his efforts to establish an independent and democratic state were rebuffed by Western leaders. During the Japanese occupation in the 1930s and 1940s, Ho maintained his struggle for an independent Vietnam.

After World War II, emboldened by Japan's defeat and inspired by the UN's pledge to end colonial rule, Ho believed his nation's time had finally come. But again he was sorely disappointed by the lack of support among the Western powers. His decision to launch a full-scale uprising against French rule quickly followed. In 1950, President Truman began providing France with economic and military aid in support of its struggle against the Vietminh. By 1954, American taxpayers were covering about 75 percent of the war costs. But French forces still could not suppress Vietnam's "revolutionary war," a reality that became clear in March 1954 when Vietminh forces launched an assault against the strategically vital French fortress at Dien Bien Phu. Clearly, the French could not hold on without U.S. intervention. Dien Bien Phu was the moment of decision for the United States.[27]

Testing the "Domino Theory"

Dwight Eisenhower, upon taking office in January 1953, had little interest in Vietnam. Similar to the many other developing countries described earlier, Vietnam was ruled by leaders who ignored the widespread poverty of their citizens. But the White House also refused to turn its back on the region, fearing that the coming to power of a communist regime in Vietnam would lead to other revolutions in southern Asia and perhaps across the entire developing world. "You have a row of dominoes set up, you knock over the first one and what will happen to the last one is the certainty that it will go ever so quickly," Eisenhower observed. "So you could have a beginning of a disintegration that would have the most profound influences."[28] The president's "domino theory" compelled military leaders to place Vietnam, still remote and unknown to most Americans, in the fulcrum of the global balance of power.

France, mired in a second war in Algeria during this period, was as weary of Vietnam as Americans had been of Korea. The only hope for a peaceful settlement came in Geneva, Switzerland, where France agreed in 1954 to a temporary division of Vietnam at the seventeenth parallel. Two separate

---

[27] For a comprehensive study of this battle, see Martin Windrow, *The Last Valley: Dien Bien Phu and the French Defeat in Vietnam* (London: Wiedenfeld and Nicolson, 2004).

[28] Quoted in the *New York Times* (April 8, 1954), 18.

governments were to be established during this transition period: a communist regime in the North and a noncommunist regime in the South. Elections were scheduled for July 1956 to bring about Vietnam's "unity and territorial integrity." Because the Geneva agreement called for general elections, the Vietminh expected the unpopular regime in South Vietnam to collapse.[29] Leaders in Hanoi, the North Vietnamese capital, assumed that the country would be reunited under Ho's leadership. His popularity compelled the United States to prevent the 1956 elections. Ngo Dinh Diem, South Vietnam's autocratic leader and a fervent anticommunist, vowed to stay in power no matter what the Geneva agreement said about elections. With the accord in tatters, in 1959 Ho mobilized his rebel army and the second Vietnam War—this one involving the United States instead of France—began.

Despite the many similarities between the Korean and Vietnamese conflicts, U.S. involvement in Vietnam began quite differently. The Korean War started with a clear-cut, aggressive attack that aroused the American public and united the principal Western Allies against a common threat. Korea also had been a conventional war in which regular communist forces were checked by regular South Korean, American, and UN troops. By contrast, the French defeat at Dien Bien Phu in 1954 was a decisive moment in military history because it demonstrated that *guerrilla* tactics could prevail against a larger and stronger army. Diem's failure to enlist the support of his population—especially the peasantry, through political, social, and economic reforms—made the ground especially fertile for such a campaign.

Not only was the American public ignorant of Vietnam; the nation's political and military leaders had only a superficial grasp of the conflict. Eisenhower assumed that the Sino-Soviet bloc was united despite strong evidence to the contrary. As a result, he exaggerated the likelihood that Vietnam would become a "puppet" of China despite the fact that the two countries, which shared a large border, were historic enemies. This oversight led Eisenhower to view Ho Chi Minh as driven by communist ideology. In fact, Ho was ultimately a Vietnamese *nationalist* whose goal was to liberate his country from external domination from all sources, whether French, Chinese, or American. But grasping these truths would have required close study of a little-known part of the world—a task that did not come naturally to American leaders secure in their hemispheric comfort zone. Eisenhower's commitment to Vietnam set the stage for further escalations. Upon taking office in January 1961, President Kennedy sent in 16,500

[29] For an instructive collection of articles published by the *New York Times* during the early years of this conflict, see Mark Lawrence, ed., *The Vietnam War*, vol. 1 (Chicago: Fitzroy Dearborn, 2001).

military advisers to help the South Vietnamese army. His successor, Lyndon Johnson, increased the force level to more than 500,000 by 1969.

Johnson, whose top priority was achieving Kennedy's domestic goals, gained congressional support for the Vietnam War by citing a faulty premise: an alleged North Vietnamese attack on an American naval destroyer in the Gulf of Tonkin in August 1964. His claims, however, proved dubious when new evidence surfaced that the attack against the *Maddox* had not taken place as reported. Subsequent investigations by the National Security Agency, which discovered faulty translations and numerous errors in intelligence reports, concluded that "the engagement was illusory."[30] Johnson's failure to confirm the attack, followed by the Gulf of Tonkin Resolution, which authorized him to use "all necessary measures . . . to prevent further aggression," set the course of the Vietnam War.

In this confused environment, American leaders failed to resolve basic questions about Vietnam: Was it vital to American security interests, and, if so, how vital? Could the situation in South Vietnam be saved militarily given its dictatorial government in Saigon (the South Vietnamese capital) and lack of popular support? How large an American military deployment would be required? Lacking concrete answers to these questions, some White House advisers urged Johnson in July 1965 to give up on this American ally. George Ball, an undersecretary of state, declared, "We cannot win, Mr. President. The war will be long and protracted. The most we can hope for is a messy conclusion."[31] Still, Johnson sided with his military aides who called for escalation rather than withdrawal. Fearing that he would be blamed for "losing Vietnam" just as Truman "lost China" and Eisenhower "lost Cuba," Johnson clung to the domino theory. Despite the president's claims, "neither friends nor foes around the world tended to see American credibility as being at stake in Vietnam."[32]

The Misconduct of Guerrilla Warfare

The United States not only failed to understand South Vietnam's cultural landscape, but also virtually ignored the nation's political structures. As described earlier, for years the United States had supported Ngo Dinh

---

[30] John Prados, *Vietnam: The History of an Unwinnable War, 1945–1975* (Lawrence: University of Kansas Press, 2009), 95.

[31] Quoted in Charles Peters, *Lyndon B. Johnson* (New York: Basic Books, 2010), 122–123.

[32] Frederik Logevall, "America Isolated: The Western Powers and the Escalation of War," in *America, the Vietnam War, and the World*, ed. Andreas W. Daum, Lloyd Gardner, and Wilfried Mausbach (New York: Cambridge University Press, 2003), 175.

Diem, the devout Catholic whose authoritarian rule and aloofness had alienated most of the mainly Buddhist population of South Vietnam. By the time the South Vietnamese military overthrew and executed Diem in 1963, the rebels already controlled most of the region; the domestic reforms needed to win the war had been neglected too long.

The possibility of achieving a quick victory over the rebels was slim, because guerrilla warfare is entirely different from traditional warfare. The aim of a guerrilla war is to capture the government from within by winning the "hearts and minds" of ordinary citizens and undermining their confidence in the regime. To achieve this objective, guerrilla forces do not have to inflict a complete defeat on enemy forces or compel them to surrender unconditionally. Guerrilla war is, then, a long-term strategy in which the rebels use hit-and-run tactics and engage only those smaller and weaker government forces they can defeat. The government's only defense against this strategy is to deploy troops to guard every town, every village, and every bridge against possible attack. Unable to come to grips with the enemy, lacking public support, and suffering one small loss after another, the national army becomes demoralized, and its mood becomes defensive.

According to Mao Zedong, guerrillas need the people "just as fish need water"; without popular support, guerrillas would not receive recruits, food, shelter, or information on the deployment of government forces. The guerrillas gain the support of the peasantry by successfully representing themselves as the liberators from colonialism or foreign rule, native despotic governments, economic deprivation, or social injustice. In this way, they isolate the government in its own country. Thus, unlike conventional warfare in which each army seeks the destruction of the other's military forces, guerrilla warfare is based on a strategy of bringing down the state from the ground up. A government that has the allegiance of its population does not provide fertile soil for guerrillas, but where social dissatisfaction exists, guerrillas find an opening.

What all this means is that U.S. forces, experienced only in conventional warfare, found guerrilla warfare hard to fight in Southeast Asia. Concerned primarily with social and political reforms, such an effort ran counter to traditional American military strategy. The length of the war caused great frustration because the U.S. government, under intense public pressure, had promised repeatedly that the war would end soon, that its leaders saw the "light at the end of the tunnel." When this very different kind of warfare did not yield swift and successful results, U.S. military leaders faced the choice of either pulling out or seeking a shortcut to victory through military escalation. Such a dilemma continued to face Washington after the Cold War as foreign adversaries resorted to terrorist attacks and "low-intensity" military tactics in such places as Afghanistan and Iraq in order to wear down the United States.

The Military Battlefield in Vietnam

During the war in Vietnam, American policymakers misplaced their confidence in U.S. military prowess and its ability to change the guerrillas' "rules of the game." In 1965, the illusion of American omnipotence had not yet died. After all, the United States had successfully confronted the Soviet Union in Cuba and compelled it to back down. Could there really be much doubt that, under the leadership of Secretary of Defense Robert McNamara, and with its sizable forces and its superior mobility and firepower, the United States would be able to beat a few thousand "peasants in black pajamas"? To win this war, however, U.S. forces had to secure villages and show their citizens that the South Vietnamese government cared about them. Instead, the military carried out massive search-and-destroy operations that left countless villages in ruin. The guerrillas, even if driven away from the villages, continued to control the countryside.[33]

American soldiers clearly did not understand the social and political nature of guerrilla warfare. They had been trained for conventional battle and to use maximum firepower to wear the enemy down in a war of attrition. The military was confident it could do this; the measure of success became the daily body count of communist dead. Still, large-scale U.S. bombing attacks did not weaken Hanoi's will to prosecute the war, nor did it cut the flow of supplies sufficiently to hamper the fighting in the South or greatly reduce troop infiltration. Hanoi's persistence, in turn, led to increased calls by Washington for more air strikes and new targets. Those who advocated intensifying the air strikes insisted that massive bombing could provide victory for the United States, but only if it were used with maximum efficiency.[34]

This objective, however, remained unattainable, as the opposition was gaining strength. In South Vietnam, even the more stable military regime of Nguyen Van Thieu failed to undertake social and economic reforms as the

---

[33] The United States would later adapt this strategy of counterinsurgency to the Afghanistan and Iraq wars, which also failed to bring peace to the various war zones. See Gregory A. Daddis, "Mired in a Quagmire: Popular Interpretations of the Vietnam War," *Orbis* 57 (Autumn 2013): 532–548.

[34] Secretary McNamara and his top aides confidently defended this strategy and predicted victory based on advanced computer models and cost-benefit calculations, most of which were proved wrong in the context of guerrilla warfare. See David Halberstam, *The Best and the Brightest* (New York: Random House, 1972).

Impact and Influence: Robert McNamara

Robert McNamara, secretary of defense from 1961 to 1968, oversaw the American war effort in Vietnam. A former president of the Ford Motor Company, McNamara joined other "whiz kids" who sought to introduce modern analytical methods and technical innovations to the armed forces. Among his other initiatives, McNamara led the effort to shift U.S. nuclear strategy from the "massive retaliation" of the Eisenhower years to a strategy based on a "flexible response."

The pressures of the war in Vietnam, however, gradually consumed McNamara's energies. An early advocate of U.S. military involvement, he began to question the war effort and called for a negotiated settlement. When this proved impossible, McNamara left the Johnson administration in February 1968 to become president of the World Bank. During his thirteen-year tenure at that institution, the World Bank greatly increased its assistance to developing countries. McNamara's 1995 memoir, *In Retrospect: The Tragedy and Lessons of Vietnam*, detailed the many mistaken assumptions, political problems, and tactical errors that led to the U.S. defeat in Southeast Asia.

conflict escalated. It was particularly remiss in waiting so long to redistribute land from the usually absentee landlords to the peasants. Without such reforms, the rebels grew stronger. Militarily, every increase in American forces was met by the wider infiltration of both guerrillas and conventional troops from the North to the South. Nevertheless, the U.S. government issued optimistic battle reports and forecasts of victory on a regular basis.

The 1968 Tet (Vietnamese New Year) Offensive, launched on the last day of January, showed once and for all that, despite the repeatedly optimistic predictions, the enemy had again been badly underestimated. The rebels launched a major countrywide offensive and attacked Saigon, Hué, and every other provincial capital. A rebel battalion even penetrated the U.S. embassy compound, thereby scoring a significant symbolic victory. The fighting that followed, however, was bloody, and the rebels were eventually worn down. Nevertheless, they had clearly demonstrated that neither an American army of half a million nor the far larger South Vietnamese army could ensure the security of the mass population.

Map 4-4 The Vietnam War

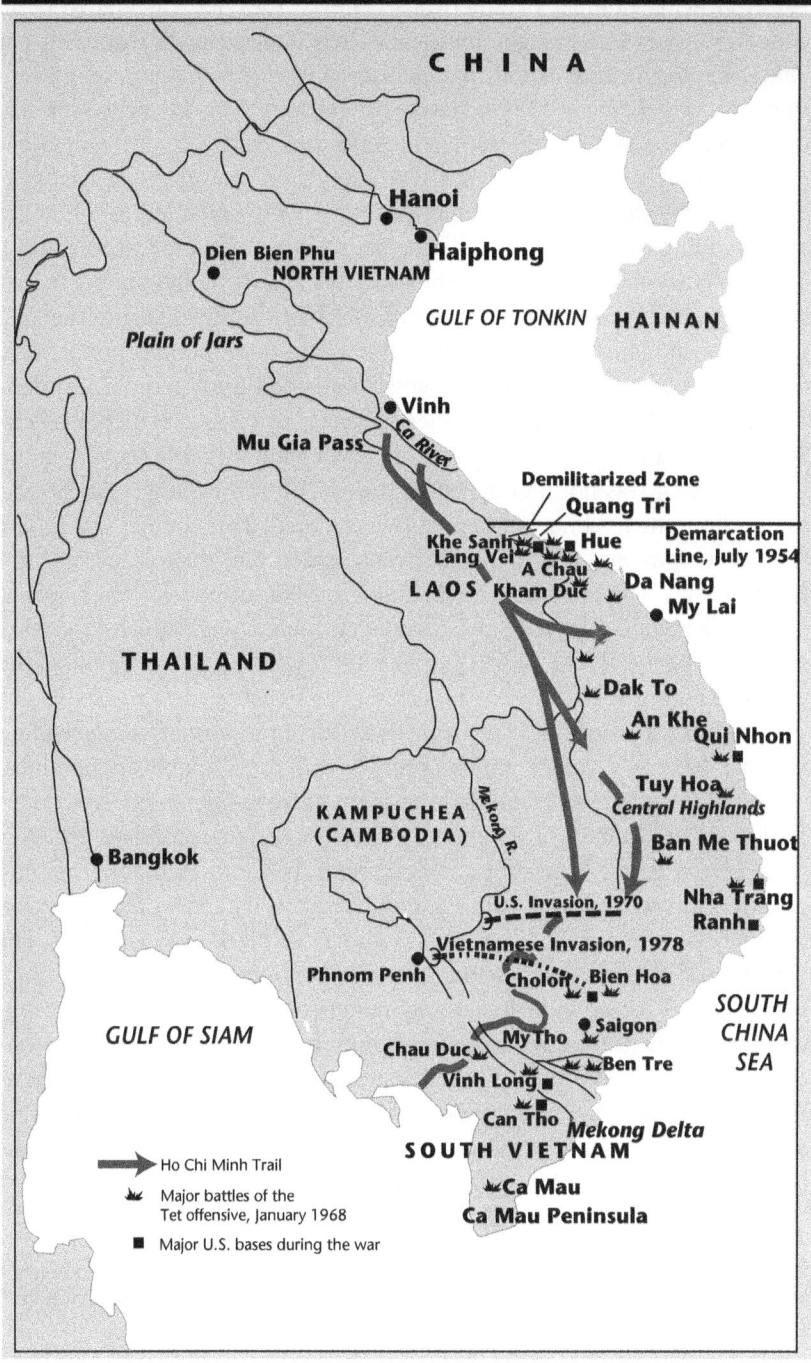

CHINA

Hanoi

Dien Bien Phu
NORTH VIETNAM
Haiphong

GULF OF TONKIN   HAINAN

Plain of Jars

Vinh

Mu Gia Pass   Ca River

Demilitarized Zone
Quang Tri

Khe Sanh   Hue   Demarcation
Lang Vei   Line, July 1954
A Chau
LAOS   Kham Duc   Da Nang
My Lai

THAILAND

Dak To

An Khe
Qui Nhon

Tuy Hoa
KAMPUCHEA   Central Highlands
(CAMBODIA)   Mekong R.   Ban Me Thuot

Bangkok

U.S. Invasion, 1970   Nha Trang
Ranh

Vietnamese Invasion, 1978

Phnom Penh   Choloin   Bien Hoa

GULF OF SIAM   Chau Duc   My Tho   Saigon   SOUTH
CHINA
Ben Tre   SEA

Vinh Long

Can Tho   Mekong Delta
SOUTH VIETNAM

Ho Chi Minh Trail

Major battles of the
Tet offensive, January 1968   Ca Mau
Ca Mau Peninsula
Major U.S. bases during the war

The Political Battlefield at Home

A growing number of Americans believed the Vietnam War to be ill conceived, if not downright immoral. There had never been a clear-cut attack across the seventeenth parallel dividing North Vietnam and South Vietnam, which made the accusation that Hanoi was an aggressor less believable. For its part, the repressive and unpopular Saigon regime lent credence to the view that the war was a rebellion against the central government. The massive use of American firepower, which led to the widespread killing of civilians, pricked the consciences of many Americans.

The guerrilla strategy of psychologically exhausting the opponent had succeeded; the American strategy of physical attrition had failed. The U.S. military won many battles, but it lost the war as the American public grew tired of the struggle in Vietnam, which remained a mysterious and confusing place. The Vietnam War, then, played out on two battlefields. The first, in Vietnam, was bloody but inconclusive militarily. The second, in the United States, was not bloody, but it was decisive politically.[35] As the war dragged on, the nation's will to continue declined. This conflict was unlike the two world wars in which Americans sensed that their security, if not their survival, was at stake. The declining public support for the war, less than 40 percent by the 1968 presidential election, coincided with the war's steadily rising death toll, which surpassed thirty thousand by the end of the year (see Figure 4-1).

With the Democratic Party split over Vietnam, former vice president Richard Nixon, a career anticommunist and the Republican nominee, promised to end the war if elected president in November 1968. Nixon and Vice President Hubert H. Humphrey, the Democratic candidate, fell over themselves offering hopes for an "honorable" peace in Vietnam. The only question was when to get out and on what terms. Nixon won the election on the basis of his pledge to resist "moral decay" in the United States. His plan to end the war in Vietnam, however, amounted to little more than reducing U.S. forces while increasing military aid to South Vietnam's fledgling army. Even as thousands of American troops returned during the president's first term in office, the United States offered ongoing aerial support to its ally in Saigon, pummeling rebel forces in the countryside with bombing attacks. Nixon vowed that he would only accept "peace with honor," meaning that the outcome of the struggle would have to be on American terms.

---

[35] For an elaboration of the domestic politics surrounding the American involvement in Vietnam, see Melvin Small, *At the Water's Edge: American Politics and the Vietnam War* (Chicago: Ivan R. Dee, 2005).

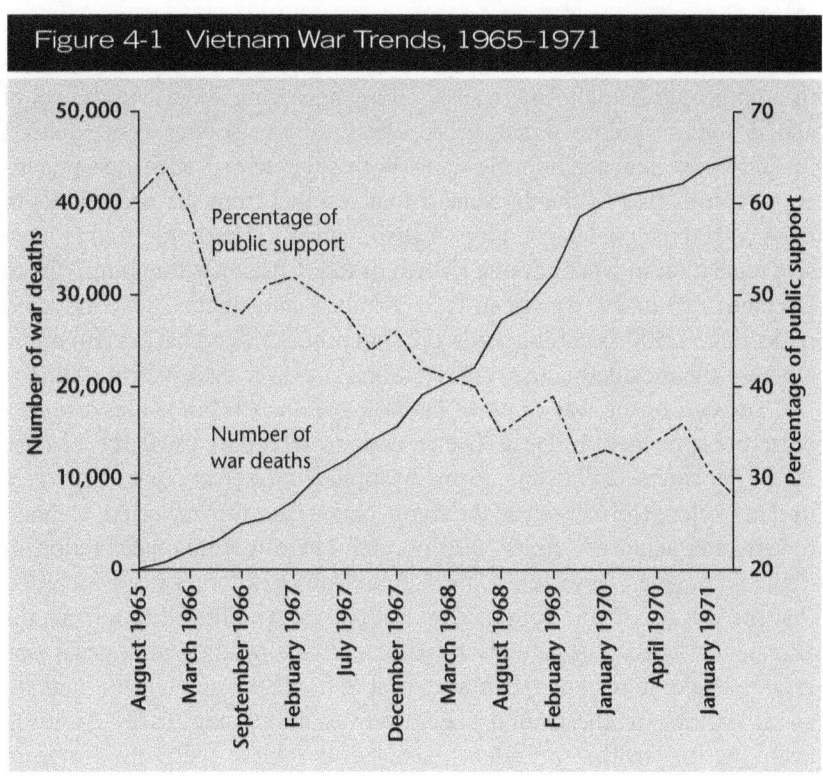

Figure 4-1 Vietnam War Trends, 1965–1971

Source: Eric V. Larson, *Casualties and Consensus: The Historical Role of Casualties in Domestic Support for U.S. Military Operations* (Santa Monica, Calif.: RAND, 1996), 111.

American Defeat and Withdrawal

Events just outside of Vietnam hastened the U.S. military failure. Cambodia's Prince Norodom Sihanouk, who had allowed rebels to create base camps just across the Vietnamese border, was overthrown in 1970 by military leaders who wanted the communist troops out of Cambodia. When the communists moved toward the Cambodian capital to unseat the new government, Nixon decided to intervene and, without public knowledge, ordered air strikes deep into Cambodia. Once this intervention became known, it reignited domestic protests. College campuses erupted nationwide, and in Ohio, national guardsmen shot and killed four Kent State University students during an antiwar rally. Nine others in the crowd were injured in the seemingly random volley of gunfire.

The Kent State tragedy of May 4, 1970, made it all too clear that the United States had to end the Vietnam War. A month before the U.S. presidential election in November 1972, Hanoi signaled its willingness to accept something less than a total victory. The terms of the agreement included a cease-fire that would halt all American bombing and bring about withdrawal of all U.S. forces within two months; separate future cease-fires were expected in Cambodia and neighboring Laos. Both sides would exchange prisoners of war as part of the agreement that resulted from the peace talks in Paris. When the final negotiations stalled, however, Nixon resorted to massive retaliation in what became known as the "Christmas Bombing." From December 18 to 29, American B-52 bombers and fighter jets conducted more than 1,500 bombing raids on Hanoi and other North Vietnamese targets—the most lethal use of the nation's airpower since World War II.

The end of the war came in January 1973 when both sides signed a cease-fire agreement in Paris. Twelve nations, including the United States, the Soviet Union, and China, formally approved the treaty that was largely in place before the Christmas Bombing. Nixon, recently reelected, claimed that he had achieved "peace with honor." There was little celebration in the United States, however, as most Americans had long since concluded that the war was a colossal mistake. For Nixon, who hoped to refocus his energies on the Soviet Union and China, regaining the public trust was essential. Like Johnson's, Nixon's attempt to frame the outcome of Vietnam as satisfactory for the United States "proved an extraordinarily daunting task, one that neither president managed to achieve with any degree of effectiveness."[36]

But Nixon did not serve out his second term in office. He resigned in August 1974 under the cloud of the Watergate scandal.[37] His successor to the presidency, Gerald R. Ford, oversaw the final U.S. withdrawal. The U.S. defeat in Vietnam had shattered long-held notions of the nation's insurmountable world power. To many, the war represented a moral turning point in American foreign policy; the United States was guilty of backing the more repressive and illegitimate side. Sen. J. William Fulbright, who had long equated American foreign policy with moral mission, now attacked America's global role as evidence of an "arrogance of power."[38] The painful legacy of Vietnam would drag on for many years as Americans

---

[36] Robert J. McMahon, "The Politics, and Geopolitics, of American Troop Withdrawals from Vietnam, 1968–72," *Diplomatic History* (June 2010): 471.

[37] This scandal involved illegal activities by the Nixon administration during its 1972 reelection campaign and the elaborate means devised by Nixon to cover up these activities.

[38] J. William Fulbright, *The Arrogance of Power* (New York: Vintage Books, 1967).

sought—often in vain—the return of prisoners of war (POWs) and soldiers listed as "missing in action" (MIAs).[39]

In searching for reforms that would prevent another Vietnam, lawmakers in Washington sought to curb presidential power in foreign policy, especially the power of the commander in chief to commit American forces to battle. Democrats especially sought to restrain the executive branch. In their opinion, the president, the "military-industrial complex," and the CIA were intent on involving the country in too many costly adventures abroad. Conservative or liberal, the remedy for the "imperial presidency" was to reassert congressional oversight of foreign policy and to restore constitutional checks and balances.[40] To that end, in 1973, Congress passed the War Powers Resolution, which allowed Congress to order American troops home if a U.S. military intervention was failing. Although denounced by later presidents as unconstitutional and rarely invoked, the War Powers Resolution symbolized the national mood that blamed the war on excessive presidential power. From this perspective, the exercise of power inevitably made the United States arrogant. Power itself was corrupting; democracy and power politics were simply incompatible. No idea could be more characteristically American.

The Vietnam experience would not be the last time American foreign policy would face unexpected challenges in the developing world. As later chapters will reveal, the same lack of historical and cultural understanding produced setbacks for the United States in Central America, sub-Saharan Africa, the Middle East, and central Asia. The failures of these military interventions could be considered paradoxical in view of the global primacy of the United States and the relatively high educational levels of its people. But perhaps it was *because* of their power and wealth that so many Americans were not curious about the world around them. Learning about foreign nations, especially those mired in poverty, seemed unnecessary in a country that was invulnerable. Time would tell, however, whether this was a luxury Americans could forever afford.

---

[39] Michael J. Allen, *Until the Last Man Comes Home: POWs, MIAs, and the Unending Vietnam War* (Chapel Hill: University of North Carolina Press, 2009). For a summary of ongoing debates regarding the war, see Gary R. Hess, *Vietnam: Explaining America's Lost War* (Malden, Mass.: Blackwell, 2009).

[40] See Arthur M. Schlesinger Jr., *The Imperial Presidency* (Boston: Houghton Mifflin, 1973).

CHAPTER 5

Détente and World-Order Politics

The debacle in Vietnam confirmed many Americans' worst fears about how the United States would behave once it joined the ranks of the great powers. The nation had emerged victorious in the two world wars of the early twentieth century, but it effectively "lost" the peace between the wars by shirking the responsibilities that came with its heightened stature. By the 1970s, it appeared as though America was ill equipped to live up to its self-proclaimed role as leader of the "free world." The lost war also raised serious doubts about using anticommunism as the all-encompassing basis for the country's foreign policy. Before Vietnam, the United States sought to contain communism at every turn. After Vietnam, American leaders became more cautious about military interventions in remote areas and looked toward other means to win the Cold War.

The U.S. containment policy had been weakened by the fragmentation of the communist bloc. It was one thing to fight a communism that seemed monolithic, but when the communist states became more numerous and divided internally, the best Western response became more difficult to define. Did the United States now have to distinguish among the communist states, determining which posed a true threat? What changes in the distribution of power could America safely allow? And where, if anywhere, did it still have to draw frontiers? These questions became difficult to answer in the 1970s as American leaders faced rapid shifts in the global balance of power.

During this period, the administrations of Richard Nixon and Gerald Ford, Nixon's successor after the Watergate scandal, pursued détente—a relaxation of tensions—in response to these shifts. The United States had become, after the Vietnam War, a weakened nation. This mood was demonstrated by attacks on the "imperial presidency" and restraints imposed on the White House by a more assertive and watchful Congress. Moreover, America's self-appointed role as a global guardian of democracy was widely criticized given the nation's own limitations and moral shortcomings as a great power. This sentiment was expressed frequently by Jimmy Carter, who, after he became president in 1977, sought to reclaim the high ground in American foreign policy.

Henry Kissinger and President Richard M. Nixon share an informal moment in September 1973 after Kissinger was sworn in as the fifty-sixth U.S. secretary of state. Kissinger, the architect of the détente policy that eased Cold War tensions, had previously served as Nixon's national security adviser.

In military terms, the Soviet Union had caught up with the United States. From the 1950s to the late 1960s, American bombers and missiles, increasingly bolstered by the navy's nuclear submarines, deterred the Soviet Union by threatening to destroy its cities. Moscow balanced America's strategic power with its massive ground forces, which could potentially overrun Western Europe and quickly defeat North Atlantic Treaty Organization forces. Thus the balance of power had been asymmetric: the United States held strategic (nuclear) superiority and an intercontinental reach; the Soviet Union maintained conventional military superiority and a regional reach. But in 1964, the Soviets began a massive weapons buildup, and by 1970, the Soviet Union's nuclear arsenal had achieved parity with that of the United States. Moreover, the Soviet buildup showed no sign of slowing even after reaching the level of *mutual assured destruction* with the United States and its allies.

Even during the period of U.S. strategic superiority, Soviet leaders were willing to risk limited challenges, such as in Berlin and Cuba, but remained cautious during confrontations. When there was resistance, the Kremlin retreated. American power, therefore, set limits as to how far the Soviets felt they could push. But because the strategic balance was now shifting, a continuation of the containment policy by means of nuclear deterrence was riskier. Indeed, the Soviet Union had now assumed a top-tier position, with the United States, in a bipolar balance of world power. Would the Soviet Union, in these new circumstances, be content to expand its influence only on land? Or would Soviet leaders, with their new might, gain confidence and act more boldly in the air and at sea? For its part, would the United States, once it lost its strategic superiority, be more reluctant to react?

Nations that have seen their power decline relative to that of other states normally adjust by reducing their commitments or by seeking new allies or greater contributions from current allies. They generally also seek to reduce threats to their interests through diplomacy. After it lost its strategic superiority, and in the aftermath of Vietnam, the United States sought to curtail its obligations as well. The détente policy adopted by Washington was aimed at securing U.S. interests at lower levels of tension and cost than through military intervention and crisis management. The bipolar U.S.-Soviet balance would be more complex and fluid than in the earlier era of U.S. strategic superiority.

Managing the Superpower Rivalry

In 1969, the incoming Nixon administration decided to adopt a foreign policy based on the traditional logic of the state system. This dramatic shift away from a moralistic style born of the nation's domestic values and experiences was surprising. As an earlier participant in Sen. Joseph R. McCarthy's ideological "witch hunts," Nixon rejected having anything to do with communists. But as president, he pursued a more pragmatic approach to foreign policy that accommodated shifts in the global balance of power. His appointment of Henry Kissinger, a German-born Jewish immigrant and refugee from Nazi Germany, reflected Nixon's desire to adopt the "power politics" of the Old World.[1] In this sense, Nixon and Kissinger were the first American leaders to openly challenge and deviate from the country's traditional style of foreign policy.[2]

---

[1] For recent studies of Kissinger's life and career, see Mario Del Pero, *The Eccentric Realist: Henry Kissinger and the Shaping of American Foreign Policy* (Ithaca, N.Y.: Cornell University Press, 2010), and Jeremi Suri, *Henry Kissinger and the American Century* (Cambridge, Mass.: Belknap Press, 2007). For critical appraisals, see Jussi Hanhimäki, *The Flawed Realist: Henry Kissinger and American Foreign Policy* (New York: Oxford University Press, 2004), and Christopher Hitchens, *The Trial of Henry Kissinger* (New York: Verso, 2001).

[2] This relationship is further elaborated in Robert Dallek, *Nixon and Kissinger: Partners in Power* (New York: HarperCollins, 2007).

Serving first as national security adviser and later as secretary of state, Kissinger carried out much of the public and private diplomacy of the Nixon and Ford administrations. He dominated the inner circles of both presidents and attacked his critics both within and outside the White House with a vengeance. "The press, the diplomatic corps, and even foreign leaders were not safe from displays of his anger."[3] Still, Kissinger's instincts as a realist were readily accepted by his only superiors, Nixon and Ford, who urgently needed a new approach to American foreign policy. Détente, a French term meaning the relaxation of tensions, seemed well suited to American needs in the post-Vietnam era.

Henry Kissinger's Worldview

Kissinger compared the Soviet Union's rise to Germany's appearance on the world scene in the early twentieth century. In both cases, the challengers were land powers ambitious to expand far beyond their borders. The United States recognized that Germany's desire to become a world power had resulted in World War I. The Soviet Union, like Germany years earlier, sought overseas clients that would become members of the Soviet bloc. Although these territories were usually of limited strategic value, they were important as symbols of communism's global advance. Therefore, the Soviet Union's military buildup raised questions not just about the military balance and its stability, but also about the Soviets' ultimate intentions.

The strategic underpinnings of American foreign policy during the Kissinger years began with the assumption that world politics was not a fight between a "good" side and a "bad" side. All states, according to this realist perspective, had the right to exist and possessed legitimate interests. A nation, therefore, did not launch moral crusades against an adversary on the assumption that differences of interests represented a conflict between good and evil. American security in the nuclear era, Kissinger believed, demanded that leaders attempt to resolve differences with other great powers and build on shared interests. Differences, admittedly, would not be easily or quickly reconciled. Good personal relations among leaders might smooth this process, but they were not a substitute for hard bargaining, and accords basically reflected the ratio of power between the nations the leaders represented.[4]

---

[3] Barbara Keys, "Henry Kissinger: The Emotional Statesman," *Diplomatic History* (September 2011): 588.

[4] For an instructive comparison of Kissinger's approach with those of other realists, see Michael Joseph Smith, *Realist Thought from Weber to Kissinger* (Baton Rouge: Louisiana State University Press, 1986). For an application of Kissinger's worldview to his actions as a policymaker, see Stephen G. Walker, "The Interface between Beliefs and Behavior: Henry Kissinger's Operational Code and the Vietnam War," *Journal of Conflict Resolution* (March 1977): 129–168.

How, then, should the United States deal with a communist dictatorship whose values it deplored? American power was too limited to transform Moscow's behavior. Thus the United States simply had to abandon its habit of crusading to democratize adversaries and coexist with the Soviet Union in order to preserve peace and security. The key was the balance of power. The United States needed to accommodate the legitimate needs of the principal challenger to that balance. Power neutralizes opposing power in this view. By satisfying the interests of other great powers, the United States would be more likely to maintain the status quo than by perpetuating external hostilities toward Washington.

In sum, Kissinger brought American foreign policy more in line with the traditional norms of the interstate system. The U.S.-Soviet balance remained the preoccupation; the Soviet Union, as a great power, still had to be contained. Coexistence with Moscow, to be achieved through negotiation and compromise, was sufficient to maintain a balance of power that preserved American security. The ultimate victory, as Kissinger's fellow realist, George Kennan, predicted a quarter of a century earlier, would stem not from an American moral crusade, but from the incremental withering of the Soviet state and society.

Exploiting the Sino-Soviet Split

Kissinger's goal was not simply to manage the Soviet Union's growing strategic power. He also sought to establish a working relationship with communist China. The United States had no official relationship with China when Nixon came to power in January 1969. Beijing's leaders refused to establish relations with the United States as long as Washington officially recognized the Nationalist regime in Taiwan. But Nixon recognized the changing strategic circumstances and considered it vital to bring mainland China, still led by Mao Zedong, into the diplomatic constellation. By calling the regime by its chosen name, the People's Republic of China (PRC); ending regular U.S. naval patrols of the Taiwan Strait; and lifting trade restrictions on the PRC, Nixon opened the way for a personal visit to China in February 1972. For the American public and Congress, long hostile to dealing with Beijing, this visit symbolized a dramatic shift in American policy. By playing the "China card," Nixon and Kissinger began clearing away mutual hostilities and exploring areas of mutual cooperation.

In executing this strategy, Nixon exploited the growing tensions between the Soviet Union and China. As the first communist-controlled state, the Kremlin had long monopolized the international communist movement. Moreover, since World War II, it controlled the states of Eastern

Europe. The Chinese leadership, although communist, was highly nationalistic and therefore not likely to subordinate itself to the Kremlin. Further, Mao's model of "rural" communism was presumably better suited to the developing countries of the Third World. The potential for a schism, then, was built into the Sino-Soviet relationship.[5] A falling-out was inevitable despite the treaty of friendship signed by the two countries in 1950. By 1970, both countries had allowed their treaty to lapse. The Soviets publicly likened Mao to Adolf Hitler, while Chinese leaders described the Soviet Union as a "dictatorship of the German fascist type." The Sino-Soviet split gave the United States leverage to play the two communist giants against each other and gain the upper hand in the triangular power struggle.

In the Shanghai communiqué released at the end of Nixon's historic visit to China in 1972, the United States and China declared their opposition to the hegemony of *any* power in Asia—but they clearly were referring to the Soviet Union. Thus Sino-American relations were established on a firm foundation of mutual self-interest. As for the United States, its eagerness to attract China into an anti-Soviet coalition was reflected in America's declaration that it would gradually remove all its forces and installations from Taiwan and would not interfere in a "peaceful settlement" between the communists and the Nationalists. The agreement ended once and for all the irrationality of a situation in which the United States had for almost a quarter-century ignored the existence of the world's most populous country, a nation with great potential power and long-standing animosity toward Moscow. Sino-Soviet quarrels reflected entrenched conflicts of interest more profound than the apparent bond of communist ideology.

On January 1, 1979, the PRC and the United States exchanged diplomatic recognition and ambassadors. This exchange was followed by an official visit to Washington by China's future leader, Deputy Premier Deng Xiaoping, who had succeeded to the chairmanship of the Communist Party two years after Mao's death in September 1976. With mutual recognition came new opportunities for trade, a top priority of the new Chinese leader. Deng looked to the West to help convert China's economy into a capitalist one, complete with private property and free enterprise. And Deng welcomed foreign investment from the United States and Western Europe in an attempt to globalize China's economy. By the 1990s, China had emerged as one of the major trading partners of the United States. The PRC's importance to Washington was revealed annually when Congress extended China

---

[5] Historical distrust between the Russian and Chinese peoples, based largely on territorial claims, preceded the Cold War and further aggravated relations between the communist states.

most-favored-nation status despite the continuation of communist rule in the country. Quite clearly, ideology in Sino-American relations had given way to mutual economic gain.

Arms Control and "Linkage"

Even though the opening of diplomatic relations with China drove the wedge deeper between Beijing and Moscow, the détente strategy adopted by Nixon and Kissinger called for closer contact with the Soviet Union on a variety of issues. In the world of *realpolitik* that Kissinger imported to American foreign policy, even proclaimed adversaries could cooperate when their interests converged. In this respect, both sides stood to benefit from the lowering of tensions and the creation of a stable working relationship. Indeed, the interstate system as a whole would gain much-needed relief from the superpower rivalry, which inflamed domestic politics in many nations and provoked regional conflicts that sometimes escalated into head-on collisions.

One area of potential U.S.-Soviet cooperation was strategic arms control, which over the years had assumed greater importance. The arms race was an expression of the deep political differences between the United States and the Soviet Union. The danger was that the arms race, fueled by continuing conflict, would at some point spill over into a nuclear war. To avoid such a cataclysmic outcome, each side built up its nuclear forces and created new ways to deliver the deadly missiles from all distances (see Figure 5-1). Because nuclear weapons were unlikely to be abolished, both sides recognized that the next best tactic was to manage the nuclear balance through arms control agreements.[6]

The Strategic Arms Limitation Talks (SALT), one of Nixon's major achievements, stood at the center of détente. The talks, which involved high-level U.S. and Soviet officials, had four objectives. The first was to make the arms race more predictable by establishing, documenting, and reporting the number of strategic weapons possessed by each side. The second objective was to ensure "parity," or military equality. In the absence of nuclear superiority, the United States and the Soviet Union would each retain a sufficient second-strike capability to ensure mutual assured destruction. The third purpose of SALT was to reduce threats to each side's

---

[6] This effort was frequently at odds with the U.S. government's traditional approach to foreign affairs, as outlined elsewhere in this volume. See Colin S. Gray, *Nuclear Strategy and National Style* (Lanham, Md.: Hamilton Press, 1986).

Figure 5-1 U.S.-Soviet Nuclear Balance, 1967–1973

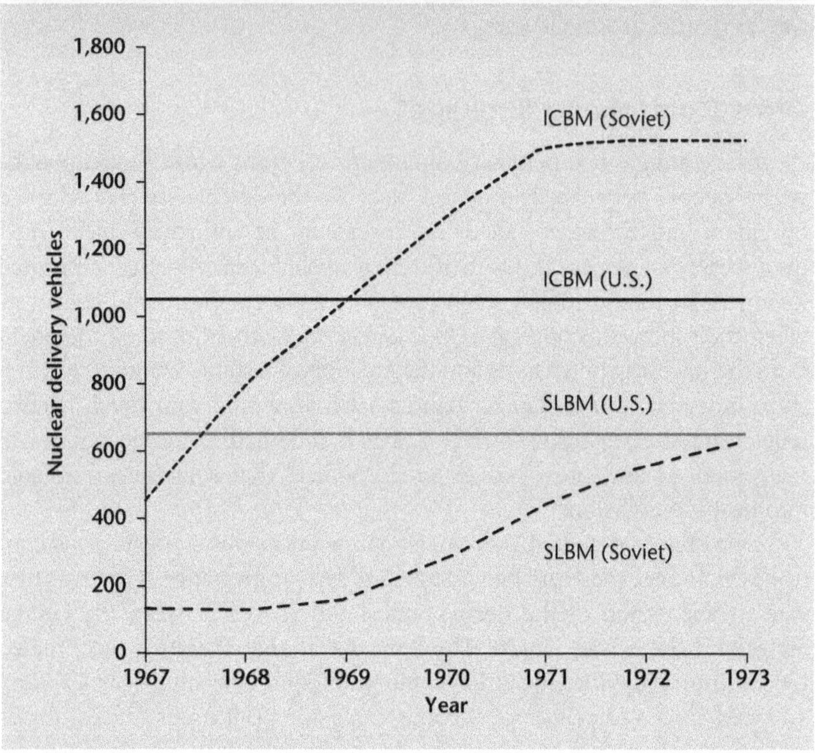

Source: International Institute for Strategic Studies (IISS), *The Military Balance*, 1973–1974, No. 2 (London: IISS, 1973), 71, 1141.

Note: ICBM = intercontinental ballistic missile; SLBM = submarine-launched ballistic missile.

deterrent forces. The development of a new defensive weapon was a concern. The Soviets had deployed antiballistic missiles (ABMs) around Moscow and were working on a second-generation ABM for possible nationwide deployment. If ABMs could shoot down American intercontinental ballistic missiles (ICBMs) and reduce the destruction inflicted on the Soviet Union to an "acceptable" level of casualties, the ABMs would undermine U.S. deterrence.[7] Finally, SALT was crucial for détente. Any failure to continue SALT was bound to hamper the overall U.S.-Soviet political relationship. Only a relaxation of tensions would enable the two nuclear giants to feel more secure.

---

[7]See Robert E. Osgood, *The Nuclear Dilemma in American Strategic Thought* (Boulder, Colo.: Westview Press, 1988), 48–55.

Nixon and Soviet leader Leonid Brezhnev signed the first set of agreements, known as SALT I, in May 1972. SALT I, which had taken two and a half years to negotiate, incorporated two agreements. The first limited each country's ABMs to two hundred launchers, later reduced to one hundred each. The second agreement froze offensive missile batteries at the number each side possessed at the time. Each side retained the right to improve its weapons within the overall quantitative agreement, thereby preserving parity. The follow-up agreement, SALT II, was approved at a 1974 meeting between President Ford and Brezhnev. The agreement called for new limits on the nuclear arsenals of both superpowers. Even though the ratification debate in Congress over SALT II became moot after the Soviet Union deployed troops into Afghanistan in late 1979 to shore up a pro-Soviet military regime, the terms of SALT II were observed into the late 1980s, when efforts to reduce nuclear stockpiles accelerated again under President Ronald Reagan (see Chapter 6).

Meanwhile, détente opened the doors to other agreements and cooperative measures beneficial to both powers. The key to such arrangements, however, would be *linkage*, directed primarily toward Moscow. If the two countries could achieve understandings on matters such as arms control and trade, the Soviet Union would gain a vested interest in good relations with the United States. Thus the Soviet Union would face, as before, a strong American military. This "stick," however, would be supplemented with enough economic "carrots" to make cooperation more rewarding. Military sanctions against the Soviet Union at a time of strategic parity were becoming riskier for the United States. The linkage strategy, which offered wide-ranging trade opportunities to Moscow, could achieve the same outcomes with far fewer risks. Progress on one front would be tied to progress on another.

By the time Nixon entered office in 1969, the Soviet economy, always particularly vulnerable, was in serious trouble. After expanding rapidly in the 1950s and early 1960s, the economy saw its 5 percent growth rate fall to 2 percent by the early 1970s. The economic decline was particularly notable in those sectors associated with the "second" industrial revolution: computers, microelectronics, and telecommunications. In short, the Soviet Union was falling further behind the West in those industries that were most important for economic growth. Moreover, the Soviet workplace was plagued by high absenteeism, drunkenness, corruption, and shoddy production. The implications of this decline, which was matched by a stagnant agricultural sector, damaged the Soviet Union's appeal as a socialist state, hampered its ability to compete with the United States, and threatened its superpower status.

The Soviet Union was the only industrial society in which the peacetime life expectancy of males was declining and infant mortality was rising. Brezhnev, who came to power in 1964, was well aware that the failure of his predecessor, Nikita Khrushchev, to achieve a higher standard of living led directly to his downfall. Khrushchev, reeling from his setback in the Cuban missile crisis, raised popular expectations about economic growth and then failed to meet them. The same thing could happen to Brezhnev, who took over as the Soviet standard of living was slipping both in absolute terms and in comparison to those enjoyed by Western capitalist states.

The Nixon administration believed these economic problems would give the United States leverage. Trade between the Cold War rivals could be quite profitable for U.S. industry and agriculture. But the main reason for establishing such ties was political. American productivity, it was hoped, would provide powerful material reinforcement for a Soviet foreign policy of restraint and accommodation. According to Kissinger, economic relations could not be separated from the political context. The United States should not be asked to reward hostile conduct with economic benefits. In return for the expansion of trade, it was not unreasonable to require the Soviets to cooperate on important foreign policy issues. In effect, the linkage strategy would give Moscow incentives to practice *self-containment*.

For its part, the United States faced serious economic problems during the Nixon-Ford years and stood to gain from the easing of U.S.-Soviet tensions. The Vietnam War had drained the Pentagon's budget, with little benefit in return, and the oil crisis of 1973 sparked high inflation and a two-year slump in the stock market. Europe, meanwhile, was no longer the weak, divided, and demoralized continent it had been just after World War II. Indeed, the emerging

Common Market—a precursor of today's European Union—had become a powerful economic competitor.[8] As a result of all these developments, the U.S. dollar was no longer considered as "good as gold" in global currency markets, bringing an end to the Bretton Woods system of fixed exchange rates. Nixon, true to his own realist instincts, recognized the limits facing the United States as well as its nemesis in Moscow.

Although détente marked a breakthrough in U.S.-Soviet relations, implementing the new strategy proved difficult for Nixon and Ford. Nixon's White House was consumed first by its futile search for an "honorable peace" in Vietnam, and later by the Watergate scandal that forced Nixon's

---

[8] For a review of Western Europe's progress toward "functional integration" during this period, see Martin Holland, *European Integration: From Community to Union* (London: Pinter, 1994), 22–59.

resignation on August 9, 1974. Ford, a former congressional leader without any foreign policy experience, devoted his start-up presidency to restoring political stability at home. Furthermore, as a strategy that combined both conflict *and* cooperation, détente was confusing to many Americans. It was easier to explain a relationship that was overtly hostile or friendly, not something in between. The Cold War aroused people; détente reassured them. This relationship, however, meant a reduction of tensions, not an absence of superpower rivalry. Expectations that détente would produce harmony were bound to be frustrated.

Carter's Quest for World Order

It was not surprising that government officials and much of the American public had become disillusioned with détente by 1976, President Ford's last year in power. As noted earlier, the United States had always wavered between opposite and mutually exclusive categories: isolation or intervention, peace or war, diplomacy or force, idealism or realism, harmony or strife. The pursuit of détente, however, was fraught with ambiguities. Meanwhile, many Americans had become cynical in the aftermath of Vietnam, the Watergate scandal, and a protracted slump in the U.S. economy.[9]

In such times of national self-doubt, Americans often turn to an outsider who appears untarnished by past government actions and who promises a fresh approach to domestic and foreign policy.[10] In the 1976 U.S. presidential campaign, Democrat Jimmy Carter, a peanut farmer and former governor of Georgia, filled this role. Carter seemed to epitomize the moral virtues Americans found lacking in previous presidents. Drawing on his experience as a Sunday school teacher in his Baptist church, Carter eloquently described the country's need for moral rejuvenation and spiritual rebirth after the traumas of Vietnam and Watergate. His words struck a chord with the American people, who elected him president over Ford.

Drawing on the idealism of President Woodrow Wilson, Carter identified human rights as the appropriate basis of American foreign policy. In equating the nation's moral principles with universal standards, Carter

---

[9] The transitions from Nixon to Ford, and from Ford to Carter, left American foreign policy in a constant state of flux. See Barbara Zanchetta, *The Transformation of American International Power in the 1970s* (New York: Cambridge University Press, 2014).

[10] In this respect, the parallels to the rise of Barack Obama are striking. Like Carter, he lacked widespread recognition prior to being elected U.S. president in November 2008. Obama also appealed to public pressure for a more "democratic" foreign policy.

personified the American style of foreign policy. The new president also offered a way out of what he called the "malaise" within the United States. The best course for the country, he argued, was to reject power politics, seek renewal by concentrating on domestic affairs, and build a fully free and socially just society whose example would radiate throughout the world. In the words of a former chair of the Senate Foreign Relations Committee, J. William Fulbright, America should "serve as an example of democracy to the world" and play its role in the world "not in its capacity as a *power*, but in its capacity as a *society*."[11] Virtue, not power, would be the hallmark of foreign policy; American influence in the world would derive from the nation's moral standing as a good and just society.

History has demonstrated that democratic states cannot conduct foreign policy effectively in the absence of domestic consensus. For most of its history, America had enjoyed such a consensus, which centered on the need for detachment from European great-power politics and the primacy of economic and political development. In the absence of an external threat, Americans wanted only to be left to their own devices. This consensus broke down, however, after the United States emerged from World War II as a predominant world power— and then began acting like one at great military, economic, and moral cost.

The task of re-creating consensus on foreign policy was embraced by Carter, who thought he could find it in America's self-proclaimed historical role as the defender of democracy and individual liberty. Rather than containment, human rights became the platform on which Carter expected to mobilize popular support for a new vision of world order.[12] Carter pledged to condition American relations with other countries, rich and poor alike, on their respect for human rights. He felt that the superpowers, by extending their Cold War to all corners of the world, had encouraged military dictators of all ideological stripes, undermined democratic reforms, and retarded economic development. In short, the Cold War only worsened the miserable conditions in much of the world. The United States once more stood for something, having reclaimed its democratic heritage and a moral basis for its foreign policy.

Jimmy Carter, the born-again Christian, thus became the redeemer of American ideals and moral principles.

---

[11] J. William Fulbright, *The Arrogance of Power* (New York: Vintage Books, 1967), 256 (emphasis in original).

[12] See Stanley Hoffmann, *Primacy or World Order: American Foreign Policy since the Cold War* (New York: McGraw-Hill, 1978).

The president was also keenly aware of general trends in world politics, particularly the growing *interdependence* of states and societies. All sides in the Cold War acknowledged that a nuclear war of any kind would affect all corners of the world and possibly render much of the planet uninhabitable. The expansion of the global economy into a single marketplace opened new markets for trade and investment while fostering a higher degree of cooperation and coordination among governments. Finally, Carter recognized that rapid population growth, worsening pollution, and other problems crossed national boundaries and thus could not be solved individually by states. Together, interdependence was not just an aspiration but also a reality in world politics. No longer could any nation prosper by going it alone.

The attraction of interdependence was its prospect of a more peaceful and harmonious world consistent with American values and an escape from the troublesome world of power politics. It was not surprising that this vision of transnational interdependence strongly influenced Carter, who came to power when the United States was recovering from the Vietnam War. Many of Carter's foreign policy advisers had participated earlier, during the Kennedy-Johnson years, in managing the war. They openly regretted the abuse of American power and the support of dictators throughout the world. Thus they dismissed Kissinger's amoral fixation with balance-of-power politics and looked instead toward a new era of global cooperation.

Carter was also deeply concerned about the developing countries, where widespread poverty and suffering persisted in the late 1970s. The optimism had faded that foreign aid would propel their modernization or, later, that expanding trade would permit them to finance their own development. For a variety of complex reasons, the billions of dollars in development aid from the North had little or no impact in the "Global South," as the vast region became known. Despite the creation of an elaborate aid "regime," gaps between the world's richest and poorest populations only widened. To Carter, the resulting tensions in North-South relations threatened his vision of "world-order politics" as much as the East-West struggle between the capitalist and communist powers.

Global interdependence featured dangers as well as opportunities, as was made clear by the first of several "oil shocks" that plagued the world economy. The latest war between Israel and its Arab neighbors in 1973, detailed below, had led to spiraling gasoline prices. These shocks to the industrialized economies were engineered by the Organization of the Petroleum Exporting Countries (OPEC), which gained control of the supply, and thus the price, of petroleum on world markets.[13] The cartel's bid to gain control over the world's oil reserves left no country untouched. In the United States, high oil prices prompted "stagflation" (simultaneous inflation and recession) and a surge in unemployment. The energy crisis of the 1970s did not merely cause occasional inconveniences such as long lines to buy gas or higher prices at the gas pump; it profoundly upset entire economies and changed ways of life, as evidenced by smaller cars and lower speed limits in the United States. Mao Zedong, who once said "power grows out of the barrel of a gun," would have been equally correct had he referred to a barrel of oil.

Carter assumed that, by adopting a more cooperative foreign policy, the United States would regain its political, economic, and moral strength. In his view, responsible American leadership would produce a more democratic world order, one that would also be more peaceful given the natural tendency of democracies to cooperate with one another. Carter's attempt to make human rights a "centerpiece" of his foreign policy, not only through rhetoric but by reshaping U.S. foreign policy agencies and their relationship with international organizations, marked a defining feature of his presidency.[14] His optimism, however, would be sorely tested as he sought to revive the U.S. economy, to maintain cordial superpower relations, and—perhaps his greatest challenge—to bring peace to the most explosive region of the world, the Middle East.

War and Peace in the Middle East

Beyond the developing regions noted earlier, the Middle East also required constant attention among the makers of American foreign policy during the Cold War. Three sets of rivalries intersected in this region: those between Israel and its Arab neighbors, those among Arab states, and those between the United States and the Soviet Union. The region's massive oil wealth, exploited by the OPEC cartel throughout the 1970s, added yet more volatility to the Middle East, the most explosive region in the world during and after the Cold War.

---

[13] See Daniel Yergin, *The Prize: The Epic Quest for Oil, Money, and Power* (New York: Simon and Schuster, 1991).

[14] Mary E. Stucker, *Jimmy Carter, Human Rights, and the National Agenda* (College Station: Texas A&M University, 2008).

Early Arab-Israeli Wars

Arab antagonism toward Israel stemmed from the Balfour Declaration of 1917, in which the British government pledged the establishment of a "national home" for the Jewish people. The declaration called for this homeland to be located in Palestine, a territory on the southeastern shore of the Mediterranean Sea that London had controlled since World War I. The declaration further promised Palestinian Arabs that their rights would also be protected. After World War II, the deaths of six million Jews in the Holocaust added new urgency to the Jewish cause and need for a secure state.

In November 1947, the United Nations partitioned Palestine into two independent states, one Jewish and the other Arab. Although the Arabs refused to accept this solution, the planning for a Jewish state continued. On May 14, 1948, Great Britain's mandate over Palestine officially ended, and the state of Israel was born. David Ben-Gurion, a leader of the Zionist movement that had long advocated for such a state, became its first prime minister.

The creation of Israel sparked the first Arab-Israeli war on the day after Israel's creation, when the armies of the Arab League (Egypt, Iraq, Jordan, Lebanon, Saudi Arabia, Syria, and Yemen) invaded the new state. With Ben-Gurion also serving as Israel's commander in chief, Israel's newly formed defense forces repelled the initial attack. By July, these forces included a modern army, navy, and air force, all of which were fortified by weapons procured from the United States and Czechoslovakia. Having gained air supremacy over the region, Israel succeeded in defeating the Arab forces and expanding its territory beyond the partition borders established by the United Nations. Israel, which scored a decisive victory in its "War of Independence," negotiated separate peace agreements with the defeated Arab states.

The Arabs, however, still refused to recognize Israel. Egypt, the leading Arab power, sought foreign armaments to prepare a second assault on the Jewish state. Egypt's leader, Col. Gamal Abdel Nasser, then tightened the ring around Israel in 1956 by forming a joint command with Saudi Arabia, Syria, and Yemen. When the United States angered Nasser by retracting its offer to finance his pet project, the Aswan High Dam, Nasser vowed to nationalize Egypt's Suez Canal, which connected the Red Sea and the Mediterranean, and use the revenues collected from it to finance the dam. Nasser, whose defiance of the United States thrilled Arab nationalists throughout the Middle East, became a heroic figure.

In this overheated environment, Israel took the offensive and marched into Egypt, where it quickly defeated the Egyptian forces on the Sinai Peninsula. British and French forces, still seeking a presence in the region, intervened on Israel's behalf and sought control of the canal. Far from receiving an American endorsement, however, the action by America's allies infuriated President Eisenhower, who feared a wider war in the Middle East. Eisenhower's opposition proved decisive in defusing the Suez crisis and establishing U.S. responsibility for regional stability. Congress followed through in 1957 by passing a joint resolution that declared the Middle East vital to U.S. security. Under the Eisenhower Doctrine, as the measure became known, the United States would use armed force to ensure peace—and Israel's security—in the Middle East.[15]

Keeping the peace, however, proved impossible. Nasser reasserted his leadership of Arab nationalism in 1967, leading to another Arab-Israeli war. Syria, which had briefly joined Egypt in creating a United Arab Republic, repeatedly called for Israel's destruction. Arab armies soon surrounded the Israelis: Syria to the north, Egypt to the south, and Jordan to the east. But their ambitions for pan-Arab unity were quickly frustrated when Israel struck first with air strikes. Israeli forces also routed the Jordanian army, and then captured half of Jerusalem and the western bank of the Jordan River. Finally, the Israelis eliminated Syrian bases on the Golan Heights from which Syria had been shelling Israel. Once again, the Israelis had won a war against their Arab neighbors—this time in just six days. Nasser's dreams of an Arab empire were shattered once and for all. Meanwhile, the United States maintained an even greater hold on the Middle East as the region's vast oil reserves became a vital security interest—and a cause of recurring conflicts—in the decades to come.

Still, the United States could not prevent yet another war in the Middle East, this time bringing the Cold War superpowers close to a direct and deadly clash. In 1973, Egypt and Syria attacked Israel on the highest of all Jewish holy days—Yom Kippur, or the Day of Atonement. Egypt entered the conflict because its leader, Anwar Sadat, was frustrated by Israel's refusal to give up the Egyptian territory it captured in the 1967 Six-Day War. The Egyptians and their Syrian allies, supported by massive military supplies from the Soviet Union, achieved initial success in restoring the previous status quo. The United States responded with a similar airlift of military supplies to Israel. After the Soviet Union threatened to deploy troops to the region, American military forces were placed on a worldwide nuclear alert. Moscow backed off, however, and the United States, also eager to avoid an escalation, pressured Israel to end its advance. These moves ensured a fragile cease-fire.

---

[15] For an elaboration, see Peter L. Hahn, *The United States, Great Britain, and Egypt, 1945–1956: Strategy and Diplomacy in the Early Cold War* (Chapel Hill: University of North Carolina Press, 1991).

Beyond its tensions with the Soviet Union, other fault lines in the Middle East ensured that the United States would find intervention in the region highly complex and unpredictable. "More often than not," historian George C. Herring observed, "the United States found itself hopelessly snarled in the raging conflicts between the Arabs and Israelis, Arabs and Arabs, and Arab nationalism and the European colonial powers."[16] Still, American leaders felt obligated to promote stability in the chaotic Middle East. Their commitment to Israel, based on moral as well as strategic objectives, was unwavering, and their economic interests in reliable oil supplies from the Middle East only grew more urgent given the dependence of the United States on petroleum. As made clear in the Eisenhower Doctrine, the status of the Middle East as a "vital interest" rendered withdrawal an impossible dream in American foreign policy.

The Camp David Accords

Taking power just four years after the Yom Kippur war, President Jimmy Carter understandably viewed the chronic Arab-Israeli dispute with alarm. He therefore proposed that all parties resume the negotiations they had begun after the war. In addition, Carter approached the Soviets to enlist their cooperation in achieving a peace settlement. This was an essential step given Moscow's influence with the Palestine Liberation Organization (PLO), which had formed to press the cause of renewed statehood for Palestine. The Soviets, therefore, could cause a lot of trouble and block negotiations. But if Moscow participated in the negotiations, the possibility of a superpower clash would be reduced, and détente with the United States would be revived.

The two superpowers reached agreement on a resolution of the Middle East conflict late in 1977, but neither Jerusalem nor Cairo was happy with the U.S.-Soviet accord. Thus Israel and Egypt decided to bypass Moscow and Washington and negotiate directly. In a dramatic and internationally televised visit to Jerusalem in November 1977, Sadat recognized the Arabs' archenemy. The mood afterward was euphoric but did not last long. Israel's new coalition government, led by Prime Minister Menachem Begin, proposed an Israeli withdrawal from the Sinai Desert but refused to offer statehood to the Palestinians on the West Bank and in the Gaza Strip, each of which contained large Arab populations. The Israeli government

---

[16]George C. Herring, *From Colony to Superpower: U.S. Foreign Relations since 1776* (New York: Oxford University Press, 2008), 671.

Map 5-1 Israel and Disputed Territories

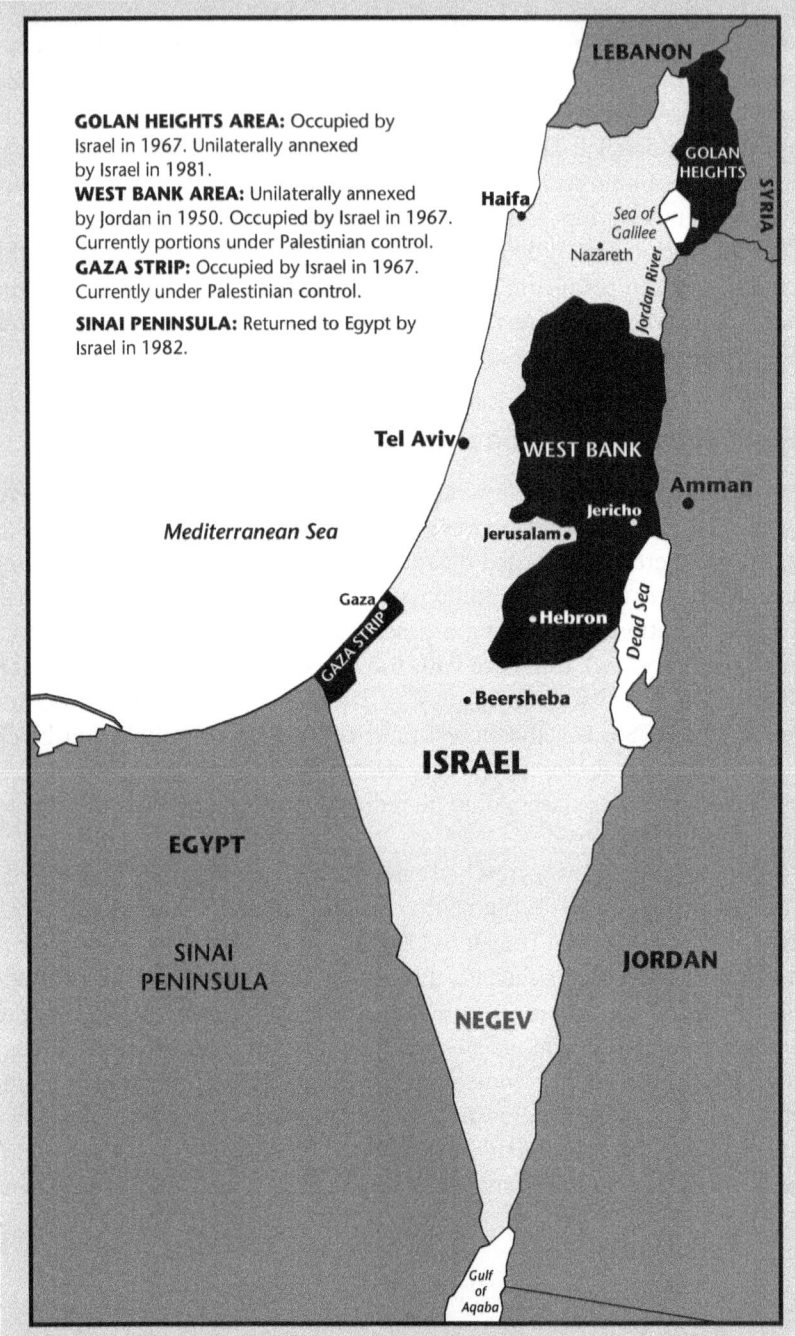

GOLAN HEIGHTS AREA: Occupied by
Israel in 1967. Unilaterally annexed
by Israel in 1981.
WEST BANK AREA: Unilaterally annexed
by Jordan in 1950. Occupied by Israel in 1967.
Currently portions under Palestinian control.
GAZA STRIP: Occupied by Israel in 1967.
Currently under Palestinian control.
SINAI PENINSULA: Returned to Egypt by
Israel in 1982.

LEBANON

GOLAN
HEIGHTS

Haifa

Sea of
Galilee

Nazareth

SYRIA

Jordan River

Tel Aviv

WEST BANK

Amman

Jericho

Mediterranean Sea

Jerusalem

Dead Sea

Gaza

GAZA STRIP

Hebron

Beersheba

ISRAEL

EGYPT

SINAI
PENINSULA

JORDAN

NEGEV

Gulf
of
Aqaba

announced that Jewish settlements in these areas would remain, and it even encouraged the establishment of new ones.

When, to no one's great surprise, bilateral negotiations broke down, the United States reentered the negotiating process. Carter felt that Sadat was offering Israel the security and peace it had so long sought, and that if this opportunity was not seized the result would be politically disastrous for Israel and economically disastrous for the West. The president thought three conditions were necessary for a solution in the Middle East. First, Israel had to return most of the Arab territory it had captured in 1967. Only minor adjustments for security reasons could be allowed. Second, the Palestinians had to participate in the peacemaking process. Carter himself declared that the Palestinians had a right to a "homeland," a deliberately vague term but one that nevertheless carried great symbolic weight. Third, in return for such Israeli concessions, the Arab states had to commit themselves not only to ending their hostilities with Israel but also to signing a peace treaty.

Begin remained opposed to a Palestinian state, which he—and indeed most Israelis—felt would endanger the existence of Israel. Moreover, he promoted his own plan for Israeli settlements in the occupied lands. Since 1967, however, the United States had consistently opposed these settlements as illegal. The Carter administration repeated this opposition while it watched in disbelief as the Israeli government, in the middle of the peace process, actively encouraged new settlements on the land the Arabs claimed to be theirs. In September 1978, Carter gambled and invited Begin and Sadat to meet with him at Camp David, the presidential retreat in Maryland. The invitation was a gamble because had this summit meeting produced no results, the president's prestige would have been seriously impaired, U.S. mediating attempts would have run their course, and U.S.-Israeli relations would have been set back even further. But the president persisted and after twelve days of patient negotiations emerged with a series of agreements, including a commitment by the two leaders to sign a peace treaty within three months.

Though Israel refused to withdraw from the West Bank and Gaza Strip, its government promised to recognize "the legitimate rights of the Palestinians," to permit Palestinians to participate in future negotiations on these areas, and to halt temporarily new Israeli settlements on the West Bank. In return, Israel gained formal recognition from the strongest of its Arab neighbors; without Egypt, the other Arab states could not by themselves take on Israel. Thus for a seemingly small investment, Israel had gained a real sense of security.

For his part, Sadat hoped that a peace agreement would prompt other Arab states to resolve their differences with Israel. But the Arab reaction to the Camp David Accords was negative, with many Arab leaders condemning Sadat. Still, Carter's courageous intervention—including his visits to Egypt and Israel—produced a historic diplomatic breakthrough and brought peace between these two historic enemies. The United States supported this peace with massive transfers of foreign aid to both governments that totaled more than $8 billion annually. For Carter, such expenses were a bargain if they bought time for expansion of the Middle East "peace process" and mutual recognition between Israel and other Arab states in the embattled region.

Blowback and the Soviet Power Play

For all of their differences, Richard Nixon and Jimmy Carter were both determined to alter the course of American foreign policy in response to changes in the interstate system and balance of power. The Vietnam War left the United States militarily, economically, and morally exhausted. At the same time, the war bolstered and emboldened the Soviet Union, which could not be displeased with the serial misjudgments by the White House and Pentagon that left the American forces deep in the quagmire of Indochina. The Soviet Union appeared upwardly mobile by comparison and seductive to the teeming, impoverished populations of postcolonial Africa, Latin America, and southern Asia. Through its vast nuclear arsenal and advanced delivery systems, the Kremlin also appeared capable of negating, for an indefinite period of time, American primacy in world politics.

Jimmy Carter's embrace of world-order politics in the mid-1970s coincided with many Americans' "crisis of confidence" in their government. The Watergate scandal tore at the nation's deeply embedded faith in the legitimacy of its political institutions, whose only functional drawbacks seemed related to the inefficiencies built into the separation of powers. Richard Nixon's cover-up, which included bugging the Oval Office and routinely tapping the phones of those on the administration's "enemies list," aimed to shield the president as he went to extreme lengths, including breaking the law, to advance his political agenda. The scandal compounded the public's cynicism in the wake of the Vietnam War and the distortions of truth that went with it from the start.

Even though President Carter sought continued détente with the Soviet Union, the term was closely identified with the disgraced Nixon administration. Carter thus rarely used the term and instead diminished the

Impact and Influence: Anwar Sadat, Jimmy Carter, and Menachem Begin

The Jimmy Carter Library

President Jimmy Carter struggled throughout most of his presidency to redirect the course of American foreign policy away from the rigid policy of anticommunist containment and Henry Kissinger's strategy of détente, which was based on amoral calculations of power politics. Although Carter's shift toward "world-order politics" and his attempt to highlight human rights were ultimately frustrated by global events, his central role in mediating the Camp David Accords in 1978 made it possible for peaceful relations to be established between Israel and its western neighbor—relations that continue today.

In awarding Sadat and Begin the Nobel Peace Prize in December 1978, the award committee's chair Aase Lionæs captured the importance of the Camp David Accords: "Never has the Peace Prize expressed a greater or more audacious hope— a hope of peace for the people of Egypt, for the people of Israel, and for all the peoples of the strife-torn and war-ravaged Middle East." Although Arab-Israeli tensions have persisted since the accords, Israel and Egypt have remained at peace.

superpower struggle as a diversion from the new realities of world politics. But the East-West struggle was not just an old, bad memory. It was still very much alive, even if the United States insisted that containment was no longer relevant in the face of global interdependence, the diffusion of power in the world, the growing nationalism in developing countries, and the shift from power politics to world-order politics. Many U.S. interventions in countries had embittered their citizens and left Washington vulnerable to "blowback," or acts of vengeance against the United States and its allies.

For their part, the Soviets shared neither the belief that international politics had changed nor the view that military force had become less relevant in foreign policy. Abroad, the Soviet Union exploited hostility among developing countries toward the North and offered those countries, for emulation, its model of communism and centrally directed industrialization. The internal decay of the Soviet economy, not yet visible to the outside world, was obscured by the heightened capacity of Soviet military power. It would take another decade for the root rot within the nation to be fully revealed.

Whereas Nixon and Kissinger followed realist tradition in charting a new course, Carter's liberal path was more in keeping with the American sense of moral mission and manifest destiny. But in acknowledging the nation's past violations of its own principles, and in pledging to uphold human rights and self-determination in deeds as well as words, Carter implicitly encouraged uprisings in foreign countries whose citizens had felt betrayed and victimized by the United States in the past and now mobilized to rectify these wrongs. The upheavals that followed posed new and unforeseen challenges to the United States. Indeed, after December 1979, when the Soviet Union responded to Carter by staging a military takeover of Afghanistan, both détente and world-order politics were in shambles. A new escalation of the Cold War had begun.

Nicaragua's Sandinista Revolution

Carter's call for human rights was well received in Central America, where decades of economic distress, military dictatorship, and ideological polarization had spawned a variety of revolutionary movements. These movements often were directed not only against the reigning rulers but also against the United States, whose support for dictators in the name of containing communism engendered widespread resentment throughout Latin America and the Caribbean. The United States, the self-proclaimed protector of the region under the Monroe Doctrine, was viewed by many in the region as more of a menace than a supportive patron. Carter hoped to change this perception by reforming U.S. policy and establishing a new reputation as a truly "good neighbor."

In Nicaragua, Carter opposed the long-standing military dictatorship of Anastasio Somoza García, whose family had ruthlessly controlled the country for nearly five decades (after the departure of U.S. Marines from the country). Carter's reversal of American policy was consistent with his overall effort to shift attention from Cold War concerns to internal social and economic problems in poorer countries. Continued U.S. support for right-wing dictatorships, he felt, would certainly doom U.S. interests in the region and throughout the developing world. Popular resentment and anger would eventually lead to the overthrow of such dictatorships, and identification of America with the status quo would only alienate the new rulers. Unlike in Vietnam, the argument went, the United States had to place itself on the "right side of history." Thus Carter favored social and political change and tried to identify U.S. policy with such change rather than oppose it.

The rebellion against Somoza accelerated in the late 1970s, despite the leader's increasingly brutal use of the Nicaraguan National Guard. The government-backed murder in January 1978 of Pedro Joaquín Chamorro Cardenal, a newspaper publisher and leading opponent of the regime, prompted a general strike and a call for free elections by the Organization of American States. The spiral of violence came home to Americans in June 1979 when Bill Stewart, an ABC News reporter, was executed by government forces on a city street in full view of camera crews. As disgust with Somoza spread far beyond Nicaragua, the regime finally collapsed in July.[17] At first, Carter favored the coalition of anti-Somoza forces led by the Sandinista National Liberation Front, which—at least initially—was supported on the domestic front by the Catholic Church, the educated middle class, and the business community. Thus in its first years under the coalition, Nicaragua received allotments of $80 million in foreign aid from the United States and promises for long-term support.

The new regime in Nicaragua, however, did not live up to Carter's expectations. The broad-based anti-Somoza coalition rapidly dissolved as the San dinistas, led by Daniel Ortega, centralized authority within a five-member "Junta of National Reconstruction." Free elections were delayed, the press was again censored, and other political restrictions were imposed by the new regime, which turned increasingly to Marxist-Leninist models for building a self-sufficient communist state. Ortega tightened his hold on power and declared common cause with Cuba and the Soviet Union. In addition, he offered to aid rebels in neighboring El Salvador, where a similar uprising had begun against its military dictator-ship. The Salvadoran dictatorship responded to the uprising by sending "death squads" into the impoverished countryside and murdering sus-pected insurgents. When their victims included a Catholic archbishop and three American nuns, the Carter administration rescinded U.S. aid to El Salvador and watched as the civil war became bloodier. No immedi-ate reversal of American policy, however well intentioned, was likely to counteract the bitterness and resentment that had developed for so long toward "*Yanqui* imperialism."

---

[17] For a more thorough treatment, see Anthony Lake, *Somoza Falling* (Boston: Houghton Mifflin, 1989).

America "Held Hostage" in Iran

The depths of anti-American hostility were further illustrated in November 1979 by the storming in the Middle East of the American embassy in Tehran by a mob of protesters. In the melee, militant students seized fifty-two American embassy workers. This event came on the heels of the ouster of Iran's pro-American leader, Mohammad Reza Shah Pahlavi, whose decades of brutal domestic repression were justified—in Tehran and Washington—on the basis of anticommunism. The ousted shah's admission to the United States in October for cancer treatment outraged Iranian nationalists and sparked the hostage crisis.[18] The seizure of American hostages paralyzed Carter, and his subsequent efforts to gain their safe release became high public drama. Nightly U.S. television networks featured images of Iranian crowds chanting anti-American slogans and burning Carter in effigy.

The newly installed revolutionary authorities, hoping to create an Islamic theocracy in Iran, gave the unprecedented hostage-taking their blessing and support. The Ayatollah Ruhollah Khomeini, Iran's chief religious leader and *imam*, or leader, of all Shiite Muslims, called America the "Great Satan," and "Death to America" was the battle cry on the streets of Tehran. Carter, who had stressed human rights in his election campaign, was caught between conflicting views. Although the shah's removal from power was consistent with Carter's rhetoric, the president's understanding of Khomeini was superficial. Neither Carter nor other world leaders in that secular age had given serious consideration to the strength of a religious movement and the possibility that it would transform Iran into an Islamic theocracy.

In the 444 days following the hostage-taking, the world watched as the Carter administration tried one means after another to gain the hostages' release. Among other things, the White House appealed to the United Nations and the International Court of Justice and applied a series of economic sanctions. But all was in vain. The holding of the hostages was a symbolic act of defiance and revenge for America's support of the shah, who was portrayed by the new regime as an American puppet who had cruelly exploited Iranians in behalf of U.S. interests. As the administration's patience wore thin, it attempted a rescue mission in the spring of 1980.

---

[18] The shah died a few months later in Egypt. For reviews of his long and intimate relationship with the United States, see Roham Alvandi, *Nixon, Kissinger, and the Shah: The United States and Iran in the Cold War* (New York: Cambridge University Press, 2014), and Mark Gasiorowski, *U.S. Foreign Policy and the Shah: Building a Client State in Iran* (Ithaca, N.Y.: Cornell University Press, 1991).

The mission was called off, however, when three of the eight helicopters in the mission malfunctioned in a desert sandstorm. Even worse, one helicopter collided on the ground with the refueling aircraft for the flight out of Iran, killing eight servicemen and injuring five others.

For a nation on edge, the failure of the rescue mission symbolized the helplessness of the United States as well as the low level of readiness, competence, and reliability of its armed forces. Secretary of State Cyrus Vance resigned in protest of the mission, revealing deepening divisions within the Carter administration. Vance's rival, national security adviser Zbigniew Brzezinski, demanded a hard line in foreign policy that would replace Carter's reliance on good intentions with the use of military power to achieve American goals. Increasingly, Carter's idealism gave way to realism as he complied with Brzezinski's "calls to be tough, to threaten, to demonstrate and prepare to use force as a means of gaining over his circumstances."[19]

Two events helped to gain the hostages' release on January 20, 1981, the day Carter left office. The first was the Iraqi attack on Iran in the fall of 1980. The war suddenly made the U.S. economic sanctions, especially the freeze on Iranian money in American banks, painful for Iran, because its military forces were largely U.S.-equipped. The need for spare parts and the cash to buy them and other goods grew as oil production in Iran fell to almost nothing. The second event was the November 1980 victory of Republican Ronald Reagan, the former governor of California, in the U.S. presidential election. Because he had run on a tough foreign policy platform and had denounced the Iranians as "barbarians" and "kidnappers," the Iranians expected harsher measures from Reagan, including military action. In these circumstances, diplomacy finally proved successful. The fifty-two hostages were released just after Reagan's inauguration in a gesture fraught with symbolism.

The Soviet Takeover in Afghanistan

The greatest challenge to Carter's world-order politics came from the Soviet Union, which chose Christmas Day 1979 to achieve its longtime goal to dominate Afghanistan, whose location in central Asia offered Moscow an expanded sphere of influence and a potential stepping-stone to

---

[19] Betty Glad, *An Outsider in the White House: Jimmy Carter, His Advisers, and the Making of American Foreign Policy* (Ithaca, N.Y.: Cornell University Press, 2009), 286. See also Jeral A. Rosati, *The Carter Administration's Quest for Global Community* (Columbia: University of South Carolina Press, 1987), 142–149.

the Middle East oil fields. Like Iran, Afghanistan had long been governed by a monarchy whose ruthlessness led to its overthrow in 1973. After several years of internal conflict, a Marxist regime came to power in 1978 that promised Soviet-style modernization in the poverty-stricken country along with cultural reforms that would diminish the role of Islam as a driving force in Afghan society. While Soviet leaders supported the new regime with military aid, President Carter approved covert funding in July 1979 to support Afghan insurgents, or *mujahidin*, who sought to overthrow the Marxist regime and to abolish its radical land reforms and efforts to create a secular, communist state.

Among their other concerns, the Soviets feared that the Islamic fundamentalism then sweeping Iran and Pakistan might engulf Afghanistan, which lay between these two countries, creating an insecure situation on the Soviet Union's southern border where some fifty million Soviet Muslims lived. In response to the situation, Moscow invoked the Brezhnev Doctrine, which asserted that once a nation had become socialist, it was not to be surrendered to "counterrevolution." Earlier, this doctrine had been invoked only in Eastern Europe—in Hungary in 1956 and Czechoslovakia in 1968. Now the Red Army was to ensure history's progress outside of the Soviet sphere in a developing country. Brezhnev, citing a 1978 "Treaty of Friendship" with Afghanistan's pro-Soviet regime, exploited the chronic disarray in Kabul by deploying nearly one hundred thousand airborne and ground forces into the city, seizing the government's centers of power, and installing a puppet regime that closely resembled Moscow's satellites in Eastern Europe.

The Soviets expected Americans to merely condemn the December 25 "liberation" of Afghanistan as deplorable. In fact, believing their own vital security interests to be at stake, the Soviets did not give much thought to the American reaction and felt they had little to lose. After all, the Soviet Union had received few of the trade, technology, and financial benefits it had expected from détente. Indeed, Moscow had been denied most-favored-nation commercial status, which China had received, despite its own lack of political and social reform. Nevertheless, such a disregard for the American reaction revealed contempt for American power.

For Carter and Vance, who had pinned so much of their hopes for world-order politics on superpower cooperation, the Soviet invasion was a shock. Chagrined, Carter called the Afghanistan invasion the greatest threat to world peace since World War II, saying, "[the Soviet action] made a more dramatic change in my opinion of what the Soviets' ultimate goals are than anything they've done in the previous time I've been in office." With those words, the president demonstrated dramatically his own naïveté. He stepped up military spending, halted high-technology sales, embargoed grain shipments, and imposed a U.S. boycott on the Olympic Games scheduled for Moscow in the summer of 1980. Meanwhile, the Senate refused to ratify the SALT II treaty with Moscow. Carter declared that any Soviet actions that sought greater control over the Persian Gulf would be considered a direct threat to America's vital interests. Most important, his approval of covert funding to the *mujahidin*, continued by Carter's successors, was crucial in turning back the Soviet Union a decade later—and in immersing the United States in Afghan domestic politics that would prove fateful in the "war on terror" long after the Cold War.[20]

Nixon's détente and Carter's world-order politics both came to an end in 1980 as superpower relations disintegrated. As noted earlier, the Nixon administration's "linkage" strategy failed to elicit goodwill from Moscow. For his part, Carter's foreign policy was based on the assumption that not all regional conflicts were tests of superpower strength and credibility. In truth, however, few purely regional quarrels existed outside the context of superpower tensions. Clearly, Soviet leaders did not consider their rivalry with the United States over. In fact, quite the opposite was true: they took advantage of America's post-Vietnam illusion that regional problems could be separated from the superpower competition. With the Cold War still on, "historical forces" were not moving in the direction of great-power cooperation, as Carter had presumed. Instead, world politics and American foreign policy remained mired in conflicting interests and tests of strength.

---

[20] Steven Coll, *Ghost Wars: The Secret History of the CIA, Afghanistan, and Bin Laden, from the Soviet Invasion to September 10, 2001* (New York: Penguin, 2004).

Breakthroughs in the Superpower Struggle

J ust as Jimmy Carter's rise to power reflected the introspective and sullen American mood of the Vietnam-Watergate era, Ronald Reagan's assumption of leadership embodied the more assertive national spirit of the early 1980s. A former movie star and pitchman for General Electric, President Reagan was known neither for his intellect nor for his long days at work in the Oval Office.[1] The contrast with his predecessor was widely apparent. Whereas Carter's worldview emphasized the complexities of interdependence, Reagan's was one-dimensional. Whereas Carter pored over background reports and anguished over policy choices, Reagan often dozed through high-level meetings. But he brought to the office two characteristics that would serve him well: strong anticommunist instincts and a powerful ability to mobilize public opinion.

Reagan attempted to restore the country's battered stature and national pride by reviving the notion that an active U.S. role in international affairs was essential to world peace. Soviet leaders, he felt, had exploited détente, the Vietnam syndrome, and Carter's attempts to place human rights at the center of American foreign policy. As Reagan's supporters saw it, a straight line could be drawn from Carter's idealism to the Sandinista revolution in Nicaragua, the seizure of American hostages in Iran, and the Soviet invasion of Afghanistan. Believing the United States must match the Soviet nuclear and conventional military buildup of the 1970s, Reagan proposed a massive buildup of U.S. armed forces. A compliant Congress approved his proposals to double American defense spending in his first term and to match recent Soviet deployments of intermediate-range nuclear missiles in Europe with a new generation of North Atlantic Treaty Organization (NATO) missiles.

Reagan often boasted that he was blessed with the luck of the Irish. Indeed, he certainly had the good fortune to take office as the torch was

---

[1] For an informative biography, see Lou Cannon, *Reagan* (New York: Putnam, 1982). For a study of Reagan's work at General Electric, where his role as a "traveling ambassador" shaped his transition from a liberal to a conservative, see Thomas W. Evans, *The Education of Ronald Reagan* (New York: Columbia University Press, 2006). A critical assessment of Reagan can be found in Robert J. McMahon, "American Foreign Policy during the Reagan Years," *Diplomatic History* (Spring 1995).

Warm personal relations between Soviet President Mikhail Gorbachev (left) and U.S. President Ronald Reagan (right) led the two adversaries to find common cause on a variety of issues. Their signing in December 1987 of a treaty banning the deployment of intermediate-range missiles in Europe set the stage for other agreements that cooled tensions in the Cold War.

being passed in Moscow from the old guard to a new generation of re formers led by Mikhail Gorbachev. The lower tensions between the superpowers, so unexpected at the beginning of the decade, often have been attributed to Gorbachev, who took over the Kremlin in 1985, during Reagan's second term in office. His generation of Soviet elites hailed from urban rather than rural backgrounds and had some exposure to foreign countries. As a result, they were more aware of the failings of the Soviet system and critical of its internal defects. Had Leonid Brezhnev or his two immediate successors survived, Gorbachev's new domestic and foreign policies might not have seen the light of day. Nor is it likely the Cold War would have ended on terms that were as peaceful or as beneficial to the West.

To some, the collapse of the Warsaw Pact and the Soviet Union in 1991 was inevitable no matter who was president of the United States in the 1980s. The ossified Soviet system was already in an advanced stage of decline, its internal problems were growing worse daily, and its hold on its clients in Eastern Europe and beyond was becoming increasingly tenuous. Thus Gorbachev—or any leader of the country—had to implement drastic reforms in the Soviet Union's political and economic systems; permit the restive populations in Warsaw, Prague, and East Berlin to express themselves;

and adopt a more cooperative posture toward the United States. These measures would, according to those holding this view, only magnify the deficiencies of the Soviet system and hasten its self-destruction.

But this interpretation of events, which minimizes the roles of both Reagan and Gorbachev, does not tell the full story. It fails to recognize the crucial part Reagan played in raising the costs of the superpower competition and in forcing the Soviet Union to reform its system. The U.S. military buildup, which began in Carter's last year, required greater Soviet investments in arms at a time when the dwindling resources of the nation were needed for domestic priorities. Moreover, the new NATO missile deployments in Western Europe negated the strategic advantages of recent Soviet installations. Reagan's proposals for a Strategic Defense Initiative further worried the Soviets because whether or not it succeeded in creating a missile-proof "shield" over the United States, the project might lead America to a quantum leap in technology at a time when the Soviet Union was struggling with growing economic problems at home. Finally, Reagan's support for anticommunist movements in many parts of the world further increased the costs of Soviet expansion.

In short, the Kremlin's foreign policy, which at first had appeared so successful, had become counterproductive: it had provoked a strong American reaction, held NATO together, and left the Soviet Union surrounded by enemies (including Japan and China). For his part, Reagan had increased the strains on the Soviet Union so much that it could no longer muddle through. He eliminated any flexibility that Gorbachev might have had and forced him to retrench abroad, cut military spending, and subordinate foreign policy to domestic affairs. Initially thought to be reckless and widely condemned as a cowboy (especially in Europe) because he appeared trigger-happy, Reagan left office in January 1989 with the United States clearly dominant in the Cold War.

Reagan's Rhetorical Offensive

When Reagan came into office, the national disillusionment with détente was widespread. The president's longtime hostility toward communism in general and the Soviet Union specifically fit the new post-détente mood. Soviet leaders would "lie, steal, cheat, and do anything else to advance their goals," warned Reagan.[2] Opposition to the Soviet Union was, therefore, a

---

[2] *New York Times* (January 30, 1981).

moral as well as a political imperative. Reagan also spoke of the march of freedom and democracy that would leave "Marxism-Leninism on the ash heap of history." Of Eastern Europe he said, "Regimes planted by bayonets do not take root"—that is, the communist regimes had no legitimacy. The United States could not accept the "permanent subjugation of the people of Eastern Europe."[3] In making the point that democracy and freedom were the waves of the future, the president was not just giving the Soviets a dose of their own medicine, for the Soviets regularly denounced the United States and forecast the "inevitable end" of Western capitalism. More important, he was questioning the legitimacy and longevity of communism as a social and political system in Eastern Europe and the Soviet Union.

Many American critics dismissed as empty rhetoric Reagan's predictions that communism would be swept aside by the tide of democracy. By the end of his second term, however, many repressive noncommunist states were being transformed along democratic lines, and communist regimes were being exposed to greater demands for liberties from within. Thus Reagan's prediction looked less like rightwing ranting than accurate insight into historical development. Although he was far from a political theorist, Reagan was a spirited polemicist whose expectation of communism's demise in Europe materialized on his watch.

Reagan's harsh denunciations of the Soviet Union also served two tactical purposes. First, the war of words was intended to remobilize American public opinion after the years of détente. Reagan, to whom détente had all along been an illusion based on the unwarranted belief that the Soviets would change their character, sought to arouse American opinion for the longer term. Second, the president's public statements were intended to send the Soviet leaders a message, one that probably was heeded all the more because the Soviet leadership was in the throes of a geriatric crisis. Three Soviet leaders died in three years: Leonid Brezhnev in late 1982, Yuri Andropov in early 1984, and Konstantin Chernenko, in ill health when he took over, in 1985. Gorbachev, who had risen rapidly to the top of the Communist Party hierarchy, now became the Soviet Union's fourth leader since Reagan had assumed office. At age fifty-four, he was the youngest man to take charge of the nation since Joseph Stalin.

Reagan bluntly informed the new Soviet leaders that the Vietnam syndrome was a thing of the past. America's will to resist Soviet expansion was

---

[3] Address to members of the British Parliament, June 8, 1982, in Strobe Talbott, *Russians and Reagan* (New York: Vintage Books, 1984), 89–104. For a recent assessment of this speech, see Robert C. Rowland and John M. Jones, *Reagan at Westminster: Foreshadowing the End of the Cold War* (College Station: Texas A&M University Press, 2010).

back. Reagan wanted to make sure the Soviet Union would not act, as it had during the 1970s, in the belief that America would not respond to its provocations. Minor U.S. military actions against Soviet proxies such as Libya and Grenada—which the United States could not lose and were not costly—were intended to drive this message home. In that sense, the tough words were essentially a substitute for riskier deeds.

The early Reagan years were characterized by rhetorical confrontations, as there were no direct encounters or crises. Despite his reputation for machismo, the president was operationally cautious. To the extent the Soviets saw him as a leader spoiling for a fight, they felt it necessary to act with restraint. Reagan's foreign policy was basically a return to the containment policy of the immediate post–World War II years. The primary emphasis was on East-West relations, on the Soviet Union as a communist expansionist state, and on the need to contain that expansion—by force if necessary.

Expanding U.S. Military Forces

The late 1970s in the United States were rife with antimilitary sentiment and cries for a renewed emphasis on domestic priorities and reductions in the defense budget. Indeed, those years witnessed "the most substantial reduction in American military capabilities relative to those of the Soviet Union in the entire postwar period."[4] American defense expenditures had fallen to the 1950 (pre–Korean War) low of 5 percent of the nation's gross national product at a time when the Soviet Union, despite having an economy only half the size of that of the United States, was spending substantially more than the United States on defense. By 1981, with the turmoil of Jimmy Carter's final years in the White House clearly in mind, any president would have been concerned about Soviet intentions and capabilities.

After a decade and a half of Soviet efforts to exploit America's Vietnam-induced malaise and a weakened presidency, the Soviet Union possessed the strategic and conventional forces needed to project its power beyond Eurasia. It was in the context of their perceptions of a changing "correlation of forces" that the Soviets had exploited unstable situations in poorer countries to increase their influence. This task was undertaken by military advisers and arms, proxies such as the Vietnamese in Cambodia and

---

[4]John Lewis Gaddis, *Strategies of Containment: A Critical Appraisal of Postwar American National Security Policy* (New York: Oxford University Press, 1982), 320–322.

the Cubans in Africa, and, of course, their own troops in Afghanistan. The Reagan administration was especially worried about the state of U.S. nuclear forces and warned that a "window of vulnerability" had opened that could leave the United States vulnerable to Soviet nuclear blackmail.

Yet Reagan's promise to revive U.S. military power alarmed many Americans, who feared the onset of a global nuclear war. Even more disturbing was Secretary of State Alexander Haig's talk of nuclear warning shots, "protracted" nuclear war, nuclear "war-fighting," and "prevailing" in a nuclear war. Thus the administration's five-year, $1 trillion defense program (which actually totaled almost $3 trillion over Reagan's two terms in constant 2000 dollars) sparked an enormous controversy (see Figure 6-1). The sharp rise in spending conveyed the impression that by relying too much on military strength Reagan was flirting with disaster, and it revived charges that the United States was largely responsible for the arms race. The momentum of the Soviet Union's arms program since the mid-1960s and its impact on the balance of forces were forgotten in the uproar over the administration's rearmament program.

Opposition to Arms Control

This uproar was intensified by Reagan's strong opposition to arms control, the centerpiece of both Nixon's and Carter's policies toward the Soviet Union. Rejection of the SALT process reflected the Reagan administration's strong distrust of the Soviets and its conviction that past arms control efforts had led to America's relative decline. Reagan announced that he would postpone any arms negotiations until the United States could "negotiate from strength." But postponing new arms control talks proved difficult, because public opinion equated arms control with a sincere search for peace. The pressure on the administration therefore grew. When negotiations finally began in 1982, the administration claimed it was shifting the emphasis from arms limitation—setting ceilings on missile launchers and warheads—to drastic reductions in both categories. Thus Reagan changed the name of the process from SALT (Strategic Arms Limitation Talks) to START (Strategic Arms Reduction Talks). The administration's real motive for this change, however, was to make its approach politically appealing at home, to deflect domestic criticism, and to weaken the newborn nuclear freeze movement while the buildup continued. The initial arms control proposals from the Reagan White House were clearly meant to be rejected by Moscow, thereby winning time for the administration to win over the American public.

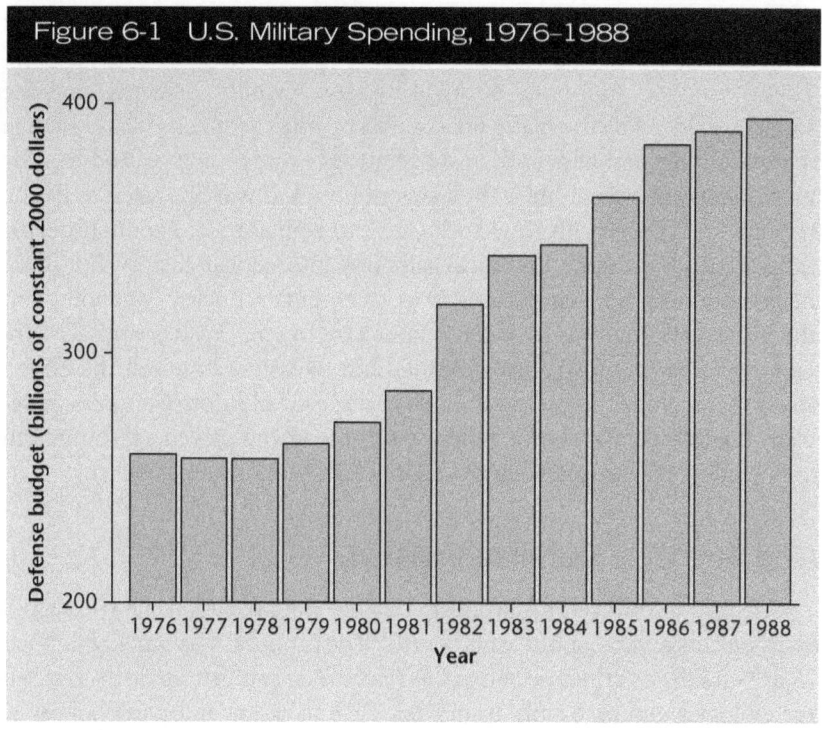

Figure 6-1   U.S. Military Spending, 1976–1988

Source: White House, Office of Management and Budget, www.whitehouse.gov/omb/budget/fy2005/pdf/hist.pdf.

Many Americans were not fooled, however, and the Reagan administration's efforts provoked a widespread peace movement in the early 1980s. Its adherents ranged from academics to religious leaders, who questioned the morality of nuclear deterrence, a policy based on the threat to use nuclear weapons in order to prevent their use. Catholic and Methodist bishops condemned not only the use of nuclear weapons, but also their very presence in the arsenals and military doctrines of both superpowers.[5] Yet if such weapons could not be used even in retaliation, how could deterrence be made credible? Was the goal of peace moral but the means of preserving it immoral? In the meantime, anti-nuclear books and films became popular, climaxing in an ABC-TV movie titled *The Day After* that depicted the nuclear devastation of an average American city.

---

[5] National Conference of Catholic Bishops, *Challenge and Peace: God's Promise and Our Response* (Washington, D.C.: United States Catholic Conference, 1983).

In addition to decrying the immorality of nuclear deterrence, the peace movement asserted that nuclear war would mean the end of civilization. This theme was supported strongly by new scientific evidence that the smoke produced by the many fires caused by nuclear attacks would plunge the world into darkness and create a "nuclear winter" that would destroy most plant and animal life.[6] The danger of nuclear war appeared to be the nation's first concern. In New York City, three-quarters of a million people turned out for the largest political gathering in American history. For those demonstrators, the ultimate goal was to eliminate nuclear weapons, but the immediate goal was to achieve a nuclear "freeze." Such proposals were endorsed in many town-hall meetings and by voters in ten of the eleven states that included freeze resolutions in the 1982 election. Congress, especially the Democratic House, reflected this mood and passed a resolution in 1983 calling for a suspension of U.S. nuclear weapons production.

The Strategic Defense Initiative

Reagan introduced his Strategic Defense Initiative (SDI) in 1983 amid swirling controversy about arms control. The proposal was quickly dubbed "Star Wars" by its critics because of its reliance on sophisticated space-based technologies glimpsed only in movies, such as lasers and particle beams. SDI was intended to render nuclear missiles "impotent and obsolete," presumably protecting America's population. According to official descriptions, SDI would be a "layered" defense using different technologies to destroy approaching missiles during each phase of the ballistic trajectory. Mutual assured *survival* would replace mutual assured destruction.

For the president, the SDI proposal served two primary purposes, the first of which was domestic and political. Criticized for increasing the defense budget while cutting social services and assailed for being a war-monger, Reagan would present himself as a man of vision who would end the threat of missile attacks and ensure that the populations of the United States and the Soviet Union would survive. His SDI proposal also served a more pragmatic function. If it worked, Americans would gain the upper hand on the Soviets, whose superpower status was based in large measure on their arsenal of intercontinental ballistic missiles. The proposed missile shield threatened the value of this Soviet investment and Moscow's claims to strategic parity with the United States. A defense against Soviet-launched

---

[6] See Carl Sagan, "Nuclear Winter and Climatic Catastrophe: Some Policy Implications," *Foreign Affairs* (Winter 1983–1984): 257–292.

missiles would increase the Soviets' uncertainty that they could launch a successful first strike, thus making the U.S. nuclear deterrent more credible.

The SDI proposal was denounced by critics for many reasons: it would be enormously expensive, it would accelerate the arms race, it would have to work perfectly the first time it was needed, and it would tempt a Soviet first strike if the Soviets felt they were on the verge of becoming "nuclear hostages" to an unassailable United States. In short, SDI would only lead to new arms races, offensive and defensive, in which the defensive technologies, even if they gained the upper hand, would do so only temporarily. Moreover, the system would be so expensive that it would threaten U.S. budgets for other strategic and conventional forces, not to mention domestic priorities. The reduction of arms through bilateral negotiations was the better course.

But if the critics were correct, why did the Soviets denounce Reagan's "arms race in space"? Why, after previously walking out of all arms control negotiations, were the Soviets so eager to resume talks? Clearly, SDI worried them; they were as fearful of an American first strike as the Americans had been of a Soviet first strike since the early 1970s. The Soviets perceived SDI to be part of an offensive, not a defensive, strategy, a prelude to an American strike that would be launched once the U.S. population could be protected. They also knew that SDI research and development would result in American technology taking a huge step forward. With their domestic economy deteriorating rapidly, the Soviets could not afford to accelerate the arms race on so great a scale.

"Rollback" in Developing Countries

Although President Reagan refocused the attention of American foreign policy on the East-West struggle, the developing countries remained a matter of concern. Among Reagan's top priorities on taking office was a reversal of what he saw as Soviet gains during the 1970s in, among other places, Afghanistan, Angola, Cambodia, Ethiopia, and Yemen after the Vietnam War. The Soviets and their allies had been using force to make inroads in these areas—direct force in Afghanistan, indirect force through proxies elsewhere. Past administrations, committed to containment, had not hesitated to intervene to save a friendly regime from being attacked from outside or from within by the Soviet Union or its friends. Yet containment remained a fundamentally defensive doctrine. Reagan's "rollback" strategy, however, called for offensive action.

Dubbed the "Reagan Doctrine," the policy aimed to reverse Soviet gains. Afghanistan, Angola, and Nicaragua had established Marxist governments that had not yet fully consolidated their power, and all faced resistance movements. The Soviets had justified their expansion in the developing world with the doctrine of "national liberation" and then asserted that communism was irreversible once a society had become Marxist. Reagan now adopted his own national liberation strategy against governments that had not come to power by means of democratic processes. In his eyes, such regimes lacked legitimacy. Moscow had placed them in power, and, unlike his predecessors (with the exception of Jimmy Carter in Afghanistan, where a U.S. program of covert assistance for resistance fighters was already in place), he refused to accept the Brezhnev Doctrine's claim that once a nation had become part of the Soviet bloc it could never leave.

The rollback strategy was based on certain assumptions: that the Soviet Union had become overextended in the 1970s; that the global balance of military power was increasingly favoring the United States; that the Soviet Union's most critical problems were domestic; that the Soviet Union would not risk a confrontation with the United States; and that a democratic tide was sweeping across the developing world. In practice, the Reagan Doctrine amounted to bleeding the targeted governments and especially Moscow.

As noted, the Reagan administration turned Marxist ideology on its head by arguing that "historical forces" were on the side of Western democracy and capitalism, not communism. For evidence, the administration pointed to Latin America, where the Reagan White House had already seen Argentina, Bolivia, Brazil, Guatemala, Honduras, Peru, and Uruguay become, at least nominally, democratic, in addition to El Salvador, Grenada, and Haiti. Whatever the reason for this phenomenon, the administration claimed it was part of an irreversible process. The Soviet bloc, by denying human freedom and dignity to its citizens, was running against the tide of history.

Drawing on the traditional hemispheric preoccupation of the Monroe Doctrine, Reagan identified Central America, South America, and the Caribbean as vital U.S. interests and vowed to turn back any outside (that is, Soviet) incursions into America's backyard. To demonstrate his resolve, Reagan intervened directly on the tiny Caribbean island of Grenada, where a military coup had led to the installation of a Marxist regime in 1983. The U.S. military operation, which ostensibly was designed to liberate American medical students from the island, took longer than expected because of logistical problems and a considerable amount of bungling by

U.S. Army, Navy, and Marine forces. But the mission achieved its main objective of eliminating the Marxist regime.

The U.S. invasion of Grenada was intended to raise the risks and the costs for the Soviets and Cubans should they continue to try to extend their political and military control into the Western Hemisphere—or elsewhere. Asserting that it had intervened to prevent Grenada from becoming a "Soviet-Cuban colony," the administration called Grenada a "warning shot" that actually was targeting the Sandinista regime in Nicaragua. The administration was convinced that the Sandinistas, led by Daniel Ortega, harbored ideologically motivated ambitions beyond their own frontiers (see Chapter 5).[7] Because they also accepted support from Havana and Moscow, they were, in Washington's eyes, a continuing source of instability and tension for the vulnerable states in the region. The Sandinistas' pledge to confine themselves to Nicaragua was regarded with skepticism by those who recalled Ortega's earlier pledges to promote political pluralism, a mixed economy, and a nonaligned foreign policy.

What the Reagan administration sought in Nicaragua was to undo the Sandinistas' growing monopolization of power and return the country to its immediate post-1979 state. The popular anti-Somoza revolution had produced a new coalition government composed of the major factions—religious groups, entrepreneurs, and large segments of the middle and working classes—that had helped to overthrow the dictator. Once in power, however, the Sandinistas began to consolidate their hold on government, gradually suppressing the voices of criticism. They postponed general elections and censored the news media while building an army larger than that of dictator Anastasio Somoza Debayle, son of Nicaragua's earlier leader. True to his father's harsh approach to order, the dynasty's new leader restricted activities by opposition political parties, extended control over worker and peasant organizations, and strengthened their police and security apparatus. They also turned toward Cuba and the Soviet Union for diplomatic support and economic assistance. But the question was not how *Marxist* the regime would become as it turned against the Catholic Church, the business community, professional organizations, trade unions, and student groups that had helped it to depose Somoza. The question was how *dictatorial* it would become and how closely it would align with Havana and Moscow.

---

[7] The Sandinistas derived their name from César Augusto Sandino, the Nicaraguan nationalist who led the resistance against the U.S. occupation of Nicaragua in the early 1930s. Sandino was killed by the U.S.-trained Nicaraguan National Guard in 1934.

The United States, which initially supported the new regime in Nicaragua with foreign aid, was increasingly distressed by the regime's consolidation of power and militaristic behavior. Thus after Reagan took office, he authorized the formation of an anti-Sandinista army known as the "contras." Trained by U.S. military advisers in neighboring Honduras, the soldiers staged a series of military offenses against the Sandinista regime. Honduras received even more U.S. military assistance for these purposes, although Reagan encouraged the public to view the contras as an indigenous, independent army of "freedom fighters."

The Reagan administration also placed the Central American country of El Salvador, a country the size of New Jersey with a population of six million, within the context of the superpower conflict. Adapting the Eisenhower administration's "domino theory" of communist expansion to Latin America, Reagan expressed concerns that the Sandinista revolution in Nicaragua would spread to El Salvador, and ultimately the rest of Central America. Furthermore, the threat was defined as applying to the wider U.S. position throughout the world. "If Central America were to fall," the president asked, "what would the consequences be for our position in Asia, Europe, and for alliances such as NATO? If the United States cannot respond to a threat near our own border, why should Europeans or Asians believe that we are seriously concerned about threats to them?"[8] Specifically, Reagan alleged that the Nicaraguan government was shipping weapons to rebels in El Salvador, and he proposed increasing the U.S. arms transfers to El Salvador to match the reported Sandinista arms transfers.

Whether El Salvador was the right place to take a stand against Soviet communism and its proxies and whether the revolution should be allowed to follow its natural course were open questions in view of the U.S. government's experience. Critics of the administration's plans argued that appalling domestic social and economic conditions and political repression were the principal cause of the civil war in El Salvador, not the Nicaraguan arms. The United States should not support the privileged few who had long exploited the poor. Social justice demanded nonintervention; so perhaps did self-interest if the United States wished to avoid being identified with the losers, as it had been so many times before. The Vietnam War served as a reminder of the dangers of supporting the wrong side—an unpopular political elite whose vested interest lay in preservation of the status quo. In any event, no purely military solution was possible.

---

[8] Ronald Reagan, "Central America: Defending Our Vital Interests," *Current Policy* (U.S. Department of State, April 27, 1983).

In the developing countries, the United States had often appeared trapped between reactionary forces, whose rigid commitment to the status quo only intensified revolutionary sentiment, and radical forces, which tended to be Marxist and to look to Havana and Moscow. The administration was saved from this trap in El Salvador by Napoléon Duarte, who was in power for most of the Reagan years and sought to pursue democratic reforms while preventing the radical left from capturing power. Duarte strengthened the Reagan case for assistance to El Salvador, because Reagan could rightfully claim that the United States was not supporting the right wing as an alternative to the radical left.

The Salvadoran precedent of support for a democratic center was widely recognized after the events of 1986 in the Philippines, where the United States had long supported the dictator Ferdinand Marcos. But his despotism, economic mismanagement, transparent corruption, and the military's abuses had fueled public discontent and a rebirth of the communist guerrilla force called the New People's Army. In the absence of basic reforms, it appeared that the guerrillas might defeat the poorly trained and badly led Philippine army. Nevertheless, Marcos refused to heed suggestions for reform and, to prove his legitimacy, called for snap elections. The opposition candidate, Corazon Cojuangco Aquino, was the widow of the popular opposition leader Benigno Aquino, who in 1983 had been assassinated upon returning from exile in the United States. After her husband's assassination, Corazon Aquino became both a symbol of democracy and a rallying point for the opposition. When it became obvious that he would not win the election, Marcos tried to alter the results with widespread fraud, but his attempts were clearly visible to international observers. Thus Marcos lost his legitimacy even while "winning" another term. The United States encouraged him to step down. When top army commanders defected, Marcos fled to Hawaii, and Corazon Aquino became president.

Also in 1986, the Reagan administration helped the Haitian people oust Jean-Claude "Baby Doc" Duvalier, who had succeeded his father as dictator of the Western Hemisphere's poorest state. The United States first advised Duvalier not to use force against protesting crowds and then furnished him with an airplane to flee to France. Previously, the U.S. government had backed the military juntas in Haiti in the name of communist containment and often had looked the other way as vicious dictators tortured, killed, and otherwise silenced their enemies, real or imagined. The Reagan administration now declared its new policy: "The American people believe in human rights and oppose tyranny in whatever form, whether of the left or the right."[9] Under this variation of Carter's human rights policy, the United States would support those struggling for democracy and oppose not just radical Marxist regimes but also pro-American military dictatorships.

And it did so. In 1987, after considerable turmoil that had flared on and off for years, the military government of South Korea was persuaded to promise free presidential elections. Administration pressure on South Korea, a key U.S. ally and beneficiary of U.S. aid, had been instrumental in the long-awaited transition. Similar pressure on Chile resulted in an election that displaced its military leader, Gen. Augusto Pinochet, and opened the way for the establishment of democratic rule.

Evaluating the Reagan Doctrine

Although the Reagan administration invoked its claim of a global pro-democratic tide to support resistance movements in Afghanistan, Angola, and Nicaragua, the insurgencies it supported in the name of spreading freedom often fell considerably short of that virtue. Indeed, the administration's emphasis on human rights was compromised in many instances by the absence of moderate factions that had any chance of taking power. For Reagan, it became a matter of identifying and supporting the lesser of two evils; "authoritarian" regimes that supported Washington were preferable to Soviet-backed "totalitarian" regimes.[10] In Afghanistan, the opponents of Soviet rule were Islamic fundamentalists, who, if they won, were more likely to establish an Iranian-style theocracy than a democracy and to fragment the Muslim world further. And in Nicaragua some of the principal contra commanders were former members of Somoza's detested National Guard. Although Reagan was initially critical of his predecessors' double standards, he later adopted many of them.

Lack of congressional and public support for the Nicaraguan contras left Reagan with only one option when the presidents of Costa Rica, El Salvador, Guatemala, Honduras, and Nicaragua agreed to a regional peace plan in 1987. Reagan had to support the Contadora initiative because if the plan failed and its failure could be clearly attributed to the Sandinistas' unwillingness to open Nicaragua to genuine democratization as stipulated by the peace plan, he might regain support for further financial assistance

---

[9] "President Reagan's March 14 Message to Congress," New York Times (March 15, 1986).

[10] This distinction was made earlier by Jeane J. Kirkpatrick, Reagan's ambassador to the United Nations, in a journal article titled "Dictatorships and Double Standards," Commentary (November 1979): 34–45.

of the contras. But the Democratic-controlled Congress remained disenchanted with the contras, whose ties to the U.S. government were obvious despite administration denials, and used the peace plan as a reason not to fund any more military aid. Such assistance, it was claimed, would only thwart efforts to bring peace to Nicaragua and the region. Thus the administration's plan to overthrow the Sandinistas seemed doomed to failure. This failure appeared even more certain after the five Central American presidents, over the protests of the United States, called for disbanding the contras and for general elections in Nicaragua.

Under continuing international pressure, Ortega finally agreed to hold multiparty elections in 1990. He and his military aides were confident about the outcome. They had gradually consolidated power during their ten years in office despite the contras' challenge and expected to exploit their control of the government, including the police and army, to ensure an electoral victory that would give them international legitimacy and eliminate any possible rationale for further U.S. interference. Like Marcos in the Philippines, the Sandinistas were confident they would not lose the general election and have to relinquish their power. But lose they did. Despite Sandinista control of the government and efforts to intimidate opposition candidates and rallies, as well as the holdup of congressionally approved funds from the United States for the opposition, Ortega lost to Violeta Chamorro, widow of the anti-Somoza newspaper editor whose assassination had rallied the Sandinista-led revolution that brought down the dictator Somoza.

It was unclear who should have received the credit for the defeat of the Sandinistas: the five Central American presidents led by Costa Rica's Oscar Arias Sánchez, the Nicaraguan people who had the courage to vote against an oppressive regime, or the Sandinistas themselves for believing they could survive an unpopular draft and a mismanaged economy in a relatively free election. But there was no doubt of the consequences. For the Salvadoran guerrillas, the loss of Nicaraguan political support and military assistance constituted a serious setback to their campaign to overthrow the government or negotiate a favorable settlement that would give them a share of the power. For Fidel Castro, who was idolized by the Sandinistas and who provided help and support, it meant further isolation now that he was the only remaining revolutionary in Latin America. As for Nicaragua, the solid defeat of the Sandinistas gave that country a second opportunity to build a democracy, to reintegrate the contras into Nicaraguan society, to reconcile political opponents, and to reestablish cordial relations with the United States.

In 1988, as Reagan prepared to leave office, many of the regional conflicts in which the United States and the Soviet Union were engaged came to an end. In Afghanistan, Gorbachev, realizing that the war was an unending drain and a political embarrassment, withdrew Soviet forces. In Angola, after years of fruitless negotiations, the Cubans agreed to pull out their forces. Meanwhile, South Africa agreed to grant independence to neighboring Namibia, which it had governed since World War I. These developments were followed by settlement of the Angolan civil war and a largely effective effort by the United Nations to hasten the region's transition to democracy. The reality was clear: Gorbachev had to resolve the Soviet Union's regional quarrels, because he needed to conserve his resources for investment in the stagnating Soviet economy. Still, Moscow did not suffer a set of total defeats, nor did the United States achieve a series of unqualified triumphs. Marxist ideology retained power and influence in many countries even as the Soviet economy and government fell into critical condition.

The Iran-Contra Scandal

In executing the Reagan Doctrine in Nicaragua, the Reagan administration managed to tarnish the president's reputation. In 1986, Reagan's competence, integrity, and sense of judgment were laid open to question when it was revealed that profits from secret arms sales to Iran, now an anti-American Islamic theocracy, had been used to fund the Nicaraguan contras between 1984 and 1986 in defiance of a congressional ban on the use of U.S. funds for this purpose. In fact, in an effort to elude Congress, the administration had shifted the conduct of the contra war from the Central Intelligence Agency to the National Security Council staff. Both operations were reputedly run by CIA director William J. Casey and his point man in the NSC, Oliver L. North, a marine lieutenant colonel.[11]

Labeled the only "five-star" lieutenant colonel in the U.S. military, North supervised the arms sales made to Iran in the hope that the U.S. hostages seized in Lebanon by pro-Iranian terrorists in the mid-1980s would be released. He also directed an effort to raise private funds for the contras from tax-exempt organizations and from wealthy U.S. citizens and foreign governments. In addition, North commanded a vast network of arms dealers, ships, and airplanes to supply the contras, for whom

---

[11] For a detailed account of this scandal by its chief investigator in the U.S. government, see Lawrence E. Walsh, *Firewall: The Iran-Contra Conspiracy and Cover-Up* (New York: Norton, 1997). For another, more recent insider account, see Edward A. Lynch, *The Cold War's Last Battlefield: Reagan, the Soviets, and Central America* (Albany: State University of New York Press, 2011).

Impact and Influence: Oliver North

AP Photo/Bob Daugherty

The Iran-contra scandal of 1986 revealed the extreme lengths to which the Reagan administration had gone in order to reverse communist gains in the developing world. As information about the scandal became known, so did the central role played by Lt. Col. Oliver North. A military aide to the National Security Council, North personally negotiated secret arms sales to Iran and used the profits to supply the U.S.-backed "contra" rebels in Nicaragua who were attempting to overthrow that country's communist government.

In testimony to a special congressional committee in 1987, North (pictured here being sworn in) defended his actions and said he was following the orders of senior Reagan administration officials. Two years later, he was tried and convicted of destroying government documents vital to the investigation, but his conviction was later overturned on the grounds that he had previously testified on the same charges under a grant of immunity. In the 1990s, North remained a highly visible public figure, espousing his conservative views on radio and television talk shows and even making a run (unsuccessful) for the U.S. Senate.

he also provided tactical intelligence and advice on how to conduct the war. Under his guidance, then, the NSC became a "shadow government" that organized a secret campaign to direct and fund the contra war effort. The NSC staff not only kept any knowledge of what they were doing from members of Congress, but also lied to them. When the "off-the-shelf" operation was finally discovered, the NSC attempted to cover up its involvement and to minimize the president's role in the affair—even resorting to shredding relevant documents or smuggling them out of NSC offices. To make matters worse, when the story broke, the president first denied knowledge of many of the details of the Iran-contra activities, making it appear as if his deputies had taken American foreign policy into their own hands.

Public opinion polls showed that most Americans thought Reagan was lying, and the hearings Congress held in 1987 to look into the matter revealed plainly that he was actively involved and informed, especially on the contras. Still, "by denying that he knew anything, (Reagan) escaped scot-free."[12] Fourteen participants in the scandal, however, were indicted for their roles, and eleven were convicted. Though not charged, Reagan was badly damaged by the scandal. He had vowed that the United States would "never negotiate with terrorists," let alone sell them weapons. Even President Reagan's admirers and supporters were puzzled. They knew that if congressional investigators had been able to find a "smoking gun" linking the scandal to the Oval Office, Reagan might, like Nixon before him, have faced impeachment for his violation of federal laws. As it was, he survived the crisis and left office with a clouded reputation. The Iran-contra scandal also haunted the administration of Reagan's successor, George H. W. Bush.[13]

Alliance Politics in the Late Cold War

The Reagan administration's early attacks on détente, its preoccupation with rearmament, its reluctance to engage in arms control negotiations, and its vigorous pursuit of the Reagan Doctrine exerted great pressure on the Soviet Union throughout the 1980s. This pressure exacerbated the already strong tensions within the Warsaw Pact countries, where long years of political repression and economic stagnation had left people increasingly frustrated and restive.

Along the way, the renewed Cold War also strained the Western alliance and provoked public demonstrations from Washington to Bonn. Old questions resurfaced about the status of Western Europe as a potential superpower battleground, about the dominant role of the United States in NATO, and about the freedom of each member of NATO to pursue its own foreign policy. But the most important confrontation came over the issue of new Soviet missile deployments, which compelled the United States to propose its own series of new installations of intermediate-range missiles in Europe. With both the NATO and Warsaw Pact alliances wavering, the outcome of the most recent standoff in Europe was very much in doubt:

---

[12] Sean Wilentz, *The Age of Reagan* (New York: Harper, 2008), 242.

[13] The U.S. government's misunderstanding of Central American politics in general, and of Nicaragua in particular, ensured that such foreign policy miscues would continue. See Robert A. Pastor, *Condemned to Repetition: The United States and Nicaragua* (Princeton, N.J.: Princeton University Press, 1987).

Would NATO disintegrate because of its members' internal differences? Or would the Warsaw Pact succumb to its own deficiencies and to the mounting pressure from the West?

As these and other questions loomed, Reagan's policies produced great volatility on both sides of the iron curtain. What few people anticipated, however, was that this latest round of alliance posturing and self-doubt was a prelude to resolution of the post–World War II division of Europe. The curtain was falling rapidly on the Cold War.

Poland and the Rise of Solidarity

The first crack in the Soviet empire came in Poland, where in 1980 a labor union, asserting first its economic rights and then its political demands, led the Soviet-backed communist government to impose martial law. This crackdown, reminiscent of past actions in Eastern Europe, further inflamed Cold War tensions.

It was ironic that it was in Poland, a so-called people's democracy and a communist state that purported to represent and protect the interests of the working class, that a truly spontaneous workers' revolution against their exploiters occurred and threatened the Communist Party's monopoly of power and control. Stimulated by a failing economy—the result of poor political leadership, inefficient bureaucratic planning, and mismanagement—Polish workers demanded the right to form their own independent trade union. Lech Walesa, the leader of the workers' uprising, resisted all efforts by the Kremlin to retain control of its client in Eastern Europe.

After labor strikes finally brought down the government, the new political leadership recognized the right of the workers to form their own union, called Solidarity.[14] In effect, this development eliminated the party's monopoly of power. Solidarity then began to issue demands that were not only economic but also political. As the party-controlled government retreated before each demand, the demands increased, and the party withdrew further in the face of threatened strikes. With each success, Solidarity grew more militant, publicly asserting that it was "the authentic voice of the working class" and announcing support for other Eastern European workers who also might wish to form independent unions. Domestically, the union demanded free elections, free speech, and a voice in government policy, including running the economy.

---

[14] See Lawrence Goodwyn, *Breaking the Barrier: The Rise of Solidarity in Poland* (New York: Oxford University Press, 1991).

Although Soviet leaders accused Solidarity of provocative behavior, they refrained from sending troops to Poland. This restraint contrasted sharply with earlier Soviet behavior in Hungary (1956) and Czechoslovakia (1968). In those countries, the Soviet army had intervened when the Communist Party's monopoly of power was threatened. Yet Poland, where the Soviets had not intervened, was far more critical geographically than the other countries. It was the nation through which every Western invader of Russia had marched and through which the Soviet Union had projected its power into the center of Europe after World War II.

Nevertheless, the risks and costs of direct Soviet intervention were great. The Soviets recognized that Solidarity was not just a trade union seeking better working conditions; it also represented a well-organized mass movement. In suppressing Solidarity, the Soviets faced the real possibility of a clash with units of the Polish army, the costs of occupation, and the difficulties of pacifying the population. In addition, the cost of paying off Poland's $27 billion debt to the West would be a drain at a time when the Soviet economy was in trouble, and any chance of establishing better relations with the United States would be jeopardized. No less important, Reagan could exploit a Soviet invasion of Poland to rally the NATO allies. Thus, for more than a year, Moscow demonstrated remarkable restraint. When the move against Solidarity finally came in December 1981, it was the Polish military and police who arrested the union leaders and imposed martial law in Poland.

Whether Moscow ordered the intervention or the Polish government acted on its own, there can be little doubt of increasing Soviet pressure to crack down on what the Soviets called "counterrevolutionary" elements. Solidarity, by winning the sympathies of its almost ten million members, about one-third of the population, was a living refutation of the party's claim of representation; it symbolized the bankruptcy of communism. Unable either to produce a decent standard of living or to tolerate a minimal degree of freedom, communism in Poland had forfeited its legitimacy. The lesson was not lost on other parts of Eastern Europe, where the struggle by Solidarity served as inspiration for and a precursor of greater challenges to come.

The Missile Debate in Europe

In Western Europe, one almost heard a collective sigh of relief that the Red Army had not invaded Poland. The Polish army's crackdown was considered a domestic affair, not a matter over which détente would be sacrificed. This reaction reflected anxieties in the region about the growing hostilities between East and West, with Western Europeans finding themselves trapped in the middle. Indeed, it had become apparent in the early 1980s that Western Europeans wanted to pursue an independent foreign policy while still counting on the United States for their defense. In other words, they wanted to "uncouple" themselves politically from Washington but to remain "coupled" militarily. But even the military relationship was called into question when public opinion in Western Europe turned against a decision, collectively agreed to by the United States and its NATO allies, to meet the threat of new intermediate-range Soviet missiles (SS-20s) with a new generation of NATO missiles to be deployed in the region.

The intermediate-range nuclear force (INF) deployments were supposed to reassure the allies, who were troubled by the Soviet SS-20s. Instead of being strengthened by new American resolve, however, the NATO "marriage," in the words of the French foreign minister, came close to a divorce. Huge crowds in many countries demonstrated for months against the proposed deployment of the new missiles, with the greatest opposition in West Germany. There, the Protestant churches, the universities, the Social Democratic opposition party, and a new political movement, the pro-peace and proenvironment Green Party, were all opposed to the deployment. Moscow was not considered the chief threat. Washington, which had defended Western Europe since 1949 and had not yet deployed a single Pershing II missile, was charged with being the bigger menace to peace.

Reagan felt compelled to respond to the demonstrations in Europe and to the Soviet initiative. He proposed a "zero-zero option" whereby the United States would not deploy any of its Pershings and cruise missiles if the Soviets dismantled all of their intermediate-range missiles, which had a maximum range of 1,500 miles. It sounded good; all such missiles were to be eliminated. What could be more beneficial for peace and more moral than doing away with a whole class of dangerous weapons? The United States, however, did not expect Moscow to accept this offer. By turning it down, the Soviets would enable the U.S. deployment to go ahead as a defensive move, and the blame for the American missile buildup in Europe would be placed at the Kremlin's door.

The intra-NATO "missile crisis," however, had by then done considerable damage to the alliance. For many Europeans, the protests against INF deployment expressed their concern about Reagan's foreign policy. Many Americans, however, felt that the Europeans refused to take the measures necessary for their own defense and preferred to rely on America's "extended" nuclear deterrent. When NATO was formed, European leaders vividly remembered their attempts to appease a totalitarian regime, the defeats and suffering of World War II, their postwar collapse, and their need for American protection against the new threat from the East. But by the 1980s, these memories had given way to fears regarding Washington's nuclear intentions.

For a time, the missile crisis faded as the INF deployments continued. Then, in a complete turnabout, Gorbachev accepted the earlier Reagan proposal for the complete elimination of intermediate-range missiles for both powers. The Soviet leader needed a relaxation of international tensions in order to give priority to domestic affairs and rebuilding the Soviet economy. The zero-zero solution was significant as it eliminated an entire class of weapons rather than placing limits on their deployment. Moscow also accepted intrusive verification procedures to monitor the agreement. The Soviet turnabout was the first sign that the Soviet Union needed a cease-fire in the Cold War.

From Confrontation to Conciliation

The tensions of the 1980s may have ruptured the cohesion of both the NATO and Warsaw Pact alliances, but, in the end, when Reagan left office in January 1989, U.S.-Soviet relations were better than they had been since the two countries had been allies against Nazi Germany during World War II. How could that be? How, in a few years, could superpower relations have been so profoundly transformed?

The rapidity of the change was astounding. The Cold War had spanned more than four decades, exceeding the time that had elapsed from the beginning of World War I (1914) to the end of World War II (1945). Moreover, the 1970s had been a period of great confusion and self-doubt for the United States. After withdrawing from Vietnam without victory, the nation was shaken further by the Watergate scandal. Meanwhile, the U.S. economy and the economies of other Western nations had suffered twice from oil shocks during the decade. Some of the most ominous events occurred in 1979: the Somoza government fell to the Sandinistas in Nicaragua; the Iranians seized the U.S. embassy and fifty-two American hostages; and the Soviets took control of Afghanistan. In general, the 1970s deflated American confidence like no other decade in the twentieth century. By contrast, the Soviet Union appeared confident and optimistic about the future course of the balance of power.

And yet the apparent successes of the Soviet Union were deceptive for two reasons. The first was the failure of the Soviet economy. Its economic growth rate, 5 percent in the 1960s and only 2 percent by the early 1970s, had stagnated by 1980. It was capable of producing only a plentiful supply of weapons and no longer able to supply basic goods and public services. After harvests came up short repeatedly in the 1970s, grains and produce had to be imported from the United States and other countries. By the late 1980s, the Soviets were importing many necessities, and basic foodstuffs were being rationed. The centralized Soviet economy was nearing a breakdown. Gorbachev, who when first appointed general secretary in 1985 had believed that economic growth could be stimulated by more discipline in the workplace, less worker absenteeism and drunkenness, and higher productivity, by 1987 realized the severity of the crisis he faced. The second reason for the Soviet turnabout was the cost of Brezhnev's foreign policy. With a gross domestic product that was half that of the United States and a military budget that the CIA estimated at 16 percent of GDP (compared with 6 percent for the United States and 3 percent for Western Europe), the civilian economy was starved.

Outside the Soviet Union, Moscow's unrelenting arms buildup and expansionist activities in developing countries had produced fear and suspicion of Soviet intentions. The result was the very encirclement Soviet leaders had long feared. In Asia, the growing Soviet threat allowed the United States to play divide-and-conquer, attracting China to the Western coalition in a decisive shift of power. Thus the Soviet Union, like Germany at the turn of the century, had created its own worst nightmare and increased its sense of vulnerability.

The United States played no small role in this scenario. American-supplied weapons had raised the price of the Afghanistan intervention, placing victory out of reach, and prolonged the civil war in Angola. Although the administration did not succeed in overthrowing the Sandinistas in Nicaragua, the Soviet effort to sustain that revolutionary faction was the only bargain in an otherwise unending financial drain. The imperial outposts that had looked so promising only ten years earlier had now lost their luster, and support for proxies such as Cuba, Ethiopia, and Vietnam had become prohibitively expensive. Reagan raised the stakes further by visiting the Berlin Wall in June 1987 and, in a rhetorical flourish, appealing directly to his Soviet counterpart to "tear down this wall!" Gorbachev had no choice but to appreciate what Marxists always had prided themselves on recognizing: objective reality. The Soviet Union—hampered by a structurally unsound economy, looking at a resurgent U.S. economy (despite its rapidly increasing federal and trade deficits), and surrounded by a strengthened Western alliance—was forced to recognize the need for conciliation with the United States.

The Soviet weakness and consequent desire to end the Cold War first became apparent in 1987, when the Soviet delegates walked back into the INF talks and accepted virtually all U.S. demands. Even more significant, Gorbachev and his supporters contradicted long-held Soviet doctrine and positions by stating that (1) the "all-human value of peace" would now take precedence over the class struggle; (2) Soviet (and American) security could not be achieved unless there was "common security"; (3) security could best be achieved not by threats of force but by political negotiation and compromise; (4) "reasonable sufficiency" would be the new standard by which the Soviet Union would judge the military strength it needed; (5) Soviet forces would be reorganized in a "nonoffensive" manner so that NATO would be reassured; and (6) superpower negotiations would seek to reduce disparities in all classes of weapons, thereby ensuring a balance of forces and further ensuring cooperation.

In the developing countries, Moscow de-emphasized the revolutionary struggle for national liberation and muted its rhetoric about the future of socialism. In addition, by withdrawing from Afghanistan and helping to resolve several other regional conflicts, Gorbachev reduced Soviet foreign policy costs and diminished the likelihood of new conflicts with the United States and the chance that current ones would undermine the emerging improvement in U.S.-Soviet relations. More broadly, Gorbachev sought to deprive the American-led coalition encircling the Soviet bloc of an enemy. His "charm offensive," including visits abroad, was very effective in Europe, especially in West Germany, where "Gorby" rated far higher as a statesman and peacemaker than either Reagan or his vice president and successor, George H. W. Bush.

Gorbachev changed priorities and launched his program of *glasnost* (openness) and *perestroika* (restructuring) to revitalize Soviet society and the economy. He realized that the two were intimately related: without more openness in Soviet society, and without harnessing the energies of its people, the Soviet economy would not recover from its stagnation. Gorbachev advocated strengthening civil liberties—more freedom in the press, arts, literature, scholarship, and even the reexamination of the darker side of Soviet history, long kept secret. He also called for decentralizing the economy, cutting back on the pervasive role of the Moscow-based central planning bureaucracy, and permitting the profit motive and market forces a greater role in stimulating production, including a degree of private owner-ship and entrepreneurship. Finally, Gorbachev restricted the Communist Party's control of the economy, tolerated competition in party and legisla-tive elections, and allowed the Soviet parliament to assert itself as an inde-pendent government body.

The shift from competition to conciliation was further propelled by the amicable personal relationship between Gorbachev and Reagan. Both leaders came to power with deeply entrenched ideological differences and suspicions regarding the other superpower. Reagan's skepticism of his Soviet counterpart, however, gradually turned to trust, as reflected in his personal diary. On April 19, 1985, Reagan noted that if Gorbachev "wasn't a confirmed ideologue he never would have been chosen by the Politburo." His tone changed by May 30, 1988, when he wrote that he was sure "a cer-tain chemistry does exist between us." On December 7, Reagan was even more upbeat after a summit meeting with Gorbachev, whom he said had "sounded as if he saw us as partners making a better world."[15] This meeting of the minds was shared by Reagan's advisers, including Secretary of State George Shultz, whose objective to reduce the superpower tensions had become within reach.[16]

Reagan's fears of nuclear war, often expressed despite his ongoing sup-port for the modernization and new deployments of nuclear weapons, also eased superpower tensions. Indeed, he became a nuclear abolitionist who, much to the chagrin of his military advisers, spoke of a world devoid of nuclear weapons as his ultimate goal. At the Reykjavík (Iceland) summit in 1986, Reagan came close to agreeing with Gorbachev to the total elimina-tion of all nuclear weapons within a ten-year period. "It would be fine with me if we eliminated all nuclear weapons," Reagan said to Gorbachev, who responded, "We can do that."[17] The deal never went further, however, due to ongoing conflicts over SDI.

Although no prospect existed for resolving the ideological rivalry, the two leaders came to respect one another through the process of summit diplomacy. Their recognition of shared interests and opportunities for

---

[15] Douglas Brinkley, ed., *The Reagan Diaries* (New York: HarperCollins, 2007), 317, 613, 675.

[16] James Graham Wilson, *The Triumph of Improvisation: Gorbachev's Adaptability, Reagan's Engagement, and the End of the Cold War* (Ithaca, N.Y.: Cornell University Press, 2014).

[17] Quoted in James Mann, *The Rebellion of Ronald Reagan: A History of the End of the Cold War* (New York: Viking Press, 2009), 45.

mutually beneficial agreements emerged gradually from these recurring face-to-face contacts. As a result, "the overwhelming suspicion characteristic of the Cold War was gradually replaced by trust—not blind trust, but trust supported and reinforced by proof that promises were kept."[18]

Gorbachev's reform efforts were not embraced by all Soviets, however. He faced strong resistance from Communist Party officials and government bureaucrats, who had a vested interest in the status quo and feared that any loosening of central controls would be political suicide.

Gorbachev, however, had other concerns, including unrest in the Baltic republics (Estonia, Latvia, and Lithuania) and similar agitation in the central Asian republics. His uneasiness was compounded by the mounting efforts of Eastern European governments to throw off their communist yokes. Contrary to Marxist analysis, the political system determined the fate of the economy rather than the other way around. The Soviet political system had become the greatest obstacle to economic modernization. That was why Gorbachev, besieged by internal problems and challenges, had to end the Cold War.

---

[18] Jack F. Matlock Jr., *Reagan and Gorbachev: How the Cold War Ended* (New York: Random House, 2004), 319.

The End of the Cold War

The implosion of the Soviet bloc had already begun by the time George H. W. Bush became president in January 1989. Mikhail Gorbachev's reforms were rapidly undermining the Communist Party's hold in Moscow, the Baltic states were demanding independence, and the first streams of Eastern Europeans were making their way across the iron curtain with the reluctant assent of their crippled political leaders. Some analysts (including George Kennan, father of the containment policy) proclaimed that the Cold War was effectively over. Others suggested more cautiously that it was coming to a close, perhaps.

President Bush was a lifelong politician who lacked Ronald Reagan's flamboyance and his convictions. But his experience as director of the Central Intelligence Agency, ambassador to China, and U.S. representative to the United Nations left little doubt that he was competent in foreign affairs. When he became president, Bush said he would not use the term *Cold War* to characterize America's latest relationship with the Soviet Union. He referred instead to a period of U.S.-Soviet relations "beyond containment" in which the principal task would be to integrate the Soviet Union into the "community of nations." In 1990, however, after citing the "Revolution of '89" in his State of the Union address, Bush said the changes in Eastern Europe had been so striking and momentous that they marked "the beginning of a new era in the world's affairs." This proclamation proved to be an understatement.[1]

In truth, very few observers, including the most experienced and perceptive analysts of international relations, anticipated the sudden collapse of the Soviet system. Most predicted a prolonged stalemate between the superpowers, a gradual convergence of the capitalist and communist systems, or, more gloomily, an apocalyptic military showdown. The suggestion that one of the two superpowers would simply disappear from the world map without a shot being fired and virtually without preconditions would have been rejected as sheer fantasy. Napoleonic France, imperial Japan, and Nazi Germany did not just vanish. They had to be defeated on the battlefield, at horrendous cost.

---

[1] For recent reflections on this tumultuous period, see Victor Sebestyen, *Revolution 1989: The Fall of the Soviet Empire* (New York: Pantheon, 2009), and Jeffrey A. Engel, ed., *The Fall of the Berlin Wall: The Revolutionary Legacy of 1989* (New York: Oxford University Press, 2009).

German citizens celebrate the opening of the Berlin Wall in November 1989. The wall, erected during the height of the Cold War, symbolized the division of Europe into two blocs, one controlled by the Soviet Union and the other within the American sphere of influence. In opening the wall, these German citizens effectively demonstrated that the Cold War was over.

For Bush, the principal task of American foreign policy would be to manage this historic transition as smoothly as possible. The president sought to ensure that the demise of the Warsaw Pact and, later, of the Soviet Union would not be followed by new crises in world politics. Bush looked forward to a harmonious new era in which the benefits of the Western political and economic system would be extended into the former communist bloc and provide the basis for global stability and prosperity.

Bush's Management of the Soviet Collapse

At first, the Bush administration was not sure what to believe about the Cold War and its apparent end. In the context of more than forty years of strained relations and of previously dashed hopes that the Cold War was over, the administration—and especially the president—tended to be cautious. If Gorbachev were to fall and be replaced by a hard-line conservative, the United States did not want to be caught off guard. Nevertheless, Secretary of State James A. Baker III, a holdover from the Reagan team, acknowledged that the "new thinking" in Soviet foreign and defense policies created opportunities for East-West cooperation that were unimaginable a few years earlier.[2] Uncertainty about Soviet reforms was all the more reason to seize the opportunities represented by Gorbachev. Thus after a period of hesitation, the Bush administration followed President Ronald Reagan's lead and embraced Gorbachev, whose continuation in power was deemed good for the United States.

Events, already moving rapidly, accelerated both within the Soviet Union and beyond as the 1980s ended. In these circumstances, predicting what lay ahead for the Soviet Union was risky business, because the changes had come so quickly and had been so unexpected. The year 1990 witnessed growing upheaval in Moscow as the communist system, seventy-three years after its inception, began to crack. It became apparent that the Soviet Union was operating from a position of grave weakness and that Gorbachev's foreign policy amounted to a diplomacy of retreat and damage control. The result was that regardless of who held power in Moscow, the United States had a golden opportunity to exploit the shifting balance of power. Any leader of the Soviet Union would face severe domestic constraints on the conduct of foreign policy.

As the victorious power in the Cold War, the United States had to give thought to its terms of peace. What kind of post–Cold War world did the United States wish to see? Washington, in short, had to define its goals. Even if Gorbachev did not survive, the United States needed to take advantage of the time he was in office to ensure that Soviet concessions would be irreversible. Granted, America's influence on Soviet internal affairs was limited, and the ultimate success of the Gorbachev policy of *perestroika* (restructuring) depended on events within the Soviet Union. But if the United States were responsive to Gorbachev's policies and proposals, it could assist the process of domestic reform and bolster his position in the Kremlin. Washington's principal recourse, therefore, was to lend its support to the peaceful reform of the Soviet state.

The Soviet Union's negotiating position was very weak—a problem that was to worsen as Eastern Europe defected, ethnic nationalism grew,

---

[2] See James A. Baker III, with Thomas M. DeFrank, *The Politics of Diplomacy: Revolution, War, and Peace, 1989–1992* (New York: Putnam, 1995), chap. 5.

and communism as a political and economic system was directly challenged inside the Kremlin. Yet Gorbachev would not surrender unconditionally. Thus American leaders could not simply impose their terms on Moscow. Moreover, a victory that humiliated the loser would result in a peace built on sand. World War I had ended with a victor's peace imposed on Germany, but it had lasted only as long as Germany remained weak. After World War II, both Germany and Japan were treated in a more conciliatory fashion. Neither, therefore, had been bent on revenge. For a durable peace, the Soviet Union also had to find the emerging international order hospitable. The two powers thus embarked upon complex negotiations about the terms on which the Cold War would end, as well as about the construction and shape of the new balance of power.

The final resolution of the Cold War depended basically on the fulfillment of three conditions: (1) dismantling Joseph Stalin's empire in Central and Eastern Europe, (2) detaching Leonid Brezhnev's outposts in developing countries, and (3) reducing arms and achieving a stable nuclear balance. When these conditions were fulfilled, Bush was thrust into the tenuous position of managing the disintegration of the Soviet Union and directing the transition of U.S. bilateral relations toward the largest successor state, Boris Yeltsin's Russia.

Dismantling Stalin's Empire

Events in China during the summer of 1989 served as a prelude to the autumn uprisings in Eastern Europe and suggested that the erosion of communism's appeal and legitimacy had extended to the world's most populous communist state. As in Moscow, dissidents in Beijing had been granted greater freedom to express their grievances in public and to exercise some degree of political freedom. After they erected a miniature Statue of Liberty in Beijing's Tiananmen Square, however, the communist government moved in with tanks and brutally quashed the growing rebellion. The worldwide television audience that witnessed these events was understandably horrified. China's decrepit regime dismissed the condemnation of foreign governments and intensified its crackdown on pro-democracy activists. When their time came, Eastern Europeans were inspired by the Chinese example to accelerate their own anticommunist revolution so it could not be turned back.

One important sign of Soviet willingness to end the Cold War was its acceptance of Eastern Europe's rapid moves away from Communist Party control. The Soviet Union's conquest and Stalinization of Eastern Europe, together with the division of Germany, had split the continent after World War II. This division was at the heart of the Cold War, and only self-determination for Poland, Hungary, Czechoslovakia, and the other Eastern European states could end it. Events in Central Europe also were critical because each of the major wars of the twentieth century had broken out there. The disintegration of the Austro-Hungarian Empire had led to the eruption of successive Balkan wars and World War I; Germany's absorption of Austria and Czechoslovakia and its invasion of Poland had sparked World War II; and the de facto Soviet annexation of Eastern Europe had led to the Cold War.

Gorbachev's escape from this struggle required that he abandon Marxist ideology as the basis and justification of the Soviet Union's national security. According to this ideology, the communist regime in Moscow could be secure only if potential class enemies—even those who frowned on relations with capitalist states—were kept out of power. As for the Soviet troops stationed throughout Eastern Europe, they were intended not merely to protect these states from perceived Western threats, but also to ensure that these states adhered to the Soviet model of centralized control. Could Moscow in the late 1980s, facing the imminent collapse of this model, separate its ideology from its definition of security?

The initial answer came in 1989 in Poland. The Communist Party there was unable to form a government after its disastrous showing in the free June elections in which the Solidarity labor movement had claimed overwhelming popular support. Because the communists had been repudiated, Solidarity, which had in effect received a mandate to govern, was asked to organize the government. Poland thus formed its first noncommunist—indeed anticommunist—government in the post–World War II era. However, Lech Walesa, Solidarity's leader and spokesman, announced that Poland would remain a member of the Warsaw Pact—just the kind of political sensitivity that Roo sevelt had in mind.

Gorbachev was willing to accept a noncommunist Poland and a more traditional sphere of influence in Eastern Europe for several reasons. One was his preoccupation with worsening domestic matters. Another was that Eastern Europe had not proved to be a security belt. Instead, the region had added to Soviet *insecurity*. Its people were sullen and resentful of the Soviet-imposed regimes, and they had not forgotten that earlier efforts to rid themselves of these regimes had been suppressed by brute force. Gorbachev did not want to be confronted with an explosive situation that would foreclose his options in salvaging his core interest: the Soviet Union.

The dominoes fell throughout 1989. In Hungary, the parliament dropped the word *People* from the country's formal name, and the Communist Party renamed itself the Democratic Socialist Party in order to survive a Polish-style disaster in the upcoming multiparty elections. (Even so, the party kept only 30,000 of its original 720,000 members.) Similarly, Czechoslovakia dropped *Socialist* from its name, and the East German Communist Party also sought to shed its Stalinist skin to better compete in the 1990 elections. In a decision of critical importance, the Hungarian foreign minister opened his country's borders with Austria on September 10, 1989. A free fall then ensued when 200,000 East Germans, mostly young, skilled workers vital to that nation's industry, fled their country—via Czechoslovakia, Hungary, and Austria—for West Germany. These events collectively foreshadowed the "terminal crisis of Communism."[3]

To make the best of the situation, Gorbachev announced that socialist countries had no right to intervene in each other's affairs; each country was responsible for its own destiny. The clear implication was that the Brezhnev Doctrine was dead. To make the point clearly, Gorbachev visited East Germany to observe its fortieth anniversary as a communist state. There, by stating the new doctrine of nonintervention, he further propelled the demise of the Warsaw Pact. The process gained even more momentum after Moscow and its four Warsaw Pact allies that had jointly invaded Czechoslovakia in 1968 condemned that invasion as "illegal" and pledged a strict policy of noninterference in each other's affairs. Moscow also issued its own declaration of repentance.

Gorbachev's actions were most keenly felt in East Germany, where the exodus of its youth threatened to depopulate the country of sixteen million and undermine its hopes for the future. Mass demonstrations finally led to the removal of its despotic communist leader, Erich Honecker, in December 1989. In what was a genuine people's revolution, Soviet troops stood by instead of propping up the regime, and the new party leader promised radical changes, including free elections in May 1990. Among the first reforms, all restrictions on travel and emigration were lifted, inciting hundreds of thousands of East Germans to scale the Berlin Wall in the hours after that announcement. Altogether, 1.5 million East Germans poured across the wall that first weekend. As for the wall itself, entire sections were leveled with sledgehammers, and fragments were taken home as souvenirs. From its construction in 1961, the wall had been the embodiment of what the Cold War was all about—tyranny versus freedom. Its

---

[3] Zbigniew Brzezinski, *The Grand Failure: The Birth and Death of Communism in the Twentieth Century* (New York: Scribner, 1989).

collapse on November 9, 1989, exactly fifty-one years after Adolf Hitler unleashed his storm troopers against German Jews, aptly foreshadowed the end of the Cold War.

After the fall of the Berlin Wall, the winds of change swept over Czechoslovakia. What happened there also had great symbolic importance, although it was not widely noted at the time because of the tumult elsewhere. The great powers had inflicted tremendous injustices on Czechoslovakia, the only central European democracy before World War II. The country had been betrayed by France and England in their efforts to appease Hitler in 1938. A decade later, it had been violently transformed into a communist nation by the Soviets. Efforts to introduce a more democratic form of communism during the Prague Spring of 1968 had been crushed by Soviet tanks. The collapse of the communist regime in Prague was, therefore, also a sign of the times.

Everywhere in Eastern Europe—in what Ronald Reagan had once called the "evil empire"—people were saying openly just how evil that empire had been. They demanded not just the reform of communist parties but their removal from office, ending what many saw as nearly a half-century of foreign occupation. They also called for free elections and interim governments composed mainly of noncommunists. Only in Bulgaria and Romania did the local communist parties manage to run under new names, promising that they had reformed, and easily win the first free elections after the collapse of the Soviet-supported governments.

The United States responded by expressing support for the new governments of Eastern Europe, and President Bush provided a visible show of support by visiting Poland and Hungary in 1989. Beyond this effort, however, Bush did not want to arouse Soviet security concerns. In fact, Gorbachev, with these concerns in mind, sought a tacit understanding with Bush. The Soviet leader would continue to support, if not encourage, the transformations in Eastern Europe, and he would not resist the changes even if they went further down the road to "decommunization" than he preferred. In return, the United States would not exploit the geopolitical transformation then under way in the Soviet empire. Because it was in Washington's interest to manage the changes in the Soviet Union and Eastern Europe peacefully, the Gorbachev-Bush bargain held.

The path of nonviolent transformation was chosen not only by the Eastern European rulers but also by the masses, even though they had been exploited and oppressed by Soviet-imposed regimes for forty years. Only Romania fell into violence as its dictator, Nicolae Ceaușescu, sought in vain to buck the trend in the rest of Eastern Europe and stay in power. But he failed; army units defected to the opposition and fought his security forces. Captured as they attempted to flee, Ceaușescu and his wife, Elena, were executed on Christmas Day 1989 after a hasty trial. With that single exception, nonviolence prevailed. Czechoslovakia's new president, the playwright Václav Havel, set the tone by calling on his fellow citizens to act with dignity, honesty, and honor. The slogan of the demonstrators massed in the streets of Prague was "We are not like them."

Another important issue was the rebirth of the "German problem." For more than forty years, East and West had lived with a divided Germany. Each side preferred a partitioned Germany, because such an arrangement ensured that Germany would not initiate another war. The "terminal crisis" of communism in Eastern Europe, however, ended this division. Thousands of East Germans poured into West Germany every month, further crippling the East German state, its economy, and its social cohesion. Moreover, as the authority of the East German government waned, the calls in East Germany for unification grew stronger. To everyone's surprise, the East German election held in March 1990 was won by the followers of West German chancellor Helmut Kohl, thereby ensuring reunification. The large votes for the Christian Democrats and the Social Democrats, both tied to their West German counterparts, amounted to a death sentence for the German Democratic Republic.

But a reunited Germany, even a democratic one, posed all sorts of problems and potential instabilities. In fact, the collapse of the Warsaw Pact and the inevitable, increasingly imminent reunification of Germany meant constructing a new European balance of power. Western officials, led by Bush and Kohl, insisted that the reunited Germany be a member of the North Atlantic Treaty Organization (NATO).[4] They did, however, offer Moscow several reassurances. First, no Western armies, including German troops assigned to NATO, would be stationed on former East German territory in view of Moscow's certain opposition to the presence of NATO troops on the Polish border. Second, during a three- to four-year transition period, the 380,000 Soviet troops already in East Germany would remain there. Germany also would guarantee its neighbors' borders, renew West Germany's pledge that it would not seek to acquire nuclear weapons, and agree to limit the size of its armed forces. Gorbachev insisted that a reunited Germany be a neutral, disarmed state, a demand that was promptly rejected. He then proposed that Germany be a member of both

---

[4]For an elaboration of Chancellor Kohl's key role in these negotiations, see Mary Elise Sarotte, *1989: The Struggle to Create Post–Cold War Europe* (Princeton, N.J.: Princeton University Press, 2009).

the Warsaw Pact and NATO. But this condition, too, was rejected as merely another formula for neutrality.

In July 1990, only four months after declaring that German membership in NATO was "absolutely out of the question," Gorbachev bowed to the inevitable and accepted a reunited Germany in NATO. His acceptance was made easier by the promise of $8 billion in German credits to help the failing Soviet economy. Nevertheless, like his acceptance of a larger number of U.S. troops than Soviet troops in the new Europe, Gorbachev's acquiescence to German membership in NATO was tantamount to Soviet surrender. This event had none of the drama of VE Day or VJ Day, which in 1945 marked the end of the war in Europe and in the Pacific, respectively. Yet history will note July 16, 1990, as the day the Soviet Union gave up.

An all-German election of an all-German parliament was set for December 2, 1990. The new year would therefore start with the convocation of the new parliament and the formation of the new government. As for the future, the reunited Germany would assume the role of Europe's most powerful economic actor and, like Japan, the other country vanquished in World War II, would quickly become a principal actor in the post–Cold War multipolar international system. The world hoped, however, that Germany's preponderant size, population, and economic power would be directed not toward fulfilling selfish interests but toward serving as a catalyst for political stability and economic growth throughout Europe and, indeed, within the Soviet Union.

Detaching Brezhnev's Outposts

The second condition for ending the Cold War was Soviet cooperation in resolving regional conflicts in the developing world. As noted earlier, Soviet support for Marxist regimes and insurgencies had hindered U.S.-Soviet relations for decades. But now the Soviet Union's desire to avoid trouble with the United States was likely to prevent further challenges.

Gorbachev's reversal of his country's expansionism was dramatic. The Soviets withdrew from Afghanistan and later admitted that the invasion had been a mistake, a result of the overreliance of Soviet foreign policy on force. In Angola, after prolonged negotiations failed to achieve the exit of fifty thousand Cuban troops from that country in return for South Africa's withdrawal from Namibia, a deal was struck under which the Cubans would withdraw in return for the independence of Namibia. In Southeast Asia, with Soviet encouragement, Vietnam withdrew from Cambodia. And in the Middle East, Moscow moved initially toward rapprochement with

Israel—it had broken diplomatic relations in 1967—and later toward the reestablishment of relations. It also supported the U.S. objective of an Israeli-Palestinian treaty and raised the possibility of increased Jewish emigration from the Soviet Union to Israel.

But in Central America, the Soviets continued to supply arms to revolutionary forces, despite soothing words about seeking peaceful settlements. Soviet arms shipments to the Nicaraguan government, although reduced, continued; shipments from Cuba made up the difference. Soviet-made weapons also reached the communist rebels in El Salvador, who launched attacks on the capital city of San Salvador in 1989. Bush strongly protested these policies of support as "Cold War relics," calling these countries "Brezhnevite clients" during the informal summit meeting that Gorbachev and Bush held in December 1989 off the Mediterranean island of Malta. Gorbachev denied sending weapons to Central America, but Bush would have none of it. Cuba and Nicaragua were Soviet clients. Washington clearly expected Moscow, which elsewhere had pressured its proxies to resolve their internal and regional differences, to do the same in the Western Hemisphere.

The more critical issue was the February 1990 election in Nicaragua, which, as noted in Chapter 6, held out the promise of easing regional tensions in Central America. Gorbachev prevailed on the Sandinistas to permit free elections like those held in Eastern Europe. When the Sandinistas lost the elections, which were closely monitored by the United Nations and the Organization of American States, the Soviet Union lost yet another overseas client. National reconciliation, disbanding the contras, rebuilding the economy, ensuring a democratic and more just society, and reestablishing good relations with the United States were to be the central tasks of Nicaragua's new government.

The only remaining source of real friction between Washington and Moscow was Cuba. Castro swore that socialism would continue to be practiced on his island even if that ideology had been "betrayed" by Gorbachev and even if it were abandoned virtually everywhere else. In 1991, Moscow discontinued its massive annual subsidies to Cuba, which were largely in the form of petroleum and other necessities, announcing that future economic relations between Cuba and the Soviet Union would be on a trade-only basis. The Soviet military training brigade also would be withdrawn. The Soviet Union, itself seeking economic help from the West, was responding to the Bush administration's insistence that it would not consider providing such assistance while Moscow continued to provide Castro with the equivalent of $5 billion annually. Thus the Soviet retreat from the developing world continued.

Stabilizing the Nuclear Balance

The third condition for ending the Cold War was a reduction in superpower arms and a stable nuclear balance—a consistent U.S. goal in the evolving new superpower relationship. More specifically, U.S. policy had three objectives. The first, especially in view of Gorbachev's uncertain tenure, was to reach agreements to reduce strategic and conventional arms; once achieved, such arms reductions would be politically and economically difficult to reverse. The second objective was to reduce the likelihood of surprise attack, a goal that was pursued by both sides through a variety of confidence-building measures. And the third objective was to reduce the burden of defense spending and to realize a "peace dividend" to be spent on domestic needs.[5]

From the beginning of the Strategic Arms Limitation Talks process, the long-term objective was to cut drastically the strategic arsenals of both powers. Renamed START (Strategic Arms Reduction Talks) by the Reagan administration to emphasize more ambitious reductions—a 50 percent cut—the treaty was aimed at eliminating Soviet land-based missiles, which, with their multiple and accurate warheads, were the principal threat to the survival of American intercontinental ballistic missiles (ICBMs). In short, reductions per se were not the objective; the aim was to *stabilize* reductions. By the time Reagan left office, the START negotiations were substantially completed. Each side had agreed to a ceiling of 1,600 delivery vehicles, an aggregate of 6,000 strategic weapons, and a ballistic missile warhead limit of 4,900. Although the overall reduction in strategic forces was closer to 30 percent, the most destabilizing forces—ballistic missiles with multiple warheads—were reduced by 50 percent.

The chief obstacle from the very beginning was the Strategic Defense Initiative (SDI), the American plan to defend its territory from incoming nuclear missiles (see Chapter 6). The Soviets insisted that they would not reduce their ICBM force until they knew whether they would have to cope with American strategic defenses. But Reagan clung to his vision of SDI, and therefore the Soviets refused to sign the START treaty. To break the deadlock, Moscow announced in 1989 its willingness to sign the treaty on the condition that the United States abide by the 1972 Antiballistic Missile Treaty.

As for conventional forces, after 1987, Gorbachev had talked repeatedly about a shift from an offensive to a defensive military doctrine and a scaling back of Soviet forces to "reasonable sufficiency." He carried out

---

[5] For Gorbachev, this financial benefit was probably the driving force behind all his arms proposals. As the U.S. budget deficit grew, Bush also wanted to see a reduction in defense spending.

unilateral reductions in Soviet forces, including the withdrawal of troops and tanks facing NATO. The Conventional Armed Forces in Europe (CFE) negotiations in the late 1980s sought to reduce Soviet forces in Eastern Europe and American forces in Western Europe to 275,000 each. But events in Eastern Europe were moving so fast that in January 1990 President Bush called for a further U.S.-Soviet troop reduction in Central Europe to fewer than 200,000. Surprisingly, Gorbachev accepted the U.S. proposal even though, compared with the Soviet Union, it would leave the United States with more troops in Europe, a first since World War II. Militarily, this was unimportant, but politically and psychologically, it provided further evidence of Soviet disintegration.

Such reductions were possible, because by 1990 the Soviet-led alliance, organized to protect the Soviet-imposed socialist systems, had little to defend as Eastern Europe defected from the Warsaw Pact. In these circumstances, Moscow could no longer count on, if it ever could, the armies of Bulgaria, Czechoslovakia, East Germany, Hungary, Poland, and Romania for any joint military action against the West. And so, in 1990, Moscow agreed to withdraw its forces from Czechoslovakia, Hungary, and Poland by the end of 1992. But this pledge became irrelevant as the Warsaw Pact self-destructed first and was formally buried in 1991.

Endgame: The Collapse of the Core

Between 1989 and 1991, the Soviet Union itself underwent a rapid and profound transformation. With the disintegration of its economy, the political regime lost its legitimacy and was further weakened by internal conflicts between Moscow and some of the Soviet republics. Demands for autonomy, if not independence, erupted in many areas, and ancient ethnic feuds reemerged. These events threatened the integrity of the Soviet state and compelled the regime to move Soviet tactical nuclear warheads out of the Baltics and to move those in the volatile southern republics to parts of Russia considered more secure.

In addition, the Communist Party, showing growing signs of disintegration, was losing its authority to impose decisions on the nation. In the Baltics, Soviet communists were faced with the defection of the Lithuanian Communist Party, which identified itself with Lithuania's demand for independence. In Azerbaijan, the Soviet army had to be deployed not only to restore order between the Azerbaijanis and Armenians, but also to prevent the communist government from falling into the hands of the Azerbaijani popular front— much as communist regimes in Eastern Europe had fallen to opposition groups. In several cities and regions, party officials had to resign because of popular outrage over their corruption and privileges. Indeed, in Moscow, Leningrad, and other cities, the emerging democratic political opposition inflicted embarrassing defeats on the communists by winning majorities in local elections.

Gorbachev, alert to popular disenchantment with the party, gradually shifted his base of power from the Communist Party, whose members continued to resist his reforms, to the elected Supreme Soviet and the presidency, a post he held in addition to that of general secretary of the party. A new Congress of People's Deputies was established to promote a more democratic government, and elections to this body in May 1989 gave the Russian people their first taste of democracy. Gorbachev then went even further by calling on the Communist Party to give up its seventy-year-long constitutional monopoly of power, although he clearly considered the party to be the most capable of guiding the nation through its turmoil. For the party to remain the political vanguard, however, it would have to earn the Soviet people's trust, and to do this, it would have to restructure itself. Gorbachev even suggested the establishment of rival political parties. His radical call was persuasive: in February 1990, the party's Central Committee opened the door to opposition parties. The political landscape of the Soviet Union was irreversibly transformed in this "February Revolution."

Gorbachev's strongest challenger for power was Boris Yeltsin, a former Communist Party leader who in May 1990 was elected president of the Russian republic. Russia occupied two-thirds of the territory of the former Soviet Union and had almost half of its population and most of its oil, natural gas reserves, and coal. Yeltsin was quick to sense the popular disaffection with the power and privileges of the Communist Party. Once Gorbachev's protégé, Yeltsin became his fiercest critic and archrival; the Soviet leader had not, in Yeltsin's judgment, moved quickly enough to change the system.

On the day after his election by the Russian parliament, Yeltsin challenged the system by proposing Russia's economic autonomy and a radical decentralization in which republic law took precedence over Soviet law and the president of the Soviet Union would have no greater authority than the presidents of the fifteen republics. Indeed, not only would Russia claim sovereignty and determine the prices of its natural resources, but it also would make its own agreements with the other members of the Soviet Union. To further enhance his challenge, Yeltsin decreed that the Russian presidency would henceforth be a popularly elected office, which he won overwhelmingly. As elected president of the Soviet Union's largest republic, Yeltsin acquired a legitimacy Gorbachev never had.

A few weeks later, Yeltsin, together with the reformist mayors of Moscow and Leningrad, resigned from the Communist Party. Their resignations were symptomatic of growing national disenchantment with the party and of Gorbachev's declining popularity. Next, Ukraine, the Soviet Union's second largest republic and its "breadbasket," with a population

Impact and Influence:
Mikhail Gorbachev and Boris Yeltsin

REUTERS/Gennady Galperin

Amid the collapse of the Soviet Union, the peaceful transfer of power from Mikhail Gorbachev (left) to Boris Yeltsin (right) proved to be an extraordinary achievement. Indeed, Yeltsin's defense of the Soviet leader during the failed coup attempt by communist hardliners in August 1991 preserved their generally cordial relations even as the Soviet Union crumbled around them.

Gorbachev, the last leader of the Soviet Union, could not prevent his democratic reforms from weakening the Communist Party's hold over Eastern Europe and, later, the Soviet Union itself. Once out of power, Gorbachev formed a private foundation and continued to advocate "democratic socialism." Mean while, Yeltsin remained president of Russia throughout the 1990s, defending his political and economic reforms against challenges from neocommunists and militant nationalists. But Russia suffered under his watch, and economic stagnation, political corruption, and a failed effort to quell a secessionist revolt in Chechnya were largely to blame. Ailing and frustrated, Yeltsin abruptly resigned on the final day of 1999 and yielded power to Prime Minister Vladimir Putin, who was elected to a full term as Russia's president in March 2000. Yeltsin died on April 23, 2007.

Gorbachev, who won the Nobel Peace Prize in 1990, remained visible on the world stage long after the Soviet Union's demise. His foundation encouraged further reforms in Russia and, in the new millennium, publicly criticized President George W. Bush's unilateral foreign policies of more than fifty million, declared its sovereignty and announced that its laws would supersede those of the Soviet Union. Ukraine also claimed an independent foreign policy role by stating it would be a neutral state, it would not participate in military blocs, and it would ban the production and deployment of nuclear weapons on its territory. These actions were followed by a similar declaration from Belarus, a small but geographically vital republic located between Ukraine and the Baltic states. Eventually, all of the Soviet Union's fifteen republics issued sovereignty declarations, asserting either outright independence or more cautious assertions of their rights. Gorbachev's Soviet Union was crumbling around him, piece by piece.

By late 1990, Gorbachev, who in the fall of that year won the Nobel Peace Prize, had become more and more irrelevant in Soviet domestic affairs. Yeltsin was setting the pace and scope of change by supporting the drive for independence of the Baltic republics and by proposing a plan for transforming the Russian economy into a market economy within five hundred days. Gorbachev found himself maneuvering between the increasingly radical forces on the left and the forces of reaction on the right, represented by the traditional instruments of Soviet power—the military, secret police, and Communist Party bureaucracy—which had survived all his attempts at reform. They were the elite and therefore had a strong vested interest in the status quo. In the meantime, Gorbachev had his hands full just trying to hold the union together and stem the republics' nationalism. Thus he shifted his original direction and aligned himself with the forces of "law and order." He dismissed many of his former liberal allies in the struggle for *glasnost* and *perestroika*, began cracking down on the Baltic republics, and reimposed censorship.

Gorbachev's new allies, however, tried to limit his power and enhance their own, because they felt he was leading the country to chaos and anarchy. More over, they despised him. After all, he had retreated from Eastern Europe and had given up the Soviet Union's World War II gains. In response, Gorbachev swung back to ally himself once more with the reformers. He made his peace with the republics and promised the presidents of the nine republics who agreed to stay within the union, including Yeltsin, to turn the Soviet Union into a new voluntary federation that all republics would have the right to join or not join. They also would be free to choose their own form of government and exercise most of the power over their natural resources, industry, foreign trade, and taxes. He promised a new constitution and a newly elected central government.

But just as the New Union Treaty was about to be signed, the hardliners struck. Fearing that their power was waning and that it soon would be too late to do anything about it, they launched a coup in August 1991, arresting Gorbachev while he was on vacation. But the coup plotters failed to understand the effects of the six years of Gorbachev's policies. Led by the popularly elected Yeltsin, who showed enormous courage in condemning the coup, the people of Moscow rallied behind Gorbachev, resisting those who would reimpose the old dictatorship. When units of the military and secret police opposed the coup, it quickly collapsed. This event struck the deathblow to the Soviet Union.

All the republics now wanted their independence from Moscow and central authority. The three Baltic republics were let go, and their independence was recognized by Moscow. At this point, seven of the twelve remaining republics, including Russia, planned to stay together in a loose confederation. They were still economically interdependent, although the agriculturally and industrially important Ukraine would not commit itself to creating a "common economic space" and a single currency, the foundation of a free-market economy.

What was absolutely clear in these times of uncertainty was that the old regime had disgraced itself by the coup attempt. Statues of Stalin and Lenin were toppled and unceremoniously removed from public squares. The old imperial flag designed by Peter the Great once again flew over the Russian parliament, the center of the resistance to the coup. Leningrad was renamed Saint Petersburg, its prerevolutionary name, in accordance with the wishes of its citizens. Many said it also was time to remove Lenin's body from the mausoleum in Red Square (a step that was not taken). For all practical purposes, the Communist Party as a governing body was dead. It could no longer block the path to democracy and radical economic reform. The revolution of 1917 had been undone in a stunning sequence of events.

The republics, however, were still grappling with their future. At the moment of decision, the seven republics that had endorsed the new union would not commit themselves, leaving its fate in the hands of their national parliaments. When Ukraine voted on December 1, 1991, for independence and instantly became Europe's fourth largest country, it became clear that nothing could stop the process of Soviet disintegration. With even a weak confederation now dead, Russia was left as the successor state to the Soviet Union. This status had become overwhelmingly clear earlier, when in November 1991 the central government of the Soviet Union had declared bankruptcy and Russia assumed its debts and promised to fund what remained of the central government's ministries. In capitalist language, this act constituted a leveraged buyout of the former Soviet Union. Russia also claimed the Soviet Union's permanent seat on the UN Security Council.

The Soviet Union's demise became official on December 8, 1991. In an act of desperation to stop the complete disintegration of the nation, the presidents of the three Slavic republics—Russia, Ukraine, and Belarus—established a commonwealth and invited other republics to join. The new Commonwealth of Independent States (CIS) was to assume all the international obligations of the Soviet Union, including control over its nuclear arsenal. Coordinating bodies would be established to decide on cooperative policies in foreign affairs, defense, and economics.[6] Later, the commonwealth agreement was signed by eleven of the remaining twelve Soviet republics after the defection of the three Baltic states; the twelfth republic, Georgia, was consumed by civil war.

The end came on Christmas Day 1991. Late in the evening, Gorbachev delivered a televised speech in which he relinquished power to the new government of Russia. "We live in a new world," Gorbachev proclaimed. "An end has been put to the Cold War, the arms race, and the insane militarization of our country, which crippled our economy, distorted our thinking, and undermined our morals. The threat of a world war is no more."[7] Twenty minutes after his speech, the red hammer-and-sickle flag that had flown over the Kremlin was lowered for the last time. Seventy-four years after the Bolshevik revolution, the Soviet Union literally disappeared from the world map.

Reasons for the Soviet Collapse

Throughout his presidency, George H. W. Bush was dogged by the accusation that he lacked a coherent vision of the future of world politics. Twenty-first-century historians probably will be kinder to Bush. A careful review of his performance reveals how skillfully he manipulated one of the crucial turning points in history, not only to the advantage of the United States but also in the interests of global stability. The three-year free fall of the Soviet system was by no means a certainty when Bush arrived in office, and its peaceful demise was without precedent. In assisting Gorbachev when he urgently needed outside support, in insisting on German unification on Western terms, and in exploiting the opportunity for drastic nuclear

---

[6] Internal tensions greatly limited the actual role of the CIS in the 1990s, although the commonwealth remained officially intact into the twenty-first century.

[7] Quoted in Conor O'Clery, *Moscow, December 25, 1991: The Last Day of the Soviet Union* (New York: Public Affairs, 2011), 223.

disarmament, Bush successfully navigated the United States and its allies through a complicated phase of international relations toward their ultimate victory in a protracted conflict of global proportions. Bush was chastised for adhering to the most "prudent" approach to world politics. But history may suggest that prudence was precisely the approach the world required.[8]

The Contending Arguments in Perspective

Immediately after the end of the Cold War, some observers asked whether the United States had "won" the war and whether its containment policy had been successful. Or was it more accurate to say that the Soviet Union, plagued by internal problems of its own making, had "lost" the Cold War? These questions—two sides of the same coin and not conducive to definitive answers—sparked a contentious debate among scholars, journalists, and policymakers.[9] But it was not merely an academic exercise, for the answers to these questions would reveal the central lessons of the Cold War, which in turn would figure in the establishment of guidelines for future American foreign policy.

Advocates of the view that the United States had "won" the Cold War claimed that the Western system of political, economic, and military organization simply had been more durable than the system of the Soviet Union and its allies. Furthermore, the U.S.-led containment policy had successfully combined pressure and patience to overwhelm Soviet capabilities.[10] In other words, containment had worked much as George Kennan predicted it would nearly fifty years earlier, preventing Soviet expansion through the selective application of Western resistance.

Conversely, those believing that the Soviet Union had "lost" the war diminished the role of the containment policy. If the United States had "won," it was merely because the Soviet Union's flawed system had made its demise inevitable. Its excessive centralization of power, bureaucratic planning, and supervision of every detail of Soviet life, economic and otherwise, as well as its command economy and ideological oppression,

---

[8] A more thorough review of Bush's performance is provided by Michael Beschloss and Strobe Talbott, *At the Highest Levels: The Inside Story of the End of the Cold War* (Boston: Little, Brown, 1993).

[9] For a review of these arguments, see Michael J. Hogan, ed., *The End of the Cold War: Its Meanings and Implications* (New York: Cambridge University Press, 1992).

[10] See John Lewis Gaddis, *The United States and the End of the Cold War* (New York: Oxford University Press, 1992), 193.

had contributed to its undoing.[11] Furthermore, for some neo-Marxists, the demise of the Soviet Union reflected its failed application of Marxist ideals and principles, not the bankruptcy of the political theory.

Both views call for a closer look at the Soviet experience in converting the aspirations of the 1917 Russian Revolution into practice. Seventy years after the revolution, the Soviet standard of living was so low that even Eastern Europe, with its own economic problems, appeared affluent by contrast. The former Soviet Union's own statistics reveal that about 40 percent of its population and almost 80 percent of its elderly citizens lived in poverty. One-third of its households had no running water. Indeed, the Soviet Union was the only industrialized society in which infant mortality had risen and male life expectancy had *declined* in the late twentieth century. In Zbigniew Brzezinski's words, "Perhaps never before in history has such a gifted people, in control of such abundant resources, labored so hard for so long to produce so little."[12]

The Soviet economy, which was supposed to have demonstrated the superiority of socialism, sputtered for decades and then collapsed. Deliberately isolating itself from the global capitalist economy, the Soviet Union had intended to build an economy that was self-sufficient and productive, ensuring a bountiful life for the workers and peasants who had been deprived for so long. Instead, the centralized command economy meant no domestic competition among firms, and its self-exclusion from the international economy ensured that it remained unchallenged by foreign competition. The Soviet economy became a textbook example of what free traders have long argued results from state control: inefficiency, lack of productivity, unresponsiveness to consumer needs, and technological stagnation.

Soviet communism, therefore, deserves much of the credit it has been given for abetting its own collapse. But to conclude from this that the containment policy was not necessary, or, if necessary, was not a key ingredient in the Soviet Union's demise, is to differ from the conclusions drawn by its potential victims. As the United States attempted to withdraw from Europe after World War II, countries such as Iran and Turkey, followed by those in Western Europe, pleaded with American leaders to help them. The collapse of the former great powers of Western Europe left the Soviet Union as the

---

[11] See Walter Laqueur, *The Dream That Failed: Reflections on the Soviet Union* (New York: Oxford University Press, 1994), 50–76. Also see Charles W. Kegley Jr., "How Did the Cold War Die? Principles for an Autopsy," *Mershon International Studies Review* (Summer 1994): 11–41.

[12] Zbigniew Brzezinski, *Game Plan: A Geostrategic Framework for the Conduct of the U.S.-Soviet Contest* (Boston: Atlantic Monthly Press, 1986), 123. Also see Brzezinski, *The Grand Failure*.

potential hegemon throughout Eurasia. All countries saw their independence and national integrity at stake; America's continued presence was their only protection. Had the United States detached itself from great-power politics as it did after World War I, the countries on the periphery of the Soviet Union would have been vulnerable to the same assertion of Soviet power being felt east of the iron curtain.

Western Europe remained the pivotal strategic stake throughout the Cold War. The Soviets repeatedly tried to intimidate these nations, to divide them (especially West Germany from the United States), and to drive the United States back to its shores. But the containment policy made Moscow cautious about expanding its power. From this perspective, the ancient rule of states is a prudent one: power must be met by countervailing power. A balance among states is the only guarantee that they will retain their independence and preserve their way of life. Without containment, the inefficiencies of the Soviet system might not have mattered as much; the Soviet Union would not have had to engage in a costly arms race.

Containment, however, was not directed just at blocking Soviet domination of Western Europe and the rest of Eurasia. It also was intended to win time for the Soviet leadership to reexamine its goals and moderate its ambitions. Thus the American strategy in the Cold War rested largely and correctly on a tactical assumption of Soviet behavior. As George Kennan had explained years earlier, the United States had "it in its power to increase enormously the strains under which Soviet policy must operate . . . and in this way *to promote tendencies which must eventually find their outlet in either the breakup or the gradual mellowing of Soviet power.*"[13]

In retrospect, these words were prophetic. The Cold War experience demonstrated the virtue of patience in foreign policy. While interpreting the Soviet threat as the country's paramount concern, Kennan foresaw no quick fixes and recommended no immediate solutions to the problem. To the contrary, he anticipated a prolonged, low-intensity struggle across several distant frontiers. The conflict would be settled most effectively—and most peacefully—through the gradual exposure of contradictions within Soviet society. Soviet communism, in his view, would ultimately *self-destruct* under the weight of these contradictions. In the meantime, the United States would have to pursue a "long-term, patient, but firm and vigilant containment of Russian expansive tendencies." From Truman to Bush, that is just what U.S. presidents did.

---

[13]George Kennan, *American Diplomacy, 1900–1950* (Chicago: University of Chicago Press, 1951), 127–128 (emphasis added).

Map 7-1 Post-Soviet Eurasia after 1991

American policy compelled Soviet caution and moderation. If the United States and its allies, especially NATO, had not opposed Soviet expansion in the wake of Vietnam, there would have been no need for Gorbachev to reassess his predecessors' policy and seek an accommodation with the West. It was obvious when he assumed power that the Soviet Union was "losing the capacity to generate the resources necessary to the leadership's three central objectives: a minimally acceptable standard of living; traditional foreign policy goals; and sufficient investment to ensure future growth."[14]

Excesses of the Containment Policy

Containment was by no means a flawless policy. Once the Cold War began, U.S. misperceptions, like those of Soviet leaders, fed the superpower conflict. For example, Washington frequently exaggerated Soviet military capabilities. Fears of Soviet superiority—the bomber gap in the 1950s, the missile gaps in the 1960s, and "the window of vulnerability" in the early 1980s—added momentum to the arms race already well under way. In addition, the U.S. government's fixation on ideology and the bipolar balance of power rendered American policy blind to the national aspirations of new nation-states that were liberated from colonial rule. American support for dictators across the developing world left the United States widely resented by the millions of people living in fear and extreme poverty.

The U.S. government also consistently exaggerated the monolithic nature of international communism. The fall of Nationalist China, the Korean War, and the communist Chinese intervention in that war transformed the containment policy—which originally was limited to responding to Soviet moves in the eastern Mediterranean and Western Europe—into global anticommunism. The events of 1949 and 1950 led to virulent anticommunism in the United States, with the Republicans (notably Sen. Joseph McCarthy) engaging in paranoid witch hunts and accusing the Democrats of being "soft on communism." Future Democratic administrations therefore would not be able to exploit the growing differences between the Soviet Union and China.

The American penchant for crusading, already demonstrated vividly in two "hot" wars, was not to be denied in the Cold War. America's failure to distinguish between vital and secondary interests—or to discriminate between different communist regimes—resulted in a war the United States

---

[14]James W. Davis and William C. Wohlforth, "German Unification," in *Ending the Cold War: Interpretations, Causation, and the Study of International Relations*, ed. Richard K. Herrmann and Richard Ned Lebow (New York: Palgrave Macmillan, 2004), 134.

could not win, dividing the country deeply and undermining the domestic consensus that had been the basis of the Cold War. Ironically, the Vietnam War destroyed the aggressive mode of American anticommunism, and U.S. policy shifted back toward a more passive containment of Soviet power—but this time in a de facto "alliance" with China. Finally, as detailed in Chapter 6, the overzealous pursuit of the Reagan Doctrine resulted in the Iran-contra scandal, which raised new doubts about the extent to which the U.S. government would go to fulfill its mission of defeating communism.

A Final Appraisal

Its shortcomings aside, the American containment policy must be pronounced, on the whole, a success. The expansion of American power and influence in the world has, despite the excesses of the Cold War, been associated with the promotion of democracy. America's World War II enemies, once dictatorial, are today stable, free, and prosperous societies. And its allies, particularly in Western Europe, have benefited from the opportunity to integrate their economies and pursue cooperative foreign relations. If one looks at the societies "liberated" by the Soviet Union during World War II, the contrast is striking. No Eastern European country, until the Gorbachev era, was granted self-determination by the Kremlin; earlier attempts by Czechoslovakia, East Germany, Hungary, and Poland to move toward greater freedom had been crushed by Soviet forces or their proxies. East Germany had to build a wall across Berlin and a barbed-wire fence along its entire border with West Germany to prevent its citizens from escaping.

The principal thrust of American foreign policy after World War II, as before the war, was to preserve a balance of power that would safeguard democratic values in the United States and other like-minded states. Indeed, this policy had been pursued consistently since World War I, whether the threat had come from the right or the left. American policymakers in the twentieth century opposed fascism and communism because those ideologies threatened not just U.S. security but, more broadly, the international environment in which democratic values could prosper. Communism, especially in the Soviet Union that Gorbachev inherited, was antithetical to individual freedoms, whether of speech or religion, to multiparty competition and genuine political choice, and to a distinction between state and society. It was America's power, not simply its democratic ideals, that protected these values.

Indeed, the end of the Cold War was witness not only to the end of the Soviet challenge but also to the defeat of the second totalitarian challenge to Western-style democracy in this century. The Nazis will forever be identified with the concentration camps of Auschwitz, Bergen-Belsen, and Treblinka, where they systematically murdered millions of people, including six million Jews, and with the unleashing of World War II, which, before it was over, took the lives of seventeen million soldiers and thirty-four million civilians. Just as the Nazi system was epitomized by Hitler, the Soviet system remains identified with Stalin and his cruel collectivization of the Soviet peasantry, the deliberate starvation of the Ukrainian peasants in the early 1930s, and the purges and other crimes that claimed the lives, conservatively estimated, of twenty million people and led to the imprisonment and deportation of twenty million more. Stalin, like Hitler, was an infamous mass murderer. His ability to impose over whelming control over such a massive territory had no historical precedent. The defeat of Stalin's successors, therefore, had global significance.

President Bush, along with his European counterparts, could take substantial credit for brokering a peaceful end to the Cold War. More broadly, the United States and its allies created a system of global governance during the decades after World War II that continues to enhance the prospects for international cooperation, free markets, and democratic reforms today. Bush's success politically was short-lived, however. As detailed in the next chapter, the American people soon turned to more immediate concerns, particularly an economic recession in 1992. Bush would suffer the same fate as Winston Churchill, Great Britain's prime minister who led his country to victory in World War II only to be promptly ejected from office after the war by voters disturbed by rising unemployment.[15]

Although the U.S. victory in the Cold War coincided with America's own economic woes, the country still had reason to be proud of its overall record. There had been no nuclear conflict during the nearly half-century of Cold War in which the United States had led the Western coalition. Soviet expansionist ambitions had been checked. Democracy had emerged in a steadily growing number of countries. And after winning the Cold War, the U.S. government refused to gloat, seeking instead to attract the former Soviet bloc as a partner in the process of economic and political reform. Although this process would be as complex, difficult, and potentially dangerous as that of containing communism, it would gradually extend the domain of European cooperation and produce a degree of stability not seen before in the twentieth century. As we will find in later chapters, this cooperation would endure for nearly two decades before succumbing to the same power struggles that typified the Cold War.

---

[15] See Timothy Naftali, *George H. W. Bush* (New York: Times Books, 2007), 139–141.

The New World "Disorder"

PART

II

CHAPTER

8

Old Tensions in a New Order

The abrupt collapse of the Cold War in the late twentieth century caught most world leaders by surprise and produced new uncertainties about world politics. Despite its perils, the rivalry between the Soviet Union and the United States had become a familiar reality that guided the foreign policies of all countries, large and small. In its absence, once-clear distinctions between friends and foes became blurred. Old alignments were either no longer necessary or, in many cases, no longer advisable. Consequently, the source and intensity of new fault lines were hard to distinguish.

A central question during this transition was the nature of the new balance of power. As noted, global stability traditionally has relied on a stable balance, or equilibrium, among the world's strongest powers and their allies. During the early nineteenth century, the Concert of Europe established a *multipolar* balance of power that produced a "long peace" among the great powers. The dissolution of this balance, beginning with the unification of Germany in 1870, set the stage for two world wars. During the Cold War, the *bipolar* balance between the American and Soviet blocs, which was bolstered by nuclear weapons and threats of "mutual assured destruction," prevented an even more cataclysmic world war.

One thing was clear about the post–Cold War balance of power: The disintegration of the Soviet Union had brought an end to the bipolar order that had persisted since the late 1940s. To many observers, the international system had again become multipolar. The Western European states retained their previous stature, and the European Union was taking shape as a single entity. Russia remained a force to be reckoned with. And a host of newly industrialized countries—primarily in East Asia—were emerging as formidable players on the global stage. The United States, in this view, was one of many countries of comparable strength and capabilities. Its foreign policy would have to adapt accordingly.

A more convincing perspective recognized that, at least for the immediate period, a *unipolar* balance of power would prevail. The United States held a variety of advantages that, when taken together and compared with the aggregate resources of any other single power, marked the arrival of America's "unipolar moment." According to the political columnist Charles Krauthammer, who coined the term, "American preeminence is based on

Bill Clinton faced a variety of foreign policy crises during his eight years (1993–2001) as U.S. president. In May 1993, he welcomed troops returning from Somalia, a country on the Horn of Africa where U.S. and other peacekeeping forces tried, but failed, to settle a bloody civil war among rival warlords.

the fact that [the United States] is the only country with the military, diplomatic, and economic assets to be a decisive player in any conflict in whatever part of the world it chooses to involve itself."[1]

The economic statistics spoke for themselves. In 1991—the last year of the Cold War—American firms produced $5.6 trillion in goods and services, or 26 percent of the world's output. Japan ranked second worldwide in gross domestic product, and yet its output of $3.4 trillion was just three-fifths of the U.S. total. As for Europe, America's GDP exceeded the combined totals of France, Germany, Italy, and the United Kingdom. In all three areas of economic output—manufacturing, agriculture, and services—the U.S. economy set the pace for its competitors. Although foreign trade and investments contributed only about 10 percent to its GDP, the United States also served as an engine of growth overseas by importing far more goods—worth $506 billion in 1991 alone—than any other country. All of this was especially noteworthy in view of the fact that the United States was home to less than 5 percent of the world's population.[2]

America's preponderance was even greater in the military realm. The United States maintained its global presence, with military forces deployed

[1] Charles Krauthammer, "The Unipolar Moment," *Foreign Affairs* (Winter 1990–1991), 24.

[2] World Bank, *World Development Report 1993* (New York: Oxford University Press, 1993), 239–265.

across the Western Hemisphere, Europe, the Middle East, and East Asia. The U.S. Navy patrolled most of the vital sea-lanes, and the U.S. Air Force had uncontested supremacy of the skies. American military spending of $280 billion in 1991 represented 27 percent of the worldwide total and was a much larger sum than that spent together by the country's potential adversaries.[3] Although the Soviet Union possessed a vast nuclear arsenal and came close to the United States in defense spending, the Central Intelligence Agency (CIA) had consistently overstated its role as a viable military competitor. Between 1989 and 1991, the Soviets' military strength plummeted as the Soviet bloc slowly dissolved, and those forces left were plagued by outdated equipment and sagging morale. Most other countries that maintained large and modern defense forces were longtime allies of the United States, adding further to U.S. power. The technical superiority of U.S. forces cemented their global might.

Finally, the United States emerged from the Cold War with a stable political system that, despite occasional controversies and scandals, had endured for more than two hundred years. Citizens of other nations who had known only oppression and dictatorial rule eagerly sought the democratic freedoms offered by the United States. America's vast network of colleges and universities attracted thousands of students from overseas. And its popular culture—expressed in fashion, music, publishing, movies, websites, and television—appealed to a worldwide audience. In this increasingly important area of "soft power," including the less tangible aspects of cultural and political influence, the United States held a sizable advantage.[4]

All of this did not suggest that the unipolar world would necessarily be a stable one, or one of long duration. Simply put, the modern nation-state system had never witnessed such a concentration of power in a single state. There was no comparable past experience from which to draw informed predictions. The few standard cases for comparison—including the Roman, Ottoman, Spanish, French, British, and Russo-Soviet empires—were hardly global in scope, nor did they possess the many reinforcing elements of hard and soft power that yielded U.S. predominance in the 1990s. The European empires had imposed a tight grip over their domains, whereas U.S. influence was generally less direct, taking the form of political and cultural role modeling and the provision of global "public

---

[3] "U.S. Arms Control and Disarmament Agency, World Military Expenditures and Arms Transfers, 1991–1992" (Washington, D.C.: Government Printing Office, 1994), 47–87.

[4] Joseph Nye Jr., *Bound to Lead: The Changing Nature of American Power* (New York: Basic Books, 1990), chap. 6.

goods" rather than conquest and formal occupation. But this difference only worked to further America's advantage. History had proved repeatedly that heavy-handed rulers who ignored the interests of their citizens ultimately became victims of their own tyranny.

Unipolarity also did not mean the United States would face no immediate challenges to its efforts to prevent its domestic base from eroding or to preserve its leading role in world politics. To the contrary, American leaders in the 1990s faced a bewildering array of problems at home and overseas during the first post–Cold War decade. The United States, however, confronted these challenges with a superior range of resources. The ultimate question at the time was how the nation's friends and foes would respond to a new world order made in America.

Great Expectations after the Cold War

The end of the Cold War not only elevated the stature of the United States, but also gave rise to a new sense of euphoria throughout the West. The world seemed on the verge of a profoundly new era of peace, prosperity, and individual freedom. This hope was based in part on the collapse of the Soviet Union and the anticipated replacement of Cold War rivalry with U.S.-Russian cooperation. The very forces that historically had fueled international tensions were themselves being transformed. As one scholar declared, "What we may be witnessing is not just the end of the Cold War, or the passing of a particular period of history, but the end of history as such: that is, the end point of mankind's ideological evolution and the universalization of Western liberal democracy as the final form of human government."[5]

Two forces would presumably characterize this "post-historical" world: democracy and free-market capitalism. Both had already taken hold in many parts of the developing world and were expected in the 1990s to spread across Eastern Europe and the former Soviet Union. Adherents of this view believed the expansion of democracy would benefit average citizens while enhancing the prospects for global stability. After all, democracies, even though they frequently engaged in armed struggles against nondemocratic states, traditionally had engaged in peaceful behavior toward other democratic states. The "democratic peace" they established with like-minded governments allowed for multiparty elections, observed

---

[5] Francis Fukuyama, "The End of History?" *National Interest* (Summer 1989), 4.

the rule of law, and respected human rights.[6] In the economic sphere, a market-based world economy would presumably tie nations together in a cooperative search for prosperity. Nuclear weapons, it was believed, had rendered warfare among the great powers suicidal and thus prohibitive. Large-scale conflict was becoming obsolete, just as dueling, once widely accepted, became viewed as "contemptible and stupid" in the nineteenth century.[7]

George H. W. Bush, the first U.S. president to serve in the aftermath of the Cold War, took all of these factors into account and proclaimed to a joint session of Congress in March 1991, "We can see a new world coming into view, a world in which there is the very real prospect of a new world order, a world where the United Nations—freed from Cold War stalemate—is poised to fulfill the historic vision of its founders; a world in which freedom and respect for human rights find a home among all nations."[8]

For a president who had long been associated with a pragmatic if not a conservative approach to foreign policy, Bush's exaltations seemed out of character. But his vision was very much in keeping with the country's traditional idealism and emphasis on moral principles. In predicting the global spread of democracy, Bush recalled the optimism of Thomas Jefferson. In expressing faith in multilateral organizations to uphold widely accepted norms of international behavior, Bush echoed Woodrow Wilson. And in placing the United States at the center of such a reformed world, Bush restated themes advanced by Franklin Roosevelt and John Kennedy. His outlook, then, fit neatly into a mold that was well established by past U.S. presidents. The only difference: for Bush, this long-awaited future had arrived.

Even as Bush announced the arrival of the "new world order," debates began about the future role of the United States. One question raised frequently was whether American foreign policy after the Cold War would resemble that of 1918, when the United States retreated into its hemispheric shell after World War I, or that of 1945, when it assumed a strong internationalist posture after World War II. Of central concern was how much attention and how many resources should be devoted to foreign

---

[6] See Bruce Russett, *Grasping the Democratic Peace: Principles for a Post–Cold War World* (Princeton, N.J.: Princeton University Press, 1993); and Michael W. Doyle, "Liberalism and World Politics," *American Political Science Review* (December 1986), 1151–1169. For a critique, see Joanne Gowa, *Ballots and Bullets: The Elusive Democratic Peace* (Princeton, N.J.: Princeton University Press, 1999).

[7] John Mueller, *Retreat from Doomsday: The Obsolescence of Major War* (New York: Basic Books, 1989), 10.

[8] Quoted in Stanley R. Sloan, "The U.S. Role in a New World Order: Prospects for George Bush's Global Vision," *Congressional Research Service* (Washington, D.C., March 28, 1991), 19.

policy when, for all practical purposes, the nation no longer confronted any formidable military threats.

In Washington and around the country, many people also questioned whether the United States needed a new grand strategy in the wake of the Cold War. At one level, this was not necessary, as the foremost mission of American foreign policy since World War II was to secure the nation's primacy in the international system. The rise of the Soviet bloc and the containment policy that followed in 1947, then, served as a secondary strategy in achieving this overriding goal of sustained primacy. Economic leadership and the promotion of multilateral cooperation and global governance were also vital elements of U.S. grand strategy.

Clearly, the United States could not pursue a coherent post–Cold War foreign policy in the dark. Vital interests must be recognized and articulated. Priorities must be established, budgets prepared, and resources deployed in a systematic fashion. Furthermore, allies must be reassured and potential adversaries put on notice by a government speaking with one voice. Otherwise, policy vacillates and drifts, government agencies move in separate directions, and public support wavers. Most troubling, challengers to the status quo inevitably exploit the void that results when a great power leads by improvisation.

To address these concerns, policy analysts inside and outside the U.S. government devised an array of possible strategies that clustered around four basic models: (1) a retreat from global leadership, (2) a campaign of liberal internationalism, (3) an effort to maintain U.S. economic and military primacy, and (4) an ad hoc policy of "selective engagement."[9] The first two positions reflected long-held but divergent feelings about America's role in world politics. As noted throughout this book, the country's foreign policy traditionally lurched between periods of detachment from great-power politics and periods of moral crusading. The third and fourth positions were specific to the post–Cold War era and suggested a significant evolution in the country's approach to world politics that reflected its experience as a great power.

Although early American foreign policy sought to distance the nation from the conflicts of the major powers, isolationism, the first approach, had never meant that the United States would not intervene in "its" Western Hemispheric sphere of influence. Nor did it mean that the United States would not be an aggressive player in the world economy. Instead, the nation would pursue a unilateral policy and lead by example whenever

---

[9] For an elaboration on these strategies, see Barry R. Posen and Andrew Ross, "Competing Visions for U.S. Grand Strategy," *International Security* (Winter 1996–1997), 5–53.

possible. In the wake of the Cold War, a large segment of the public supported a return to this more modest role and relief from what, for most of the twentieth century, had been a demanding and exceedingly troublesome world beyond the Western Hemisphere.[10]

An alternative approach, liberal internationalism, related to America's self-image as the "city on a hill." As noted earlier, many Americans believed their nation to be an exceptional one whose foreign policy must pursue a moral course, even if other nations did not. Because of the human and economic sacrifices borne by the United States during its rise as a great power, America should exploit its hard-fought victory by supporting democracy and improving social welfare throughout the world. The United States was uniquely capable of putting its moral principles into practice. The "peace dividend" stemming from the collapse of the Cold War could be used to ensure the continued spread of democratic institutions, to solve transnational problems such as pollution and the AIDS epidemic, and to hasten the economic growth of developing countries.

The third model went in the opposite direction, seeking an even more active role in world politics, but one that sought to preserve the gains of the Cold War primarily through the assertion of U.S. power. This so-called "primacy" school presumed that an American withdrawal into an isolationist mode, or an open-ended campaign of global altruism, would tempt potential enemies to challenge America's status as the world's lone superpower. The best hope—for both U.S. security and global stability—was for the United States to prolong its "unipolar moment" by exploiting its military predominance, imposing itself in regional power struggles, and aggressively containing potential challengers. In short, only through a *Pax Americana* could the anarchic world be saved from itself. "A world without U.S. primacy," wrote political scientist Samuel Huntington, "will be a world with more violence and disorder and less democracy and economic growth than a world where the United States continues to have more influence than any other country in shaping global affairs."[11]

The fourth option called for the United States to pursue a middle course of selective engagement in which American leaders would respond to international problems on a case-by-case basis.[12] This course became

---

[10] The isolationist view was most fully articulated by Eric A. Nordlinger in *Isolationism Reconfigured: American Foreign Policy for a New Century* (Princeton, N.J.: Princeton University Press, 1995).

[11] Samuel Huntington, "Why International Primacy Matters," *International Security* (Spring 1993), 83.

[12] See Stephen Van Evera, "Why Europe Matters, Why the Third World Doesn't: American Grand Strategy after the Cold War," *Journal of Strategic Studies* (June 1990), 1–51.

attractive to many in light of the country's experience as a world power during the twentieth century. The attempted escape of the United States from great-power politics after World War I only encouraged the fascist challengers to the status quo, who then ignited the Second World War. By contrast, America's escalation of the Cold War from a geopolitical struggle against the Soviet Union into a global anticommunist crusade produced its own calamities.

Into this void came the closely contested presidential campaign of 1992. Bush's public approval ratings were generally positive as he managed the fall of communism, negotiated German unification, and organized a multilateral effort to reverse Iraq's invasion of Kuwait (see below). At the same time, however, the U.S. economy had fallen into a recession that produced high unemployment and accelerating trade and budget deficits. These concerns opened the door for Arkansas governor Bill Clinton, who promised to concentrate on domestic problems rather than foreign policy.

Upon taking office, President Clinton knew Americans longed to be free of the conflicts that frequently dragged the nation into regional conflicts and close to a cataclysmic showdown with the Soviet Union. Yet he also recognized that the United States had enormous stakes in the rapidly changing system and must play a role commensurate with its stature. Three other assertions shaped his foreign policy. First, the country's primary goal in the mid-1990s would be strong economic growth, which would depend on a robust global economy. Second, many global problems neglected during the Cold War—ecological decay, rapid population growth, and political repression (in capitalist as well as communist states), among others—were also urgent. Finally, cooperation with other nations and global institutions must play a key foreign policy role. Thus, Clinton adopted a fifth foreign policy model, assertive multilateralism, to serve American and global interests.

Bill Clinton's Embrace of "Geoeconomics"

The future of the U.S. economy figured prominently in the foreign policy of President Clinton, who was keenly aware of the deep national anxieties about the country's economic outlook. This sense of unease, reflected consistently in public opinion polls, was truly remarkable. One might have expected the American people to feel jubilant after the country's victory in the Cold War. After all, "the Soviet Union wasn't just beaten on points, it was dismembered. Communism wasn't just relegated to second place—it was utterly delegitimized. And all with remarkably little bloodshed."[13]

Many Americans, however, were preoccupied with the country's internal health. Smokestack industries had fallen to foreign competition, and the high-technology sector had faltered in the late 1980s. The rise of many industrializing states meant a loss of jobs and opportunities to improve America's standard of living. As never before, the country was aware of its dependence on exports for employment and economic growth. With these concerns in mind, Clinton had made the U.S. economy the centerpiece of his bid for the presidency. He laid out a program of domestic reforms and emphasized that without a strong and growing economy accompanied by declining budget and trade deficits, the United States could not afford to play an influential role in world politics.

As Clinton and others acknowledged during this period, the "decline" of the U.S. economy during the Cold War was in many respects inevitable.[14] The overwhelming strength of the U.S. economy just after World War II, when it accounted for half of global production, stemmed from the wreckage of the Western European and Pacific economies. That strength, however, lasted only until these economies recovered; by the early 1990s, the U.S. share of global production was about the same as just before World War I. Thus, the country's economic predominance after World War II was a historical aberration. Its *relative* economic decline was not a harbinger of economic collapse. On an absolute basis, the U.S. economy continued to grow.

The Course of America's Economic Troubles

The post–World War II period featured unprecedented prosperity in the United States. Wages rose rapidly as trade unions grew powerful and negotiated sizable annual raises paid by industries that apparently could afford them while still earning handsome profits. In the 1960s, John Kennedy and Lyndon Johnson vastly expanded the welfare state in their efforts to build a "Great Society." They established new entitlement programs and hiked spending on older programs such as Social Security. Some newer programs, such as Medicare and Medicaid, started small but grew rapidly as their clientele and services multiplied.

---

[13] Owen Harries, "My So-Called Foreign Policy," *New Republic* (October 10, 1994), 24.

[14] Concern about a national decline, unusual for a great power but typically American, was reflected in the strong response to Paul M. Kennedy's *The Rise and Fall of the Great Powers: Economic Change and Military Conflict from 1500 to 2000* (New York: Random House, 1987). It suggested that the United States was on the verge of "imperial overstretch."

The bubble burst in the early 1970s. The enormous expense of the Vietnam War combined with the dramatic rise in oil prices produced soaring inflation, interest rates, and unemployment. "Stagflation" set in as economic growth slowed. Meanwhile, the war-ravaged industrial economies of Western Europe had recovered, and new competitors in East Asia were entering the global marketplace. American leaders knew that the country no longer could afford an unlimited supply of both guns and butter. Richard Nixon first responded in 1971 by suspending the gold standard and ending the U.S. dollar's role as the basis of the world's monetary system. He also extricated the United States from Vietnam, lowered tensions with Moscow, and transformed China from an adversary into an ally, thereby reducing the cost of foreign policy.

In the late 1970s, Jimmy Carter tried to revive the economy by reducing military spending and keeping taxes in line with growing entitlement programs. But a second oil shock in 1978–1979 produced a new round of inflation, punctuated by double-digit interest rates and unemployment. The resurgence of Soviet expansionism and anti-American revolutions in Iran and Nicaragua then forced Carter to reverse his military cutbacks. His successor, Ronald Reagan, accelerated expansion of the military in the early 1980s and simultaneously cut taxes, thereby fulfilling two campaign promises. Yet despite his efforts to reduce domestic spending, the United States suffered from rising budget deficits that would grow for more than a decade. A string of trade deficits also plagued the U.S. economy as manufacturing moved overseas and as East Asian states, particularly Japan, experienced an "economic miracle" based largely on government support for major corporations.

The reasons for the twin deficits were similar to those for the overall deterioration of American industry: low capital investments in nonmilitary research and development; the preoccupation of corporate leaders with quarterly profits to the detriment of long-term growth; and the exodus of manufacturing jobs. As for American consumers, despite the stagnation of their disposable incomes, they continued to spend freely, often with credit cards, draining the economy of an essential pool of national savings. But not all the blame for America's lethargy could be directed inward, as this period coincided with rapid economic globalization. Commerce no longer had political boundaries; firms competed not only with others at home but also with those based overseas. "There is coming to be no such thing as an American corporation or an American industry," wrote the economist Robert B. Reich, who became secretary of labor in the Clinton administration. "The American economy is but a region of the global economy."[15]

---

[15] Robert B. Reich, *The Work of Nations: Preparing Ourselves for 21st Century Capitalism* (New York: Knopf, 1991), 243.

Responses by the Clinton Administration

The superior production capacity of the United States underwrote its victory in World War II and its successful Cold War campaign against the Soviet Union. But economic stagnation in the 1980s and early 1990s raised the critical question of whether the economy could still support a foreign policy that maintained three hundred thousand U.S. soldiers in Western Europe, defended Japan and South Korea, policed the Persian Gulf and the Middle East, and retained the traditional sphere of influence in Latin America. Could the United States do all this while supporting ever-growing domestic programs and keeping up with interest payments on the national debt, the fastest-growing area of federal spending?

As Clinton sought an economic rebound at home, he was also determined to see U.S. economic relations assume the same institutional prominence as U.S. diplomatic and military relations. He elevated the status of the U.S. trade representative and granted his Treasury, Commerce, and Labor secretaries unprecedented power to shape the nation's foreign economic policies. He also created the National Economic Council to serve as a counterpart to the National Security Council. Taken together, these steps reflected the president's concern for "geoeconomics."

Among Clinton's other priorities in foreign economic policy was expanding the U.S. role in regional trading blocs. The early 1990s witnessed a wave of regional economic integration, much of it based on the success of the European Union, which had linked its member states into a single economic market (see Chapter 9). By removing barriers to trade and investment within the bloc, by encouraging the movement of workers and services across national borders, and by unifying regulations, these states hoped to increase economic efficiency and raise overall levels of production.

The first such achievement for the United States was the passage in 1993 of the North American Free Trade Agreement (NAFTA). Conceived and negotiated by the Bush administration, NAFTA was aimed at reducing or eliminating the tariffs that had limited trade among the United States, Canada, and Mexico. American critics of NAFTA charged that it would encourage U.S. manufacturers to relocate their factories in Mexico, where labor was far cheaper, thereby crippling American firms and their surrounding communities. Supporters argued that in Mexico the treaty would stimulate growth and relieve poverty while creating new markets for American goods. In the end, the NAFTA treaty passed narrowly in Congress and went into effect in 1994. The United States also became actively involved in a second, but more loosely knit, organization known as

Asia-Pacific Economic Cooperation (APEC), which also pursued expanded regional trade.

Clinton took a further step in this direction in 1994 when Congress ratified the latest General Agreement on Tariffs and Trade (GATT), which reduced tariffs on most products sold by member states overseas. Passage of GATT was placed in doubt after Congress criticized its provisions for a World Trade Organization (WTO) to monitor trade practices and enforce compliance. The criticisms were silenced, however, after Clinton assured Congress that the United States would not surrender its sovereign authority to the WTO. In fact, the United States would be in a strong position to use the WTO as a vehicle to promote its economic model of free enterprise and open markets.

Sources of Global Fragmentation

The mid-1990s in the United States saw the euphoria surrounding the end of the Cold War quickly succumb to an outbreak of conflicts overseas. Ethnic and religious disputes sparked violence across the developing world, challenging ruling elites and threatening regional power balances. Meanwhile, the jockeying continued among the great powers for power and strategic advantage. Western leaders expressed concern about the sluggish reform movement in Russia, lest the country slip back into its old dictatorial ways and expansionism. The same leaders also became alarmed by China's rise as a major power with growing economic and military strength.

Among those who felt the "end of history" was at hand after the Cold War, the defining trend in world politics was the technological revolution that was rapidly drawing the far reaches of the world closer together. This process of global *integration* was welcomed for several reasons: World leaders would increasingly recognize and solve problems that crossed national boundaries, integration would discourage self-serving and nationalistic behavior, nongovernmental organizations would mobilize global public opinion and highlight human rights and environmental concerns, economic globalization would increase prosperity, and the spread of democratic rule would reduce the likelihood of war.

It was not long, however, before the equal but opposite forces of global *fragmentation* raised doubts about these rosy scenarios. The reason: The shift in the global balance of power had produced a volatile and violent international order.[16] Bipolarity had been relatively stable because

---

[16] See Benjamin Barber, *Jihad vs. McWorld: How Globalism and Tribalism Are Reshaping the World* (New York: Times Books, 1995), chaps. 10–14.

of its very simplicity. Watching each other constantly, the superpowers maintained the balance, always aware of the danger of nuclear war and its suicidal potential. Consequently, there was no third world war; after the 1962 Cuban missile crisis, there were no comparable crises between the superpowers; and despite tensions, Europe experienced the longest period of peace in the twentieth century. But all of this changed with the collapse of the Soviet Union, leading some analysts to express nostalgia for the Cold War.[17]

The breakdown of bipolarity wrought instability and encouraged fragmentation in three distinct ways. First, the retreat of the Soviet Union revived the nationalist, ethnic, and religious tensions that had accompanied the breakup of the Austro-Hungarian, Russian, and Ottoman (Turkish) empires after World War I but that were kept largely in check during the Cold War. The breakup of the Soviet Union into fifteen republics produced armed clashes between Armenia and Azerbaijan, a war of secession in the Russian province of Chechnya, civil war in Tajikistan, and new tensions between Russia and its formidable neighbors China and India. The end of communist rule in Yugoslavia sparked a new and ghastly round of religious warfare. In fact, the reemergence of the fault lines separating ethnic and religious groups in many parts of the world suggested that a "clash of civilizations" was imminent.[18]

A second consequence of the breakdown of bipolarity was that aspirants to regional hegemony felt free to pursue their aggressive designs. It was no longer true that each superpower, dominant in its own sphere of influence, could restrain its clients and prevent local conflicts. Expansionist middle powers were now free to fill the void left by the superpowers. Iraq's invasion of Kuwait in 1990, an event described later in this chapter, was unthinkable so long as the Soviet Union remained a key regional player that wished to avoid a confrontation with the United States. Similarly, the resurgence of ethnic conflict across Africa and the escalation of tensions between India and Pakistan coincided with the withdrawal of the great powers.

Finally, the fragmented world order tested the resilience of U.S. alliances. Organized to counter the power of the Soviet Union and China, these alliances gave priority to common interests in collective security. With the Cold War over, the mission of the North Atlantic Treaty Organization

---

[17] See John Mearsheimer, "Why We Will Soon Miss the Cold War," *Atlantic Monthly* (August 1990), 33–50.

[18] Samuel Huntington, "The Clash of Civilizations?" *Foreign Affairs* (Summer 1993), 22–49.

(NATO) became unclear as other security arrangements were devised for the European Union. The fears of U.S. leaders that NATO would become obsolete explained much of their enthusiasm for its eastward expansion. Meanwhile, the web of multilateral alliances created by the United States across the Pacific Ocean had long ceased to exist in any meaningful sense, and the durability of its bilateral ties to several nations in East Asia was thrown into question. The United States reaffirmed its regional presence by extending its security pact with Japan in 1996 and keeping its troops in South Korea.

The contradictory forces of global integration and fragmentation had far deeper roots than the Cold War and its aftermath.[19] Advances in transportation and communication had been making the world "smaller" for centuries. By the same token, the outbreak of civil wars was a logical result of the spread of democracy and its calls for self-determination, which first became a strong political force during the Enlightenment era of the eighteenth century. The end of the Cold War, however, ruptured the geopolitical basis for world order and allowed both forces to find full expression.

War and Peace in the Middle East

The first trouble spot to disrupt the "new world order" was the Middle East. Ample and inexpensive oil from the Persian Gulf had powered the twentieth century's Industrial Revolution. But after the Arab members of the Organization of the Petroleum Exporting Countries (OPEC) embargoed oil shipments to the United States in 1973 and provoked a second oil shock in 1978, the West recognized all too well its dependence on Middle East oil and its vulnerability to future disruptions of oil flows. In the 1990s, the absence of a superpower rivalry left a power vacuum in the Middle East that one regional leader, Iraq's Saddam Hussein, attempted to fill. Saddam's bid for hegemony produced the first world crisis of the post–Cold War era. Meanwhile, the peace process between Israel and its Arab neighbors inched forward between spasms of violence and political crisis.

War in the Persian Gulf

The end of the Cold War encouraged some foreign leaders to test the limits of U.S. resolve, forcing military action in both the George H. W. Bush and Clinton presidencies. The first of these was Iraqi leader Saddam

---

[19] See John Lewis Gaddis, "Toward the Post–Cold War World," *Foreign Affairs* (Spring 1991), 102–122.

Hussein, whose country suffered an $80 billion debt from his eight-year war (1980–1988) with Iran. On August 2, 1990, Saddam ordered his battle-tested army to invade his oil-rich neighbor, the emirate of Kuwait. The Iraqi army quickly overran the largely undefended Kuwaiti capital, Kuwait City. With his troops poised on the border of Saudi Arabia and many Arab neighbors afraid of him, Saddam then sought to intimidate the Persian Gulf oil kingdoms and assert his dominance over the entire region.

Saddam expected little resistance from the United States. After being ejected from Iran in 1979, Washington sought vengeance against Tehran and a new U.S. support base in the Persian Gulf.[20] Toward both ends, President Ronald Reagan provided Saddam with intelligence, military equipment, and agriculture credits worth billions, many of which Saddam bartered for military supplies.[21] Meanwhile, export licenses allowed Saddam to buy "dual-use" technology that could be used to produce biological and chemical weapons, and he repeatedly used these weapons against Iranian targets. Saddam also launched such weapons of mass destruction (WMDs) against Kurdish citizens in his own country, who opposed his regime. A single gas attack on the Kurdish city of Halabja in March 1988 left an estimated five thousand dead and ten thousand injured.

In return for Washington's support, Saddam had pledged to keep the Persian Gulf free of communist influence and to provide America with a discount on Iraqi oil. This marriage of convenience ended with the conclusion of the Iran-Iraq War. Concerned about Iraq's WMD program, Congress threatened the Iraqi leader with economic sanctions. But Saddam still received positive signals from the White House and expected U.S. leaders to look the other way when he set his sights on Kuwait in 1990. This proved to be a fateful miscalculation.[22] Bush, heir to Reagan's hands-off policy toward Saddam, abruptly reversed course and announced that Iraq's blatant aggression "would not stand."

As Iraqi forces massed near Saudi Arabia's border, the possibility that Saddam might soon control 40 percent of the world's oil reserves and dictate the terms of OPEC production forced an aggressive response. Japan and the Western powers froze Iraqi assets in their countries and those of the deposed government of Kuwait. This measure was accompanied by an

---

[20] For a look at Iranian culture, see Laura Secor, *Children of Paradise: The Struggle for the Soul of Iran* (New York: Penguin, 2016).

[21] See Bruce W. Jentleson, *With Friends Like These: Reagan, Bush, and Saddam, 1982–1990* (New York: Norton, 1994).

[22] Rick Francona, *Ally to Adversary: An Eyewitness Account of Iraq's Fall from Grace* (Annapolis, Md.: U.S. Naval Institute Press, 1999), 5–6.

embargo on Iraqi oil and other economic sanctions, to be enforced by a naval blockade of the Persian Gulf. The two central questions were whether Iraq's customers would honor the embargo long enough to bankrupt the Iraqi economy and whether Saddam ultimately would succumb to the economic sanctions or allow his people to suffer indefinitely, like Fidel Castro in Cuba. Meanwhile, the United States proceeded with its largest troop buildup (dubbed Operation Desert Shield) since the Vietnam War; 250,000 troops were deployed to deter an Iraqi attack on Saudi Arabia. American officials hoped the prospect of war with the United Nations (UN) coalition—composed mainly of U.S., British, and French forces and those from several Arab states—would persuade Saddam to withdraw from Kuwait.

Map 8-1   The Persian Gulf, with Key Oil Fields and Pipelines

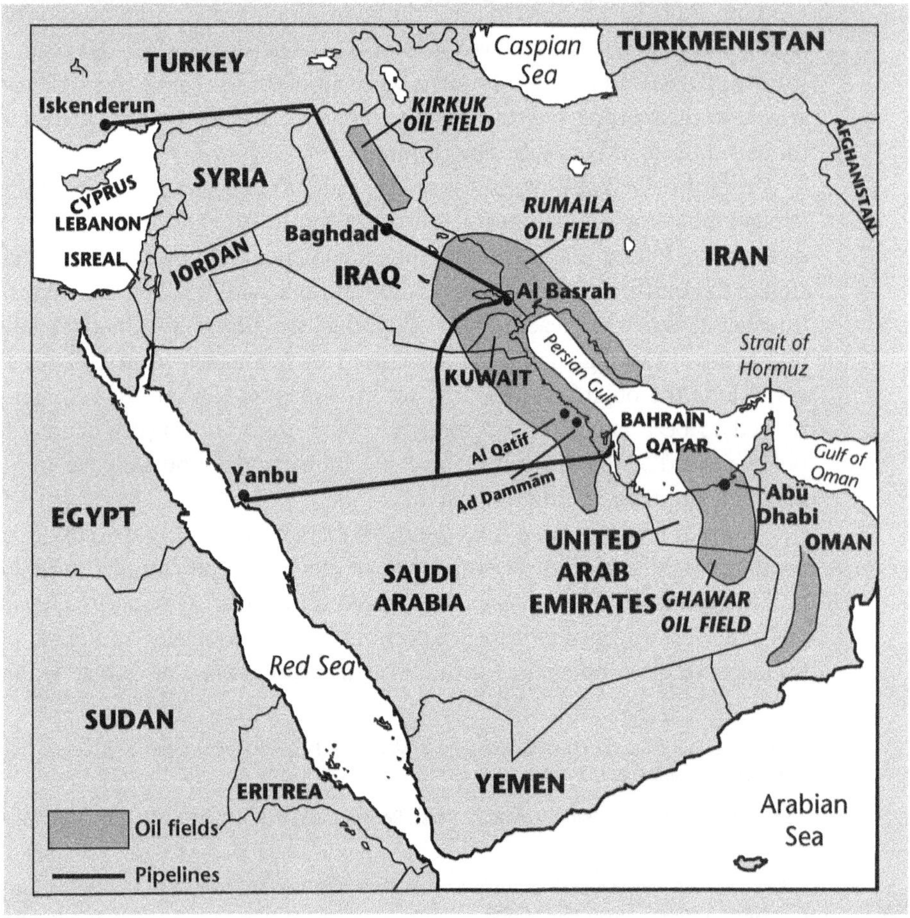

The stakes in this confrontation were clear: possible Iraqi control of oil production and prices, the stability of moderate Arab regimes and Israel, and the durability of the post–Cold War balance of power. Having rhetorically accepted the challenge, the United States could not afford to back down. If it did, it would endanger its security, its economic growth as well as that of its major trading partners, and its status as the world's lone remaining superpower. If its Arab allies and Israel were neglected in their moment of peril, they might not trust the United States again. The stage was set for a showdown.

The UN gave Saddam a deadline of January 15, 1991, to withdraw from Kuwait. If he refused, he would be ejected by force. The unanimity within the UN Security Council was remarkable and clearly demonstrated how great-power politics had changed with the end of the Cold War. Previously, the council's five permanent members—the United States, the Soviet Union, Britain, France, and China—had agreed on virtually nothing, and the two superpowers had vetoed any call for collective action. But with Mikhail Gorbachev clinging to power in the Soviet Union and seeking accommodation with the West, the great powers were for once able to cooperate. Saddam, hoping to disrupt this marriage of the great powers, instead provided a rationale for the UN to test its long-dormant system of collective security.

The unprecedented UN solidarity was not matched within Congress, however. It insisted that President Bush gain its assent before using force. Many members, still haunted by memories of Vietnam, argued that economic sanctions would be sufficient to dislodge Iraq. Their arguments were shared by thousands of peace activists, who held candlelight vigils and public demonstrations to denounce the impending war. With the UN deadline nearing and the U.S. troop deployment increasing to nearly five hundred thousand, Congress held a historic debate about the Iraqi challenge and narrowly approved the military operation. When the January 15 deadline passed with Iraqi forces still in Kuwait, the United States and coalition partners transformed Operation Desert Shield into Operation Desert Storm.

The massive air assault that began on January 17 sent Saddam's forces fleeing for cover. Allied air forces flew more than one hundred thousand sorties, devastating Iraqi targets from the front lines to Baghdad. In the first phase, they took out Iraqi command-and-control posts, airfields, communication centers, and other military installations. In the second phase, they destroyed the bridges and roads being used to supply the Iraqi forces in Kuwait. Cut off, those forces were then subjected to constant pounding. Their poorly concealed tanks and armored personnel carriers were destroyed by U.S. laser-guided missiles, which either killed the Iraqi soldiers or left them stranded in the desert. Not until February 24 did the coalition's tank forces launch their ground attack across the Saudi border.

The results of this military response exceeded the expectations of the most optimistic military planners. Within one hundred hours, the ground forces had surrounded the Iraqis, most of whom surrendered quickly. Once feared as the world's fourth-largest fighting force, these troops were only too glad to throw down their arms in return for food and water. Facing almost no opposition, coalition convoys rolled toward Kuwait City, past oil fields set ablaze by Iraq's retreating forces. When the first wave of liberation forces, mostly from Arab countries, reached the Kuwaiti capital, they were greeted and embraced by cheering mobs. The Gulf War had lasted forty-three days. More than one hundred thousand Iraqi soldiers were killed in the *blitzkrieg*; coalition casualties numbered fewer than two hundred. In the end, Saddam was forced to revoke his annexation of Kuwait and withdraw what was left of his occupation force.

The war, however, did not result in Saddam's removal from power; that had never been the goal of the UN. Indeed, had the tank columns rolled on to Baghdad, the coalition likely would have come apart. The Arabs wanted to ensure that Saddam would no longer pose a threat, but they were against his overthrow. And Washington wanted no part in governing a nation in civil war, which appeared likely in the wake of Saddam's defeat. Iraq's Kurds and Shiite Muslims, constituting the majority of the country's population, rebelled in separate regions against Saddam, a Sunni Muslim. But they were not strong enough to defeat the remnants of Saddam's Republican Guard, many of whom were saved at the last moment by the abrupt cease-fire.

Despite Saddam's undisguised brutality toward his own people, the United States and its allies, as noted, did not want to see Iraq disintegrate. They expected the country to maintain its pivotal role in the Middle East balance of power, a role not possible if it were partitioned. More important, they did not want the surrounding countries, especially Iran and Syria, to carve up Iraq in their own bids for regional dominance. Iraqi Kurds and Shiites charged the United States with encouraging them to revolt against Saddam and then ignoring them once they were engaged in battle and ultimately defeated. But the realities of the regional power balance overrode those criticisms.

After the war, Saddam defied a series of international demands, making it clear that despite the coalition's victory he would remain a threat. In late 1994, he displayed his capacity to menace the Persian Gulf region at will when he again massed troops on the Kuwaiti border, this time to protest continuing UN sanctions against Iraq. The United States, now led by President Bill Clinton, responded by mobilizing its remaining forces in the Persian Gulf and deploying thousands of additional troops to the region. Saddam then backed down and ordered his Republican Guard soldiers to return to their bases. Two years later, he sponsored attacks against the Kurdish population of northern Iraq, a region declared off-limits by the UN and occupied by a U.S.-led relief force. After the United States responded with air strikes against Iraqi military installations, Saddam withdrew once more.

Despite the coalition's spectacular success in routing Iraq from Kuwait in 1991, Saddam remained firmly in power and demonstrated repeatedly his ability to create havoc. He recognized Iraq's importance to the strategic interests of the Western powers. And he openly exploited his freedom to inflame the region at the time and place of his choosing. As he did so, Saddam wore down the UN coalition. Two factors aided his divide-and-conquer strategy. First, the United States was steadily losing support within the UN Security Council. Among the permanent members, Russia and China were growing more supportive of Iraq—less because of their affinity for Saddam than because of their desire to curb U.S. influence. They were joined in their defiance by France, which used any opportunity to display its independence from Washington. Only Britain, led by Prime Minister Tony Blair, remained loyal to the United States in the Security Council.

In 1997, Saddam directed his wrath toward the UN Special Commission (UNSCOM), which had been given the difficult task of ensuring that Iraq dismantle its weapons of mass destruction. The role of UNSCOM was vital because Iraq had used biological weapons against Iran and its own Kurdish population. There also was evidence that since the 1980s, Iraq had filled missile warheads with botulism, anthrax, and other deadly biological agents. The fears that Iraq was secretly storing such weapons and would use them if given the opportunity were therefore justified. Saddam had agreed to the creation of UNSCOM, but he soon resisted inspections of Iraqi military installations. A cat-and-mouse game quickly ensued, with UNSCOM agents arriving at suspected Iraqi weapons facilities only to find they had been recently vacated. Saddam turned up the heat late in 1997 by expelling the U.S. members of UNSCOM, whom he accused of dominating the inspections and conspiring with the CIA to overthrow him.

Clinton was clearly losing this standoff with Iraq. His lack of political support at home and overseas left him with little room to maneuver. More than anything, Clinton feared he would be condemned for launching a military attack on Iraq at a time when Saddam was widely viewed as seeking reconciliation. Political concerns took precedence over military strategy, and in the political sphere Clinton's hand was growing weaker every day. His concessions to Iraq only stiffened Saddam's resolve and energized the anti-American coalition in the UN. When Clinton resorted to force, as in the December 1998 aerial bombardments code-named Operation Desert Fox, he was accused of trying to distract attention from domestic problems and scandals.

Obstacles to an Arab-Israeli Peace

In the wake of Operation Desert Storm, the United States judged the time right for a new effort to gain a comprehensive peace between Israel and its neighbors. The oil kingdoms owed Washington a favor for saving them from Saddam. Syria, deprived of Soviet patronage and protection, also seemed ready for a settlement. Moreover, shortly after the Gulf War, Israel's hard-line Likud government, which had a cool relationship with the United States, was replaced by a more accommodating Labor Party government headed by Yitzhak Rabin.

The unexpected breakthrough came in September 1993 when the Palestine Liberation Organization (PLO) and Israel agreed to mutual recognition. In the historic Oslo Declaration of Principles, which was facilitated by the Norwegian government, the PLO abandoned its call for the destruction of Israel and renounced terrorism. In return, Israel would withdraw from the Gaza Strip and the West Bank town of Jericho and allow the Palestinians to govern themselves. It was assumed that, over time, Palestinian control over education, health, social services, taxation, and tourism would be extended over the West Bank except in the areas settled by the Israelis. It also was assumed that the Palestinians would keep order, police themselves, and, in particular, end the *intifada* (uprising) against Israel and its supporters. If these expectations were realized, the two sides eventually would hold "final-status" talks about whether the Palestinians would be allowed to establish a state of their own.

Why did these two deadly enemies finally decide to negotiate their differences? For one thing, the end of the Cold War deprived the PLO of a strong political supporter—the Soviet Union. For another, the Gulf War had left the organization almost broke; PLO leader Yasir Arafat had made the disastrous decision to support Iraq against the oil kingdoms that provided the PLO with most of its funds. Arafat established a Palestinian Authority in the occupied areas, thereby suggesting a two-state solution instead of Israel's elimination. For their part, the Israelis were tired of the conflict and the costs of the six-year-old *intifada*. If Israel could achieve a stable peace, the country's economy would prosper. Talks with the PLO had therefore become inevitable, and the hope was that these would lead to a comprehensive peace agreement.

Over the opposition of extremists in Israel, the Middle East peace process edged further forward in 1994 when Israel resolved its major differences with Jordan. Under the terms of this second agreement, both countries acknowledged the right of the other to exist, bringing their de facto state of war to an end. In addition, Jordan's King Hussein and Israel's Yitzhak Rabin agreed on the boundaries between the two states and divided control over underground water reservoirs and other natural resources; they also established the basis for bilateral trade and tourism. As part of the treaty, the United States agreed to forgive its portion of Jordan's foreign debt, which had soared after years of economic stagnation.

As in the past, the progress toward Arab-Israeli peace was shattered by violence and tragedy. On November 4, 1995, a Jewish extremist assassinated Rabin in order to halt the peace process. In the spring of 1996, Palestinian terrorists staged four suicide bombings in nine days, killing fifty-nine Israelis and wounding more than two hundred. Israelis, now doubtful about the peace process, showed their misgivings at the polls. The conservative Likud Party was restored to power with the election of its leader, Benjamin Netanyahu, to the office of prime minister. Netanyahu pledged to bring "peace with security" to Israel, meaning he would not support further concessions to the Arabs without explicit guarantees that Israel's security would be protected on all fronts.

When these guarantees were not forthcoming, Netanyahu delayed the withdrawal of Israeli troops from the West Bank. As each side accused the other of trying to scuttle the agreements, a new round of bloody attacks by both sides occurred in 1996. Netanyahu's insistence on building new Jewish settlements in East Jerusalem, home to many Palestinians, led to yet another round of violence. Despite the best efforts of the United States, a resolution of the Arab-Israeli conflict remained elusive, leaving the prospects of a "two-state solution" in the hands of future leaders in Tel Aviv, Israel's capital, and in the Palestinian territories.

The Plight of "Failed States"

Among the most notable trends in world politics after World War II was the steady rise in the number of nation-states—from fifty-five in 1946 to

Impact and Influence: Yasir Arafat

Claude Salhani/Sygma via Getty Images

For most of his life, Yasir Arafat personified the struggle among Palestinians to gain statehood in territories granted to Israel upon its creation in 1948. Arafat was born in Egypt in 1929, but he spent much of his childhood in Jerusalem. He fought briefly for the Egyptian army, but once he received his engineering degree in 1956, he moved to Kuwait to begin work as a building contractor. Arafat continued, however, to be committed to the Palestinian cause, and in 1957, he helped to found Fatah, an underground network of activists engaged in armed struggle against Israel. Fatah became the primary faction within the Palestine Liberation Organization, created in 1964, and Arafat rose to become the PLO's leader in 1969. He spent the next two decades seeking international support for the PLO and organizing its ongoing low-intensity war against Israel, along with terrorist attacks on Israeli targets in other areas. Arafat maintained the status of an influential and colorful world leader during this period, visiting foreign capitals and, in 1988, speaking before the UN General Assembly in his military fatigues and familiar Arab headdress.

In the early 1990s, prospects for peace brightened between the Israelis and Palestinians—both sides were exhausted by the endless political violence. The Oslo Accords of 1993, described in this chapter, raised hopes for a "two-state solution" that would one day bring peace to the embattled region. But Arafat later proved unable, or unwilling, to restrain his own deputies from sponsoring terrorist attacks on Israelis. His refusal to compromise on key issues in the final-status talks in 2000 left him politically isolated and under virtual house arrest by Israeli forces in his Ramallah compound. American leaders, who had struggled since the days of the Camp David Accords to mediate an end to the conflict, looked to other Palestinian leaders for a lasting peace. Arafat died in 2004 with the Arab-Israeli peace process far from complete.

nearly two hundred by the turn of the millennium. Most of the new countries were created from former European colonies in Africa and southern Asia. Others, such as the Czech Republic and Slovakia, emerged after the Cold War in Eastern Europe. Still others were carved out of the former

Soviet Union. This proliferation of nation-states dramatically changed the face of world politics during the late twentieth century. The new countries, often located in the world's poorest areas, received large volumes of foreign aid from wealthier nations and accepted their help in the complicated task of "nation building." Yet despite some progress in their living conditions, these developing countries remained generally hostile to the industrialized North. In the UN, the new states united with other developing countries to form a majority in the General Assembly, which served as a forum to express their grievances against the United States and other industrialized nations.

This resentment steadily intensified during the Cold War, when many developing countries became battlegrounds for the superpower conflict, illustrating the aphorism that "when two elephants fight, the grass suffers." The ideological nature of these conflicts polarized the developing countries and often pitted neo-Marxist revolutionaries against right-wing military juntas, which became ever more repressive when challenged for power. Neither a middle class nor a moderate political center was possible under these circumstances. Frequently, extremists on both sides received modern weaponry from the superpowers or their allies, which further inflamed the conflicts.

In this respect, the end of the Cold War was welcomed by the most impoverished nations, which were still reeling from the punishing economic distress of the 1980s, widely labeled the "lost decade" of development. By the late 1990s, however, the social and economic problems plaguing many poor countries had only worsened. Contrary to widespread expectations, the accommodation between Washington and Moscow had produced lower levels of foreign aid to the world's poor; indeed, the United States had all but eliminated aid to "nonstrategic allies." Instead, U.S. policy makers called on developing countries to seek private investments to boost their economies. But such investment was unlikely where poverty and political unrest prevailed. In contrast to the flood of foreign investment that flowed to the newly industrialized countries of East Asia, the poorest states received barely a trickle.

Some observers suggested dismantling what was left of the most desperate developing countries and putting them under UN trusteeship. Such a response was highly unlikely, but it revealed the depths to which many of these countries had fallen. Indeed, in many areas, the post–Cold War era witnessed the emergence of the "failed state":

> From Haiti in the Western Hemisphere to the remnants of Yugoslavia in Europe, from Somalia, Sudan, and Liberia in Africa

to Cambodia in Southeast Asia, a disturbing new phenomenon is emerging: the failed nation-state, utterly incapable of sustaining itself as a member of the international community. . . . [T]hose states descend into violence and anarchy—imperiling their own citizens and threatening their neighbors through refugee flows, political instability, and random warfare.[23]

These crises raised questions about the arrangements that had created these countries in the first place, particularly those in Africa, whose ethnic groups overlapped state boundaries drawn by colonial rulers. For the United States, which had sought support from these impoverished states to counter Soviet influence in the region, their plight was suddenly remote to its strategic self-interests. Americans, however, could not escape the scenes of warfare and starvation appearing on their televisions daily and crying out for action by the world's richest and most powerful country. Yet what form, if any, this help should take remained unclear.

Political Collapse and Genocide in Africa

One of the first states to arouse international attention was the impoverished country of Somalia, located along the Horn of Africa at the entrance to the Red Sea (see the map "Africa Today" in Chapter 4). During the Cold War, the Soviets had supported the government of Somalia because its larger neighbor to the north, Ethiopia, was aligned with the United States. But when a pro-Soviet military regime came into power in Ethiopia, Somalia's ruler switched sides as well. Gen. Mohamed Siad Barre became a loyal client of the United States despite his ruthless oppression of the Somali people.

All of this perversely made sense in the context of Cold War rivalry. But when the Cold War ended and Barre was overthrown, Somalia became embroiled in a war of succession among rival factions. The government ceased to function and chaos prevailed. Widespread starvation followed when the rival militias prevented farmers from planting, disrupted the activities of nomadic traders, and killed most of the nation's livestock. An estimated three hundred thousand Somalis died of starvation; another two million were in immediate danger. For months, the world looked

---

[23] Gerald B. Helman and Steven R. Ratner, "Saving Failed States," *Foreign Policy* (Winter 1992–1993), 3. Also see *Collapsed States: The Disintegration and Restoration of Legitimate Authority,* ed. I. William Zartman (Boulder, Colo.: Lynne Rienner, 1995).

the other way. But media attention finally compelled a Western response through the UN. More than twenty-seven thousand troops, at first mainly American, were dispatched in late 1992 to provide order and food. After they had accomplished the mission of Operation Restore Hope, the U.S. forces were to be withdrawn and replaced by a temporary contingent of UN forces.

It soon became clear that, once the outside forces were withdrawn, the Somali warlords would resume their struggle for power, leading to renewed killing and hunger. Thus, in 1993, the UN changed its mission from one of humanitarian relief to one of rebuilding Somalia's political and economic structures. But the country's principal warlord, Gen. Mohammed Farah Aidid, who controlled Somalia's capital, Mogadishu, resisted the enlarged UN mission because it called for his own removal from power. In the fighting that followed, twenty-four Pakistani peacekeepers were ambushed and killed. Later, more UN troops were killed, including U.S. soldiers who were deployed to capture the elusive general. As the number of U.S. casualties mounted—and after a slain U.S. soldier was dragged through the streets of Mogadishu before cheering crowds and television cameras—demands began for the withdrawal of U.S. troops. Clinton responded by accelerating their departure, and the UN suspended the mission in the spring of 1995.

How did the Somali operation go so tragically wrong? The international peacekeepers, initially dispatched for the humanitarian purpose of feeding the people, ignored the political situation that had created the hunger in the first place. Food shortages had not stemmed from a natural disaster; they were man made. Indeed, it should have been clear from the beginning that resolving the anarchic political situation was a prerequisite to resolving the humanitarian crisis. What was originally thought to be a short mission ended up taking two and a half years, underlining the fact that there was no such thing as an apolitical, purely humanitarian intervention. A lasting solution to the Somali conflict was possible only through internal reconciliation undertaken by the Somalis themselves.

In the waning days of the Somalia debacle, the world was confronted with an even more grotesque humanitarian nightmare in the African state of Rwanda. In 1994, over a period of less than three months, violence between the Hutus, who dominated the government, and the minority Tutsi population had resulted in more than eight hundred thousand casualties, mainly Tutsi. This death toll far exceeded that in Bosnia, where the killing of about two hundred thousand Muslims by the Serbs had been labeled genocide (see Chapter 9). Because the multilateral response had proved unworkable in Somalia, a concerted peacekeeping effort in Rwanda was out of the question. Personal apologies by President Clinton in 1998 for the lack of a U.S. response did nothing to relieve the suffering of the Rwandans; nor did the UN's admission in December 1999 that it made "serious mistakes" in failing to prevent the catastrophe.[24]

Haiti's Descent into Anarchy

The Clinton administration was confronted with yet another crisis in the failed state of Haiti, the poorest country in the Western Hemisphere. Ruled by the U.S.-backed Duvalier dictatorship until 1986, the Haitian people had their first democratic elections in 1990. The Reverend Jean-Bertrand Aristide became the country's new president. But Aristide's proposed reforms, including his plans to demilitarize the country and redistribute wealth, resulted in his overthrow six months later by the military. With Aristide in exile in the United States, Haiti's military leaders, led by Gen. Raoul Cédras, launched a campaign of terror across the island, killing, torturing, and imprisoning those who had fought for reforms and who continued to resist the new rulers. In response, thousands of Haitians constructed makeshift boats and fled to the United States. In his final months in office, President Bush announced that the United States was unprepared to accommodate these "boat people" and ordered the U.S. Coast Guard to turn them back. His decision angered many human rights groups, as well as candidate Bill Clinton, who declared that as president he would allow the Haitians to seek asylum in the United States.

But just as in other areas of foreign policy, Clinton's position on Haiti changed once he took office. Suddenly, he shared Bush's reservations about absorbing the mass emigration of Haitians. While continuing to demand Aristide's return to Haiti and denouncing the military rulers, Clinton announced he would not allow Haitian refugees to enter the United States. Instead, a UN-sponsored economic embargo was imposed on Haiti, but it had little effect on the political and social crisis. In July 1993, Clinton and the Haitian leadership reached an agreement that would have brought about Aristide's return to power in exchange for amnesty for Cédras and other military leaders. When the 270 U.S. and Canadian peacekeepers arrived in Haiti on the USS *Harlan County* to oversee the transition back to

---

[24] See United Nations, *Independent Inquiry into the Actions of the United Nations during the 1994 Genocide in Rwanda* (New York: United Nations, 1999).

civilian rule, they were greeted by armed demonstrators. Under Clinton's orders, the ship beat an ignominious retreat.

The tentative U.S. response to disorder in Haiti became a symbol of the Clinton administration's general lack of resolve in foreign policy. The *New York Times*, which supported most of Clinton's domestic initiatives, expressed dismay at his reversals in handling the deepening crisis in Haiti: "After months of vacillating from one policy to another, America faces the troubling prospect that Mr. Clinton is drifting into using troops in Haiti because he wants to compensate for other policy embarrassments and does not have a better idea."[25] The turmoil in Haiti continued into the fall of 1994, when Clinton finally concluded that the Haitian problem could only be resolved by U.S. military intervention. The military assault on Haiti was then transformed into a "semipermissive occupation" by twenty thousand U.S. troops that extended well into 1995. Stability on the island depended on the presence of U.S. troops, a steady stream of Western foreign aid, and the deployment in March 1996 of six thousand UN peacekeepers. By the end of the decade, any hopes that Haiti could be converted into a stable state and society had vanished.

Lessons from the Regional Crises

The regional conflicts just described collectively deflated the euphoria that followed the end of the Cold War. Many members of Congress—including Clinton's allies in the Democratic Party—openly doubted that the United States had vital interests in the failed states. But they generally supported the humanitarian interventions in the early 1990s, which appealed to the nation's historical sense of mission and moral responsibility. Support for U.S. involvement quickly evaporated, however, when it became clear the United States could not resolve the underlying problems in these countries. For many Americans, a retreat from the chaotic struggles overseas was appealing.

Although the restraints on U.S. power were few, it became clear that Washington could not solve the many problems in developing countries that were sparking widespread violence after the Cold War. America's vast military arsenal was of little or no use in most trouble spots; constructive, long-term solutions were required. Moreover, most of the conflicts were civil wars, not disputes between states—a fact further demonstrating that homegrown solutions, not those imposed by other states, were needed.

---

[25] "Which Haiti Policy?" (editorial), *New York Times* (July 7, 1994), A18.

This stubborn reality challenged the view among many Americans that, once America committed its military forces to battle, their overwhelming strength could subdue any foe.

The failed military intervention in Somalia reminded American leaders that they must pay attention to the interests at stake in any conflict—as well as the cost, level of public support, likelihood of success, and existence of a coherent exit strategy. These preconditions became part of the "Powell Doctrine," named after Gen. Colin L. Powell, chairman of the Joint Chiefs of Staff under Presidents Bush and Clinton. The regional conflicts also demonstrated the limits of multilateral intervention and peacekeeping. As in the early 1930s, when the League of Nations failed to resist Japan's invasion of Manchuria, pledges by UN members to act collectively in the 1990s turned out to be hollow. The reasons for such reneging were eerily similar to the League of Nations' precedent: the primacy of national self-interests over transnational concerns, unresolved disputes among the great powers, and doubts about the world body's political and military leadership. Congressional leaders, who controlled the country's purse strings, viewed the UN with suspicion—if not contempt—and refused to meet U.S. financial obligations to that organization.[26]

While the lessons from the regional conflicts prescribed a healthy dose of moderation for U.S. military policy, in other respects the wrong lessons were learned. The failure of the humanitarian interventions provoked a general backlash against U.S. activism in developing areas. As the pendulum swung toward the other extreme—global *disengagement*—Congress cut deeply into the State Department's budget and closed dozens of foreign embassies, consulates, and missions. Many foreign aid programs to the poorest countries of Africa, South Asia, and Latin America were eliminated.[27] As a result, the United States deprived itself of a key resource with which to address the underlying problems in the poor countries and contribute to constructive, peaceful, and long-term change. The fact that the world's most prosperous country scaled back its foreign service and foreign aid programs sent a troubling message about Washington's future intentions.

---

[26] In late 1999, the United States began to pay off its overdue financial commitment to the UN, which amounted to more than $1 billion, but only after being faced with the loss of its vote in the General Assembly.

[27] As a percentage of economic output, U.S. foreign aid spending was by 1995 lower than that of all other industrialized countries. Michael O'Hanlon and Carol Graham, *A Half Penny on the Dollar: The Future of Development Aid* (Washington, D.C.: Brookings, 1997), 25.

CHAPTER 9

The Shifting European Landscape

A fter the Cold War, the United States continued to maintain a visible presence on the European continent, hoping to exploit the gains stemming from the collapse of the Soviet Union and to prevent the emergence of new fault lines. The U.S. effort, however, yielded contradictory results. As Europeans became stronger and more unified, they also grew wary of their American caretaker and sought to become more self-sufficient. Above all, they hoped to regain their place among the great powers after being trapped for nearly a half-century in the middle of the East-West struggle.

America's preoccupation with Europe was, of course, nothing new. It always had viewed a stable Europe as essential to its security. Specifically, a *balance* among the European powers was required to prevent a single country from dominating the continent and, in turn, threatening the United States. Throughout the nineteenth century, this geopolitical concern had led U.S. leaders to avoid alliances with the European powers, a strategy clearly laid out in President George Washington's Farewell Address (1796) and in the Monroe Doctrine (1823). American detachment from the great powers of Europe was further justified on moral terms: the European monarchs had brazenly denied their citizens fundamental political rights and routinely placed them in harm's way in their deadly game of power politics. The United States, by contrast, would remain true to its democratic principles by refusing to play this game. This strategy worked so long as the Concert of Europe maintained a balance of power and the British navy protected the Atlantic sea-lanes. But American fears that one country would try to dominate the European continent were affirmed in the two world wars, which forced the United States to abandon its policy of "splendid isolation" once and for all.

As the Cold War set in, the makers of American foreign policy faced a dilemma in contemplating future relations with Europe. With the United States the strongest world power in 1945 and with the Soviet Union quickly emerging as its chief rival, U.S. isolation from Europe *even in peacetime* was no longer conceivable. This dilemma forced the United States to prolong its presence in Western Europe, where it sought to enmesh those states in a variety of international organizations that would reward regional cooperation, suppress nationalism, and discourage self-serving economic and security policies.

David Turnley/Corbis/VCG via Getty Images

Bosnian refugees clog a rural highway in 1995 trying to avoid the devastation of the civil war between the former Yugoslav province and the Ser-bled government based in Belgrade. The conflict, reviving memories of World War II in Europe, required U.S. intervention because the European powers proved unable to quell Serbia's campaign of "ethnic cleansing" against Muslims.

This strategy of European "institutionalism" served the vital function of strengthening Western Europeans against the Soviet Union, but it also contained a logic that extended beyond the Cold War. Having Europeans cooperate rather than fight one another would mark a historic break for the region and a relief for the United States. It was not surprising, then, that Presidents George H. W. Bush and Bill Clinton adhered to this strategy throughout the 1990s amid rapidly changing circumstances in Europe. As this chapter describes, the Western European states edged closer toward a confederation by creating in 1992 the European Union (EU), which eventually adopted a common currency. Meanwhile, their neighbors in Eastern Europe were rebuilding their political institutions and economies largely along the lines of the EU states. They also were taking a keen interest in the North Atlantic Treaty Organization (NATO), which, far from dissolving along with the Soviet Union, expanded into Eastern Europe and became embroiled in "out-of-area" conflicts. All the while, the Russian government lurched from crisis to crisis, thereby keeping tensions high all across Europe.

First Bush and then Clinton tried to play a stabilizing role as Europe adjusted to the new strategic landscape. Both presidents knew that a democratic Europe that embraced free markets not only would benefit

Europeans, but also would make the United States more secure. Yet the United States could not prevent conflicts from breaking out in the Balkan Peninsula and within the former Soviet Union. Nor could it prevent its European allies from erecting new military structures and devising new strategies that would, if fully implemented, amount to a declaration of independence from Washington. "The EU is no longer merely a client of the United States and now often takes the lead on major issues in international gatherings," wrote an official in the European Parliament. "This can have advantages or disadvantages for U.S. policy, but whatever the outcome, it is a new fact of political life that Washington must now consider."[1]

Western Europe: From Community to Union

The integration of Western Europe into a more cohesive European Union brought those states closer and provided them with a forum in which to resolve their long-standing political differences. In 1992, the twelve members of the European Commission ratified the Maastricht Treaty, which created the European Union and moved the alliance beyond economic integration to include goals such as a unified legal code and a common foreign policy.[2] In 1995, three previously neutral countries—Austria, Finland, and Sweden—joined the European Union, bringing its full membership to fifteen.[3] With the EU growing in both numbers and responsibilities, a system of "dual sovereignty" emerged. Although member states retained ultimate political control over their territories and citizens, they transferred an ever-growing share of their authority to the EU's central government in Brussels. By 2000, it appeared that the historical vision of a "United States of Europe," long dismissed by skeptics, might actually come to pass.

---

[1] Christopher Piening, *Global Europe: The European Union in World Affairs* (Boulder, Colo.: Lynne Rienner, 1997), 102.

[2] The twelve countries were Belgium, Denmark, France, Germany, Greece, Ireland, Italy, Luxembourg, the Netherlands, Portugal, Spain, and the United Kingdom. The three new members admitted in 1995 included Austria, Finland, and Sweden.

[3] Another thirteen countries had formally applied for EU membership by 2000. Of these, ten were cleared for membership in 2004: Cyprus, the Czech Republic, Estonia, Hungary, Latvia, Lithuania, Malta, Poland, Slovakia, and Slovenia. Bulgaria, Croatia, and Romania were approved to join the EU between 2007 and 2013. Five other countries were being considered as of 2014: Albania, Iceland, Montenegro, Turkey, and the former Yugoslav Republic of Macedonia. Their membership would raise the total EU membership to thirty-three, about two-thirds of all the European countries.

Map 9-1 The European Union

| | European Union members |
| | Under review for future membership |

From the standpoint of Washington, Europe's gradual move toward confederation was both welcome and potentially troubling. As noted, American leaders had long encouraged regional integration as a means of defusing the bitter rivalries among the European powers. The Truman administration explicitly made regional cooperation a condition for Marshall Plan funding and military aid. But a revitalized Europe could very well seek to chart an independent course, even if it meant alienating the United States.

Changes in the European landscape also produced a changing of the political guard. The leaders of the new generation that took power in the 1990s sought to put the Cold War behind them and enter the new millennium with a clean slate. These leaders included Prime Minister Tony Blair of Britain, President Jacques Chirac of France, and Chancellor Gerhard Schröder of Germany. All three supported the continued push toward European integration, and they used their political advantages within the EU to pressure the smaller states. The leaders of the "big three" European governments had something else in common: they were appalled by the disabling conflict between Bill Clinton and the U.S. Congress, irritated by the resulting stalemate in U.S. foreign policy, and determined to pursue their own interests with or without the United States.

The greatest leap forward in European integration came in January 1999 with the introduction of a common currency, the euro.[4] Because a national currency represents one of the central pillars of sovereignty, it always has been closely guarded by political leaders, especially in Europe, where the nation-state system evolved during the seventeenth century. But the presence of many national currencies, all with different and wildly fluctuating values, became a nuisance after the Europeans created a single internal market. A common currency would be the most efficient way to do business (see Table 9-1). By 2014, eighteen EU governments had adopted the euro as their currency.

The euro, however, came at a hefty price: each government was forced to relinquish its fiscal and monetary authority and rein in public spending, reduce debts, and lower inflation. Welfare programs were scaled back and government subsidies reduced in all eleven participating countries. In the past, external pressures to undertake such reforms had incited charges of imperialism, and austerity measures often had sparked demonstrations or riots when spending cuts increased unemployment or reduced popular social services.

---

[4]Four EU members did not immediately adopt the common currency. The governments of the United Kingdom and Denmark chose not to participate, and Sweden and Greece initially did not meet the economic requirements for entry. (Greece has since met these requirements and adopted the euro.) For the eleven other member states of the EU, the euro became the basis of foreign exchange in 1999 and began circulation in January 2002.

Table 9-1 United States and European Union: A Comparison of Basic Indicators, 2000

	United States	European Union
Population (millions)	282	377
GDP (trillions of constant 2000 U.S. dollars)	$9.8	$7.9
Per capita GDP (constant 2000 U.S. dollars)	$34,599	$22,756
Military expenditure (billions of current U.S. dollars)	$302	$209

Source: World Bank, *World Development Indicators* (Washington, D.C.: World Bank, 2005).
Note: EU figures exclude trade among member states.

But European leaders and their constituencies willingly accepted these curbs on their autonomy in exchange for the promise of greater prosperity.

Internal harmony among the European economies did not mean their chronic trade disputes with the United States suddenly vanished. Quite the contrary, these disputes became even more contentious, only this time U.S. trade negotiators faced a united front instead of separate foreign ministries. In 1999, the growing strains between Washington and the EU led to a "banana war" in which the United States imposed 100 percent tariffs on many European goods in retaliation for the EU's refusal to import bananas from U.S.-based corporations. A second dispute over the sale of aircraft engines prompted U.S. officials to ban Europe's supersonic Concorde from landing in the United States. Mean while, European investors ignored the U.S.-led economic embargo against Cuba and other sanctions that targeted Cuban leader Fidel Castro's trading partners. Taken together, these problems made it clear that a united Europe whose population and economic output exceeded that of the United States could become a formidable rival in the intensifying competition for world markets.

The EU's pursuit of a "common foreign and security policy," mandated in the Maastricht Treaty, was even more ambitious than its adoption of a common currency. By pledging to pool their diplomat corps and military forces, EU members seemed prepared to surrender the last and most vital element of their national sovereignty. But large, familiar hurdles to an all-European foreign policy remained. The nationality of the armed forces would become irrelevant, but that of the military leadership would not. Which of the major powers would lead the all-European forces? What roles would the other EU members play in the command structure?[5] Furthermore, it was never clearly established how the Europeans would pay for such a military force or, more fundamentally, what the substance of a "common" foreign policy would actually be.

These ambiguities had had little effect so long as the United States ran things from Washington—and from NATO headquarters in Brussels. The alliance not only had spared Europeans a perilous decision over military leadership, but also had allowed them to skimp on military spending, thereby freeing up funds for the more generous social programs favored by European citizens. In the wake of the Cold War, however, a growing number of Europeans, particularly the French, associated NATO with American hegemony. Thus France moved forward on a joint defense force with Germany that would bring the common foreign policy to life. Its efforts, if successful, threatened to make the United States a victim of its own success. "Where the mark, the franc, the lira, and the guilder are headed, armies, fleets, and air squadrons will eventually follow," one scholar observed. "A Europe moving toward real economic integration may be a less reliable and less predictable partner for the United States—or perhaps not even a partner at all."[6]

Jump-Starting Democracy in Eastern Europe

The fate of the "transition" countries of Eastern Europe also was of great importance to the United States. Long viewed as a fulcrum in the power balance between East and West, Eastern Europe had twice been turned into a bloodbath by the Russian and German armies. The same nations then served as Soviet pawns in the Cold War, enduring decades of political repression and economic decay under communist rule. For all the major powers, then, the fate of the wide-ranging reforms undertaken in the early 1990s in Eastern Europe had implications that extended well beyond that region.

Because most Eastern European governments lacked historical experience with either democratic rule or market economics, they faced

---

[5] France and Germany had already sparked a political crisis by clashing at the last minute over the leadership of the European Central Bank. The German-backed candidate, Willem Duisenberg, was finally appointed in May 1998, but only after agreeing to "retire" halfway through his eight-year term and to be replaced by the French candidate.

[6] Ronald Steel, "Eurotrash," *New Republic* (June 1, 1998): 12.

enormous difficulties in instituting reforms. But the demise of the Cold War suggested that better times lay ahead. Francis Fukuyama's vision of the "end of history," out lined in Chapter 8, was therefore welcomed by most Eastern Europeans, whose histories had consisted largely of foreign conquest and domination.

The newly liberated Eastern European states quickly put into place the variety of institutional components required of democratic governments. They wrote and approved constitutions that provided for basic political and civil rights, and they established modern legal codes and court systems to ensure that the rule of law prevailed. They also created legislatures in which elected leaders from competing political parties could debate and enact the new laws. By and large, their efforts to build the structural foundations of democracy, mostly from scratch, were fruitful. But the success of these political reforms depended on the progress of the simultaneous economic reforms that sought to replace the centrally planned economies of the Soviet era with those based on private enterprise. This task proved quite difficult in many parts of Eastern Europe and threatened the region's move toward democratic rule.

The difficulties stemmed from several sources. First, the cost of rebuilding these economies was far greater than expected. Economic conditions after the Cold War were dismal throughout Eastern Europe. Decaying factories, crumbling roads, outdated utilities, and widespread environmental damage blighted the landscape. School systems had fallen into disrepair, course materials were out of date, and teachers were paid barely enough to survive. It soon became clear that educating and training the productive workforce required for long-term economic growth would take many years, possibly more than a generation.[7]

Second, many citizens of Eastern Europe were demoralized by the half-century of communist rule that had deprived them of the political power and prosperity enjoyed in the West. They had little experience in forming independent trade unions, rival political parties, and other democratic movements—and no experience at all in campaigning for elected positions of their own. As a result, they often were unprepared to manage the demands of political leadership that came with their freedom from Soviet rule. The widespread layoffs and cutbacks in social services that followed from the "structural adjustments" produced mass protests against

---

[7] These problems persisted despite a massive inflow of aid funds from the EU to Eastern Europe. See Karen E. Smith, *The Making of EU Foreign Policy: The Case of Eastern Europe* (New York: St. Martin's Press, 1999).

national leaders, many of whom had been exalted as saviors during Eastern Europe's rise against communism.

Third, further hampering the recovery, most Eastern European countries were not immediately attractive to large-scale foreign investment, which at the time was flowing primarily to the United States, Western Europe, and the newly industrialized countries of East Asia. Private investors and multinational corporations generally adopted a wait-and-see attitude toward the former communist countries. Only Poland, Hungary, and—to a lesser extent—the Czech Republic received large volumes of foreign investment. Thus it was not surprising that by 2000 each had emerged as a market economy that could compete with its counterparts in Western Europe. Poland, with by far the largest level of economic output in Eastern Europe, had introduced reforms quickly, through "shock therapy." After several sluggish years, its economy grew in the late 1990s at an annual rate of more than 5 percent, and inflation and unemployment rates fell steadily. In Hungary, more than $17 billion in foreign investments fueled a similar resurgence. It was no coincidence that these countries quickly rose to the top of the EU's list of candidates and were welcomed into NATO (described in the next section).

Elsewhere, what little private capital was invested was quickly withdrawn at the first sign of trouble. The smaller economies in Eastern Europe were especially vulnerable. Economic output in Bulgaria and Romania declined throughout the 1990s, forcing their leaders to rely on emergency aid from the International Monetary Fund to prevent economic collapse. Meanwhile, government corruption and organized crime undermined public confidence in reform efforts. Many became nostalgic for the communist regimes of the Cold War era, which at least assured them of jobs and a minimal level of income. Thus in 1994 the Bulgarian Socialist Party gained control of that nation's legislature. In Romania, the National Salvation Front, led by high-ranking members of the former Communist Party, became the most popular political party.

All of this was tied in to the fourth problem affecting reform—a problem that became evident long after the transitions had begun. Throughout Eastern Europe, the most powerful government officials often were former communists who had, at least rhetorically, rejected communism and embraced free markets. In practice, however, these former members of the communist *nomenklatura* exploited their status and connections to ensure for themselves a sizable share of the public enterprises that were placed in private hands. But once they obtained control, the former communist technocrats were no better able to stimulate productivity and economic growth than they had been during the Cold War. "Crony capitalism" prolonged the economic stagnation of many Eastern European economies and failed to improve living standards.

NATO's Search for a New Mission

Beyond the economic realm, the future of European military security remained uncertain after the Cold War. Of central concern was the status of NATO, which had accomplished its stated mission of protecting the Western European states from possible Soviet aggression. In view of this achievement, many felt the alliance should be disbanded. But to others, including Presidents Bush and Clinton, NATO remained useful in confronting potential new threats to its members on both sides of the Atlantic Ocean.

Confusion over NATO's future reflected widespread misunderstandings about its past. Contrary to official proclamations, containing the Soviet bloc was not the only purpose served by NATO during the Cold War (see Chapter 3). Lord Hastings Ismay, its first secretary general, aptly summarized its broader functions when he pointed out that NATO was needed "to keep the Americans in, the Russians out, and the Germans down." Only the second function was directly related to the Cold War; the first and third had deeper roots. These functions, combined with nagging doubts about Russia in the 1990s, propelled the alliance into a new and ambiguous future.

The military "umbrella" offered by the United States was critical to NATO's founding and eagerly welcomed by Western European leaders at the time. Not only did the U.S. presence in NATO fortify the front lines of the Cold War; it also stifled the chronic *internal* rivalries that had twice led to world war. Protected by the alliance, Western Europeans were able to focus their energies on economic recovery and political cooperation. In this sense, the United States provided "a sense of reassurance to the Europeans that they would not otherwise have and thereby helped make security relations, and also political and economic relations, within Western Europe more stable than they would otherwise be."[8]

Germany also figured prominently in the NATO equation. Through NATO, German leaders rejoined the Western European community

---

[8]Robert J. Art, "Why Western Europe Needs the United States and NATO," *Political Science Quarterly* (Spring 1998): 12.

without provoking new fears of expansionism. In so doing, German chancellors from Konrad Adenauer to Gerhard Schröder also sought to strengthen Germany's fragile democracy and ensure its success in a country with a dictatorial history. The alliance, in effect, adopted a policy of "double containment" of Germany and Russia.

But, like America's role as a regional caretaker, the need to keep Germany "down" was rarely mentioned publicly.

NATO, then, provided for the collective *defense* of Western Europe against foreign attack and for the region's collective *security* against its own self-destructive tendencies. Both roles, as it turned out, remained valid after the Cold War. Developments in Russia, described later in this chapter, were hardly reassuring to the other European states. Nor was Germany's emergence as the EU's economic powerhouse. NATO was thus seen as a guarantor against another German-Russian collision (like that before World War I) or further collusion (like that before World War II). The alliance also could soothe tensions between other members. For example, disputes between Greece and Turkey over Cyprus and other matters simmered during and after the Cold War. These and other points of contention required a continued and pervasive U.S. presence in Europe.

An immediate rationale for NATO's continued survival was found in the desire of former Soviet bloc states to become part of the "West." Thus the question quickly became not whether the alliance should disband, but whether it should *expand*. The timing for "enlargement" (the term favored by military planners) seemed right because of the new power vacuum in Eastern Europe created by the abolition of the Warsaw Pact. Unless NATO stepped in to fill this vacuum, countries such as Poland and Hungary would have to build independent military forces. They also might be tempted to create another regional bloc. Neither scenario was appealing to NATO members, or to Eastern Europeans themselves who saw NATO as a stepping-stone to EU membership.

The decision to expand NATO beyond its sixteen members was complicated by Russia, whose leaders had always feared encirclement by hostile neighbors. Thus any move to add the Eastern European states to NATO threatened to inflame Russian nationalism and to isolate Russian moderates. This development would, in turn, introduce pressures for Russia to rearm and divert resources badly needed to ensure the success of its political and economic reforms. Clinton and other NATO leaders arrived at a compromise solution in October 1993. Under the rubric of a "Partnership for Peace," the former War-saw Pact members and Soviet republics were invited to become junior partners of NATO. In this capacity, they would participate in some NATO deliberations and training exercises. But they would not receive the security guarantees of full members. If the "partnerships" proved successful, these auxiliary states would be considered for full membership.[9]

Russian president Boris Yeltsin first rejected the partnership concept, but he soon recognized the futility of his position. He then insisted, also in vain, that Russia receive preferential treatment because of its military strength and permanent membership in the UN Security Council. Yeltsin further protested NATO's plans to invite Poland, Hungary, and the Czech Republic to join the alliance as its first new full members. Exploiting the tensions within NATO, the Russian president warned all Europeans about subjecting themselves to continued U.S. military control. He declared that a "cold peace" was setting in between Moscow and Washington and suggested that it would thaw only after suspension of the proposed eastward expansion of NATO.

The United States and its NATO allies dismissed Yeltsin's thinly veiled threats, which were attributed to his need to appease nationalists at a time when his hold on power was tenuous. They moved forward on their plan to add the three Eastern European countries to NATO membership by 1999, the alliance's fiftieth anniversary, and to leave the door open for other new members. Faced with the inevitable, Yeltsin again softened his stance. Instead of blocking NATO expansion, he successfully negotiated a separate treaty that would prevent the placement of foreign troops or nuclear weapons in Eastern Europe. The Russia-NATO Founding Act of 1997 called for military cooperation rather than competition between the former Cold War adversaries. Under the agreement, Russia would be given a "voice, but not a veto" over NATO policy.

Yeltsin's surrender on NATO expansion revealed the depths to which his country had fallen. One need only consider how Washington would have reacted if the Soviet Union had won the Cold War and then invited Mexico and other Latin American countries to join the Warsaw Pact. In reality, NATO's offer not to place nuclear weapons in the Eastern European states was hollow, because the offer could be quickly withdrawn in a crisis. Yet Russia still accepted the face-saving agreement and reaped the rewards: billions of dollars in continued economic aid from the West.

---

[9] Twenty-seven countries had agreed to join the partnership by 2003: Albania, Armenia, Austria, Azerbaijan, Belarus, Bulgaria, Croatia, Estonia, Finland, Georgia, Ireland, Kazakhstan, Kyrgyzstan (the Kyrgyz Republic), Latvia, Lithuania, (the former Yugoslav Republic of) Macedonia, Moldova, Romania, Russia, Slovakia, Slovenia, Sweden, Switzerland, Tajikistan, Turkmenistan, Ukraine, and Uzbekistan. By 2014, nine of these countries had joined NATO.

Having attained Russia's compliance, NATO welcomed Poland, Hungary, and the Czech Republic into its fold in March 1999. The expansion was quickly approved by all the European states and Canada. In the United States, even the Senate, which had opposed Clinton on nearly every foreign policy issue, approved the expansion by a vote of 80–19. Secretary of State Madeleine Albright declared that Europe had taken a giant step toward becoming "whole and free."

But what was to be the mission of the enlarged NATO? Its new "Strategic Concept" omitted the previous objective—to preserve a "strategic balance in Europe"—yet it failed to outline a coherent future role. If, as the document proclaimed, the meaning of regional security would be broadened beyond military concerns, how would the alliance solve the vast array of political and social problems it would then confront? And how exactly would the alliance conduct a global crackdown against weapons of mass destruction, as Albright had proposed? No clear answers were forthcoming for the uncomfortable reason just noted: the real driving forces behind NATO's endurance—restraining Russia and Germany while preserving a dominant U.S. military presence in Europe—were too politically sensitive to acknowledge openly.

Yet another question raised during the expansion debate—whether NATO would intervene in conflicts beyond the borders of its member states—was answered by NATO jet fighters. At the very time of the anniversary celebration, they were bombing Yugoslavia in southeastern Europe. This was the second round of NATO assaults on the former communist country, which had become embroiled in a brutal civil war. The protracted conflict in the Balkan Peninsula, long known as the "tinderbox of Europe," put NATO and its hazy new mission to the ultimate test. By 2014, twenty-eight countries had joined NATO, with many others remaining candidates for membership. Of these, Ukraine sought immediate membership after Russia's government seized control of its territory in Crimea and supported efforts by Ukrainian separatists to become part of "Mother Russia" (see Chapter 14).

"Ethnic Cleansing" in the Balkans

The violent disintegration of Yugoslavia in the 1990s served as a frightening example of how the removal of Cold War restraints could unleash nationalistic rivalries. Yugoslavia, created in the aftermath of World War I, was a diverse federation of ethnic and religious groups—mainly Serbs (Eastern Orthodox), Slovenes and Croats (Catholic), and Bosnians and

Albanians (Muslim). During the Cold War, the country was held together under Marshal Josip Broz Tito, who had relied on Marxist ideology and a monopoly of political power to suppress any divisions. But Tito's make-shift arrangements began crumbling soon after his death in 1980. They collapsed altogether in 1989 along with the communist regimes in other Eastern European states. Ancient religious hatreds quickly returned to the surface, and Yugoslavia's descent into a spiral of violence soon followed.[10]

The dominant Serbs, who still controlled the capital of Belgrade and the country's formidable armed forces, opposed Yugoslavia's disintegration and sought instead to create a Greater Serbia that would include territories occupied primarily by non-Serbs. After the provinces of Slovenia and Croatia declared independence in 1991 and were immediately recognized by the European Community, the Yugoslav army intervened in both territories. Serbian troops inflicted great damage but were unable to prevent the secession of the two new states, both of which were promptly admitted to the United Nations. The Serbs then directed their military campaign to the heart of Bosnia and Herzegovina (referred to as Bosnia here), the most multinational of the Yugoslav provinces, which also had declared its independence from Belgrade. There, the Bosnian Serbs launched a self-described campaign of "ethnic cleansing" that consisted of driving Muslims from their communities in order to expand Serbian territory. Masked paramilitary forces burned and looted villages, tortured and starved non-Serbs in concentration camps, raped Islamic women, and besieged the Bosnian capital, Sarajevo, for three years, depriving its citizens of food, water, and electricity.

These actions appalled outside observers and drew widespread condemnation. Many Americans, including presidential candidate Bill Clinton, called in 1992 for military intervention. Horrified onlookers charged that the systematic expulsion of Muslims constituted genocide, which was explicitly prohibited by the UN Charter, and they called on all countries to intervene and prevent the mass slaughter, which was based on ethnic or religious differences. But charges of widespread war crimes went both ways, because Croat and Muslim forces also committed atrocities against the Serbs—a familiar pattern in the region's history.

Opponents of intervention argued that this was a civil war, not one between countries, despite the establishment of new states recognized by

---

[10]For an account by the former U.S. ambassador to Yugoslavia, see Warren Zimmerman, *Origins of a Catastrophe: Yugoslavia and Its Destroyers—America's Last Ambassador Tells What Happened and Why* (New York: Times Books, 1996). For another historical perspective, see Robert D. Kaplan, *Balkan Ghosts: A Journey through History* (New York: Vintage Books, 1993).

the European Community and United Nations. The Pentagon asserted that any military intervention to separate the combatants and restore order would entail a massive commitment of between two hundred thousand and four hundred thousand troops, heavy fighting, and extensive casualties. Moreover, the foreign troops probably would have to remain in the treacherous mountain territory for many years, and no coherent "exit strategy" was evident. Most important, the conflict appeared to be contained within the Balkan Peninsula, posing little threat to the great powers, especially the United States. The Bush administration generally adopted this cautious view and pursued a negotiated outcome. Likewise, once elected, Clinton soon retracted his earlier calls for outside intervention and pressed for a diplomatic solution, preferably mediated by the newly reorganized European Union. Later, he would be gravely disappointed when the EU member states, preoccupied with regional integration and plagued by conflicting allegiances in the Balkans, failed to take a united stand.

An international arms embargo imposed on Yugoslavia in the early days of the conflict favored the Serbs, because the Yugoslav army—well equipped from its years of association with a communist dictatorship—supplied the Bosnian Serbs with weapons from its arsenal. The Muslims, by contrast, could not acquire sufficient arms to protect themselves. Nevertheless, European leaders opposed lifting the embargo, arguing it would only broaden the violence and endanger their own peacekeeping forces, which were protecting so-called safe havens in the remaining Muslimheld areas. The arms embargo continued into 1995, along with an economic boycott against the Serbian regime in Belgrade.

When Clinton occasionally advanced proposals for multilateral military action and for lifting the arms embargo against Bosnia, he was opposed by most Western European governments and many influential members of the United Nations, including Russia, a traditional ally of the Slavic Serbs. Most experts in the Defense Department also opposed a military response, because, in their view, air strikes would have little effect without the massive deployment of U.S. ground forces. Within Congress and among the general public, domestic issues were of greater concern than the seemingly intractable problems in the Balkans. In short, many Americans asked the same question: if the Europeans did not feel sufficiently threatened by events in Bosnia to intervene, why should the United States?

For all these reasons, Clinton was unwilling to assert himself and demand action as Bush had done in Kuwait. Instead, he wavered, sometimes threatening to intervene with air power and to lift the arms embargo, at other times retracting these positions, citing allied reluctance as his reason for inaction. Clinton knew that if the United States intervened unilaterally, the war would soon become "America's war." Like President Lyndon Johnson in Vietnam, he might become stuck in military quicksand, jeopardizing his domestic priorities, stimulating a peace movement, and endangering his chances for reelection in 1996.

Map 9-2 The Former Yugoslavia

*The last remaining provinces of the former Yugoslavia, Serbia and Montenegro, became separate nation-states following Montenegro's declaration of independence in June 2006.

Meanwhile, the United Nations pressed forward with a plan to partition Bosnia along ethnic lines, but the Serbs continued shelling Muslim enclaves that the UN had promised to protect. UN peacekeepers provided the besieged Muslims with medicine and food, but only the threat of air strikes against Serbian positions in the mountains surrounding Sarajevo temporarily brought relief to that city and other safe havens. Serbian defiance resumed, however, when the few air strikes authorized by the UN and undertaken by NATO revealed that the foreign powers did not have the will to stop the Serbian aggression. To deter future air attacks, the Serbs seized hundreds of UN peacekeepers and placed them around bombing targets as human shields. The Serbs thus accomplished their goal of displacing the Muslims from their homes throughout Bosnia and succeeded in humiliating the UN by demonstrating that its peacekeeping forces never had a peace to keep. In a final turn of the screw, the Serbs overran the Muslim safe havens of Srebrenica and Žepa in July 1995. While UN peacekeepers watched helplessly—under orders to use force only in self-defense—the Serbs separated Muslim families and herded thousands of men and boys into concentration camps, where they were later executed and buried in mass graves.

The Dayton Accords

Suddenly in late 1995, a shift in the regional balance of power transformed this situation. The Croatian army, showing surprising strength, launched a successful ground attack against the Serbs, depriving them of many of their earlier territorial gains. Muslim forces joined the counteroffensive, which produced a new flood of refugees, this time Serbs fleeing the Croats and Muslims. Recognizing the shifting power balance and outraged by the most recent Serbian atrocities, NATO launched a sustained bombing campaign against Serbian munitions dumps, bridges, and air defenses that further weakened the Serbs. By this time, the multilateral economic sanctions against Belgrade had begun taking their toll and forced Serbian president Slobodan Milosevic to assert his authority over the Bosnian Serbs.

In this improved climate, American leaders seized their opportunity to negotiate a deal among the Balkan rivals. Despite the violence and the deepening mutual hatreds, each of the factions had strong reasons to end the fighting: for the Serbs, to consolidate the Bosnian Serb gains before they were lost or reversed and to end the economic sanctions; for the Croats, to secure their independent state and the safety of their nationals in other areas; and for the Muslims, to relieve the suffering of their people and to

Impact and Influence: Madeleine Albright

Scott J. Ferrell/Congressional Quarterly/Getty Images

Among the most forceful proponents of an activist U.S. world role after the Cold War was Secretary of State Madeleine Albright, the first woman to hold the post and the highest-ranking woman in the U.S. government. As the world's "indispensable nation," she argued, the United States was duty bound to promote democratic freedoms far from its borders, even through the use of military force.

Albright's personal history profoundly shaped her worldview. Her family fled Czechoslovakia in 1939 after Adolf Hitler's takeover of the country, and three of her Jewish grandparents died in German concentration camps. Upon Hitler's defeat, Albright's family returned home, but soon became refugees again when the Soviet Union seized control of the government in a 1948 communist coup. The daughter of a Czech diplomat, Albright served during Clinton's first term as U.S. ambassador to the United Nations. Her calls for U.S. participation in several UN peacekeeping missions resulted in frequent clashes with Republican leaders in Congress. Yet she remained well respected on Capitol Hill and was easily confirmed as secretary of state in 1997.

create a Bosnian state with strong Muslim representation. Forced to negotiate face-to-face at a U.S.

Air Force base in Dayton, Ohio, leaders of the three factions signed a complex agreement in November 1995 that led to a cease-fire in 1996. Under the Dayton Accords, nearly sixty thousand NATO troops were deployed to the region as part of Operation Joint Endeavor. Once in place, they separated the armed factions, protected civilian populations, and delivered economic assistance to the warravaged Bosnian communities. Bosnian leaders then created a new government led by a three-member presidency, one from each ethnic group, to be chosen by the Bosnian people in national elections.

Shortly after his reelection in November 1996, Clinton extended the NATO mission in Bosnia through June 1998, a move that surprised no one and was followed by longer extensions of the foreign presence. Clinton argued that the troops were still needed to buy time for the new civilian-led government to take full control. Thus NATO troops, accompanied by Russian peacekeepers, would continue to separate and disarm the combatants in three zones supervised by the United States, Britain, and France, respectively. The United States and Western European governments formally put the Bosnians on notice: continue the peace process or face new economic sanctions and the with-drawal of the peacekeeping force.

The Bosnian war revealed critical shortcomings in the system of collective security that was supposed to guarantee peace in the post–Cold War era. The United Nations was incapable of harnessing a united response to aggression, much less ending and punishing "ethnic cleansing." This failure of the UN reflected the failure of the Western great powers, which, until forced into action, were deeply divided by the crisis. The European Union, which at the same time was trying to create a "common foreign and security policy," proved especially impotent. Because of all these shortcomings, it was doubtful that the externally imposed peace would provide a basis for long-term reconciliation.

The Kosovo Showdown

Tragically, the Balkan wars did not end in Bosnia. As many feared, Milosevic simply redirected his military machine against another Yugoslav province, Kosovo. The province held great symbolic value to Belgrade despite its chronic poverty and small Serbian population, for it was there that Serbian armies had made their last stand against the Ottoman Turks in the 1389 Battle of Kosovo. After the Serbian defeat, most Kosovars converted to Islam. The remaining Serbs adhered to Christianity and submitted to five centuries of repressive rule by the Ottoman Empire, all the while plotting their revenge. They received their first chance when Kosovo was folded into the new federation of Yugoslavia after World War I. The Serb-dominated government immediately sought to settle the score, ejecting the majority population of ethnic Albanians from Kosovo and repopulating their villages with Serbs. But this early round of ethnic cleansing was cut short by the Second World War, as the region again became a battleground for the great powers.

Tito allowed the conflict in Kosovo to smolder during the early stages of the Cold War and even permitted the region's autonomy under the new Yugoslav constitution of 1974. But Milosevic had other ideas once he assumed power fifteen years later. He quickly rescinded the constitution, nullified the rights of Kosovar Albanians, and installed Serbs in key provincial offices. Yet Serbs, because of their mass exodus from Kosovo over a period of centuries, made up only about 10 percent of the province's population; ethnic Albanians made up the other 90 percent. In this respect, the crackdown that began in 1989 was doomed from the start.

The Kosovars responded by declaring independence and organizing a defense force that became known as the Kosovo Liberation Army (KLA). Their appeals for statehood, however, were drowned out—first by the jubilation that attended the collapse of the Soviet Union, and then by the eruption of violence elsewhere in Yugoslavia.

For Milosevic, revenge in Kosovo was the only way to overcome his humiliating defeats in Slovenia, Croatia, and Bosnia. His paramilitary troops forced Albanian families from their homes, seized their possessions, and then set entire villages on fire. The KLA responded by conducting raids against the small population of Serbs, primarily police and government officials. In February 1999, attempting to prevent a full-scale war, the United States and several European powers brought the rival factions together in Rambouillet, France. The deal proposed by the mediators—the retreat of Serbian forces from Kosovo, the introduction of a NATO-led peacekeeping force, and renewed autonomy (but not independence) for Kosovo—appealed to neither the Serbs nor the Kosovars. Under intense pressure from U.S. and European leaders, the Kosovar delegation agreed to the deal anyway, but only because Milosevic's rejection of the accords was a foregone conclusion.

With the Rambouillet Accords in tatters, NATO faced little choice but to act on its threats to respond with military force. Withholding military intervention would have revealed the threats as empty. Furthermore, in doing nothing NATO ran the risk of undermining the alliance at the very time it was seeking new life—and new members. The threatened NATO bombardment, code-named Operation Allied Force, began in late March. President Clinton, under pressure from domestic critics and many anxious European leaders, publicly ruled out a ground offensive.[11] In gaining support for the intervention by minimizing the risk of NATO casualties, however, Clinton and his NATO counterparts provided cover for Milosevic to create the very cataclysm NATO sought to avoid: widespread destruction in Kosovo and the displacement of more than one million citizens.

The events were ghastly, but familiar. Thousands of Muslim men were rounded up, tortured, and murdered. Serbian troops raped Muslim women, often in front of their children. Homes and businesses were pillaged and burned. Entire cities such as Peć and Djakovica, and even Kosovo's capital, Pristina, were reduced to ashes. Those who escaped the onslaught were

---

[11] The German government, in particular, insisted that ground forces be avoided. The mere prospect of introducing ground troops to Kosovo was certain to incite a backlash against Chancellor Gerhard Schröder's new administration.

stripped of their identification papers and sent wandering into the mine-filled mountain passes out of Kosovo. Many elderly refugees fell to their deaths along the way, their bodies compounding the horror of the survivors. Other refugees were separated from their families, stuffed into locked trains, and shuttled to refugee camps in Albania and Macedonia that could not adequately feed or house them, or provide them with medical care. Although seemingly random and spontaneous, and contrary to Serbian claims that the exodus was caused by NATO bombing, the campaign of terror had been "meticulously organized and aimed, from the outset, at expelling huge numbers of people."[12]

Clinton soon confronted the consequences of NATO's decision to adopt a bombing campaign based on gradual escalation rather than an immediate and overwhelming destructive force that would have inflicted real pain on the civilian population. Based on the successful experience in Bosnia, the president had wrongly assumed that a modest show of NATO muscle—lasting just two or three days—would again drive Milosevic to the bargaining table. But this time the pinprick attacks on Serbian artillery and command centers only accelerated the gutting of Kosovo. Clinton therefore had only one option: to intensify the bombing campaign by directing NATO air strikes against the heart of Serbia. Early on, however, a series of targeting errors by NATO bombers, including the destruction of passenger trains and of the Chinese embassy in downtown Belgrade, had left scores of civilians dead and prompted widespread condemnation. Such mistakes were to be expected, however, because pilots were prevented from flying below fifteen thousand feet, within the reach of Serbian antiaircraft missiles. Meanwhile, by this point the NATO barrage and its commitment to a final victory were irreversible.

After lengthy internal negotiations, the NATO states finally acknowledged in May that ground forces might be required to support the air campaign. The alliance also assented to a renewed ground campaign by KLA forces that would flush Serbian forces from their concealed positions in Kosovo and expose them to a crippling round of NATO attacks. As in Bosnia, where aerial attacks had been bolstered by the Croat-Muslim counteroffensive, the military campaign in Kosovo finally produced results. Repeated attacks on Belgrade's electrical grid, which literally "turned off the lights" in the Yugoslav capital, were especially helpful in demonstrating NATO's heightened resolve. Faced with another defeat and under pressure by Russian officials to end the war, Milosevic agreed in June to withdraw

---

[12] John Kifner, "How Serb Forces Purged One Million Albanians," *New York Times* (May 29, 1999), 1A.

the Serbian forces and allow the displaced Kosovars to return to the remnants of their communities.

This latest round of the Balkan ordeal achieved the general objectives of NATO. Serbia's ten-year campaign of terror and intimidation was finally brought to an end, and fears of a widened conflict beyond Yugoslavia were dispelled. In gaining Milosevic's final surrender, Western leaders had delivered their message that ethnic cleansing in Europe was a thing of the past. In defeating Serbia without a single NATO casualty, Clinton and his European counterparts had prevented their domestic opponents from mobilizing against the war, challenging their leadership, and threatening the future of the alliance.

In other respects, the NATO victory was partial and highly qualified. Kosovo was "liberated," but it would remain—at least in name—a part of Yugoslavia. Milosevic and his top military aides still held the reins of power, even after being indicted by a UN court for crimes against humanity. As for the European governments, the Kosovo intervention clearly showed them how far they had to go to attain any semblance of a common foreign policy. In tactical terms, it was significant that U.S. aircraft had carried out most of the estimated six thousand bombing missions, and that nearly every target had been identified by U.S. intelligence sources. The European states, by contrast, had had little to offer in the way of skilled manpower and weapons systems. "The Kosovo war was mainly an experience of Europe's own insufficiency and weakness," German foreign minister Joschka Fischer observed. "We as Europeans never could have coped with the Balkan wars that were caused by Milosevic without the help of the United States. The sad truth is that Kosovo showed Europe is still not able to solve its own problems."[13]

U.S.-Russian Relations under Stress

One of the most bizarre episodes of the war in Kosovo occurred after the fighting had ended and the peace treaty had been signed. Before dawn on June 12, 1999, an armored column of Russian troops entered the smoldering ruins of Pristina, the capital city. The city's remaining Serbs cheered the soldiers as they rolled toward the airport, where they took up their position as an occupying force.

---

[13] Quoted in Ivo H. Daalder and Michael E. O'Hanlon, "Unlearning the Lessons of Kosovo," *Foreign Policy* (Fall 1999): 137.

But there was a problem: the Russians were not supposed to be in Pristina; they were supposed to be at their peacekeeping posts in Bosnia. Their surprise arrival several hours ahead of the NATO contingent—including British, French, Italian, and U.S. troops—stole the spotlight from the very forces whose military campaign had brought about Milosevic's surrender of Kosovo. Russian leaders, who considered the Slavic people of Serbia to be allies, had consistently *opposed* the bombing campaign and promised to veto any UN effort to prevent the ethnic cleansing of Kosovar Albanians. The Russian "liberation" of Pristina was, therefore, a farce. But it offered the Russian troops and their leaders in Moscow a brief moment of glory, along with a barely concealed sense of satisfaction that they had beaten the NATO powers to their prize.

This misplaced show of force illustrated just how decrepit Russia had become during its torturous period of transition after the Cold War. Eight years of political and economic crises had produced almost daily political struggles in Moscow, a declining economic output, and a string of military challenges inside and beyond Russia's borders. Were it not for a steady supply of economic aid from Western countries, Boris Yeltsin's faltering regime—and his democratic reforms—would likely have collapsed long before the Kosovo conflict and its surreal aftermath. Yet Yeltsin somehow had managed to remain in power until after the Balkan wars, and his country retained the one source of power that could not be denied: a massive nuclear stockpile. As a result, Russia continued to preoccupy American leaders into the new millennium.

Internal Challenges to Reform

The collapse of communist rule exposed deep fault lines within the former Soviet Union. Just as the breakup of the Ottoman and Austro-Hungarian Empires contributed to the onset of World War I, and just as the dismantling of the European colonial empires after 1945 set off violence between and within many new states, new possibilities for conflict appeared after the Soviet Union fractured into fifteen republics, all claiming sovereignty. The Baltic states of Estonia, Latvia, and Lithuania reclaimed their pre–World War II independence. Because the Russians had long controlled both the czarist and communist states, ethnic Russians were left scattered throughout the Commonwealth of Independent States (CIS), the loose-knit group of twelve non-Baltic republics formed after the fall of the Soviet Union. In addition to the Russians, dozens of other ethnic groups inhabited its vast frontiers.

This intermingling of ethnic groups inflamed the hatreds between the Russians and the peoples they had long dominated, particularly Muslims living in the southern tier of CIS states. In Russia, the revival of ethnic tensions gave xenophobic nationalists and former communists bent on destroying the liberal state and market economy the reformers were trying to create a strong emotional issue with which to bring down Yeltsin's centrist regime. Moldova and Georgia (a non-CIS state) immediately faced secessionist movements. Ukraine was internally divided between its own ethnic group and a sizable Russian population. Belarus, Turkmenistan, and Uzbekistan came under dictatorial rule. Tajikistan was engulfed in civil war. And Armenia and Azerbaijan fought a costly war over an enclave—Nagorno-Karabakh—each claiming it as a rightful possession.

But despite all of these conflicts, Russia remained a potentially formidable military power with the ability to destroy the fragile political arrangements that were emerging in the 1990s. The Russian government continued to command an army of more than one million soldiers, two hundred thousand of whom remained outside its borders within the CIS. Yeltsin instituted ambitious political and economic reforms, but they proved difficult to impose on a society that had never been exposed to democracy or the free market. Prominent communists, elected under the old Soviet constitution, still dominated the legisla-ture and state bureaucracy, and they blocked the Russian president's reform efforts. Also opposed to Yeltsin's efforts were Russian nationalists, who shared the communists' resentment at the loss of empire and status, and a powerful "mafia" that exploited the vast black market in Russia's largest cities.

Boris Yeltsin was caught in the middle of a political cyclone.[14] In September 1993, the Russian president dissolved the Russian parliament, whose members were elected under the Soviet system and opposed many of his political and economic reforms. The dissidents then called for armed insurrection against Yeltsin and barricaded themselves within the "White House," as the building that housed the parliament was known. Yeltsin, faced with growing unrest on the streets of Moscow, responded by declaring a state of emergency and ordering Russian troops to shell the White House, which had served as a symbol of democracy and resistance to the communist regime prior to the collapse of the Soviet Union. More than one

---

[14] On the debilitating effect of Russia's internal politics, see Lilia Shevtsova, *Yeltsin's Russia: Myths and Reality* (Washington, D.C.: Carnegie Endowment for International Peace, 1999). Also see Dimitri K. Simes, *After the Collapse: Russia Seeks Its Place as a Great Power* (New York: Simon and Schuster, 1999).

hundred people were killed in the assault, and the leading political opponents were arrested. Yeltsin then quickly introduced a new constitution that greatly enhanced his powers and called for elections to a new bicameral federal assembly. These actions, he argued, were necessary to ensure the success of Russia's experiment with democracy.

The elections in December, however, only made matters worse. Extremists from both the right and the left dominated the new federal assembly. The most outspoken nationalist, Vladimir Zhirinovsky, pledged to restore the old Russian empire, even suggesting he would gain the return of Alaska. As conditions worsened across the country, many Russians welcomed his appeals and longed openly for the more "orderly" system under Lenin, Stalin, and Brezhnev.

In the United States and Western Europe, questions were raised about the continuing flow of Western aid to Russia. Should the new Russia be left to wallow in its economic misery, perhaps to emerge some day as a resentful state—like Germany after World War I? Or should Russia's former adversaries furnish the support Russia needed to grow economically and become politically stable—in much the same way the United States helped Germany after World War II? The Western powers adopted the latter course and agreed that Russia should receive economic assistance, but only so long as the money was used effectively. They demanded that Yeltsin's political reforms move forward and that Russian leaders hold inflation in check and stop subsidizing inefficient or Mafia-controlled industries. Even though they were faced with their own economic problems, Western leaders, led by the German government, promised Russia more than $30 billion in aid. Meanwhile, the International Monetary Fund approved an additional $10 billion in low-interest loans.

Despite Yeltsin's reelection in 1995, the Russian president could not prevent his nation's continued slide into disarray. Economic output finally increased by 1997, but then it plunged again in 1998 amid a collapse of the ruble, renewed inflation, and Russia's default on its foreign debt. Much of the Russian economy had been reduced to barter transactions. Tax collection was sporadic and selective, and government regulators routinely supplemented their meager incomes by demanding bribes. The "crony capitalism" that was sweeping across Eastern Europe became an art form in Russia, where former communists gobbled up huge public industries such as the Gazprom energy consortium and kept the profits for themselves. Meanwhile, Yeltsin's behavior became ever more erratic as he battled not only his domestic enemies but also a series of health problems that left him frail and often incapacitated.

Unrest in the "Near Abroad"

Yeltsin's problems were further aggravated by turmoil in the "near abroad" region of central Asia, home to the largely Islamic states of the CIS whose people had struggled against Russian domination ever since the Cossacks first entered the Caucasus Mountains in the sixteenth century. The sparse and impoverished Muslim population had succumbed to the brute strength of czarist Russia, and during the Cold War it had suffered even worse repression as a captive member of the Soviet Union. Because of this history, it is no wonder that the liberated republics of central Asia welcomed the collapse of the Soviet Union and seized their opportunity to be finally free of Moscow's control.

Moscow worried that other Islamic powers in the region, including Iran and Turkey, would exploit the vacuum created by the Soviet Union's demise and attempt to impose their own hegemonic designs on the region. All of central Asia seemed up for grabs in the 1990s as militant Islamic groups seized control of Afghanistan and civil wars raged in neighboring CIS republics. In the meantime, the United States and European powers quietly pursued their own interests in the rich oil fields of the Caspian Sea and sought to construct pipelines out of the area that would not be subject to Russian control.

The threat of Islamic movements within Russia itself quickly became real in the territory of Chechnya, which had long struggled against Moscow's hegemony.[15] After Chechen leaders declared "our independence is forever" in 1994, Yeltsin sent Russian troops to the Chechen capital, Grozny, and the Russian air force bombed residential neighborhoods. But his poorly organized and underequipped troops faltered against the more determined Chechens, who drew support from neighboring Islamic states and continued to press their case for independence into the late 1990s.

Such independence would set a dangerous precedent for other dissatisfied ethnic groups. Yet nothing the Russian troops did was sufficient to overcome the Chechen fighters, whose defiance in the face of a stronger enemy was reminiscent of the Afghan *mujahidin*. The Chechens stood firm, held elections in January 1997, and then issued an even more explicit declaration of independence. Humiliated, Yeltsin unleashed another attack in 1999. The military campaign served as the only rallying point for the Russian people, who were otherwise demoralized and destitute after years of stalled economic reforms.

---

[15] See Anatol Lieven, *Chechnya: Tombstone of Russian Power* (New Haven, Conn.: Yale University Press, 1998).

The United States clung to Yeltsin throughout this ordeal, viewing the Russian leader as the best and perhaps only hope for the country's peaceful reform. Although Clinton and Yeltsin bickered over issues such as NATO expansion and Yugoslavia, they agreed on the basic designs of the new Russia. And they knew that Russia would need continued infusions of aid—accompanied by exceptional patience—from the West in order to prevent a catastrophe. From the standpoint of U.S. leaders, only Yeltsin could keep bilateral arms control talks from coming apart and prevent Russia's nuclear technology from being sold to the highest bidders. The latter was especially important to the United States. It had spent nearly $3 billion between 1992 and 1999 to "denuclearize" Belarus, Kazakhstan, and Ukraine and to remove other weapons of mass destruction from across the former Soviet Union. But more work was needed to prevent the sale of nuclear technology, which had become an attractive prospect to the cash-starved economies of the region. Clinton was therefore restrained in criticizing Yeltsin. After first condemning the crackdown in Chechnya, Clinton defended the Russian leader's sovereign right to keep the province and only asked that Yeltsin avoid excessive force.

Clinton's hands-off stance could not disguise Russia's military humiliation or the futility of its effort to defeat the Chechen nationalists. Facing mounting domestic problems and seizing his chance to shape his own succession, Yeltsin abruptly resigned on the last day of 1999 and transferred power to his latest prime minister, Vladimir Putin. The former KGB officer had become a hero for leading the most recent crackdown in Chechnya, despite the mission's tactical failures that were not reported in the Russian press. Putin also had just consolidated his political power in parliamentary elections, giving him a distinct advantage in the March 2000 presidential elections, which he won easily after pledging to revive Russia's economy at home and in world markets, root out corruption, and strengthen the military forces.

While such a brazen power play would have been widely condemned in the United States, Yeltsin's timely resignation received little fanfare within or outside Russia. The mere fact that power had been transferred peacefully was considered a major achievement—and a source of relief. Nevertheless, the prospects for Russia in the post–Yeltsin era were highly uncertain. The aging Russian leader had kept his tenuous hold on power only by resorting to many of the same autocratic measures that had sustained his predecessors. But none of this would work for Russia in the future, under Putin or any other Russian leader, because, as one historian aptly noted, at the end of the twentieth century international power rests not on the extent of territory a state controls but on its level of economic and technological developments. Politically, economically, and morally the age of territorial empires is over: crossing frontiers with armies is no longer a permissible road to national aggrandizement. . . . Thus Russia, no matter how organized politically, must first become rich if she wishes again to be powerful; and getting rich, with the handicap of a Soviet legacy, will take no small length of time.[16]

Faced with this stubborn reality, the United States remained patient with Russia into the twenty-first century. It was simply too large, too well stocked with nuclear weapons, and too politically volatile to be ignored. Put more positively, a democratic Russia with a vibrant economy would be a force for global stability. For different reasons, U.S. leaders also had no choice but to maintain their close contacts with the Eastern European governments, which still claimed allegiance to the democratic values long espoused by the United States even as their economic reforms came under fire. America's vision of democratic governance and market economics had finally been given its chance on the dividing line between East and West. This was no time for the United States to retreat into its hemispheric shell.

---

[16] Martin Malia, *Russia under Western Eyes: From the Bronze Horseman to the Lenin Mausoleum* (Cambridge, Mass.: Belknap Press, 1999), 417.

America under Fire

The "unipolar moment" proclaimed at the Cold War's end was not a moment at all. If anything, the global primacy of the United States *increased* during the decade that followed the Soviet Union's collapse. The U.S. economy grew steadily in the 1990s, fueled by greater worker productivity, soaring foreign investment, and an end (temporarily) to federal budget deficits. Wall Street enjoyed a decade-long bull market, while American firms enjoyed the largest market shares of the computer industry and other high-technology sectors. The United States also extended its lead in military power, spending more on defense in 1997 than the next six countries combined.[1] American military supremacy was especially pronounced in the area of weapons technology, which allowed the nation to enhance the firepower and precision of its vast arsenal while reducing the size of its armed forces. In addition, the influence of America's democratic values and the cultural impact of its civil society demonstrated its enduring "soft power."

Global developments accentuated these advantages. Russia's government floundered in the 1990s amid economic stagnation, political corruption, and the endless civil war in Chechnya. The European Union (EU) suffered through the growing pains of monetary union and the launch of a common currency, the euro. Despite the EU's call for a "common foreign and security policy," its members could not form a united front even as ethnic warfare raged across Yugoslavia.

Meanwhile, economic troubles in East Asia extended the gap in global production between the United States and other industrial powers. Japan, the longtime regional "locomotive," was battered by economic scandals and overheated capital markets, and its rupture quickly spread far beyond East Asia. Only the People's Republic of China emerged from the 1990s with greater world power. Military spending in China grew steadily during the decade, with much of this expansion directed toward high-technology

---

[1] U.S. Arms Control and Disarmament Agency, *World Military Expenditures and Arms Transfers* (Washington, D.C.: USACDA, 1998), 40. Four of these six countries—France, Japan, Britain, and Germany (listed in order of spending amounts)—were allies of the United States during this period. China and Russia were second and third on the list, respectively.

The north tower of the World Trade Center collapses after being struck by a hijacked jet on September 11, 2001. The terrorist attacks on New York City and Washington, D.C., prompted a swift response by the Bush administration and a new era in American foreign policy.

weapons systems and enhanced "3CI" (command, control, communications, and intelligence). Beijing's ability to project this power, however, was constrained by its repressive political system and its crushing domestic burdens. Although China's economy was booming—it grew at an annual rate of nearly 10 percent between 1980 and 2000—the daily task of feeding more than 1.3 billion citizens (more than four times the U.S. population) remained the government's primary focus. For the time being, Chinese leaders were content with economic and military modernization, and with lending an appearance of political moderation. They knew the time was not right, not yet anyway, for challenging American interests in the Taiwan Strait, the Korean Peninsula, or other regional hot spots.

242   Part II | The New World "Disorder"

The unipolar balance of world power had thus become an entrenched fact of geopolitical life. To many analysts, it was a force for global stability. Because of the wide lead of the United States in so many categories of national power, rational second-tier states would "bandwagon" with Washington rather than challenge it, either alone or by creating rival blocs. As one scholar put it,

> The raw power advantage of the United States means that an important source of conflict in previous systems is absent: hegemonic rivalry over leadership of the international system. No other major power is in a position to follow any policy that depends for its success on prevailing against the United States in a war or an extended rivalry. None is likely to take any step that might invite the focused enmity of the United States.[2]

In the popular imagination, the United States was more immune than ever to the perils of the outside world and more capable of fulfilling its self-appointed mission to lead the world toward freedom, peace, and prosperity. The experience of the 1990s convinced many, inside and outside of government, to believe this mission could be accomplished with little effort or sacrifice. Opinion polls consistently found that most Americans, while believing the nation should play a leadership role abroad, were more concerned about domestic problems than foreign policy. News organizations closed overseas news bureaus and cut back on world news. Congress cut foreign aid. Despite President Bill Clinton's adoption of an ambitious foreign policy agenda based on global "engagement" and democratic "enlargement," the State Department's budget in 1997 fell to its lowest level in twenty years.[3]

Such a casual approach to global leadership seemed reasonable in view of the resounding victory of the United States in the Cold War, its swift success in the Persian Gulf War, and its halting of ethnic violence in Bosnia and Kosovo with few American casualties. Clinton, stung politically by the abrupt U.S. withdrawal from Somalia (see Chapter 8) and aware that the public would not accept casualties in other humanitarian interventions, had refused to place U.S. troops in harm's way in the Balkans (see Chapter 9). Yet he had achieved his goal of ending both conflicts, largely through the

---

[2] William Wohlforth, "The Stability of a Unipolar World," *International Security* 24 (Summer 1999), 7.

[3] See Steven W. Hook, "Domestic Obstacles to International Affairs: The State Department under Fire at Home," *PS: Political Science and Politics* (January 2003), 23–29.

use of high-altitude bombing raids that reinforced the sense that wars could be won painlessly, at least for the United States. In other cases, such as the 1998 terrorist attacks on American embassies in Kenya and Tanzania, a few long-range cruise missiles delivered to enemy targets were deemed sufficient to keep the peace.

The United States, it appeared, could enjoy an unprecedented degree of global dominance while taking or leaving the burdens of leadership as it saw fit. All this seemed natural for a nation whose political, economic, and social systems were widely believed to be superior to others. As a rising power, the United States had lurched between periods of activism and detachment. Global hegemony, it seemed, allowed the makers of American foreign policy to have it both ways.

Strains in the Unipolar Order

The relative calm of the late 1990s affirmed Americans' long-standing belief that peace, not war, is the natural state of global affairs, and that the spread of democracy and free markets would suppress violent conflict. But beneath this veneer of commitment and solidarity, antagonism was setting in between the United States and the international community. American preeminence provoked resentment—and a certain measure of envy—within states and societies with fewer resources and less clout. Much of the discontent was directed toward the agents of American soft power, the multinational corporations and media outlets whose promotion of consumer culture threatened traditional customs and forms of expression in many societies. But critics also denounced American foreign policy, particularly the government's selective adherence to free trade, its antagonism toward the United Nations, its cornering of the global arms market, the enormous gap between its defense and foreign aid spending, and its opposition to international agreements favored by most other countries. Above all, critics perceived American officials to be overly moralistic—not because the government's proclaimed democratic values were misplaced, but because U.S. actions often contradicted them.

These controversies tarnished America's image at the peak of its world power. Americans traditionally viewed the nation as an exceptional "city on a hill," but foreign governments and citizens saw a Washington arrogant with power and indifferent to problems such as global warming, mass starvation in Africa, the AIDS epidemic, and weapons proliferation. Some analysts in the United States warned of *blowback*, a term used by the Central

Intelligence Agency (CIA) to describe retaliation against the nation by vindictive foreign governments and groups.[4] Whatever the outcome, it was clear that the unipolar order was far from a harmony of interests, let alone a universal embrace of American leadership.

The Globalization Backlash

The Clinton presidency will long be associated with "globalization"—the linking of national and regional markets into an integrated world economy. Toward that end, the World Trade Organization (WTO) held particular allure for Clinton. He had argued that the WTO, with 135 members in 1999, would bolster a world economy based on private enterprise and free trade. Trade disputes would be resolved in an orderly fashion, agreements would be reached on regulating global financial transfers, and new standards would be adopted to protect workers and preserve the environment. Most important, the WTO would mesh with other international organizations, ensuring political stability and harmony worldwide.

Directly challenging this logic was a vast network of local, national, and transnational interest groups. Widely dispersed, but closely connected through the Internet, these groups had little in common except their shared disdain for the WTO. Environmental activists viewed the organization as an agent of global warming and deforestation. Labor unions saw their jobs being shipped away by WTO bureaucrats. Human rights advocates accused the WTO of tolerating sweatshop labor. And self-styled anarchists alleged that the WTO represented a stepping-stone toward an oppressive world government. To critics, globalization threatened cultural diversity and prevented local and national leaders from controlling their own political, economic, and cultural development. Multinational corporations would be given free rein, and the world would effectively be made safe for McDonald's, Walmart, Coca-Cola, and General Motors.

Distracted by domestic upheavals and regional conflicts, Clinton failed to recognize this rising tide of dissent. He had assumed that the growing networks of nongovernmental organizations (NGOs) would *advance*, not oppose, the globalist cause. Nor did Clinton appreciate the deep divisions between rich and poor countries over issues such as labor standards and the costs of environmental protection, or the strained trade relations between the United States and the European Union that were engulfing

---

[4]For an application of this concept, see Chalmers Johnson, *Blowback: The Costs and Consequences of American Empire* (Boston: Little, Brown, 2000).

the WTO. The president also disregarded the lesson from the East Asian economic crisis that unfettered foreign investments, especially short-term stock and bond purchases, often cause more problems than they solve. His apparent obliviousness to these points came back to haunt him, however, after he made the fateful decision to host the annual meeting of the WTO in Seattle, Washington.

The December 1999 conference was a fiasco from start to finish. First, Clinton aides waited until the last minute to invite foreign leaders. Thus, by the time the aides tried to arrange a "Millennium Round" of trade negotiations, most heads of government had other plans. Second, Clinton failed to achieve even a minimal consensus on the agenda, which ensured that the conference would also lack any sense of focus. Third, by the time the meeting began, widespread protests were overwhelming the Seattle police, who had ignored the problems at the most recent WTO summit in Geneva and failed to take the necessary precautions against civil disobedience. Storefronts were smashed and looted, police were pelted by rocks, and hundreds of protesters were injured or arrested. Many WTO delegates, including Secretary of State Madeleine Albright and UN Secretary-General Kofi Annan, were confined to their hotels for much of the conference, unable to pass through the chaos.

Disillusionment also set in at the International Monetary Fund (IMF), whose actions before and during the economic recession that plagued Japan and other East Asian countries in the late 1990s were widely criticized. In encouraging the tidal wave of private investments in East Asia, which then proved unable to absorb the funds, the IMF helped to spark the economic wildfire. And in providing vast sums of aid after the bottom fell out, the IMF rewarded the same state bureaucrats and foreign investors whose reckless behavior had produced the crisis. Under the terms of its aid, the IMF was ensured of eventual repayment; the East Asian countries were left to pick up the pieces. The painful readjustments fell most heavily on the laborers, property owners, and small merchants who had nothing to do with creating the economic meltdown. This experience was similar to that in Russia and many parts of Eastern Europe, where IMF funds effectively rewarded government corruption and ineptitude.

The turmoil within the IMF and WTO provided ample evidence that the honeymoon for globalization was over. If for every action there is an equal and opposite reaction, it should not have been surprising that globalization sparked opposition. Ironically, the same forces that propelled the trend—computer technologies, multinational corporations, massive cash flows across borders, and transnational interest groups—also were vital to the backlash. Globalization came to be negatively identified with the United States, which had long anticipated a single world marketplace as the realization of the country's historical vision.

Retreat from Multilateralism

In addition to the unrest over globalization, a second source of tension confronted the makers of American foreign policy after the Cold War: the growing rift between Washington and the array of international institutions the United States had actively supported since World War II. In turning against these multilateral institutions (involving three or more governments) and the agreements they produced, American leaders seemed to be turning their backs on the more democratic world order that, like globalization, also represented a long-standing American dream.

This unilateral turn in American foreign policy occurred despite Clinton's continued calls for engagement with the international community. But the president could not overcome pressure from Congress, still controlled by the Republican Party, to scale back the nation's nonmilitary commitments. In fact, Clinton, who was generally more concerned with domestic policy, did not strongly resist this pressure and effectively surrendered his grand strategy to legislators.[5] Even then, Clinton's relations with Congress grew worse with time. The Monica Lewinsky scandal, which led in 1998 to the president's impeachment by the House of Representatives for not being open about his extramarital affair, left Clinton humiliated and politically wounded for the remainder of his presidency.[6]

The depth of Clinton's downfall in foreign policy was demonstrated by the Senate's October 1999 rejection of the Comprehensive Nuclear Test-Ban Treaty (CTBT), which Clinton had praised three years earlier as "the longest-sought, hardest-fought prize in the history of arms control." More than 150 foreign governments had pledged to support the treaty, which was based on the premise that a ban on testing would prevent potential proliferators from building weapons in the first place. Critics predicted that

---

[5] On grand strategy, see Lukas Milevski, *The Evolution of Modern Grand Strategic Thought* (Oxford, UK: Oxford University Press, 2016).

[6] Clinton maintained broad public approval during this period despite the scandal, and public surveys found that most Americans believed the House's impeachment was politically motivated and unjustified. See Nancy Gibbs and Michael Duffy, "The Great Disconnect," *Time* (January 25, 1999). The president was not convicted by the Senate and thus completed his second term in January 2001.

hostile nations would exploit American restraint and threaten the United States when its guard was down. But the primary motive of Clinton's Republican opponents was political: The treaty gave them a golden opportunity to humiliate the president on the world stage. The Senate defeat of the CTBT marked its first repudiation of a major treaty in eighty years and its first-ever rejection of a nuclear treaty. The refusal of the world's foremost nuclear superpower to join the moratorium on nuclear testing sent a strong signal to would-be nuclear powers: If the United States reserved the right to test these weapons, why shouldn't others?

The United States also found itself an outcast on a wide variety of other international agreements. Under pressure from the Pentagon, Clinton refused to sign the Anti-Personnel Mine Ban Convention calling for a worldwide ban on land mines, whose primary victims were civilians in war-torn developing countries. The U.S. government's opposition was ironic—an American citizen, Jody Williams, won the Nobel Peace Prize in 1997 for organizing the public campaign that garnered support for the treaty from more than 120 other countries.[7] However, the Department of Defense opposed the land mines treaty on the grounds that "antipersonnel" mines were vital to preventing a North Korean invasion of South Korea.

Washington's retreat from multilateralism gained momentum when Republican George W. Bush became president in January 2001. The governor of Texas and the son of Clinton's predecessor in office, Bush was in no mood to mend fences with the "international community," a term his national security adviser, Condoleezza Rice, had dismissed during the campaign as an illusion.[8] In her view, the multilateral cooperation and institution building embraced by the United States since the end of World War II had not brought the rest of the world in line with the nation's democratic values. Instead, they had produced open-ended commitments and mounting obligations that threatened U.S. sovereignty while empowering countries hostile to the United States. The second Bush administration, therefore, would be selective in observing such commitments and making new ones. Rather than working through formal organizations such as the United Nations or the North Atlantic Treaty Organization (NATO), the United States would form "coalitions of the willing" on a case-by-case basis

---

[7] The treaty entered into force in March 1999 and was ratified by 148 governments by 2006. For the most recent figures, see the website of the International Campaign to Ban Landmines, www .icbl.org.

[8] Condoleezza Rice, "Promoting the National Interest," *Foreign Affairs* 79 (January–February 2000), 45–62.

and dismantle them when their missions were accomplished. When help from other nations was not deemed necessary or was not forthcoming, the United States would go its own way.

Bush, with a Republican majority in Congress, eagerly joined the legislative attacks on multilateral commitments that had begun in 1995. Claiming that American chemical companies would face intrusive visits by international inspectors, the president blocked new measures to strengthen the 1972 Biological Weapons Convention. He also opposed a global treaty that restricted the trafficking of small arms, and he nullified a prior U.S. commitment to the Rome Statute of the International Criminal Court on the grounds that U.S. troops on peacekeeping missions would be unfairly singled out for prosecution. Bush was supported in these actions by "neoconservatives" in Washington who had spoken out harshly against Clinton's engagement strategy and gained high-level positions in the Bush administration. The only dissenter in the new president's inner circle was Secretary of State Colin Powell, who adopted the conventional view that diplomatic agreements establishing standards of appropriate behavior in world politics served both U.S. national interests and the greater cause of international stability.

Of greatest concern to the new president was the 1972 Antiballistic Missile Treaty (ABM Treaty) with Russia, signed along with other nuclear arms control agreements by Richard Nixon and Leonid Brezhnev. The Bush administration concluded that the treaty, based on deterrence and mutual assured destruction (see Chapter 3), was obsolete in the new era of "rogue states" and freelancing terrorists with appetites for weapons of mass destruction. Thus, Bush withdrew from the ABM Treaty, despite protests by Russian leaders and warnings by strategic analysts of a new global arms race, this time in antimissile technologies. The Department of Defense promptly stepped up its testing of missile defenses and planned for the deployment of a national missile defense system in Alaska and California by 2004.

Two events in the spring of 2001 dramatized the deepening isolation of the United States. In March, Bush renounced the Kyoto Protocol to the UN Framework Convention on Climate Change, which had been signed by Vice President Al Gore in 1997 but never submitted to the Senate for ratification.[9] The treaty, approved by eighty-three other governments, required industrialized countries to reduce their greenhouse gas emissions.

---

[9] Clinton knew that the Senate most likely would reject the treaty and for this reason did not submit it for ratification. See http://unfccc.int/kyoto_protocol/items/2830.php for the full text of the Kyoto Protocol.

The Clinton administration had agreed to reduce U.S. emissions by 7 percent of their 1990 levels by 2012. In rejecting the treaty, Bush disputed the scientific evidence linking greenhouse gases to global warming.[10] He charged instead that the protocol would merely slow U.S. economic growth and unfairly burden the United States while exempting developing nations, including China. The president also claimed that verifying compliance and enforcing the mandatory emission cutbacks would be impossible. No treaty at all, he argued, was better than a flawed one.

The president's dismissal of the Kyoto Protocol and his failure to propose a more rigorous alternative despite earlier pledges to do so incited widespread criticism from abroad. The United States was producing about one-quarter of the world's greenhouse gases—by far the largest share. Indeed, at the very time America renounced the Kyoto Protocol, U.S. highways were filled with gas-guzzling minivans and SUVs that, due to the political muscle of domestic automakers, were exempt from federal fuel efficiency standards. This spectacle was especially offensive to government leaders and environmental groups in Europe, where conservation and the use of alternative energy sources had become a way of life.

The second revealing episode occurred in May 2001, when the UN Human Rights Council denied the United States a seat on the panel for the first time since its creation in 1947 under the leadership of Eleanor Roosevelt. The move was clearly political payback for Washington's refusal to pay past UN dues, for its effort to force the resignation of the previous secretary general in 1996, and for its opposition to international agreements, most of which had nothing to do with human rights. The fact that repressive states such as Sudan and Syria were voted onto the commission made it clear that human rights were not a primary concern to the governments that denied the United States its customary seat. The incident further convinced Bush that the policy of "assertive multilateralism" so favored by his predecessor was a dead-end street.

John Bolton's appointment as undersecretary of state for arms control and international security in 2001 further underscored Bush's mistrust of global commitments. A prominent critic of agreements that restricted Washington's freedom of action, Bolton spent most of his time at the State Department blocking, weakening, and withdrawing from them. This approach was in direct contrast to the actions of previous undersecretaries, who had pursued *closer* ties and formal agreements with other

---

[10]See, for example, the Intergovernmental Panel on Climate Change, "Climate Change 2001: Impacts, Adaptation, and Vulnerability" (New York: United Nations, February 2001).

governments. Bolton's adversarial approach often clashed with that of his boss, Colin Powell. But Bolton's appointment to his position in the State Department, and his temporary appointment in 2005 as ambassador to the United Nations, was very much in keeping with the unilateral turn in American foreign policy.

The Growing Threat of "Sacred Terror"

As we have seen, after the Cold War, many Americans believed the nation's primary threat stemmed from attempts by the United Nations and other global institutions to stifle American sovereignty in the name of "global governance." Such concerns, however, merely distracted the United States from another transnational force. Adherents of militant Islam, based in the Middle East but extending in disillusioned pockets across the Muslim world, had for years expressed ill will toward the West on several counts. For one thing, they resented the role of earlier Western leaders in redrawing the map of the Middle East after the downfall of the Ottoman Empire and after the two world wars of the twentieth century. Similarly, they strongly opposed the UN's creation of the state of Israel in 1948 and the support given by Western leaders, especially those in Washington, to the Jewish state.

Islamic militants also charged the industrialized countries, primarily the United States, with exploiting the Middle East's vast petroleum reserves, often with the approval of autocratic monarchs and military dictators who enriched themselves at their people's expense. Living standards in the former empire stagnated for decades despite the accelerating extraction of this oil wealth, which literally fueled the West's industrial boom and rapid economic growth.

Finally, the militants believed that Western cultural influence was corrupting their societies with its materialism, permissive lifestyles, and political freedoms that violated the strictures of the Koran, the Islamic sacred text. As these dissidents and their spiritual mentors in the Islamic mosques and *madrassas* (religious schools) saw it, the Western states and societies were preventing Muslims everywhere from recapturing the Ottoman Empire's promises and creating a new and enduring caliphate, or sphere of Islamic rule.

American leaders were aware of these antagonistic feelings, which had surfaced earlier with the Iranian revolution of 1979 and then the siege of the U.S. embassy in Tehran. But the rise of militant Islam was only of secondary concern to the makers of foreign policy, whose focus during the Cold War remained on containing Soviet communism. More generally, the threat posed by advocates of *jihad*, or holy war, was not given much priority in Washington because American leaders thought of the balance of world power in terms of nation-states. From this perspective, no country in the Middle East, or anywhere else for that matter, came close to presenting a clear and present danger to the United States. Certainly, no private organization, however vengeful, could hope to contend with American power.

Early Warnings and Responses

The euphoria surrounding the end of the Cold War further distracted American leaders from the threat of militant Islamists, whose tactics of choice—terrorist attacks—were not readily understood by a defense establishment hardwired for conventional war. Indeed, the United States, a secular state despite its cultural attachment to Christian principles, was especially ill equipped to anticipate the onslaught of "sacred terror" on its own territory.[11]

But developments at home exposed Americans to the mounting danger of international terrorism (see Table 10-1). A series of attacks in 1993, including an attempt to topple New York City's World Trade Center by means of underground explosives and a shooting spree outside CIA headquarters in Langley, Virginia, forced Clinton to confront the problem. By June 1995, he was sufficiently alarmed to issue a Presidential Decision Directive (PDD-39) calling for greater coordination among federal agencies in anticipating future attacks and responding effectively should they occur. "The United States," Clinton's directive stated, "regards all such terrorism as a potential threat to national security as well as a criminal act and will apply all appropriate means to combat it."[12] In May 1998, Clinton issued another directive that created the position of national coordinator for security, infrastructure protection, and counterterrorism, a move designed in part to demonstrate the president's resolve in fighting terrorism.

These measures aside, the White House had a difficult time persuading members of Congress that the threat was urgent. According to the first "counterterrorism czar," Richard A. Clarke, his position was accompanied

---

[11] Daniel Benjamin and Steven Simon, *The Age of Sacred Terror* (New York: Random House, 2002).

[12] White House, "U.S. Policy on Counterterrorism," Presidential Decision Directive 39 (June 21, 1995), www.fas.org/irp/offdocs/pdd39.htm.

Year	Terrorist incident	Chief suspect or claimant of responsibility
1983	*(April)* Car bomb destroys U.S. embassy in Beirut, Lebanon, killing seventeen Americans, including CIA's Middle East director.	Hezbollah (Lebanon)
	(October) Suicide bombing of U.S. military compound in Beirut, Lebanon, kills 241 marines.	Hezbollah (Lebanon)
1984	*(March)* CIA agent William Buckley kidnapped, tortured, and killed in Beirut.	Islamic Jihad (Syria)
	(September) Twenty-four workers at U.S. embassy in Beirut killed by bomb blast.	Hezbollah (Lebanon)
1985	*(October)* Italian cruise ship *Achille Lauro* hijacked off Egyptian coast; wheelchair-bound American tourist Leon Klinghoffer killed.	Palestinian Liberation Front
1986	*(April)* Bomb attack on discotheque in West Berlin kills one U.S. serviceman and injures forty-four others.	Libyan government
1988	*(December)* Passenger jet destroyed in midair bomb attack over Lockerbie, Scotland; death toll of 270 includes 189 Americans.	Libyan government
1993	*(January)* Two CIA employees shot to death outside CIA headquarters in Langley, Virginia.	Pakistani militant
	(February) Bomb attack damages World Trade Center in New York City; six killed and 1,049 injured.	Followers of Egyptian sheik Omar Abdel-Rahman
	(April) Former president George H. W. Bush is target of assassination attempt during visit to Kuwait.	Iraqi government
1995	*(March)* Two U.S. diplomats killed in U.S. consulate in Karachi, Pakistan.	Unknown
1996	*(June)* Car bomb near U.S. Army compound in Al Khobar, Saudi Arabia, kills or wounds more than 250 U.S. military personnel.	Saudi Hezbollah, Iranian government

(Continued)

Table 10-1   (Continued)

Year	Terrorist incident	Chief suspect or claimant of responsibility
1997	*(February)* Tourists at Empire State Building in New York City are target of machine gun attacks; one visitor killed and several others wounded.	Palestinian militant
1998	*(August)* U.S. embassies in Dar es Salaam, Tanzania, and Nairobi, Kenya, attacked in nearly simultaneous bombings. Death toll of nearly three hundred includes twelve Americans; more than five thousand are wounded.	al Qaeda (Afghanistan)
1999	*(February)* Three American human rights activists in Venezuela kidnapped and then killed.	Revolutionary Armed Forces of Colombia
2000	*(October)* USS *Cole* bombed while refueling in Aden, Yemen; seventeen sailors killed and thirty-nine others injured.	al Qaeda (Afghanistan)
2001	*(September)* Suicide aircraft attacks on World Trade Center and Pentagon kill more than three thousand and injure thousands more.	al Qaeda (Afghanistan)

Sources: U.S. State Department, "Significant Terrorist Incidents, 1961–2003: A Brief Chronology," http://www.fas.org/irp/threat/terror_chron.html; Center for Defense Information, "Chronology of Major Terrorist Attacks against U.S. Targets," http://www.freerepublic.com/focus/f-news/1087538/posts; and Public Broadcasting Service, "Target America: Terrorist Attacks on Americans, 1979–1988," *Frontline*, www.pbs.org/wgbh/pages/frontline/shows/target/.

Note: Although the countries most closely linked to Hezbollah, Islamic Jihad, and al Qaeda at the time of attacks are noted in parentheses, the state sponsors of these groups vary over time and in connection with different attacks.

by "no budget, only a dozen staff, and no ability to direct actions by the departments or agencies."[13] After a high-level task force warned of impending terrorist strikes in 2000, legislators expressed alarm but approved no major initiatives or funding measures to fortify U.S. counterterrorism

---

[13]"Testimony of Richard A. Clarke before the National Commission on Terrorist Attacks upon the United States" (March 24, 2004), www.9-11commission.gov/hearings/hearing8/clarke_statement.pdf.

programs.[14] Meanwhile, emergency responders received little or no training in handling terrorist attacks. Depending almost entirely on scarce local funds, these units maintained tight budgets largely designed for routine matters such as house fires and automobile accidents.

Basic statistics will help to explain this complacent attitude. Although international terrorists occasionally targeted Americans in the 1980s and 1990s, the 666 deaths from these attacks were modest compared with the battle deaths resulting from World War II (291,557) and the wars in Korea (33,651) and Vietnam (47,378).[15] Indeed, the victims of terrorism during these two decades were vastly outnumbered by the deaths caused by highway accidents, which averaged about 40,000 annually. The deadliest single act of terrorism, the bombing of the U.S. Marine barracks in Beirut in 1983, killed 241 Americans, but it was overshadowed the next day by the U.S. invasion of Grenada. Public and political reaction was also muted because the Beirut attack, like the later bombings of the Khobar Towers in Saudi Arabia in 1996 and the USS *Cole* off the Yemen coast in 2000, occurred far from the United States. Still, it is significant that the death toll from terrorist attacks between 1980 and 2000 greatly exceeded the combined casualties that resulted from U.S. military actions in Grenada, Haiti, Kuwait, Panama, Somalia, and the former Yugoslavia.

It is well known that open societies are by their nature highly vulnerable to terrorism. This certainly applied to the United States before the terrorist attacks of September 11, 2001. America's borders with Canada and Mexico were lightly guarded, as were its coastlines and airports. Foreign citizens traveled to and from the United States with little scrutiny, attaining work permits, student visas, and even American citizenship with relative ease. Furthermore, the U.S. economy was highly dependent on overseas markets, particularly on oil. Any disruption of economic activity in these markets would jeopardize American prosperity. The global reach of the U.S. government—its worldwide web of embassies, consulates, diplomatic missions, and military bases—provided terrorists with a multitude of potential targets. The same could be said of private American citizens, who traveled the world in numbers that greatly exceeded those from any other country.

Other factors placing the United States at risk of terrorist attacks stemmed, paradoxically, from its democratic political system. The openness of American government—most congressional proceedings and

---

[14] National Commission on Terrorism, *Countering the Changing Threat of International Terrorism* (Washington, D.C.: National Commission on Terrorism, June 2000).

[15] Paul R. Pillar, *Terrorism and U.S. Foreign Policy* (Washington, D.C.: Brookings, 2001), 18–19.

records were open to the public—provided potential enemies with ample information. The *Congressional Record* and C-SPAN revealed daily the bitter divisions within the federal government, and commercial media sources fueled debilitating political scandals with nonstop coverage. Government agencies, of course, were expected to operate within the law and according to standard operating procedures. But none of these constraints, so vital to the preservation of democracy, applied to terrorist groups, whose deliberations and movements were hidden and whose members operated without regard to legal restrictions. Furthermore, terrorist groups adapted quickly to changing circumstances in stark contrast to the notoriously risk-averse agencies of the U.S. government.

The al Qaeda Connection

American investigators discovered a common link among many of the acts of Islamic terrorism in the 1990s: the terrorist group al Qaeda, based in Afghanistan. Like other militant Islamic groups, al Qaeda rejected Western cultural, social, and economic values and openly declared its intention to destroy Western political institutions, military forces, and economic assets.[16] Initially composed largely of veterans of the Soviet resistance, al Qaeda expanded in the 1990s, opening training camps in Sudan, Yemen, and other countries with large, impoverished, and embittered Muslim populations. At least sixty al Qaeda cells existed worldwide in 2001 and formed their own coalitions of the willing with like-minded groups in Bosnia, Chechnya, Somalia, and other hotbeds of Islamic unrest. The group was linked to the anti-American resistance in Somalia in 1993, the bombing of the World Trade Center in the same year, the 1998 bombings of American embassies in Kenya and Tanzania, and the 2000 bombing of the USS *Cole* off the coast of Yemen.[17] The attacks of September 11 served as a natural extension of al Qaeda's mounting aggression.

The campaign to bring al Qaeda to justice soon took on a human dimension. Osama bin Laden, the group's leader, grew up in a wealthy

---

[16] See Gilles Kepel, *Jihad: The Trail of Political Islam* (Cambridge, Mass.: Belknap Press, 2002), chap. 13.

[17] Terrorists linked to al Qaeda were involved in the 1993 bombing of the World Trade Center in New York City. The person convicted of the attack, Ramzi Yousef, had also planned with other al Qaeda members to bomb the Lincoln and Holland Tunnels and the United Nations headquarters in New York City. The al Qaeda cell in the city was led by Sheik Omar Abdel-Rahman, a spiritual leader who had developed a working relationship with al Qaeda leader Osama bin Laden during the "blind sheik's" years as a member of Egyptian Islamic Jihad. Richard A. Clarke, *Against All Enemies: Inside America's War on Terror* (New York: Free Press, 2004), 78–79.

Saudi Arabian family and was well known to the U.S. government since the days when he organized the *mujahidin*, or "holy warriors," against the Soviet occupation of Afghanistan in the 1980s. The CIA secretly provided logistical and financial support to the *mujahidin*, which helped them to overcome the larger and more technologically advanced Soviet forces.

This marriage of convenience ended, however, after the Soviet Union's defeat in 1989. Bin Laden returned to Saudi Arabia, where he spoke out against the monarchy's secular form of government and close ties to the United States. His criticism so angered Saudi officials that they ejected him from the kingdom in 1991. Undeterred, bin Laden moved to the North African country of Sudan, whose government, dominated by the National Islamic Front, was engaged in a genocidal crackdown against its black population, who followed Christian and other non-Islamic religious traditions. Safe in Sudan, bin Laden had ample freedom and resources to organize al Qaeda, whose English translation—"the base"—neatly captured the organization's intended role as a foundation for Islamic *jihad*. Al Qaeda soon created cells in other countries, including Egypt, Russia, and the former Yugoslavia, providing soldiers, weaponry, and other forms of assistance to Muslim insurgents seeking to gain political power by force. Al Qaeda also established a presence in European cities, including London, Milan, and Vienna, funding "charitable organizations" that served as fronts for al Qaeda operations. In Afghanistan, years of civil war after the war against the Soviet Union led to the rise of the Taliban, whose leaders welcomed bin Laden's return in 1996 after he was forced by international pressure to leave Sudan. With his globalized network of al Qaeda cells now fully mobilized, bin Laden used his sanctuary in Afghanistan to begin planning his frontal assault on the American infidels.

Terror in the Morning Sky

Despite the diplomatic tensions that accompanied Washington's rejection of multilateral engagement, the first months of George W. Bush's presidency were relatively quiet ones. The nation remained focused on domestic problems, particularly an economic slowdown after a decade of rapid growth. Although foreign leaders scoffed at the unilateral turn in American foreign policy, they continued to support Washington on most issues. An extended period of global stability, albeit one of occasional discord, was widely expected.

All this changed on September 11, 2001, when nineteen terrorists turned four hijacked airliners into weapons of mass destruction. Their assaults on New York City and Washington, D.C., shattered America's sense of invulnerability. Not only was the United States attacked with devastating effect, but the strikes also targeted its commercial and political centers. The fact that an invisible adversary—lacking national sovereignty, formal armies, or territory—committed the attacks exposed the limits of America's ability to defend itself despite its overwhelming power and influence.

The four airliners used in the attacks took off within a two-hour period—two from Boston, a third from Washington, and the fourth from Newark, New Jersey. All were bound for California and were loaded with fuel. In each case, the terrorists hijacked the jets shortly after takeoff, using box cutters to subdue the flight crews, enter the cockpits, and take the controls. The first jet left Boston for Los Angeles, but suddenly changed course toward New York City before flying into the north tower of the World Trade Center at 8:48 A.M. Initial news reports suggested the collision was accidental. But fears of a terrorist attack were confirmed eighteen minutes later, when a second jetliner crashed into the south tower. Half an hour later, a third jet plunged into the Pentagon, where 125 people died. The fourth jet, hijacked over Ohio and set on a course toward Washington, crash-landed at 10:10 A.M. in rural Pennsylvania. Passengers on the plane tried to overpower the hijackers, and although they could not save themselves, they likely spared the U.S. Capitol or the White House. In all, 266 people died in the four planes.

Images of the crippled World Trade Center, the workplace of some fifty thousand people, transfixed the nation and the world. Thousands of rescue workers descended on the area, and hundreds raced up the stairways toward the fires, hoping somehow to reach the office workers trapped above the flames. But as the burning jet fuel melted the towers' steel supports, the twin skyscrapers gave way. The upper floors simply fell onto the floors beneath, causing a downward chain reaction that extended to the basements of both towers. The south tower was the first to go, at 10:05 A.M. After the north tower followed at 10:28 A.M., a cloud of smoke and debris enveloped Manhattan for the rest of the day. At the World Trade Center, 2,606 people died.

President Bush was in Florida at the time of the attacks, reading to schoolchildren as part of a campaign to promote his education reforms. Amid the confusion, he was flown secretly to air force bases in Louisiana and Nebraska before it was considered safe for him to return to Washington. Vice President Dick Cheney, working in the White House, was rushed to an underground bunker. Cabinet members were moved to various locations around the capital to ensure that they would not all be in one place in the event of another strike. The attacks paralyzed routine activities across the nation. All 4,546 airplanes aloft at the time were ordered to land immediately. The Mexican and Canadian borders were closed, along with federal offices, foreign embassies, and highly visible landmarks such as the Golden Gate Bridge, the Sears Tower (now the Willis Tower), and Disney World. The New York Stock Exchange, located blocks away from "ground zero," suspended trading indefinitely. Schools and private businesses across the country closed early as the gravity of the terrorist attacks set in.

The United States received immediate global support. The French newspaper *Le Monde* featured a banner headline on September 12 that declared, "We Are All Americans." The United Nations condemned the attacks and called for swift and concerted retaliation. For the first time in its history, the North Atlantic Council, the executive body of NATO, invoked Article 5 of its charter that declared an attack on any NATO member to be an attack on the entire alliance. Congress also responded quickly, passing a joint resolution that authorized Bush to use "all necessary and appropriate force" against the terrorists.

Bush declared the terrorist attacks to be an act of war. In a televised address on the night of the attacks, the president vowed to wage war against terrorism, not simply against those who were behind the assaults on New York City and Washington. Bush then widened the scope of the U.S. response by announcing that he would "make no distinction between the terrorists who committed these acts and those who harbor them." Thus, state sponsors of terrorism would also be targeted by the United States. "Every nation, in every region, now has a decision to make," Bush declared to a joint session of Congress on September 20. "Either you are with us, or you are with the terrorists." With these words, Bush set the course of an American counteroffensive that would take many forms against many adversaries throughout much of the world.

For all of their horrible consequences, the attacks of September 11 ended the decade-long drift in American foreign policy. No longer could this period in history be regarded vaguely as the "post–Cold War era," a term that related to the past rather than the present. No longer could the U.S. public turn its back on threats from overseas previously thought unimportant. No longer could the U.S. government veer from one grand strategy to another. Henceforth, the war against terrorism would consume the government's attention, providing the basis for foreign policy and many aspects of domestic policy.

Impact and Influence: Osama bin Laden

Not long after the September 11, 2001, attacks on New York City and Washington, D.C., American leaders became aware of their source: the terrorist group al Qaeda and its leader, Osama bin Laden. Born the seventeenth of fifty-two children to the wealthiest construction magnate in Saudi Arabia, bin Laden enjoyed a childhood of privilege. He received a college degree in civil engineering in 1980 and then moved to Afghanistan to help the Islamic *mujahidin* wage war against Soviet invaders. It was there that bin Laden first put his university training to use, along with the machinery and financial assets of his father's construction empire. By 1986, he was leading his own band of guerrilla forces from Syria and Egypt in combat operations that ultimately forced the Soviet Union's retreat from Afghanistan.

Having overcome one Cold War superpower, bin Laden set his sights on the other. He condemned U.S. support for Israel, its close ties to secular Arab regimes, and its military presence in the oil-rich Persian Gulf. Creating al Qaeda, he instructed Muslims in all countries "to kill the Americans and plunder their money wherever and whenever they find it." Efforts by the United States to apprehend bin Laden failed as the scale of his attacks steadily escalated, culminating in the events of September 11. He remained at large long after the United States ousted the Taliban from Afghanistan and offered large rewards for his capture, "dead or alive." Bin Laden was finally captured and killed in Pakistan on May 2, 2011 (see Chapter 11).

Elements of Counterterrorism

The prospect of an imminent war against terrorism raised questions about how such a war would differ from the conventional wars previously fought by the United States. As noted earlier, the distinctive style of American foreign policy traditionally viewed warfare as an exception to the general rule of peaceful coexistence among states and societies. The "war on terror" declared by Bush would depart from this tradition in several ways, including the open-ended nature of the conflict. Fighting "terror" as opposed to a definitive enemy would commit the United States to an extended struggle in any number of areas. Indeed, the remote prospect of vanquishing terrorism altogether made it likely that the struggle would never be fully "won" or "lost" and instead would continue indefinitely.

Definitions of *terrorism* vary widely, based in large part on disagreements over what constitutes a "terrorist" as opposed to a "freedom fighter" or the like.[18] American officials formally defined the term as "premeditated, politically motivated violence perpetrated against noncombatant targets by subnational groups or clandestine agents, usually intended to influence an audience."[19] According to this definition, acts of terrorism share the following elements: the involvement of private individuals and groups as opposed to government agents, extensive prior planning, an intent to change government policy, the willful use of violence, and the targeting of civilians or off-duty military personnel.

Beyond these elements, three other aspects of terrorist activity also must be considered. First, neglected in the U.S. government's definition is the importance of symbolism in many acts of terrorism. The World Trade Center towers were not only New York City's tallest buildings, but also a symbol of American-led global commerce. The Pentagon was the ultimate symbol of U.S. military power. Their destruction was meant to symbolize, in turn, the failings of American values and the limits of American power. To terrorist groups that lack the resources to challenge a superpower directly, such statements are invaluable. Second, the psychological impact of terrorism is vital. Terrorists aim to incite mass anxiety, or in some cases panic, as a means of disrupting government policy and creating doubts about the ability of political leaders to protect their citizens. The fact that civilians, not military personnel, were killed *en masse* on September 11 had enormous appeal to the terrorists because from that day on, Americans would feel a little less secure as they went about their normal daily routines. Such mass anxiety could not have been achieved had military forces rather than civilians been targeted. As one author describes it,

> The distinction between the fair fight of an open military confrontation and the unfair one of a terrorist attack comes into play. Ask the average American if the life of a soldier who dies in battle is worth the same as the life of a countryman who has died from terrorism, and the answer will be yes. But ask after each type of event

---

[18] For an elaboration, see Walter Laqueur, *The New Terrorism: Fanaticism and the Arms of Mass Destruction* (New York: Oxford University Press, 1999); and Bruce Hoffman, *Inside Terrorism* (New York: Columbia University Press, 1998).

[19] *U.S. Code,* 22 (2000), § 2656f (d).

how much shock and revulsion that American is feeling, and the reaction will be stronger after the terrorist incident. . . . [H]owever much one might try to talk down the subject, some of the special shock of a terrorist attack will always be there; it is in the nature of the event.[20]

Finally, the messianic nature of the Islamic *jihad* cannot be ignored. Angry, disgruntled groups of many kinds have resorted to terrorism in modern history to achieve a variety of goals—for example, secession from a nation-state or changes in government policies.[21] By contrast, al Qaeda's motivation for the September 11 attacks "was neither political calculation, strategic advantage, nor wanton bloodshed," wrote two former National Security Council analysts. "It was to humiliate and slaughter those who defied the hegemony of God. . . . It was an act of cosmic war."[22] To the United States, which had long equated its own global ambitions with a "manifest destiny," the Islamists' presumption of divine guidance was not entirely unfamiliar.

No one doubted that the United States maintained overwhelming military superiority, vast economic wealth, and close political ties with other powerful governments. With these advantages, the United States could not be defeated in a conventional war. An alternative battle plan was needed. Just like those waging guerrilla warfare (see Chapter 4), the challenger would have to exploit the element of surprise, appeal to popular opinion, and have knowledge of the local terrain. Unlike the large armies deployed by the superior power, which could easily bog down in a protracted conflict, the terrorists could afford to be patient. In the parlance of military strategists, the war against al Qaeda would be an *asymmetric* war in which calculations based on standard ratios of power would not apply. "In its basic form, asymmetrical warfare utilizes one side's comparative advantage against its enemy's relative weakness. Successful asymmetrical warfare exploits vulnerabilities—which are easy to determine—by using weapons and tactics that are unplanned or unexpected."[23]

Unlike Clinton, Bush did not have the luxury of taking pot shots at the terrorists and relegating counterterrorism to the back burner. The

---

[20] Pillar, *Terrorism and U.S. Foreign Policy,* 24.

[21] See Andrew Sinclair, *The Anatomy of Terror: A History of Terrorism* (New York: Macmillan, 2003).

[22] Benjamin and Simon, *The Age of Sacred Terror,* 357–360.

[23] Rob de Wijk, "The Limits of Military Power," *Washington Quarterly* 25 (Winter 2002), 79.

war on terror would be Bush's primary concern for the remainder of his presidency. But the White House would need both the public's support and its understanding because of the likelihood of military setbacks and additional terrorist attacks—not to mention the high cost of such an undertaking. Maintaining this support would not be easy because the United States could not hope to destroy the enemy in one blow. Instead, it would have to fight a war of attrition over an extended period of time.[24] In summary, the war against al Qaeda forced the United States to abandon its traditional approach to warfare based on the use of overwhelming force against a discernible enemy in a clearly defined location. Beyond the need of the United States to gain public support and patience, three other factors would determine its success or failure in the coming struggle: intelligence, diplomacy, and homeland security.

Intelligence

Among the first questions raised after September 11 was how the most vital centers of American government and commerce could have been attacked so decisively and unexpectedly. Press reports shortly after the attacks revealed that the CIA knew of al Qaeda's threats to U.S. territory and of its heightened activities in the summer of 2001.[25] Other reports disclosed that the Federal Bureau of Investigation (FBI) and local and state law enforcement agencies also were aware of growing terrorist activity during this period. The failure of these organizations, and of the federal government as a whole, to "connect the dots" not only demonstrated the fragmentation of the U.S. intelligence community, but also unquestionably contributed to the success of the terrorist attacks.[26]

The obstacles to prompt reform, however, were daunting. Fourteen federal agencies were engaged in different aspects of intelligence gathering and analysis—and none was eager to compare notes with the others. The CIA and FBI rigidly adhered to separate missions, as did the intelligence units of the four armed services. The chronic failure of federal, state, and local law enforcement agencies to coordinate their efforts further

---

[24] See Barry R. Posen, "The Struggle against Terrorism: Grand Strategy, Strategy, and Tactics," *International Security* 26 (Winter 2001/2002), 39–55.

[25] James Risen, "In Hindsight, C.I.A. Sees Flaws That Hindered Effects on Terror," *New York Times* (October 7, 2001), A1, B2.

[26] Paul R. Pillar, *Intelligence and U.S. Foreign Policy: Iraq, 9/11, and Misguided Reform* (New York: Columbia University Press, 2011).

widened the intelligence gap. A joint House-Senate congressional investigation reported in 2002 a "breakdown in communication" that resulted from "a number of factors, including differences in agencies' missions, legal authorities, and cultures. Information was not sufficiently shared, not only between Intelligence Community agencies, but also within agencies, and between the intelligence and law-enforcement agencies."[27]

Despite these obstacles, sound intelligence was essential for the United States to meet the threat posed by terrorist groups. High-altitude satellite imagery, intercepted communications, and other forms of technical surveillance were of limited utility; the groups themselves had to be penetrated directly. Only "human intelligence," or face-to-face contacts with the enemy, would produce real results. A flood of new agents with expertise and experience in the Arab world, militant Islam, and counterterrorism were required. The work of undercover agents and informants would be difficult, costly, and extremely dangerous. The United States would also have to cooperate with foreign intelligence agencies. Pakistan's Inter-Services Intelligence (ISI), for example, maintained close ties with informants on both sides of the Afghan border, a crucial region for U.S. counterterrorist operations.

Even if the U.S. intelligence "community" connected all the dots, there were still no guarantees they would foil future terrorist attacks on the United States or its allies. Secretary of Defense Donald H. Rumsfeld frequently observed that, with regard to foreign threats, there were "knowns, known unknowns, and unknown unknowns." As for the latter, "We don't even know we don't know them."[28] CIA director George Tenet also pointed out that U.S. intelligence analysts suffered from such a bad case of "threat fatigue" that they could not be sure which of the thousands of warning signs that appeared daily should be acted upon. Thus, it was not surprising that when the CIA's August 6, 2001, "President's Daily Brief" featured the headline "Bin Laden Determined to Strike in U.S.," it prompted little decisive action by the president.[29]

[27] U.S. Congress, Senate Select Committee on Intelligence and U.S. House Permanent Select Committee on Intelligence, *Joint Inquiry into Intelligence Community Activities before and after the Terrorist Attacks of September 11, 2001* (107th Cong., 2nd sess., December 2002), xvii.

[28] Quoted in Jeffrey Goldberg, "The Unknown," *New Yorker* (February 10, 2003), 42–43.

[29] For the full text, see "Text: President's Daily Brief on August 6, 2001," *Washington Post* (April 10, 2004), http://www.cnn.com/2004/ALLPOLITICS/04/10/august6.memo/.

Diplomacy

Bush also faced an uphill battle in gaining the political cooperation he needed from other governments in the war on terror. The United States simply did not have the option of going it alone in this struggle. Dozens of other countries were needed to provide intelligence, military assets such as base rights, and political support for the United States in international organizations. Because militant Islamists were threatening not only the United States but also the West in general and "infidels" within many Islamic societies, it initially appeared that more than just rhetorical support would be forthcoming. It was one thing for foreign leaders to declare common cause in the war on terror; it was quite another for them to commit resources or risk the lives of their citizens. Too close a connection to the United States exposed these leaders to political challenges by anti-American groups or even to terrorist attacks within their borders. This tendency was especially noticeable after the U.S. government retreated from many international agreements and increasingly chose unilateral solutions to foreign policy problems.

Nevertheless, the war on terror did provide opportunities for foreign leaders to align their own agendas with the U.S. antiterrorism efforts. In Russia, President Vladimir Putin welcomed the chance to portray his ongoing struggle against Chechen rebels as a struggle against terrorism. So did Chinese leaders, who faced challenges from Muslim separatists on their western frontier. By identifying their respective enemies as terrorists, the Indian and Pakistani governments each sought support from the United States in their decades-long struggle over Kashmir. The same could be said for the leaders of Israel, Peru, the Philippines, Turkey, and other countries with long histories of security cooperation with the United States. The more these governments could identify themselves as partners in America's war on terror, the more material support they could expect to receive from Washington. Even so, "checkbook diplomacy" would not be enough in this conflict. The United States needed real allies, not simply clients whose allegiance would end when the last check was cashed.

Homeland Security

The third key factor in fighting the war on terror was the home front. Unlike the Japanese attack on the U.S. naval base at Pearl Harbor in Hawaii in 1941, the attacks of September 11 targeted the continental United States. Civilians rather than military personnel were the primary victims, and the terrorists themselves had been openly engaged in American society prior to their deadly assaults. In this context, strict new measures were clearly needed to protect airports, coastlines, electrical utilities, communication networks, and government buildings from future attacks. Domestic law enforcement agencies had to identify potential terrorists in their communities and share their leads with federal authorities. Local first responders had to devise new methods to handle terrorist attacks, some of which might involve chemical, biological, or even nuclear weapons. And the American public had to prepare for possible new attacks.

The scale of this effort would be immense. Few areas of American society would not be affected, and often the routine conveniences to which Americans had long been accustomed would have to be eliminated. Indeed, the U.S. government was forced to adopt many measures, such as intrusive searches at airports and the "profiling" of minority groups associated with terrorism, that were common in other countries. The White House placed new limits on public information, expanded the scope of domestic surveillance, and curbed the legal protections of suspected terrorists. These measures, stemming from the USA PATRIOT Act passed shortly after the attacks, provoked charges that civil liberties had become an additional casualty of the war on terror.[30] It was also unclear how the new Department of Homeland Security, whose creation involved the largest reorganization of the federal government since the early days of the Cold War, would make Americans safer. The most visible early actions of Homeland Security Secretary Tom Ridge—he devised color-coded terrorist alerts and urged Americans to buy duct tape and other necessities in preparation for extended stays in shelters—simply heightened public apprehensions.[31]

The worst fears of domestic terrorism were realized in October 2001 when dozens of Americans were exposed to anthrax. The deadly bacteria were sent through the mail. The first exposure occurred at a newspaper office in Florida, where it killed one employee and disabled two others. Within weeks, powdery traces of anthrax were found in envelopes addressed to the NBC and CBS news studios, the Microsoft Corporation, and the office of New York governor George Pataki. The opening of an anthrax-laced envelope in the office of Senate majority leader Tom Daschle led to mass evacuations and the almost otherworldly spectacle of FBI agents in biohazard suits swarming into congressional offices. Traces of anthrax were later found in the mailrooms of the Supreme Court, the State

---

[30] The formal name of the act was the Uniting and Strengthening America by Providing Appropriate Tools Required to Intercept and Obstruct Terrorism (USA PATRIOT) Act of 2001.

[31] Dan Reuter and John Yoo, eds., *Confronting Terror: 9/11 and the Future of American National Security* (New York: Encounter Books, 2011).

Department, and the CIA. Two postal workers in Washington, D.C., died from inhaling the bacteria, and others were afflicted at sorting facilities in New Jersey and New York.

Still reeling from the trauma of September 11, Americans faced the immediate risk of bioterrorism in their own homes. No one felt secure as news of the anthrax attacks dominated the headlines. The Bush administration, caught off guard by the wave of terrorism, issued a series of public alerts that only reinforced public fears. The first warning referred to a "credible" but unspecified threat; subsequent alerts identified suspension bridges and nuclear power plants as possible targets. In a satellite speech to Eastern Europeans, Bush warned of a potential threat "to civilization itself." As for the terrorists, the high anxiety this speech produced around the world represented a victory of its own kind.

Meanwhile, American military strategists devised a war plan that would unfold in several stages, first against the Taliban regime in Afghanistan, then in other parts of the world where al Qaeda cells were believed to be organized. Both the terrorists and their state sponsors would be targeted. Large numbers of U.S. troops would be required in some of these missions. In others, smaller special forces would take the lead, often in tactical alliances with indigenous forces. As in the case of guerrilla warfare (see Chapter 4), the line between civilians and military forces would always be blurry because the terrorists were embedded in civilian areas and were, in the strictest sense of the word, civilians themselves. "Collateral damage," military jargon for civilian casualties, would be inevitable, possibly on a large scale.

A Grand Strategy of Primacy and Preemption

As noted earlier, even before the terrorists struck, President Bush had changed the direction of American foreign policy. As a presidential candidate in 2000, he had rejected the "assertive multilateralism" of the Clinton-Gore years and called instead for unilateral action based on U.S. self-interests. Later, President Bush, Vice President Cheney, and other members of the Bush foreign policy team complained that the deck was stacked against the United States in international organizations, which provided hostile governments with a forum to gang up on Washington. These adversaries were located not only in less developed countries, which held a majority in most intergovernmental bodies, but also in wealthy nations such as France that openly assailed the American "hyperpower." Bush's message upon taking office in January 2001 was clear: The United States would be concerned primarily with its own interests and would go it alone to secure these interests whenever necessary. Realism, not idealism, would guide American foreign policy on his watch. Still, Bush did not initially proclaim a new foreign policy "doctrine" that provided a clear basis for action.

The terrorist attacks provided just this opportunity, lending credence to the dark vision of mounting global threats long claimed by the president and his advisers. When these threats became a reality on September 11, few doubts remained that a new grand strategy, a new statement of the ends and means of American foreign policy, was required. A new grand strategy, however, presented Bush with two grand dilemmas. First, although the president's pessimistic worldview was affirmed on September 11, his previous elevation of U.S. self-interests over global concerns had alienated foreign leaders whose support the United States needed. Among many other ironies of the new era, the United States could not succeed in the war against terrorism without help from the same international community that Bush had derided, to great effect, during his campaign for office.

The second dilemma was more deeply rooted. Bush's embrace of minimal realism, of coldly calculated national interests and the means to achieve them, contradicted America's long-standing sense of universal moral purpose. The American people had always viewed the United States as an exceptional nation that stood for more than just maintaining its own territorial integrity. World politics from the American perspective ultimately involved a struggle over values, not raw power. America's core values of political liberty, spiritual tolerance, and economic opportunity were meant for export. Their adoption overseas represented the fulfillment of America's historic mission, not the "second-order effect" identified by Bush's national security adviser, Condoleezza Rice.[32] The new grand strategy, therefore, had to appeal to a wider community than the United States. And it had to exalt values and principles that transcended American self-interests.

Fortunately for Bush, the resolution of the twin dilemmas could be found in the hated ideology of Osama bin Laden, in the Taliban torture chambers, and, most of all, in the mass murder committed by the terrorists on September 11. As in the past, where American principles were rejected, tyranny and carnage reigned. The United States again confronted a foreign movement—this time in the form of a religious faction—that rejected the values and lifestyles of American citizens and the political principles,

---

[32] Rice, "Promoting the National Interest," 47.

institutions, and actions of the U.S. government. The disciples of militant Islam had declared holy war not only against Americans, but also against all others who did not subscribe to the dictates of their radical ideology.

The very nature of this latest challenge allowed Bush to meld his realist instincts with traditional American idealism, thereby forming a new basis for American foreign policy. The United States, Bush proclaimed, was thrust into yet another struggle between good and evil. "Freedom and fear, justice and cruelty, have always been at war, and we know that God is not neutral between them," Bush declared to Congress nine days after the terrorist attacks. In his January 2002 State of the Union address, Bush proclaimed that the United States confronted an "axis of evil" linking the governments of Iran, Iraq, and North Korea, along with terrorist groups, in a global conspiracy to destroy the United States. The task before the nation, Bush argued, went far beyond simply capturing Osama bin Laden and putting al Qaeda out of business. A global fight against terrorism and the evil it represented had to be mounted on all fronts. In making these claims, Bush echoed Ronald Reagan's earlier charges of an "evil empire" led by the Soviet Union. Bush also revived memories of the Truman Doctrine, proclaimed fifty-five years earlier, which envisioned two clashing global systems, one founded on freedom and the other on hatred and persecution.

These statements formed the pretext of a grand strategy that was formally unveiled in September 2002.[33] The strategy, which amounted to a Bush Doctrine, covered all aspects of foreign policy and affected relations with every country and international organization. Two pillars—the virtues of American primacy and the nation's right to wage preemptive war against perceived threats—captured the essential ends and means, respectively, of the new strategy.

The first of these pillars, American primacy, viewed the unipolar balance of power as the defining aspect of world politics after the Cold War and into the new millennium. As Bush noted in his introduction to the grand strategy, U.S. victories against fascism and communism left the world with "a single sustainable model for national success—freedom, democracy, and free enterprise." The U.S. government, the champion and embodiment of this model, would not exploit its advantages to dominate the world in a tyrannical fashion, as did empires of the past, but would serve these universal interests by shaping a "balance of power that favors human freedom." Competing against the United

---

[33] White House, "The National Security Strategy of the United States of America" (September 2002).

States in a unipolar world would be self-defeating and would divert the resources of would-be challengers from constructive purposes. "Our forces will be strong enough to dissuade potential adversaries from pursuing a military build-up in hopes of surpassing, or equaling, the power of the United States."[34]

The second pillar of the Bush Doctrine called for preemptive war, or striking first against enemies determined to inflict imminent harm on the United States. To the administration, the rise of private terrorist groups and their state sponsors changed the calculus of world politics to such an extent that conventional instruments of coercive statecraft no longer applied. In particular, nuclear deterrence and containment had been rendered null and void in a world of suicide bombers and proliferating weapons of mass destruction.[35] What would work in this perilous new world? Only taking the offensive:

> The United States has long maintained the option of preemptive action to counter a sufficient threat to our national security. The greater the threat, the greater the risk of inaction—and the more compelling the case for taking anticipatory action to defend ourselves, even if uncertainty remains as to the time and place of the enemy's attack. To prevent or forestall such hostile acts by our adversaries, the United States will, if necessary, act preemptively.[36]

In justifying preemptive war, the Bush Doctrine challenged a central tenet of international law that required nation-states to identify an imminent danger before they could legitimately resort to military force. But such clarity is not possible, the Bush Doctrine argued, because weapons of mass destruction can be easily concealed and delivered suddenly with catastrophic results. The call for preemptive war also brought into question the concept of national sovereignty, which had formed a centerpiece of the nation-state system for more than three centuries. As Richard Haass, director of policy planning for the State Department, had observed earlier, "Sovereignty entails obligations. One is not to massacre your own people. Another is not to support terrorism in any way. If a government fails to

---

[34] Ibid., 30.

[35] For an analysis of suicide terrorism, the most common tactic used in recent years, see Robert Pape, "The Strategic Logic of Suicide Terrorism," *American Political Science Review* 97 (August 2003), 343–361.

[36] White House, "National Security Strategy," 15.

meet these obligations, then it forfeits some of the normal advantages of sovereignty, including the right to be left alone in your own territory."[37]

Few Americans were aware that this was not the first time a strategy founded on U.S. primacy and preemption had been proposed. A decade earlier, officials in the first Bush administration had devised a similar formula. "Our strategy must now refocus on precluding the emergence of any future global competitor," wrote Paul D. Wolfowitz, the undersecretary of defense for policy who became Defense Secretary Rumsfeld's deputy in 2001. American leaders "must establish and protect a new order that holds the promise of convincing potential competitors that they need not aspire to a greater role."[38] Although favored by then–secretary of defense Cheney, the "defense guidance" was replaced by a softer version after it was leaked to the press and sparked public charges that the elder Bush was seeking world domination.[39] With much the same cast reassembled for the second Bush administration, and with the terrorist attacks providing a compelling pretext, the time for this new grand strategy had finally come.

In effect, the Bush Doctrine called for an American protectorate of the interstate system for an indefinite period of time, possibly on a permanent basis. The proclaimed goal of this grand strategy—U.S. primacy—would presumably be welcomed by leaders overseas, who could then turn their defense needs over to the global police force in Washington. American primacy would, in this respect, globalize America's security "umbrella" that earlier had relieved the NATO states and Japan of the burdens of national defense. And the same allies who shared Washington's view that a strictly defensive posture in the age of terrorism was a prescription for suicide would presumably embrace the means of the new strategy—preemptive war against those who threatened this world order. Foreign governments would face few risks in coming to this conclusion because the United States would handle the dirty work.

No other document in American diplomatic history, including the Monroe Doctrine, had ever made such bold assumptions or advanced such ambitious claims. Indeed, the scope of the new grand strategy was unprecedented in world history. The fact that it was accepted with little debate

---

[37] Quoted in Nicholas Lemann, "The Next World Order: The Bush Administration May Have a Brand-New Doctrine of Power," *New Yorker* (April 1, 2002), 45.

[38] "Excerpts from Pentagon's Plan: Prevent the Re-emergence of a New Rival," *New York Times* (March 8, 1992), A14.

[39] See David Armstrong, "Dick Cheney's Song of America: Drafting a Plan for Global Dominance," *Harper's* (October 2002), 76–82.

or fanfare in Congress, by the press, and among the public provides stark evidence of the hubris, or unbridled zeal, that was felt across the United States even after the September 11 attacks.

The Bush Doctrine, however, came into being as global uncertainties were mounting and fears of a growing spiral of violence were becoming more acute. The war on terror, although taking several high-profile prisoners, failed to break the back of al Qaeda or prevent calamitous terrorist attacks in many parts of the world. At the same time, a deepening slump in the world economy, combined with widening gaps between the world's rich and poor, was further dampening the prospects for stability. The new grand strategy, which was designed to stabilize the international system by asserting the benevolent intentions of its most powerful state, initially appeared to have the opposite effect. Global anxieties would intensify further as the U.S. counteroffensive extended beyond Afghanistan to Iraq, the subject of the next chapter.

Hot Wars in Afghanistan and Iraq

For President Bush, the proven threat of Islamist terrorism did not just threaten U.S. interests. Also at risk was his vision of a democratic and prosperous world order whose stability would be underwritten by U.S. military might. One did not need to be an expert in world politics to grasp the moment of opportunity for the United States. Destroying the threats that originated from a variety of failed, xenophobic, and repressive states would further propel the spread of freedom that accompanied the Soviet bloc's collapse. The United States, then, would at last realize the ambitions of its founders to remake the international system in its own image. The Bush Doctrine, based on the predominance of American power, viewed U.S. national interests as synonymous with global justice, peace, and prosperity. In short, American interests were universal.

The doctrine's general effect, however, was to alarm the very governments it was meant to reassure. Instead of eliciting goodwill toward Washington, the prospect of world domination by any single government, whatever its declared motives or intentions, troubled large and small countries alike. It was one thing for the United States to serve as a role model, a provider of public goods, and a strong advocate for global governance. It was quite another for American leaders to wield global hegemony through political coercion and military force. Still, President Bush, Vice President Cheney, and a swarm of White House advisers fervently believed the war on terror would open the door to a new American century. Their collective transformation from "pragmatists" to "crusaders" in American foreign policy assumed its most fateful form with their decision to invade Iraq in 2003.[1] Bush's conduct of the war on terror would have profound but uncertain consequences for American foreign policy. The legacy of this conflict, both overseas and within the United States, will remain for many years to come.

Bush did not wait to unveil his new foreign policy doctrine before launching the global "war on terror." As the U.S. invasion of Afghanistan in November 2001 revealed, the planners of the September 11 attacks

---

[1] For an elaboration of these presidential styles, see John Stoessinger, *Crusaders and Pragmatists: Movers of Modern American Foreign Policy*, 2nd ed. (New York: Norton, 1985).

U.S. Army soldiers from the Eighty-Second Airborne Division hike on Afghanistan's mountain trails in November 2002 in search of Taliban and al Qaeda forces. Their search-and-destroy effort in Afghanistan proved futile, however, because the enemy forces continued to control the rugged mountain region along the Afghan-Pakistani border.

on the United States earlier that year had to be pursued and destroyed in order to realize Bush's ambitious dream of security at home and enduring U.S. primacy abroad. Yet in the Middle East, Saddam Hussein's Iraq soon became the true litmus test of the Bush Doctrine. Starting in March 2003, the Iraq War would consume the attention of the White House—along with an immense share of the nation's military power, economic wealth, and diplomatic clout. Invading Iraq without the UN Security Council's blessing would leave the United States isolated from the global community. Most ominously, battling insurgents in Afghanistan and Iraq would limit Washington's capacity to manage other trouble spots around the world.[2]

Although the U.S. invasions of Afghanistan and Iraq touted distinct short-term goals—destroying al Qaeda's sanctuary and removing Saddam's weapons of mass destruction (WMDs), respectively—their long-term objectives aligned: Afghanistan and Iraq, home to two of the world's most repressive governments, had to be made "safe for democracy." The Muslim belt from North Africa across the Middle East and southwest Asia had resisted the trend of democratic reform that had swept across other

---

[2] Noah Coburn, *Losing Afghanistan: An Obituary for the Intervention* (Stanford, Calif.: Stanford University Press, 2016).

developing regions in the late twentieth century. Douglas J. Feith, Bush's undersecretary of defense for policy, believed an Iraq ruled by, and for, its newly empowered citizens "might be inspirational for people throughout the Middle East to try to increase the amount of freedom that they have."[3]

The domino theory, first adopted by President Dwight Eisenhower and applied to the war in Vietnam (see Chapter 4), found new life in the war on terror. Yet, this time, the dominoes would presumably fall in favor of American interests and America's moral mission. The spread of democracy to Afghanistan and Iraq, even through U.S. military force, would inspire democratic revolutions in other Islamic states. Not only would they establish mutually beneficial relations with one another, but, in accordance with democratic peace theory, they would make amends with Western powers, including the United States.

The Afghanistan Campaign

The U.S. military response to the 9/11 attacks first targeted the government of Afghanistan, whose overthrow was deemed essential if the al Qaeda terrorists based in the country were to be captured. Bush's initial demands to Afghan leaders—that they "hand over the terrorists" or "share their fate"—quickly yielded to a more aggressive strategy based on the regime's ejection from power. For better or worse, American forces would soon be thrust into the same mountainous terrain and impenetrable tribal societies that earlier thwarted the imperial ambitions of Great Britain and the Soviet Union.

Afghanistan entered the twenty-first century utterly exhausted by two decades of warfare, first against the Soviet occupiers, and then against internal warlords and rivals for power. Most of the country's infrastructure—roads, bridges, electrical utilities, communication systems, schools, and hospitals—had been damaged or destroyed in the conflicts. Meanwhile, the Afghan people had one of the world's shortest life expectancies (forty-three years), a literacy rate of less than 40 percent, and annual per capita incomes of less than $1,000. Hundreds of thousands of Afghans died in the tribal violence of the 1990s; millions more fled the nation as refugees. Even so, time would not allow for national recovery at the dawn of the new millennium, as Afghanistan quickly became the prime target of America's war on terror.

---

[3]Quoted in Nicholas Lemann, "After Iraq: The Plan to Remake the Middle East," *New Yorker* (February 17, 2003), 71–72.

Benign Neglect after the Cold War

As described in Chapters 5 and 6, Presidents Jimmy Carter and Ronald Reagan refused to accept the Soviet Union's 1979 invasion of Afghanistan, which was prompted by the demise of the pro-Soviet regime in Kabul. The covert operation undertaken in Afghanistan by the U.S. Central Intelligence Agency (CIA) during the 1980s on behalf of the Afghan *mujahidin*, or "freedom fighters" as they were then known in Washington, was crucial in diminishing the Soviet Union's sphere of influence. William Casey, Reagan's CIA director, saw the Soviet intervention as a monumental blunder and a golden opportunity for the United States to gain the strategic advantage in South Asia. Not only would Afghanistan become the Kremlin's Vietnam, but the economic and military costs of the occupation would sap what little was left of its strength. Thus for American leaders, the few billions of dollars required to support the *mujahidin* would be well spent, even if some of this money funded shadowy figures with uncertain agendas, including Osama bin Laden.

The American government's clarity of purpose blurred, however, once the Soviet tanks left Afghanistan in 1989 and the Soviet Union's downward spiral began. In South Asia, like elsewhere in the world, the end of the Cold War reshaped American interests. The State Department found itself opening diplomatic posts in new post-Soviet states such as Kazakhstan, while loosening U.S. ties with other governments. President George H. W. Bush, preoccupied with Russia and Eastern Europe, had little interest in Afghanistan after the Soviet withdrawal. In his view, the U.S. mission there had been accomplished. What happened later was up to the Afghans.[4]

This policy of benign neglect, typical of the United States in the aftermath of major conflicts, would come back to haunt American leaders. Even before the last Soviet troops had departed, the regional warlords across Afghanistan, who had united against their common Soviet enemy, turned on each other. Supported by the Pashtuns in the southern plains to the ethnic Uzbeks and Tajiks in the north, well-armed militias, including the so-called Northern Alliance, sought to protect their territorial enclaves and, wherever possible, to carve out larger spheres of influence. Controlling the central government in Kabul, which was reduced to rubble after a decade of Soviet occupation and armed struggle, was of secondary interest.

---

[4] It is revealing that James Baker, Bush's secretary of state, made only two references to Afghanistan in his 672-page memoir, *The Politics of Diplomacy: Revolution, War, and Peace, 1989–1992*, written with Thomas M. DeFrank (New York: Putnam, 1995).

Afghanistan remained in the hands of the crumbling Marxist regime, which was finally overthrown in February 1992 after northern rebels, led by Ahmad Shah Massoud, shot their way into the presidential palace. Although Massoud preached the gospel of national unity, he lacked support across Afghanistan's splintered society. As a result, his state soon succumbed to civil war and lawlessness. Heroin and opium became the nation's chief exports, along with the huge stockpiles of Soviet and American weapons that were no longer needed in the post-occupation era. Still, plenty of those weapons remained in the hands of the Afghan outlaws who filled the void in government control.

The anarchy continued until September 1996, when a well-organized political and religious movement known as the Taliban seized power in Kabul and gradually, but viciously, established order across Afghanistan. The Taliban ("religious students" in English) imposed a strict doctrine of Islamic law, or *Sharia*, which became the basis of government policy. Women were forbidden to attend schools, pursue occupations, or leave their homes without a male relative. Men were forced to wear beards maintained at a certain length. "Frivolous" activities such as flying kites and playing cards were banned, along with watching television, playing music, or using the Internet. The Taliban enforced these laws by means of public floggings, amputations, and mass executions held in soccer stadiums. Meanwhile, the government crushed religious movements that did not follow the *Sharia* code and expelled dozens of international aid agencies from Afghanistan.

In Washington, President Bill Clinton watched these developments unfold and, lacking moderate contacts in Afghanistan, initially sought friendly relations with the Taliban. From Clinton's perspective, the new rulers at least seemed able to maintain order in the country and possibly to shut down its flourishing narcotics trade. The Sunni Muslims who led the Taliban, though supported by Pakistan and Saudi Arabia, were contemptuous of the Shiite clerics who ruled Iran, so the emergence of a monolithic Islamic theocracy across central Asia was unlikely. Perhaps the United States, which ordinarily would be a sworn enemy of such a regime, could find common cause with the religious zealots in Kabul.

Clinton's chief regional concern at the time centered on bin Laden and his al Qaeda followers, whose pursuit of Islamic "purification" through violent means found a receptive home in Afghanistan. The president, who had linked al Qaeda to a growing wave of anti-American terrorist attacks, proposed a deal to the Taliban: American political and economic support in return for bin Laden's surrender. But only the most naive members of Clinton's National Security Council expected the offer to be accepted.

Mullah Mohammad Omar, the Taliban's spiritual and political leader, denied having a close relationship with bin Laden. His assurances were contradicted by the growing presence of al Qaeda, which opened training camps for aspiring *jihadists* from across the Islamic world.

Clinton's domestic troubles, particularly the Monica Lewinsky sex scandal during his second term, denied him the political support he needed to act forcefully against the Taliban and al Qaeda. Members of Congress, still dominated by the rival Republican Party, criticized Clinton's Pentagon for missing its al Qaeda targets in the August 1998 cruise missile strikes after the terrorist attacks on U.S. embassies in Kenya and Tanzania. Clinton was also preoccupied with other foreign policy concerns such as trade with China and the war in Kosovo. The effect of these distractions was to diminish the al Qaeda threat in the minds of top decision makers. When George W. Bush entered the presidency in January 2001, he considered Islamic terrorism a major but not an urgent concern, and he adopted a strategy of pursuing al Qaeda with the help of Massoud's armies in Afghanistan, along with a hefty infusion of CIA funding. This strategy was nullified on September 9, 2001, when al Qaeda agents posing as sympathetic Arab journalists murdered Massoud in his bungalow. His assassination left the United States without influential friends in Afghanistan or any hope of restraining bin Laden's wildest ambitions.

Phase 1: Dislodging the Taliban

The perpetrators of the September 11 attacks were traced immediately to Afghanistan, making a large-scale U.S. invasion of the country inevitable. The counterattack would unfold in two stages. First, American forces would help antigovernment Afghan militias overthrow the Taliban and round up the al Qaeda terrorists responsible for the September 11 attacks. Second, the U.S. government would lead an effort, presumably with the United Nations, to create a new, democratic regime that would not threaten its neighbors or serve as a sanctuary for Islamic terrorists. The military commanders' goal in the first phase was to apply enough muscle to topple the Taliban, but not so much force that neighboring Islamic countries would feel threatened. The plan for Operation Enduring Freedom called for U.S. ground forces to be limited to special operations, such as identifying targets for aerial attacks. The ground offensive would be conducted by homegrown forces, including the Northern Alliance and a second flank of southern Pashtun forces. The combination of U.S. bombing raids and pressure on the ground would send the enemy fleeing for refuge to Pakistan, where enemy forces would be captured and turned over to the United States.

The U.S.-led offensive against Afghanistan's Taliban regime began on September 22, 2001, less than two weeks after the September 11 terrorist attacks, when members of the Northern Alliance initiated attacks on government positions. The bombing raids on Afghanistan, conducted by American and British air forces, began in early October. The first wave disabled the Taliban's transportation and communication networks in the urban centers around Kandahar and Kabul. Troops from the Northern Alliance then swept into Kalafghan and Mazar-e-Sharif, capturing both strategic cities with little resistance. Kabul, the capital city, fell on November 12, and Afghanistan was freed from the grip of the Taliban regime.

Several factors led to the Taliban's surprisingly prompt surrender. American and British air forces flew more than twenty thousand bombing sorties in this first phase of the conflict, exceeding the combined number of strikes against Serbian targets in Bosnia in 1995 and Kosovo in 1999. Laser-guided "bunker busters" destroyed many of the underground caves that sheltered the regime, while fifteen-thousand-pound "daisy cutters," the biggest conventional bombs in the U.S. arsenal, decimated the ground forces. The bombing campaign was aided by unmanned intelligence drones that hovered above targets and provided precise coordinates to American and British pilots. And in a technological feat without historical precedent, other drones dropped guided missiles on enemy targets, including al Qaeda commanders. An estimated fifteen thousand enemy forces died in the U.S.-led attacks; about seven thousand others were sent to a makeshift prison camp at the U.S. military base in Guantánamo Bay, Cuba. The death toll among American troops was far smaller—about fifty.[5]

The central task of bringing the al Qaeda leaders to justice still lay ahead, and this proved far more difficult. The second phase of the military campaign, Operation Anaconda, was designed to round up the terrorists, including bin Laden, as they fled from their headquarters and training centers. But the mission failed. In the climactic battle at Tora Bora, U.S. special forces were overmatched by bin Laden's armed supporters in the rugged mountain peaks. Meanwhile, the supposedly pro-American Afghan militias did not stop members of al Qaeda from crossing into Pakistan. Thus bin Laden, who was believed to be pinned down in the area, escaped. Even a

---

[5] Michael E. O'Hanlon, "A Flawed Masterpiece," *Foreign Affairs* (May–June 2002), 47–63.

U.S. reward of $5 million for his capture proved inadequate in a region where bin Laden retained widespread support. Rather than seeing newscasts of the al Qaeda leader's arrest, the U.S. public watched bin Laden boast about the September 11 attacks and vow that Americans "will never dream of security [until] the infidel armies leave the land of Muhammad"—an explicit reference to Saudi Arabia, bin Laden's birthplace.

Phase 2: Nation Building in Rugged Terrain

Even if American forces had captured bin Laden, the United States still had to put Afghanistan back together. A common Western expression, taken from the sign at a Pottery Barn and repeated occasionally by Secretary of State Colin Powell, seemed apt: "You break it, you own it." Thus, whatever came of the military mission, a new regime was needed in Kabul to run the government while assuming the role of a cooperative international "citizen." As American leaders saw it, Afghanistan must be converted into a Western-style democracy, replete with a constitution, elected leaders, and a legal system that protected human rights. By helping to create a democratic Afghanistan that was presumably friendlier toward the West, the United States and its allies would also gain a higher measure of security.

The Bonn Agreement, sponsored by the UN and approved by regional leaders in December 2001, called for a "gender-sensitive, multi-ethnic, and fully representative" Afghan government that would cooperate with "the international community in the fight against terrorism, drugs, and organized crime."[6] The agreement called for an interim government that would keep the state functioning until elections could be held for a president and parliament. The task of overseeing the electoral process fell to Hamid Karzai, a Pashtun tribal leader whose friendly relations with the West made him a natural choice to lead the interim government.

But the very notion of national elections was unfamiliar to most Afghans, who identified more closely with tribal leaders. For the architects of Afghanistan's political future, truly representative government meant holding "free and fair" national elections open to all citizens. This kind of election transpired when a majority of Afghans elected Karzai president in October 2004 and returned to the polls in September 2005 to elect members of parliament. The newly elected legislators, a quarter of whom had to be women under new election rules, admitted they did "not know even

---

[6]United Nations, "Agreement on Provisional Arrangements in Afghanistan Pending the Re-establishment of Permanent Government Institutions" (December 5, 2001).

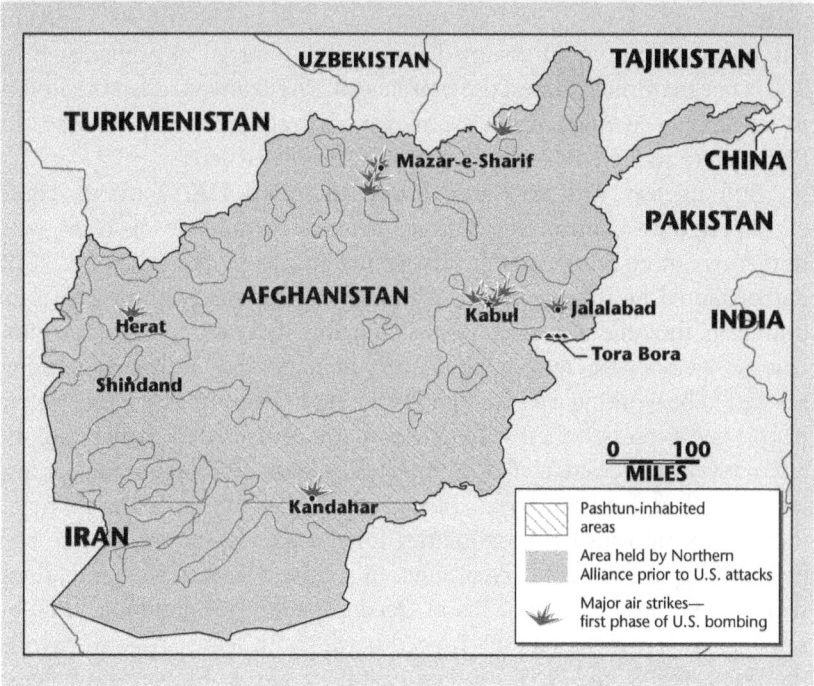

Map 11-1   The War in Afghanistan, Autumn 2001

UZBEKISTAN

TAJIKISTAN

TURKMENISTAN

Mazar-e-Sharif

CHINA

PAKISTAN

AFGHANISTAN

Jalalabad

Kabul

INDIA

Herat

Tora Bora

Shindand

Kandahar

IRAN

0   100
MILES

Pashtun-inhabited areas

Area held by Northern Alliance prior to U.S. attacks

Major air strikes— first phase of U.S. bombing

the basics of democracy, in particular how a Western-devised Parliament works."[7] They were willing to learn, however, and that alone was a cause for hope among Western state builders. The political reforms left open the question of military control of Afghanistan, which remained deeply divided by power struggles among regional factions, primarily the southern Pashtuns and members of the Northern Alliance. There was also the question of the Taliban. Like the *mujahidin* during the Soviet occupation, the Taliban leaders retreated to the surrounding mountains and valleys, where they regrouped and plotted their return to power. Karzai's authority extended barely past the city limits of Kabul. No central government could survive for long under such circumstances.

American and British forces, therefore, faced an extended mission to keep the new Afghan government from succumbing to internal pressures. In 2003, the two allies turned for help to the North Atlantic Treaty Organization, which dispatched troops to Afghanistan in the first

---

[7]Carlotta Gall, "Afghan Legislators Get Crash Course in Ways of Democracy," *New York Times* (December 19, 2005), A11.

"out of area" deployments in the alliance's history. The NATO contingent was initially limited to Kabul and the northwestern areas of Afghanistan, with American forces patrolling the treacherous southern region and the Pakistani border. NATO assumed responsibility for all of Afghanistan by 2007. For the United States, the presence of NATO forces added credibility to its mission in Afghanistan. Moreover, the reinforcements allowed the Pentagon to redirect its energies and resources elsewhere.

Still unclear was how just fifteen thousand NATO troops could be expected to control Afghanistan, a territory the size of Texas with immensely more hostile terrain. Escalating attacks by the Taliban in 2006 demonstrated its staying power. Although history offered little cause for optimism, the American strategy of stabilizing Afghanistan through regime change, democratic reform, and U.S. military and economic support seemed to be working well enough. By voting in large numbers, the Afghan people had expressed their willingness to give democracy a chance.[8] All the alternatives—renewed civil war, the restoration of Taliban rule, or the takeover of Afghanistan by al Qaeda terrorists—were far more ominous, though not implausible, possibilities for the nation's future. By the end of 2008, the Taliban controlled much of southern Afghanistan and, along with Osama bin Laden and his al Qaeda operatives, continued to enjoy safe havens across the nation's rugged border with Pakistan—still beyond the reach of U.S. and NATO forces. Gaining control of this unruly region would require a much larger military operation.

Renewed Hostilities against Iraq

Shortly after the U.S. invasion of Afghanistan, Bush's foreign policy advisers turned their attention to the second front in the war on terror—Iraq. Preemptive war was a central element of the Bush Doctrine, but it was controversial because, under international law, nations must not invade other nations unless they are attacked first or face the near certainty of imminent attack. Just-war doctrine, which dates back to the Middle Ages and remains a common point of reference, forbids the use of force unless all peaceful alternatives have been exhausted. From Bush's standpoint, waiting to be attacked in the age of terrorism merely invited aggression, a lesson learned at a terrible cost on September 11.

---

[8]United Nations Assistance Mission for Afghanistan, *UNAMA Report: Number of Afghan Civilian Casualties Rises by 24 Percent in First Half of 2014* (New York: United Nations, July 9, 2014).

Impact and Influence: Gen. David Petraeus

AP Photo/Evan Vucci, File

Few recent leaders in the U.S. Defense Department have had more impact on American foreign policy than Gen. David Petraeus. As commanding general of U.S. and allied forces in Iraq in 2007, Petraeus organized a military "surge" that gradually reduced the level of violence among insurgents, Iraqi forces, and the U.S.-led military coalition. His surge strategy—to win the "hearts and minds" of war-weary Iraqi citizens through cooperative support—departed from the Bush administration's previous emphasis of using overwhelming force against insurgents even within large population centers. Petraeus later became commander of the U.S. Central Command, which extended from Egypt to Kazakhstan, and then assumed control over NATO and U.S. forces in Afghanistan.

In 2011, President Obama nominated Petraeus to become director of the Central Intelligence Agency. His selection to lead the CIA symbolized the agency's increasing role in conducting military operations in many parts of the world. Previously, the armed services were designated to conduct such military operations, with the CIA's role limited to providing accurate intelligence to guide American troops. This applied especially to covert (secret) operations for which the agency drew public and congressional criticism during the Cold War. Modern technologies in gathering and using intelligence, including aerial reconnaissance conducted by unmanned "drone" aircraft, further blurred the distinction between intelligence gathering and war fighting.

The doctrine of preemptive war seemed tailor-made for Iraq.[9] Saddam Hussein remained firmly in control of the country despite the virtual collapse of its military forces and of its economy from years of UN sanctions. Although American and British air forces kept Iraq bottled up by rigidly enforcing

---

[9] Although the Bush administration freely applied the doctrine of preemptive war to Iraq, the 2003 invasion would actually constitute *preventive*—not preemptive—war. Preemptive war is launched against a foreign power that is clearly on the verge of attacking one's own territory—that is, its forces are about to storm the gates. Saddam's forces did not pose that kind of immediate threat to the United States. He would thus be overthrown to *prevent* Iraq from developing a long-term threat to U.S. security.

no-fly zones across most of the country, their containment of Saddam did not weaken his resolve. On the contrary, the Iraqi leader became more deeply entrenched, more brutal in suppressing internal dissent, and more contemptuous of the United States and other Western powers. After he ejected UN weapons inspectors in 1998, it was impossible for outside observers to know whether Iraq was reassembling the WMD stockpiles that UN crews had found earlier and removed. It was also not clear what had happened to the large quantities of hazardous materials that could be used to develop biological and chemical weapons. Past experience, the absolute secrecy of the Iraqi government, and Saddam's defiant posture all suggested that he still possessed such weapons and would freely use them, as he had in the past.

President Clinton had spent his entire presidency in a frustrating and ultimately futile effort to manage Saddam, the Sunni-led Ba'ath Party that represented his power base, and the tangle of UN sanctions imposed on Iraq. Clinton's containment policy, much like George Kennan's strategy for the Soviet Union, presumed that, in time, external isolation would ultimately suffocate the enemy. In Iraq's case, however, it was the United States that was being worn down. Clinton, preoccupied with the crisis in Kosovo and his own political problems, clung to his containment policy.

After Bush's election in November 2000 and the attacks of September 2001, some U.S. officials were so driven to invade Iraq that they called for the invasion to begin *before* the Afghanistan campaign. Deputy Secretary of Defense Paul Wolfowitz reportedly made this case to the Bush war cabinet on September 15, 2001. "He worried about 100,000 American troops bogged down in mountain fighting in Afghanistan six months from then," journalist Bob Woodward reported. "In contrast, Iraq was a brittle, oppressive regime that might break easily. It was doable."[10] Although Afghanistan did come first, the White House quickly turned its attention to Iraq. "Simply stated, there is no doubt that Saddam Hussein now has weapons of mass destruction," Vice President Dick Cheney told war veterans on August 26, 2002. "There is no doubt he is amassing them to use against our friends, against our allies, and against us."[11]

Advocates of regime change believed that overthrowing Saddam would produce other benefits beyond putting to rest fears of Iraq's arsenal and ties to al Qaeda. First, military action would send a clear signal to other "rogue states" that the United States had taken the offensive. Second, the action would affirm the legitimacy of the UN, whose Security Council had

---

[10] Bob Woodward, *Bush at War* (New York: Simon and Schuster, 2002), 83.

[11] White House, "Vice President Speaks at VFW 103rd National Convention" (August 26, 2002).

threatened Saddam with "serious consequences" if he did not fully cooperate with weapons inspectors. Third, a takeover of Iraq would give U.S. military forces a forward staging area in the heart of the Middle East from which it could conduct other antiterrorism operations. Fourth, with the birth of a new regime, the Iraqi people would be spared further dictatorial rule, economic privation, and human rights abuses—a moral victory of its own.[12] Finally, as noted earlier, a democratic transition in Iraq would trigger a democratic domino effect in the Arab world; Iraq would serve as a role model for other political reformers in the region.

The presumed benefits of a second war against Iraq in 2003 were offset by an array of political problems. The primary strategic concern was that military action in Iraq would divert the U.S. government from the war on terror. Tactical obstacles to regime change also existed. Even if the invasion succeeded without much resistance, it was unclear how long the postwar occupation would last, how much it would cost, and who would foot the bill. Diplomatic obstacles raised further doubts. Moderate Arab states refused to endorse a U.S.-led invasion of Iraq at a time when Washington was doing little to prevent Israel from cracking down on Palestinians. And most other governments were skeptical of the plan to invade Iraq. Even the NATO allies wavered. Among the other major powers, only British prime minister Tony Blair supported the White House. But Blair's pledge on behalf of Britain's "special relationship" with Washington crippled him politically.

Making the Case for War

None of these concerns stopped Bush from pressing forward with his plan for regime change in Iraq. The White House believed continued containment was doomed to failure because of the eroding grip of economic sanctions and the mounting international pressure to ease or lift them altogether. Bush also rejected deterrence because of Saddam's past erratic behavior and the possibility that he might share his WMD arsenal with terrorists. A covert operation by Iraqi dissidents to stage a coup was dismissed as an option because Saddam maintained total control over his internal enemies. For lack of better choices, preemptive war was the "least bad" alternative.[13]

---

[12] In April 2002, the UN Commission on Human Rights condemned the "all-pervasive repression and suppression" of Iraqi citizens that was "sustained by broad-based discrimination and widespread terror." UN Commission on Human Rights, "Resolution: Situation of Human Rights in Iraq" (April 11, 2002).

[13] For an elaboration of this rationale, see Kenneth M. Pollack, *The Threatening Storm: The Case for Invading Iraq* (New York: Random House, 2002).

Impact and Influence: Saddam Hussein

1991

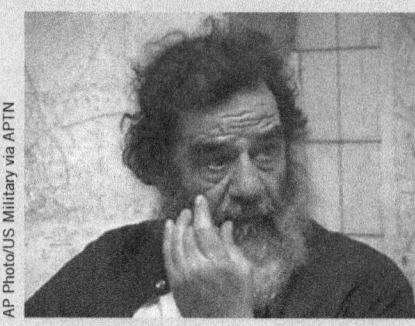

December 2003

For all of its advantages as the world's "lone superpower" after the Cold War, the United States could not prevent hostile foreign leaders from sparking regional conflicts and prompting intervention by U.S. military forces. Among these leaders, Iraqi president Saddam Hussein provoked the first post–Cold War crisis by invading Kuwait in 1990 and threatening to seize control of the Persian Gulf's vast oil supplies.

Saddam originally achieved prominence as a leader of the Ba'ath Party, an Arab nationalist movement. After taking power in Iraq in 1979, he quickly prepared its army to invade neighboring Iran and topple its newly installed Islamic government, which he viewed as a threat. The ensuing Iran-Iraq War produced hundreds of thousands of casualties. It was soon followed by another conflict, this time arising from Iraq's invasion of Kuwait, which was reversed by a UN coalition led by the United States. After his defeat, Saddam remained firmly in power despite harsh UN economic sanctions against Iraq. The terrorist attacks of September 2001 prompted President George W. Bush to invade Iraq. Saddam eluded his enemies until December 2003, when he was captured and then tried and executed for his crimes against his Iraqi enemies.

Although Bush remained determined to oust Saddam, he initially bowed to pressure for a multilateral approach to the standoff. Secretary of State Powell, echoing the stated concerns of most foreign leaders, insisted that the United States gain the UN Security Council's endorsement of military action against Iraq. A U.S. invasion without such an endorsement, Powell argued, would lack legitimacy and turn much of the world against the presumed "liberators" of Baghdad. Bush reluctantly agreed and supported a UN resolution that gave Saddam another, and presumably final, chance to disarm. In a speech to the General Assembly on September 12, 2002, the president issued a direct challenge: "All the world faces a test, and the United Nations a difficult and defining moment. Are Security Council resolutions to be honored and enforced, or cast aside without consequence? Will the United Nations serve the purposes of its founding, or will it be irrelevant?"

The strength of the White House's case depended on the latest intelligence about the threat posed by Saddam. Pentagon officials doubted the inconclusive findings of the CIA and even the Defense Intelligence Agency. Thus in September 2002, they opened their own unit, the Office of Special Plans, whose probe extended beyond conventional sources to include Iraqi exiles who had long advocated Saddam's overthrow. Ahmed Chalabi, the most prominent of these exiles, met frequently with U.S. officials and was widely viewed in the White House as Saddam's ideal successor.[14] The information provided by Iraqi exiles became part of a National Intelligence Estimate (NIE), issued in October, whose opening lines summarized the case against Saddam:

> Iraq has continued its WMD programs in defiance of UN resolutions and restrictions. Baghdad has chemical and biological weapons as well as missiles with ranges in excess of UN restrictions; if left unchecked, it probably will have a nuclear weapon during this decade. Baghdad hides large portions of Iraq's WMD efforts. Revelations after the Gulf War starkly demonstrate the extensive efforts undertaken by Iraq to deny information. Since inspections ended in 1998, Iraq has maintained its chemical weapons effort, energized its missile program, and invested heavily in biological weapons; most analysts assess Iraq is reconstituting its nuclear weapons program.[15]

The political calendar was on Bush's side as he pressed for war against Iraq. Midterm elections were scheduled for November 5, and members of Congress knew that opposing a popular president in wartime was political suicide. Bush appealed directly to voters in Cincinnati on October 7: "America must not ignore the threat against us. Facing clear evidence of

---

[14]George Packer, *The Assassin's Gate: America in Iraq* (New York: Farrar, Straus and Giroux, 2005), 105–109.

[15]Director of Central Intelligence, "Iraq's Weapons of Mass Destruction Programs" (October 2002).

peril, we cannot wait for the final proof—the smoking gun—that could come in the form of a mushroom cloud." Within days, Congress approved a joint resolution calling for military action against Iraq with or without the UN's blessing. Republican candidates swept most races in November, securing control of both chambers and ensuring a united front against Iraq.

Bush's electoral triumph led to his success in the UN on November 8. Without the prospect of dividing and conquering the U.S. government, the Security Council declared Iraq in "material breach" of past UN resolutions and required Saddam to provide "immediate, unconditional, and unrestricted" access to government offices, military installations, factories, and the dozens of presidential palaces previously off limits to the UN. Iraq faced "serious consequences" if it failed to cooperate with the inspectors. Although these consequences were not identified, there was little doubt what form they would take: a full-scale attack by the United States and any countries that chose to follow its lead into Baghdad.

The UN resolution prompted Saddam to adopt a strategy that ultimately cost him control of his country. According to information gathered after the U.S. invasion, in December 2002, Saddam secretly informed his military commanders that Iraq's WMD stockpiles had been destroyed in order to deprive the United States of a legitimate *casus belli*, or rationale for war. Saddam ordered his commanders to "scrub the country so that the UN inspectors did not discover any vestiges of old WMD."[16] Still, Saddam remained evasive in his contacts with weapons inspectors. His reason for adopting this stance was revealing: Saddam hoped to maintain leverage in his rivalry with neighboring Iran, which, fourteen years after the Iran-Iraq War, he still considered Iraq's primary threat. By leaving some doubt about his alleged WMD arsenal, Saddam felt protected against a second war with Iran. In so doing, however, he opened the door to the U.S. invasion and his own overthrow.

Unaware of Saddam's secret meetings, Bush was confident that the UN inspectors, who visited three hundred sites without notice in December 2002 and January 2003, would confirm his allegations of an Iraqi WMD arsenal. But the president also played his military card. He ordered nearly two hundred thousand U.S. troops to the Persian Gulf in a mobilization that included four army divisions, five aircraft carrier battle groups, six hundred strike aircraft, and thirty ships from which cruise missiles could be launched. The British government moved thirty thousand troops and

---

[16]Michael R. Gordon and Gen. Bernard E. Trainor, *Cobra II: The Inside Story of the Invasion and Occupation of Iraq* (New York: Pantheon, 2006), 119. On Iran, see ibid., 64–65.

scores of additional bombers to the Persian Gulf as well. The combined forces, Bush said, provided the muscle needed to back up the UN ultimatum. The advance deployments were also necessary because military action in the winter and spring would be preferable to fighting in the stifling heat of an Iraqi summer.

In keeping with Saddam's secret strategy, the eagerly awaited interim report of the UN weapons inspectors did not provide clear evidence one way or another. Hans Blix, head of the inspection team, told the Security Council on January 27 that he had found no WMD stockpiles in Iraq that would justify a military response. This finding did not mean, however, that Saddam fully cooperated with the inspectors or resolved all doubts about his weapons arsenal. To the contrary, Blix accused the Iraqi leader of hindering inspections, not fully accounting for suspected caches of chemical and biological agents, and preventing Blix's team from interviewing scientists without government "minders" present. Mohamed ElBaradei, chief inspector of the International Atomic Energy Agency, also reported mixed results. His team of inspectors had found no trace of an Iraqi nuclear weapons program. Like Blix, he appealed for more time and more inspections.

Nevertheless, the White House rejected these calls and declared that further delays would only prolong the cat-and-mouse game Saddam had mastered in the 1990s. But the president faced stiff opposition in the UN Security Council. French president Jacques Chirac vowed to use his veto power to defeat a war resolution, and German leaders also refused to support war without further evidence of Iraqi violations. Secretary of Defense Donald Rumsfeld then poured salt in the diplomatic wounds by dismissing France and Germany as remnants of the "old Europe" and likening Germany's defiance to that of Libya and Cuba. The strains within the Atlantic alliance were open for all to see even as NATO approved, in November 2002, a new round of eastward expansion.[17]

Back in the UN Security Council, French resistance to the Iraq invasion was joined with the resistance of China and Russia, two other veto-wielding members. All three countries maintained political and economic contacts with Saddam, and all three feared the outbreak of terrorist attacks within their borders that might follow such an invasion. The task of convincing the Security Council fell to Secretary of State Powell, who addressed the council on February 5. He described U.S. intelligence

---

[17]The new NATO members inducted in 2004 were the Baltic states of Estonia, Latvia, and Lithuania, along with Bulgaria, Romania, Slovakia, and Slovenia.

reports of Saddam "disbursing rocket launchers and warheads containing biological warfare agents," of WMD laboratories in railroad cars, and of shipments of aluminum tubes to Iraq for the production of nuclear fuel. "Leaving Saddam in possession of weapons of mass destruction for a few more months or years is not an option, not in a post–September 11 world," Powell concluded.[18] But his words failed to convince the Security Council that Iraq could not be contained by expanded UN inspections and "smarter" sanctions.[19]

The United States was clearly losing the battle over world public opinion. Massive antiwar rallies were held across Europe on February 15, a peculiar spectacle given that war had not yet broken out. Nearly one million protesters turned out in London, while six hundred thousand filled the streets of Rome and five hundred thousand rallied in Berlin. A central concern of would-be allies was that their own citizens would rise up if their governments supported preventive war against Iraq. Turkish legislators so feared allying with the United States that they refused to offer their territory to stage a northern front against Iraq. Large demonstrations also took place across the United States. More than one hundred city councils, including those of Chicago, Detroit, Los Angeles, and Philadelphia, approved resolutions opposing action against Iraq without UN endorsement. Although most public opinion polls found Americans supportive of regime change, those polled generally preferred a war sanctioned by the UN and supported by America's key allies.

Disputes within the Pentagon also erupted into public view in February. The army's chief of staff, Gen. Eric Shinseki, told the Senate Armed Services Committee on February 25 that "several hundred thousand" troops were required to topple Saddam, maintain order, and provide security long enough to elect a new government that could assume sovereign authority. Two days later, Deputy Defense Secretary Wolfowitz contradicted the army chief, calling his estimates "wildly off the mark." In the end, the invasion force comprised fewer than two hundred thousand troops, less than half the number used to eject Iraq from Kuwait in 1991.

---

[18]White House, "U.S. Secretary of State Colin Powell Addresses the UN Security Council" (February 5, 2003).

[19]Although this critique had always prevailed among liberals, many realists—who normally favored the assertion of U.S. power—also believed Iraq did not pose an imminent threat to the United States. See John J. Mearsheimer and Stephen M. Walt, "Iraq: An Unnecessary War," *Foreign Policy* (January–February 2003), 50–59.

Operation Iraqi Freedom

The invasion of Iraq, dubbed Operation Iraqi Freedom, began early on March 20, 2003, with a U.S. attempt to decapitate Iraq. Intelligence reports had indicated that Saddam and his two sons, Qusay and Uday, were meeting at the Dora Farms military compound outside of Baghdad. President Bush approved a sneak attack on the compound with two-thousand-pound "bunker busters" and other cruise missiles. Although the bombs did reach their targets, it later became clear that the intelligence reports were wrong; Saddam and his sons were not at the compound. Even without reaching their targets, however, the bombs provided a thunderous signal that the invasion of Iraq had begun.

A sustained bombing campaign, dubbed "shock and awe" by U.S. military commanders, followed on March 21 and coincided with a massive ground offensive by coalition forces on a trajectory from Kuwait through the desert to Baghdad. As American tanks from the Third Infantry Division rolled toward Baghdad on April 6, British forces took control of Basra, Iraq's second largest city located near the Persian Gulf. Early resistance by Iraqi forces soon withered and cleared the path to the Iraqi capital, where U.S. Marines toppled a statue of Saddam on April 9. Meanwhile, Saddam's whereabouts remained unknown, and no one was certain whether he was dead or alive. Whatever Saddam's status, his reign of terror was over. The success of Operation Iraqi Freedom demonstrated once again the supremacy of U.S. military power. The simultaneous air and ground attacks permitted coalition forces to capture Iraqi oil fields before they could be destroyed by retreating Iraqi forces. All of Iraq's major cities were under allied control by the end of April. On May 1, President Bush, dressed in a flight suit, made a dramatic landing on an aircraft carrier off the coast of California to celebrate the overthrow of Saddam's regime. Under a banner proclaiming "Mission Accomplished," Bush announced that "major combat operations in Iraq have ended."

But the routing of Saddam's regime did not settle matters. Allied forces could not simply declare victory and return home as they had done twelve years earlier. The troops had to restore order to and ultimately rebuild Iraq's cities, which erupted not only in celebration, but also in widespread looting, violent reprisals against Saddam loyalists, and attacks on U.S. soldiers. Armed Iraqis ransacked stores, government ministries, hospitals, military installations, and the National Museum of Iraq. Attacks on media outlets and electrical utilities left Baghdad literally in the dark and lacking a telephone system or other means of internal communication. The chaos in Baghdad and other cities revealed a darker reality for the occupation forces, who were not "greeted as liberators" as Vice President Cheney had predicted just before the invasion.

The Bush administration's post-invasion plan called for a short period of U.S. military occupation, followed by the drafting of a constitution and the holding of national elections. Instead of turning this process over to the State Department, which traditionally has managed post-conflict recovery efforts, Bush ordered the Pentagon to assume this responsibility. But military leaders were quickly overwhelmed by the demands of governing Iraq. Jay Garner, the retired lieutenant general appointed to oversee postwar Iraq, lasted only one month in the post. His replacement, L. Paul Bremer, created the Coalition Provisional Authority on April 21 to manage the reconstruction efforts and in July formed the Iraqi Governing Council, composed largely of regional leaders who shared a common hatred of Saddam. Although the council provided the appearance of power sharing, Bremer alone made the critical decisions regarding Iraq's future. Clad in a pinstriped suit even in the scorching heat of the Iraqi desert, he assumed the image of a colonial viceroy.

The American occupation quickly faced new problems. Contrary to the Bush administration's assurances that, in the words of CIA director George J. Tenet, uncovering evidence of WMDs in Iraq was a "slam dunk," weapons inspectors failed to find any stockpiles in the weeks and months following the invasion. The absence of WMDs shattered the White House's rationale for invading Iraq. At the end of 2003, with no such weapons found, chief weapons inspector David Kay testified to Congress that the prewar intelligence was "almost all wrong." The White House then quickly shifted its rationale for the war to democratic nation building, a goal that was part of the original war justification but secondary to WMD concerns and Saddam's alleged links to the September 11 terrorists.

But even nation building soon proved impossible for coalition forces and the civilian contractors hired to rebuild Iraq. Well-armed insurgents launched virtually constant attacks on the troops and contractors, largely in the form of suicide attacks and the detonation of "improvised explosive devices." Insurgents bombed the UN headquarters in August and the international Red Cross headquarters in October, both located in Baghdad. By attacking recruitment stations for military and police officers, the insurgents sent a separate message to Iraqis: Cooperate with the foreign invaders and you will be killed. The December 13, 2003, capture of Saddam, who was hiding in an underground bunker near his hometown of Tikrit, acted as a temporary source of relief. But news of failed WMD searches, a growing insurgency, and mounting casualties—nearly five hundred by the end of the year—confirmed that the Iraqi mission had veered perilously off course.

Who were the insurgents? Many were identified as members of Saddam's ousted government, the Ba'ath Party, and the Republican Guard. These Sunni Muslims, who represented just 20 percent of Iraq's population, had dominated Iraq for decades from their territorial base in the central region (see Map 11-2). They had the most to lose from Saddam's overthrow and the most to gain from preventing the creation of a democratic government that would leave them with little political power. Other insurgents fought on behalf of the Shiite cleric Moqtada Sadr, and still others were aligned with Kurdish militants in northern Iraq. Together, the insurgents frustrated attempts by coalition forces to control Iraq after Saddam's overthrow. Indeed, the U.S. strategy focused almost entirely on the capture of Baghdad. It paid relatively little attention to occupying and rebuilding the country.

Two fateful decisions by American leaders added fuel to the insurgency. First, Secretary of Defense Rumsfeld opted to deploy a small invading force that did not include enough troops to control Iraq's external borders. This decision literally opened the door to Saddam's foreign supporters, Islamists, and soldiers of fortune, who seized their golden opportunity to thwart the U.S.-led occupation. Thus, if Iraq was not a "nest of terrorists" before Operation Iraqi Freedom, it became one soon afterward. Second, in May 2003, Bremer decided to abruptly disband Iraq's military and police forces, which allowed the insurgency to attract a horde of indigenous recruits. Intending to start from scratch with entirely new security forces, Bremer left more than three hundred thousand Iraqis suddenly unemployed and deeply resentful. They retained their weapons, however, along with their experience and contacts within Iraqi society, all of which could now be turned against the invaders and occupiers.

White House attempts to salvage the Iraq mission faltered a year after the invasion when a new scandal erupted. In April 2004, photographs of the widespread abuse of Iraqis by U.S. troops stationed at Abu Ghraib prison outside of Baghdad filled newspapers and Internet sites. The photographs depicted bound Iraqi prisoners being taunted by attack dogs, forced to lie naked on bare floors, and exposed to electric shock, often in the company of American military police who smiled for the cameras and displayed the thumbs-up sign.[20] The graphic images, which directly contradicted the

---

[20] See Seymour M. Hersh, "Torture at Abu Ghraib," *New Yorker* (May 10, 2004).

U.S. government's claims that it was introducing civility and the rule of law to Iraq, inflamed anti-American passions worldwide.

While running for reelection late in 2004, the president insisted that U.S. forces were gaining the upper hand against the Iraqi insurgents. Bush criticized his opponent, Sen. John Kerry of Massachusetts, for questioning the war effort while U.S. troops remained in harm's way. As polls showed Kerry leading in the final week of the campaign, Bush received a boost from the most unlikely of sources: Osama bin Laden. The al Qaeda leader appeared on a videotape three days before the election ridiculing his American enemies and predicting his own victory in the war on terror. Bush, perceived by many citizens as tougher than Kerry in the war effort, gained just enough popular support to win a second term and another four years to achieve his goals in Iraq.

A Race against Time

The Bush administration began its second term in a race against time in Iraq. American troops continued to struggle in the face of insurgent attacks, and most large cities remained chaotic and largely ungovernable. Iraq formally regained its sovereignty in June 2004, however, and the first round of legislative elections held in January 2005 attracted more than eight million Iraqis to the polls. The purple ink–stained fingers of voters, which verified their participation in the election, instantly became a symbol of political freedom in Iraq. Voter turnout was almost 60 percent, higher than that for most American national elections since World War II.

But the outcome of the election presented more troubling news for those seeking a peaceful transition of power. More than 70 percent of the seats in the assembly were won by Shiite candidates, most of whom favored a government that closely followed Islamic law and customs, thereby mirroring the theocratic regime that had ruled Iran since its 1979 revolution. Another quarter of the seats went to ethnic Kurds in the north, whose vision of an Iraqi state granted them almost complete autonomy. Conspicuously absent were votes from Sunnis and members of Saddam's ousted Ba'ath Party, who boycotted the election. Taken together, the results did not bode well for Washington's model of a moderate secular state that would unify the Iraqi people. Indeed, the results seemed to codify Iraq's fragmentation.

By the end of the war's third year, in February 2006, nearly 2,300 Americans had died in Iraq, and nearly 17,000 others had been wounded.

Map 11-2 Ethnic and Religious Groups in Iraq

These numbers were damaging to Bush, whose public approval tumbled below 40 percent in 2005 and below 30 percent in 2006. A majority of Americans reported in surveys that they felt going to war in Iraq was a mistake, a sentiment that grew with the death toll. For the first time, most survey respondents expressed doubts about Bush's honesty in leading the nation to war. Members of Congress also tired of the U.S. presence in Iraq. Senators passed a resolution on November 15, 2005, calling for faster progress toward "full Iraqi sovereignty" in 2006.

Adding to the difficulties, Bush's war coalition was shrinking. Several countries withdrew their forces in 2004. Among the most prominent of these defections was Spain, where multiple terrorist attacks on March 11, 2004, killed nearly two hundred citizens. The exodus continued in 2005 with the departure of troops from Italy, the Netherlands, New Zealand, Portugal, Thailand, and Ukraine, among other countries. A series of July 2005 terrorist attacks in London left British citizens on edge, but Prime Minister Tony Blair refused to back away from his commitment to the war.

Continuing problems with Iraq's reconstruction further suggested the United States was losing its race against time. A January 2006 U.S. government report found that many projects were behind schedule or had been cancelled entirely.[21] The effort was also plagued by widespread corruption, with some funds diverted to insurgents and others paid to American contractors who did not render the contracted services. From electrical generation to sewage treatment and road maintenance, public services by 2006 had yet to reach their prewar levels. Much of Baghdad was literally in the dark much of the time, not a good sign for an occupying superpower trying to win the "hearts and minds" of the people. Meanwhile, insurgent attacks continued at a rate of more than three hundred a week. Larry Diamond, an expert on democratic reform who had served as a senior adviser to the Coalition Provisional Authority, concluded that "America's quest to stabilize and democratize Iraq seemed to be becoming one of the major overseas blunders in U.S. history."[22]

The "New Way Forward"

The quagmire deepened in 2006 as Sunnis and Shiites descended into an "all-out struggle for political and economic power in Iraq."[23] At home, public dismay over the Iraq War led to political problems for Bush and a fundamental shift in his Iraq strategy. In the November 2006 congressional elections, Democrats reclaimed the legislative majority

---

[21] Special Inspector General for Iraq Reconstruction, "Quarterly and Semiannual Report to Congress" (January 30, 2006).

[22] Larry Diamond, *Squandered Victory: The American Occupation and the Bungled Effort to Bring Democracy to Iraq* (New York: Times Books, 2005), 279.

[23] Kenneth Katzman, "Iraq: Post-Saddam Governance and Security," *CRS Report for Congress* (Washington, D.C.: Congressional Research Service, October 2, 2008), 34.

they had lost twelve years earlier under President Clinton. Opposition to the war figured prominently in exit polls, and Bush acknowledged this link by firing Defense Secretary Rumsfeld on the day after the elections. In his place, Bush appointed Robert M. Gates, a former CIA director whose cautious views on the use of force stood in stark contrast to Rumsfeld's "muscular" approach to military policy. Democrats in Congress predictably demanded troop withdrawals from Iraq, and Bush predictably refused. Still, the president knew his place in history would depend on the war's outcome. Fearful of being known for "losing Iraq," Bush became more open to advice beyond his neoconservative White House advisers.

Two reports in December 2006 provided the guidance Bush needed. The first report was produced by the Iraq Study Group, co-chaired by former secretary of state James Baker and Lee Hamilton, a retired Democratic congressman with expertise in foreign affairs. "The situation in Iraq is grave and deteriorating," the report began. "There is no path that can guarantee success, but the prospects can be improved."[24] The report called for a "new way forward" that would lower expectations about democratic reforms in Iraq while emphasizing, instead, an accelerated timetable for transferring military authority to Iraqi security forces.

The second report had even greater impact on Bush's war strategy. Lt. Gen. David H. Petraeus, a respected military leader, fundamentally changed U.S. counterinsurgency strategy in a revised field manual that would be required reading from the war colleges to the front lines. The report, coauthored by Lt. Gen. James F. Amos of the U.S. Marine Corps, rejected the U.S. military's traditional reliance on overwhelming force as a means to prevail in unconventional wars such as those being fought in Iraq and Afghanistan.[25] Instead, U.S. troops should move out of their fortress-like military bases and live among the people.[26] By placing American "boots on the ground" while securing neighborhoods from terrorist attacks, the troops would gain the trust of civilians and turn them against the insurgents.

As Bush's presidency drew to a close, both governments approved a timetable for the withdrawal of U.S. combat troops from most cities by

---

[24] Iraq Study Group, *The Iraq Study Group Report* (Washington, D.C.: U.S. Institute of Peace, 2006), 6.

[25] David H. Petraeus and James F. Amos, *Counterinsurgency* (Washington, D.C.: U.S. Department of the Army, December 2006).

[26] For a critical view, see Rajiv Chandrasekaran, *Imperial Life in the Emerald City* (New York: Knopf, 2006).

June 30, 2009, and from all of Iraq by December 31, 2011. By this time, nearly 4,500 American troops had been killed, mostly as the result of sneak attacks by insurgents (see Figure 11-1). The departure of U.S. troops came as a relief to Americans, but there was no guarantee that enduring peace would come to Iraq anytime soon. As described in Chapter 13, U.S. efforts to transform Iraq into an island of democracy in a sea of repressive states proved futile. Instead, Iraq became a "failed state," unable to provide basic services, let alone field an army that would fend off threats to Iraq from within and outside its borders.

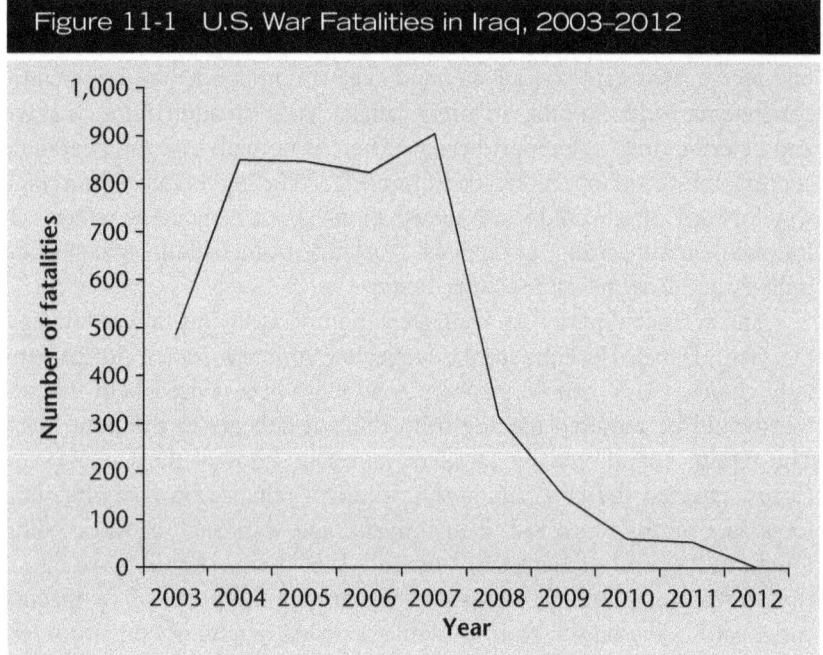

Figure 11-1   U.S. War Fatalities in Iraq, 2003–2012

Source: Iraq Coalition Casualty Count, http://icasualties.org/Iraq/index.aspx.

Flashbacks to Vietnam

The American experience in Iraq invites a comparison with the Vietnam War, described in Chapter 4. The two conflicts, which produced the longest large-scale deployments of American forces since World War II, are alike in many ways. These similarities and the shared lessons that can be derived from both conflicts are worth considering as the struggle in Iraq, as well as those in Afghanistan and on other fronts in the war on terror, continues.[27]

This discussion will begin, however, by identifying some basic *differences* between the conflicts in Iraq and Vietnam. First, before the U.S. intervention in Vietnam, the nation was little known to most Americans and of little geopolitical interest to the United States. And yet the opposite can be said of Iraq, whose regime led by Saddam Hussein was very familiar to Americans and whose vast oil deposits cast Iraq as a vital American interest, whether as friend or foe. A second difference is the demographic features of the two countries. Vietnam's population was ethnically homogeneous and thus maintained a keen sense of national identity, even under centuries of colonial rule. Iraq's people, by contrast, were divided between Arabs and Kurds. Even the Arab population, divided between the two Islamic sects, lacked a common identity.

The circumstances of each U.S. intervention also differed in important respects. Whereas the Vietnamese opposition produced a unifying figure—Ho Chi Minh—no such leader emerged in Iraq after Saddam's overthrow. Instead, the disparate insurgents were led by a variety of figures with very different goals for Iraq, from the restoration of "Saddamism" to the creation of an Iranian-style theocracy or Afghan-style Taliban. And whereas in Vietnam, the United States intervened on behalf of a pro-American regime that was beset by domestic rivals (the Vietcong), in Iraq the United States overthrew a hostile regime whose departure, and the power vacuum that resulted, sparked a previously dormant insurgency. These differences posed distinct problems for the United States in Vietnam and Iraq. The strong sense of Vietnamese nationalism undercut American efforts to win the population's "hearts and minds," whereas the divisions among Iraqis prevented them from creating a united central government.

All that said, the similarities between the conflicts in Iraq and Vietnam are more troublesome in that the many presumed lessons of the Vietnam War were neglected in the conflict with Iraq. Five similarities can be identified. First, the makers of American foreign policy cast regional conflicts in the context of a global dispute—the Cold War for Vietnam, the war on terror for Iraq. By framing the conflicts in this way, policymakers ignored the unique historical, cultural, and political dynamics at work in each society. The depths of Vietnamese nationalism surprised American leaders, who

---

[27]For an elaboration of these similarities, see Kenneth J. Campbell, *A Tale of Two Quagmires: Iraq, Vietnam, and the Hard Lessons of War* (Boulder, Colo.: Paradigm, 2007); John Dumbrell and David Ryan, eds., *Vietnam in Iraq: Tactics, Lessons, Legacies, and Ghosts* (New York: Routledge, 2006); and Robert K. Brigham, *Is Iraq Another Vietnam?* (New York: Public Affairs, 2006).

naively assumed the conflict was all about ideology. Likewise, the confrontation with Iraq was considered meaningful only as a front in the U.S. war on terror. In both conflicts, Americans, wearing their cross-cultural blinders, placed excessive faith in military solutions to problems that were social and cultural in origin. In Iraq, the war planners failed to anticipate sectarian conflicts between Shiites and Sunnis, and so they were overly optimistic about a peaceful and democratic reconstruction of the Iraqi state after Saddam was overthrown.

Second, in both cases, decision makers suffered from "groupthink," or a tendency to limit outside advice to those who already supported the administration's viewpoint and policy preferences. Irving L. Janis, the psychologist who coined the term, found that a small "in-group" within the administration of Lyndon Johnson dominated policy toward Vietnam and prevented skeptics in the "out-group" from influencing the president.[28] The same pattern was evident in the Bush administration, which, like the administrations of Johnson and Nixon in the Vietnam years, was more receptive to guidance from military advisers than from the State Department. Lawrence B. Wilkerson, Secretary of State Colin Powell's chief of staff, found that key decisions about Iraq were made by a "secretive, little-known cabal" of Pentagon strategists.[29] Also like its predecessors, the Bush administration cited intelligence reports on Iraq selectively in order to bolster its arguments for military intervention, as demonstrated by Powell's presentation to the UN Security Council.[30]

The nature of the military opposition represents a third similarity in the Vietnam and Iraq conflicts. In both, American forces were better prepared for conventional wars than for the asymmetric wars that followed, in which enemy forces used their relatively small size, lack of formal military organization, and grassroots bases of support as tactical advantages. In Vietnam, guerrilla warriors melded with sympathetic civilian populations, took advantage of familiar terrain, and staged hit-and-run attacks on American forces rather than large-scale offensives. Similarly, the Iraqi insurgents adopted evasive military tactics, killing American troops with remote-controlled bombs and recruiting suicide bombers to destroy military and civilian targets. The U.S. military's failure to manage this

---

[28] Irving L. Janis, *Groupthink*, 2nd rev. ed. (Boston: Houghton Mifflin, 1973), chap. 5.

[29] Lawrence B. Wilkerson, "The White House Cabal," *Los Angeles Times* (October 25, 2005), B11.

[30] By 2007, the White House had overcome its groupthink problem as it became clear that past efforts to stabilize and reform Iraq had failed. Thomas A. Ricks, *The Gamble* (New York: Penguin, 2009), chap. 4.

unconventional form of warfare in Iraq further suggests that the lessons of Vietnam failed to take hold in the minds of Pentagon strategists.

Fourth, the scale and timing of military deployments in Vietnam and Iraq worked to the advantage of insurgents. As noted earlier, U.S. troops were sent to Vietnam in a piecemeal fashion, buying time for Vietminh forces to mobilize and plan their attacks. That experience prompted the Weinberger and Powell Doctrines of the post-Vietnam era that called for nothing less than overwhelming force in American interventions.[31] That lesson was lost on Iraq War planners. Soon after the invasion of Iraq, it became clear that the relatively small invasion force was inadequate to bring order to the nation and allow for long-term reconstruction. As the Pentagon's dominant voice, Donald Rumsfeld believed American wars should be fought with the lighter, more mobile forces that were central to his "transformation" of U.S. defense. Although such forces captured Baghdad with remarkable alacrity, they were ill prepared to manage the insurgency that followed.

Finally, the outcome of American actions in each case was precisely what the United States had sought to avoid. In Vietnam, a communist regime took power—albeit one that did not start the dominoes falling as American leaders had predicted. In Iraq, a despotic but strong state that had previously suppressed Islamist terrorism was replaced by a state so feeble that it virtually invited Islamists to gain political control, whether by force or, perversely, by the electoral procedures put into place by the occupying power. These developments further clouded the prospects for an exit strategy in Iraq that would achieve Washington's goals.

To this list of historical parallels one might add yet another: Each conflict was initiated under false pretenses. In the Gulf of Tonkin Resolution, Congress authorized President Johnson to "take all necessary measures" to protect U.S. forces in Vietnam—an authorization based on reports that later proved to be misleading.[32] Similarly, much of the Bush administration's "weapons of mass destruction"–based rationale for war—claims about nuclear deals in Africa, intercepted aluminum tubes, mobile germ warfare laboratories, and Iraqi–al Qaeda contacts—were refuted after hostilities had begun.

Fully informed assessments of the wars in Afghanistan and Iraq will require a greater accumulation of evidence. At a minimum, however, American leaders exhibited a remarkable degree of naiveté in planning both wars that was in keeping with the nation's traditional style of foreign policy. From Washington's vantage point, the wartime goals of the United

---

[31] Caspar Weinberger served as secretary of defense in the Reagan administration.

[32] Stanley Karnow, *Vietnam: A History* (New York: Viking, 1983), 366–373.

States would be achieved simply because they represented universal moral values such as human freedom, democracy, and legal equality. In the words of the administration's 2006 "National Security Strategy," "[t]he United States must defend liberty and justice because these principles are right and true for all people everywhere."[33]

Success was further ensured by the paradoxical fruits of American exceptionalism: the world's most productive economy combined with the world's most destructive military forces. With these assets in hand, along with their providential blessings, why worry about such mundane matters as power generation and sewage treatment? These details would take care of themselves. And why try to understand the foreign culture or society when the American intervention offered a superior model that could be readily adopted abroad? As Daniel P. Bolger, a former Army lieutenant general, summed up the nation's missteps in Iraq, "We did not understand the enemy, a guerilla network embedded in a quarrelsome, suspicious, civilian population. We didn't understand our own forces, which are built for rapid, decisive conventional operations, not lingering, ill-defined counterinsurgencies. We're made for Desert Storm, not Vietnam."[34]

---

[33] National Security Council, "National Security Strategy of the United States" (Washington, D.C.: White House, March 2006), 2.

[34] Daniel P. Bolger, "The Truth about Wars," New York Times (November 10, 2014). See also various authors, "Lessons from a Decade of War," special section in Foreign Affairs 93 (November–December 2014), 2–54.

CHAPTER 12

Aftershocks of the Arab Spring

This book describes how the United States behaves as a great power, not just in breaking stalemates in world wars, but in seeking to realize America's historic ambition to remake the international system in its own image. The chapters in Part I examined the conflict between the United States and the Soviet Union. Their nearly half-century of Cold War enveloped all other countries in a bipolar balance of power and ended just as George Kennan, the architect of the U.S. containment policy, predicted: not with an apocalyptic bang, but with a whimper; not with a military victory of one over the other, but with the demoralization of Soviet citizens and the collapse of the Soviet state.

Part II of the book, covering a shorter time span, has a more complex story line. As with the first two world wars of the twentieth century, the United States prevailed in the Cold War. This time, Washington towered over the interstate system without a peer competitor in sight. Contrary to expectations that this "new world order" would bring global harmony to world politics, a common aspiration of early American leaders, the post–Cold War period quickly became plagued by revived ethnic conflicts, the settling of old scores, and the emergence of Islamist terrorism as a clear and present danger to the United States and its allies. Once again, the U.S. won a great-power war only to find itself laboring over the peace that followed. With President Trump taking power in 2017, the future of the Middle East was even less clear.

Obama's Call for "Renewal"

The many swings in American foreign policy since World War II have originated with the choices made by citizens in the voting booth. For example, Jimmy Carter's election as president in 1976 reflected voters' desires to shift from the power politics of the Nixon-Kissinger years toward a renewed focus on human rights and the UN. Four years later, with the United States mired in economic distress and foreign policy crises (see Chapter 6), Americans turned to Ronald Reagan, who promised to restore American power on its own terms. The pendulum-like pattern continued in 1992

Pete Souza, The White House

Members of the National Security Council monitor the capture of Osama bin Laden in May 2011. The group included, among others, Vice President Joe Biden and President Barack Obama (far left), along with Secretary of State Hillary Clinton and Defense Secretary Robert Gates (far right).

when Bill Clinton promised globalized economic growth and again in 2000 when candidate George W. Bush vowed to free U.S. sovereignty from the shackles of UN bureaucrats and "global governance."

As this chapter describes, President Obama came into power when most Americans were tired of the endless wars in Afghanistan and Iraq that started after the 9/11 attacks. In the new environment, domestic problems would be of greatest concern for most citizens. As for foreign policy, public sentiments were captured in a July 2008 survey that found "improving America's standing in the world" the public's foreign policy priority.[1] This changed in 2011 when a spontaneous democratic uprising in North Africa and the Middle East sparked a radical shift that became known as the Arab Spring.[2] The popular demands for freedom and subsequent regime changes injected new tensions throughout the region. Iraq's political collapse opened the door for the Islamic State of Iraq and Syria (ISIS), a well-financed terrorist group that captured territories in both countries.

---

[1] Chicago Council on Global Affairs, "Anxious Americans Seek a New Direction in United States Foreign Policy" (www.thechicagocouncil.org, 2009).

[2] These events are also labeled the Arab "awakening" or "uprising" by analysts.

The black flag of the Islamic was housed in the old city of Mosul.

Obama's image as an outsider served him well in the 2008 election. His opponent, Sen. John McCain, suffered a reputation as a "Washington Insider." Presidential transitions are always difficult in the United States.[3] The road for Obama was treacherous, given the nation's diminished stature after the failed Iraq War and the dragging war in Afghanistan. The near-collapse of the U.S. financial system before the election sealed Obama's victory. No recent president faced such daunting obstacles upon taking office, and no president since the Vietnam War had confronted a steeper climb in restoring the power and principles of American foreign policy.

Three General Principles

Three general principles dominated the new president's agenda. First, the United States should rejoin the international community after years of isolation. "America is a friend of each nation," Obama said at his inauguration on January 20, "and we are ready to lead once more." The United States would again adhere to the "constitutional" world order created by

---

[3]The United States is unique among other countries for both the length of its presidential campaigns and, following the election, the nearly three-month waiting period for the new president to take office. See Kurt M. Campbell and James B. Steinberg, *Difficult Transitions: Foreign Policy Troubles at the Outset of Presidential Power* (Washington, D.C.: Brookings, 2008).

American leaders after World War II.[4] Most countries participated in that order and accepted standards of behavior to be backed by international law and institutions such as the UN, the World Trade Organization, and the International Criminal Court. Bush had claimed that such organizations restricted U.S. sovereignty; his successor believed they would make the United States more secure.

Second, the nation would live up to its democratic principles and, by its own example, seek to inspire political reforms overseas. Simply by expressing themselves in various facets of civil society—political parties, interest groups, religious centers, the arts and news media, and the Internet—Americans would become more powerful couriers of the nation's values than the U.S. government's most expensive state-building programs. By halting practices in foreign policy that contradicted U.S. national values, the United States would stymie the anti-American movements overseas that threatened the nation's security.

Third, Obama proclaimed that the United States should revive diplomacy as a core instrument of foreign policy. He had raised eyebrows by saying he would discuss bilateral problems with any foreign leaders, including those who openly renounced the United States. "We will extend a hand if you are willing to unclench your fist," he told a world audience at his inauguration. The new president promised to treat his detractors with mutual respect, a carefully worded signal that set him apart from his predecessor.

These general principles were consistent with the American foreign policy tradition. From this perspective, wars in a democratic world order would be a rare exception to the rule of peaceful coexistence. All states would recognize their mutual interests in freedom and a prosperous economy. "America has not succeeded by stepping outside the currents of international cooperation," Obama stated in May 2010. "We have succeeded by steering those currents in the direction of liberty and justice."[5] In vowing to reclaim the nation's moral leadership, Obama reclaimed America's style of foreign policy.

The Financial Collapse of 2007–2008

Despite the growing doubts about free trade, other core features of America's market-based economy remained intact. Private firms and their senior executives enjoyed generous tax breaks. Regulations were curtailed

---

[4] See G. John Ikenberry, *After Victory: Institutions, Strategic Restraint, and the Rebuilding of Order after Major Wars* (Princeton, N.J.: Princeton University Press, 2001).

[5] Barack Obama, "Remarks by the President at United States Military Academy at West Point Commencement" (May 22, 2010).

Impact and Influence: Henry Paulson

The 2008 financial crisis forced American leaders to take drastic steps to prevent a collapse of the nation's financial system. No U.S. official had more impact on the crisis's outcome than Treasury Secretary Henry Paulson, who previously served as the chief executive officer of Goldman Sachs, a multinational investment bank based in New York City.

In the face of strong criticism by the general public and many members of Congress, Paulson pushed through legislation that authorized the Treasury Department to release nearly $1 trillion in funds to prevent the nation's largest financial institutions from bankruptcy. He also engineered the government's take-over of Fannie Mae and Freddie Mac, two of the nation's largest mortgage companies whose reckless lending practices led to the financial meltdown. Paulson ended his term in 2009 defending his actions as essential not only to save the U.S. financial system, but also to limit the financial crisis's spillover effects on economies worldwide. Still, the crisis led to the deepest recession in the United States since the Great Depression and slowed global economic growth for several years to come.

to expedite commerce. Central bankers kept interest rates low in order to keep consumers borrowing and buying. Foreign economies also benefited from American investments in their own firms and from growing exports to free-spending consumers in the United States.

All this changed, however, when a "bubble" in the U.S. housing market burst. The ensuing economic collapse left millions of Americans without homes, millions of workers unemployed, and the global economy facing its worst crisis since the Great Depression of the 1930s. The bubble originated in the high-tech boom of the 1990s. Major investors, primarily countries in East Asia and the Persian Gulf that had amassed large cash reserves, sought shelter from the economic storm by investing in U.S. government bonds that ensured a modest return on their investments. As this private capital saturated U.S. banks, government officials eased many regulations that, they argued, hindered economic growth. As the Independent Institute reported, "Mortgages seemed to require virtually no down payments; . . . [and there were] few restrictions on the size of monthly payments relative to income, little examination of credit scores, [and] little examination of employment history."[6]

---

[6] Stan J. Liebowitz, *Anatomy of a Train Wreck: Causes of the Mortgage Meltdown* (Oakland, Calif.: Independent Institute, October 3, 2008), 4.

The rollback of regulations coincided with a White House campaign to encourage home ownership, a vital part of the American Dream that could be financed with "subprime" interest rates.[7] The accelerating pace of home sales inflated the real estate bubble. Housing prices soared in most major cities even as economic indicators signaled trouble ahead. The first sign of impending crisis appeared in July 2008, when the Federal Deposit Insurance Corporation (FDIC) assumed control of a California bank, IndyMac, whose loss of $32 billion in assets marked the second largest bank failure in U.S. history. By August 2008, the top one hundred U.S. banks were facing potential losses of more than $500 billion from unpaid loans. The downward spiral continued in the weeks that followed:

- On September 7, the U.S. Treasury announced it was taking over Fannie Mae and Freddie Mac, two government-sponsored mortgage lenders whose massive investment portfolios, which grew to an estimated $1.8 trillion by 2004, included more than $300 billion in "risky loans" issued mostly to low-income buyers.

- On September 15, the investment bank Lehman Brothers declared bankruptcy. The lost assets of the company, approximately $650 billion, marked the largest financial collapse in U.S. history. The next day, the U.S. government took over the American International Group (AIG), an insurance giant whose faltering assets included complicated investment schemes known as "credit default swaps."[8]

- On September 18, the U.S. Treasury proposed a $700 billion bailout of the banking system. The proposal called for government purchases of "toxic assets" that threatened to destroy dozens of banks and other financial institutions. President Bush approved the Troubled Asset Relief Program (TARP) on October 3, marking a government intervention in the economy with no historical precedent.

---

[7] The interest rate on a conventional thirty-year mortgage reached an all-time low of 5.25 percent in 2003, a year that also saw the fastest pace of new home construction in twenty-five years. U.S. Congress, House of Representatives, Committee on the Budget, Republican Caucus, "Roots of the Financial Crisis: The Role of Government Policy" (January 8, 2009).

[8] By 2007, the combined value of such financial "swaps" had reached $62 trillion, a larger volume than the combined economic output of all countries that year. Dick K. Nanto et al., "The U.S. Financial Crisis: The Global Dimension with Implications for U.S. Policy," *CRS Report for Congress* (Washington, D.C.: Congressional Research Service, November 10, 2008), 9.

This financial meltdown affected American citizens in many ways. Many lost their jobs; others lost their homes or watched their retirement funds nearly vanish along with the college tuition they had saved over many years for their children. The least fortunate lost all of these and sought out minimum-wage jobs merely to escape bankruptcy. Although Americans had saved little during the previous decade, millions had invested in stocks and mutual funds—a profitable venture until the tide turned. The Dow Jones Industrial Average, which peaked at 14,169 in October 2007, had fallen below 7,000 by the end of February 2008. The NASDAQ index, which had surged during the dot-com boom of the late 1990s, had lost three-quarters of its value since 2000. Foreign stock markets also plummeted as the U.S. financial crisis went global, ominously revealing how the American "locomotive" of the world economy could lead not just to spreading prosperity, but also to a calamitous train wreck (see Figure 12-1).

Figure 12-1   Falling Fortunes: Index of Four Global Stock Markets, September 30–October 27, 2008

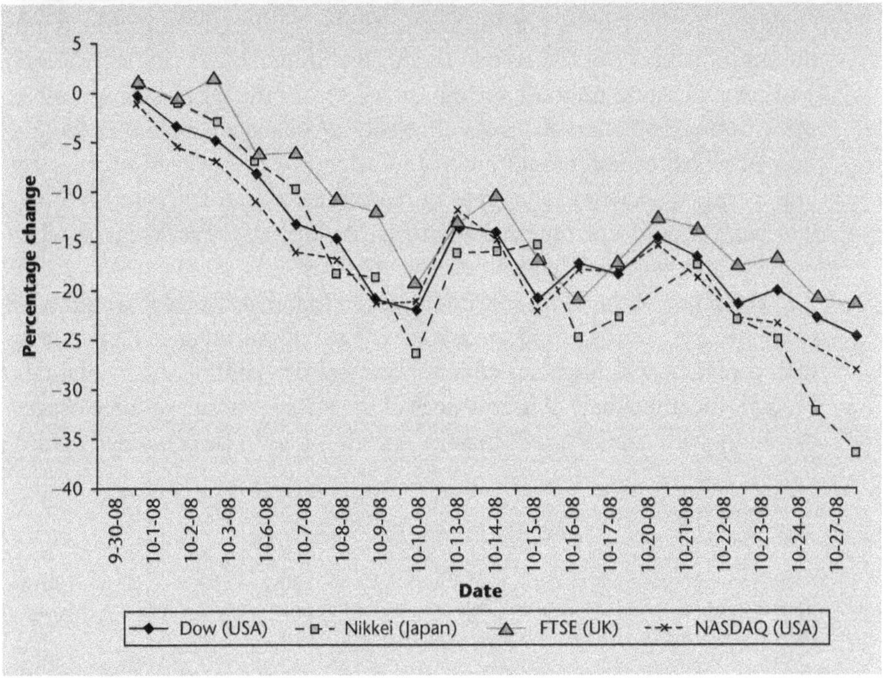

Source: msn.money. http://moneycentral.msn.com/detail/stock_quote.

The chaos in U.S. financial markets thus produced a domino effect very different from that foreseen by Eisenhower. Instead of the feared communist revolutions of the Cold War, the dominoes in this case were the financial bubbles that burst across the industrialized world. From Tokyo to London, the grim sequence was eerily similar: mounting capital reserves, reckless bank lending, overheated markets, and—after the crash—the rescue of the shattered economies by governments and global financial institutions. In October 2008 alone, the International Monetary Fund provided emergency loans to Hungary, Iceland, and Ukraine. Only drastic measures saved Australia, Chile, India, Kazakhstan, and Russia from financial catastrophe.[9] The downward spiral crushed many developing countries, whose meager export markets dried up while commodity prices plunged along with the flows of foreign investment. Few still expected that the United Nations would achieve the most vital of its Millennium Development Goals: to reduce by half the rate of "extreme poverty" (income of less than $1 a day) by 2015.[10]

Although economic managers overseas bore much of the responsibility for their distress, the financial crisis was clearly made in America. "Everything happening now in the economic and financial sphere began in the United States," Vladimir Putin complained from the Kremlin in October 2008. "This is not the responsibility of specific individuals but the irresponsibility of the system that claims leadership."[11] Putin's rhetoric aside, the bursting bubbles sprung directly from the false assumptions of the Washington consensus that minimally regulated markets and the free flow of global capital would inevitably bring prosperity even to the most impoverished societies. The crisis demonstrated that Adam Smith's "invisible hand" could not only foster prosperity, but also wreak havoc when financial markets were left to their own devices.

The scope of the economic crisis was so vast that recovery would have to proceed in four complicated stages. First, governments had to stop the "contagion" of financial collapse and restore confidence in markets. Second, the immediate consequences of the crisis—mortgage foreclosures, corporate bankruptcies, and massive layoffs—had to be contained. Third,

---

[9] Ibid., 14–40.

[10] With each percentage of reduced economic growth, twenty million more people fell into extreme poverty. Jayshree Bajoria, "Financial Crisis May Worsen Poverty in India, China," *Backgrounder* (New York: Council on Foreign Relations, January 2009).

[11] Suzy Jagger, "Vladimir Putin Blames America for World Economic Crisis," *TimesOnline* (October 2, 2008), http://business.timesonline.co.uk/tol/business/markets/russia/article4863967.ece.

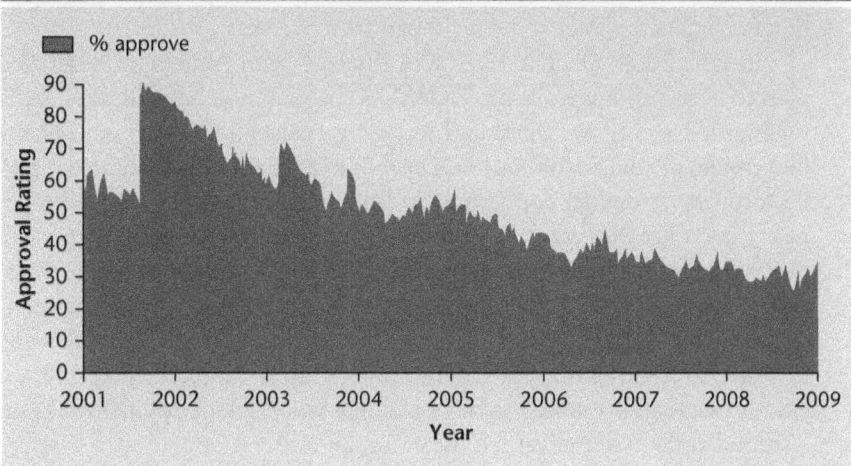

Figure 12-2　George W. Bush's Job Approval Ratings Trend

banking practices had to be "re-regulated" in order to prevent recurrences of the crisis. And finally, world leaders had to manage the long-term social and political effects of the crisis, including widespread public dismay and unrest. Although these leaders agreed on a recovery plan in November 2008, they could not tame the market forces that had spun out of control.[12]

The economic crisis was the final blow to Bush's presidency, already battered by the ongoing wars in Afghanistan and Iraq and controversies over the treatment of war prisoners. Many conservatives condemned the steps taken by Bush to prevent an even greater calamity, which amounted to a virtual nationalization of the financial system. Such actions were historically associated with socialist economies, not those based on the "magic of the market." But Bush had no choice in the matter. Only a massive government bailout stood in the way of another Great Depression.

Target bin Laden

President Obama could not ignore the continuing threat posed by Osama bin Laden, who remained at large after nearly a decade of pursuit by American military forces and intelligence agents from multiple allied governments. Capturing, and possibly killing, the leader of al Qaeda would bring some comfort to many Americans who remained haunted by the 9/11

---

[12] See Alan S. Blinder, *After the Music Stopped: The Financial Crisis, the Response, and the Work Ahead* (New York: Penguin, 2013).

attacks. Settling this score would also send a signal around the world that the United States, though weakened by economic and political struggles at home, remained a force to be reckoned with overseas.

In June 2009, Obama asked CIA director Leon Panetta for a detailed plan to locate and capture bin Laden. As the plan was being drafted, U.S. intelligence agents identified and located a Pakistani motorist who fit the description of bin Laden's courier. The motorist led the U.S. agents to a heavily fortified residential compound in Abbottabad, Pakistan, a small town near the capital that was home to the nation's military academy. American officials found it strange that the compound, surrounded by concrete walls, was only visited by this courier, that it had no telephone or Internet connections, and that the residents burned their own trash rather than leaving it at the street for collection. Aerial photographs captured images of an elderly resident, presumed to be bin Laden, who took occasional walks on a shrouded patio but never left the compound.[13]

It has been said that the first casualty of war is the battle plan. This reality was affirmed when, during the early-morning attack on May 2, the first helicopter crash-landed inside the walls of the compound. Although the SEALs were able to carry out their assault, the second helicopter abandoned its plan to hover over the building and release its crew of commandos by rope ladder onto the roof. Instead, the helicopter landed on a nearby field, forcing the SEALs to use explosives to enter the compound.

The actual assault took less than twenty minutes. As members of the National Security Council looked on via satellite from the White House, the SEALs forced their way onto the grounds and into the building that housed bin Laden. In several exchanges of gunfire, they killed three armed guards, including bin Laden's son, Khalid. They also shot, in the calf, one of bin Laden's wives, who stood between her husband and the commandos who stormed bin Laden's third-floor suite. Finally, a U.S. sharpshooter shot and killed the aged, bearded man who had brought global terror to American shores a decade earlier. The death of bin Laden, and the subsequent disposal of his corpse in the Red Sea, ended a terrible chapter in American foreign policy.

While the news of bin Laden's death produced celebrations in much of the world, several questions confronted American leaders. Would bin Laden's capture produce violent retaliation and possible terrorist attacks

---

[13] This account is drawn from Nicholas Schmidle, "Getting bin Laden: What Happened That Night in Abbottabad," *New Yorker* (August 8, 2011). According to Schmidle's interviews with numerous U.S. officials and military officers, the Navy SEALs were instructed to kill bin Laden even if he was unarmed at the time of his capture, a finding denied by the Pentagon.

against the United States? How could Washington maintain trust toward Pakistan after it became clear that bin Laden had long been residing an hour's drive away from Islamabad? And what would become of al Qaeda? The president knew the struggle against al Qaeda and other terrorist groups would continue indefinitely. The United States was still at war with al Qaeda, and counterterrorism would remain a centerpiece of American foreign policy.

Obama reminded Americans that the nation's traditional sense of being at peace in between periodic spasms of conventional war was a thing of the past. Barring an unlikely shift in the strategic landscape, the United States would likely be at war against terrorists and their proven ability to create havoc around the world and on American soil.

Mass Demands for Democracy

As with his predecessors, the spread of democracy was a central aspiration of Barack Obama's foreign policy. He differed from Bush, however, regarding the means by which the United States would shape a more democratic world. In particular, Obama opposed Bush's choice to overthrow Iraq's government in 2003. The following state-building effort relied on U.S. military power to force democratic reforms on the nation. Such an approach, the president believed, was unlikely to be successful even for the preeminent world power. Obama made this point clear on June 4, 2009, when he addressed a large audience in Cairo, Egypt. In his words,

> No system of government can or should be imposed on one nation by any other. . . . America does not presume to know what is best for everyone, just as we would not presume to pick the outcome of a peaceful election. But I do have an unyielding belief that all people yearn for certain things: the ability to speak your mind and have a say in how you are governed; confidence in the rule of law and the equal administration of justice; government that is transparent and doesn't steal from the people; the freedom to live as you choose. These are not just American ideas; they are human rights. And that is why we will support them everywhere.[14]

---

[14] The White House, Office of the Press Secretary, "Remarks by the President on a New Beginning" (June 4, 2009).

It was fitting that Obama made these remarks in the heart of the Arab world, a region that had resisted much of the spread of democracy taking place elsewhere. According to political scientist Samuel Huntington, this expansion of democratic rule proceeded in three historical "waves." The first of these occurred in the late 1700s and early 1800s with the creation of constitutional and representative governments in the United States and many Western European countries. The second wave of democracy followed the world wars as several European empires collapsed and gave way to sovereign nation-states. Finally, the third wave crested at the end of the Cold War with the transformation of Soviet client states in Eastern Europe into multiparty democracies.[15] Several factors contributed to this trend, including rapid economic growth in many countries that improved living standards, produced large middle classes, and made public education and uncensored mass media available to all citizens.

By 2010, nearly one-half of the world's population lived in "free" governments, according to Freedom House, a prominent human rights group. "The Middle East, meanwhile, stands apart from the rest of the world in its resistance to fair elections, freedom of speech, minority rights, freedom of belief, and gender inequality."[16] The same could be said for Arab states in North Africa, home to some of the world's most entrenched rulers. They included Muammar al-Qaddafi (forty-one years) of Libya and Hosni Mubarak of Egypt (twenty-nine years). For many reasons, and through a variety of coercive tactics, these and other Arab leaders denied their citizens the most basic political and human rights.

This all changed in 2011 when disgruntled masses in North Africa took to the streets and sparked the Arab Spring. The democratic brush fire was sparked in Iran, where citizens organized in many cities to protest the rigging of presidential elections there shortly after Obama delivered his Cairo speech. Although the "Green Movement" was crushed by Iranian forces, the ability of citizens to make their voices heard under the harshest of circumstances inspired dissenters elsewhere in the region. The uprisings began in North Africa and spread into the Middle East, challenging entrenched states and rigidly controlled societies.

---

[15] Samuel P. Huntington, *The Third Wave: Democratization in the Late Twentieth Century* (Norman: University of Oklahoma Press, 1991).

[16] Freedom House, *Suffocated by Dictatorship: The Middle East's Freedom Deficit* (Washington, D.C.: Author, 2011), 2. The group's annual survey, *Freedom in the World*, applies a formula of political freedom that includes elections, political pluralism, effective governance, freedom of expression, freedom of association, rule of law, and personal autonomy.

While ousting entrenched regimes solved one problem, more daunting was the challenge of creating new governments virtually from scratch. For centuries, whether under *Sharia* (Islamic) law or the grip of monarchs and military leaders,[17] citizens were deprived of civil societies—the interest groups, public service agencies, arts and media outlets, political parties, and other groups that provided citizens an independent voice in society.[18] Islamic scholar Timur Kuran predicted that "viable Arab democracies—or leaders who could govern them—will not emerge anytime soon."[19] Such pessimism was lost on mass publics in the Arab world who were fixated on ejecting their despotic leaders from power. The future, they reasoned, would take care of itself.

The appropriate role of the United States in this expected convulsion was problematic given its controversial history and reputation in the Arab world. Aside from providing moral and rhetorical support for the pro-democracy movements, a more assertive response risked familiar allegations of American imperialism. Simply allowing events to run their course, however, could increase the likelihood of greater chaos, protracted civil wars, and attempts by other powers to exploit the region's upheavals for their own, self-interested purposes. In his memo, Obama ordered his advisers to develop a "country-by-country" plan in the case of pro-democracy uprisings. No single strategy, he concluded, would adequately serve American interests. Still, as the dominoes of repression fell eastward from Tunisia, the president found himself trying to manage a historic transformation that was out of his control.

Regime Change in Dangerous Places

Historical revolutions often occur in two stages. First, the existing and unpopular regime is swept from power, often violently. The second phase is even more daunting: creating a new regime that satisfies popular expectations. As historian Crane Brinton found in the English (1640s), French (1789–1799), and Russian (1917) revolutions, the first phase was filled with "hope and moderation" for a brighter future. This optimism was crushed in the second phase, however, as radicals launched "reigns of terror" in the pursuit of extreme goals not shared by most citizens. The radicals, "better organized, better staffed, and better obeyed," ultimately dictated the type of governments established

---

[17] Barack Obama, *National Strategy for Counterterrorism* (Washington, D.C.: White House, June 2011), 2.

[18] Some, but not all, nations enforce *Sharia* law. For a broader description of *Sharia* law, see Elizabeth Stewart, "FAQ: Sharia Law," *The Guardian* (February 7, 2008).

[19] Timur Kuran, "The Weak Foundation of Arab Democracy," *New York Times* (May 29, 2011), WK8.

in these countries.[20] The same patterns characterized the Chinese (1949) and Cuban (1959) revolutions, which became dominated by communist forces and governments. The course of the Arab Spring provided more recent evidence that overthrowing regimes is a simpler task than creating new ones.

The Rise in Tunisa and Egypt

The "awakening" of Arab democracy began in Tunisia, a former French colony on North Africa's Mediterranean coast. Ever since their liberation from France in 1956, Tunisian citizens suffered under authoritarian rule and economic stagnation. Their first president, Habib Bourguiba, monopolized the one-party state for more than three decades. He remained secure only with support from the United States and its Cold War allies that were grateful for his forceful suppression of Arab nationalism, Islamic fundamentalism, and, most of all, communism. No amount of foreign aid, however, could overcome the root rot within Tunisia. Its government, infested with corruption, left much of its population without work, unable to afford even the most basic housing and food supplies.

The moment of truth for Tunisia came on December 17, 2010, when a street vendor, Mohamed Bouazizi, was apprehended by local police in the rural town of Sidi Bouzid for not holding a business license. His refusal to pay bribes to stay in business prompted the police to seize the vendor's fruits and vegetables, thus depriving him of his only means of income. Enraged, Bouazizi set himself on fire on a crowded street, an act of defiance that cost him his life. News of the incident quickly went viral on Facebook and other forms of social media, prompting protests and demonstrations that grew daily and spread to other cities and ultimately the capital of Tunis. The protesters, comprising unemployed workers, students, union leaders, and human rights advocates, demanded a variety of political and economic reforms, along with the immediate resignation of Zine el-Abidine Ben Ali, Tunisia's second president, who had ruled since 1987.

Government efforts to suppress the uprising grew more violent as the protests gained strength and worldwide attention. On January 5, 2011, nearly eight thousand Tunisian lawyers went on strike, signaling their solidarity with the pro-democracy movement. Government efforts to enforce daily curfews and subdue news coverage of the swelling protests proved futile.

---

[20] Crane Brinton, *The Anatomy of Revolution* (New York: Vintage, 1952), 134. The American Revolution did not follow this pattern as there was consensus regarding the shape of the postrevolutionary government and selection of its leaders.

The government's demise was assured as a growing number of police joined the protesters and the nation's army chief vowed to "defend the revolution." Lacking any support and fearing for his life, Ben Ali fled Tunisia for Saudi Arabia on January 14. As the rest of the world looked on, Tunisia became a role model for democratic movements elsewhere in the region.

Political reforms did not come easily to Tunisia's government, which is no surprise given its lack of experience with democratic rule and an empowered civil society. As other Arab Spring states would discover, the immediate postrevolution challenge was striking a balance between secular (nonreligious) governance and that based on Islamic laws. A coalition government, installed in October 2011, was led by an Islamist party (*Ennahda*) that proved unpopular among secularists and more radical Islamists alike. The result was a series of public demonstrations, political assassinations, and demands for a new government. As the "new" Tunisia teetered on the brink of collapse in 2013, *Ennahda* yielded to new elections and the creation of a moderate government. A new constitution, approved in January 2014, restored freedom of worship and equality for women while also declaring Islam to be the state religion. With this compromise, the state of emergency declared a year earlier was lifted, and Tunisia tried again to set the pace of reform in the Arab world. As a Tunisian policy analyst observed, "While the rest of the Arab Spring countries have slid either into chaos and civil strife—sectarian and ethnic—or back into the bleak and brutal era of military coups, Tunisia seems to have withstood the powerful storms raging around it."[21]

There was very little daylight between Tunisia's "Jasmine Revolution" and a simultaneous movement to displace the government of Egypt, whose leader, Hosni Mubarak, had ruled the nation since the assassination of Anwar Sadat in 1981. Mubarak's tenure, like that of many other Arab autocrats, featured an all-too-familiar fusion of state brutality, rampant corruption, and chronic poverty. The Egyptian government, however, could count on billions of dollars annually in foreign aid from the U.S. government, which considered these payments a bargain so long as Egypt continued to recognize Israel in keeping with the 1978 Camp David Accords (see Chapter 5). Contrary to the wishful thinking that followed the historic agreement, other Middle East states failed to join the Arab-Israeli peace process. The White House in 2011 feared, with some justification, that a seizure of power by Egyptian dissidents would bring not only political

---

[21] Soumaya Ghannoushi, "Tunisia: The Arab World's Full-Fledged Democracy?" *Al Jazeera* (October 24, 2014).

change to Cairo, but also the loss of a vital source of security for Israel and its patron in Washington.

Encouraged by the success of "people power" in Tunisia, opponents of Egypt's repressive regime filled organized mass rallies throughout the country. On January 31, more than 250,000 protesters occupied Tahrir Square in Cairo and vowed to stay there until Mubarak stepped down. As the rallies grew larger, Mubarak's attacks on the protesters grew more forceful. It was no secret that Mubarak was utterly dependent on Egypt's armed forces, which had come to dominate the government and much of the nation's social fabric. Simply put, the army was all that stood between Mubarak and the throngs of protesters who sought not only his ouster but his prosecution and severe punishment.

The Obama administration, which had adopted a hands-off posture toward Tunisia, initially clung to its ally in Cairo. As Secretary of State Hillary Clinton declared on January 25, "Our assessment is that the Egyptian government is stable and is looking for ways to respond to the legitimate needs and interests of the Egyptian people." This benign tone quickly changed, however, as public demands for regime change escalated and Mubarak refused to budge. On February 1, Obama signaled his loss of confidence in the Egyptian leader by stating that "an orderly transition must be meaningful, it must be peaceful, and it must begin now." His message predictably alarmed the Israeli government and others in the Middle East, such as Saudi Arabia, that were wedded to the status quo. At the same time, however, the rebuke of Mubarak's benefactor doomed his prospects for political survival. His departure from office on February 11 brought cheers to Tahrir Square and other hotbeds of rebellion across Egypt.

As in Tunisia, however, the jubilation rapidly gave way to doubts about the process of crafting a new government and constitution. For the moment, the Egyptian military remained the only source of institutional stability and thus retained control of the state. Elections in June 2012 were won by members of the Muslim Brotherhood, an Islamist group that sought to establish the Islamic Koran as the "sole reference point for ordering the life of the Muslim family, individual, community, and state."[22] The group's leader and first president, Mohamed Morsi, promised instead to focus on reviving Egypt's economy, which left about one-quarter of the population in poverty. Despite these promises, Morsi's first actions were to concentrate power in his office, dissolve the House of Representatives, and draft

---

[22] Steven Kull, *Feeling Betrayed: The Roots of Muslim Anger at America* (Washington, D.C.: Brookings, 2011), 168.

a constitution based on Islamist principles. Better living conditions for all Egyptians became a secondary concern.

Morsi's actions offended most of Egypt's eighty-five million citizens, and political activists once again staged mass demonstrations in town squares across the country demanding regime change. The Egyptian army, a sworn enemy of the Muslim Brotherhood, responded in June 2013 by deposing Morsi and replacing him with a military general, Abdel Fattah al-Sisi. Like Morsi, Sisi pledged economic reforms and an end to the endemic corruption that enriched government cronies and contractors. Instead, Sisi launched a violent crackdown on the banished Muslim Brotherhood, jailed an estimated sixteen thousand political opponents, killed an estimated one thousand civilians, and sentenced more than five hundred enemies to death.[23] Upon his formal election in May 2014, in which he was effectively unopposed, Sisi declared that democracy in Egypt would not be possible for at least twenty-five years.

Once again, Obama left the Egyptian ordeal to run its course. The nation's primary concern involved the future of the Camp David Accords that kept a fragile peace between Egypt and Israel. Sisi pleased Washington by honoring this agreement, which ensured his government a continuation of $1.3 billion in military aid from the United States.[24] This aid was renewed in June 2014 after Secretary of State John Kerry reaffirmed Washington's "historic partnership" with Cairo. While he praised Sisi's actions in clamping down on Islamist militants, Kerry was vague about the U.S. government's earlier calls for a "sustainable, inclusive, and nonviolent transition to democracy" in Egypt. More to the point, American foreign policy had little leverage over domestic conditions in Egypt. Its only real influence came from the delivery of high-tech weapons that preserved Cairo's regional power while also standing ready for use against domestic enemies of the ruling regime.[25]

Washington's mixed signals extended to the Arabian Peninsula, where uprisings produced very different outcomes. Later in November, intensifying protests led to the resignation of Yemini's President Ali Abdullah Saleh,

---

[23] Human Rights Watch, "Egypt: Shocking Death Sentences Follow Sham Trial" (New York: Human Rights Watch, March 24, 2014).

[24] This weaponry included American-made F-15 fighter jets, M1A1 battle tanks, and Apache attack helicopters that were seen by Washington as vital for maintaining stability, the utmost priority of American foreign policy in the region.

[25] Between 1948 and 2013, the U.S. government provided Egypt with a total of $73 billion in economic and military aid. Jeremy M. Sharp, *Egypt: Background and U.S. Relations* (Washington, D.C.: Congressional Research Service, June 5, 2014), 19.

who ruled the tiny country for decades. Obama had tolerated the leader until he turned on his own people. Facing an inevitable downfall, Saleh was forced from his office. The outcome of the revolt in Bahrain, a small island kingdom in the Persian Gulf, was less benign. Pro-democracy activists, seeking greater freedoms, were crushed by the Sunni Muslims who composed the royal family. Bahrain's close ties to Saudi Arabia ensured an endless supply of weapons and ammunition that were used freely by government forces loyal to the monarchy. Obama, primarily concerned with retaining close ties to Saudi Arabia and a major U.S. naval base in Bahrain, did not stand in the way. In all of these cases, Obama's realism trumped his liberal rhetoric.

NATO's Libya Gambit

The democratic revolutions of the Arab Spring also spread to Libya, whose leader—Muammar al-Qaddafi—epitomized the style of autocratic rule and brutal repression that was deeply entrenched across the Arab world. It was fitting that Libya, sandwiched between Tunisia and Egypt on the northern coast of Africa, became the next scene in the political drama. For the United States, it was also fitting that Libya, a bitter enemy for most of the post–World War II era, took center stage. Qaddafi would not go easily. His overthrow would take eight months and require a concerted effort extending far beyond the angry mobs that took to the streets in February 2011.

More than four decades earlier, Qaddafi led a revolution against Libya's monarchy and quickly declared himself the liberated state's founding father. Far from ushering in a new era of democracy, however, he wielded the same absolute power enjoyed by the king. American leaders, while denouncing Qaddafi's iron grip on his people, tolerated him because he refused close ties to the Soviet Union. This fragile *entente* did not last, however, as Qaddafi aligned himself with radical Islamists who launched a succession of terrorist attacks in the 1980s against U.S. and European targets. After an April 1986 bombing of a nightclub in West Berlin left three dead and 230 wounded, many of them Americans, retaliatory air strikes ordered by President Reagan only strengthened Qaddafi's resolve.

The lethality of these terrorist attacks peaked in December 1988, when a suitcase bomb exploded aboard a commercial jetliner over Lockerbie, Scotland, killing 259 passengers and crew members. Of these victims, 189 were Americans, four of whom were U.S. government officials. From that point on, Qaddafi's Libya was branded an outlaw state and subjected to diplomatic and economic isolation. Finally exhausted by the sanctions, Qaddafi succumbed in December 2003 to U.S. and European demands that he dismantle his nuclear and chemical weapons programs and renounce terrorism. In return, President Bush agreed to remove Libya from the list of state sponsors of terrorism and to restore trade ties between the two countries.

Neglected in these foreign intrigues, however, were the Libyan people who still suffered from Qaddafi's tyrannical rule. Their discontent, energized by the ouster of Mubarak in Egypt days earlier, boiled over as angry mobs, again connected by social media, organized mass demonstrations across northern Libya. A national "day of rage" on February 17, 2011, unleashed widespread violence after Qaddafi ordered his troops to open fire on the protesters. Within days, several Libyan cities and the entire eastern region were in rebel hands. Rapidly losing control of his nation, Qaddafi vowed to commit mass summary executions in cities that had aligned with the opposition. He made this point chillingly clear on March 17 when he warned the citizens of Benghazi, the largest rebel stronghold: "We are coming tonight. You will come out from inside. Prepare yourselves for tonight. We will find you in your closets."

The prospect of imminent slaughter prompted the United States, along with Canada and several European countries, to launch air strikes against Libya. The UN Security Council authorized the attacks, citing a widely accepted norm that sovereign states have a "responsibility to protect" their citizens. Failure to do so would empower other UN members to protect threatened citizens.[26] On March 24, the North Atlantic Treaty Organization assumed control over this effort by enforcing a no-fly zone over the country and conducting large-scale aerial attacks on Qaddafi's military bases, tank columns, and other military assets. Enforcing the no-fly zone, which was also supported by nine members of the Arab League, allowed NATO to continue its air strikes with impunity.

Obama's decision to intervene in Libya was problematic given that the United States was still at war with two other Islamic nations, Iraq and Afghanistan. Yet his previous strategy—to stay at arm's length from the Tunisian and Egyptian uprisings and let them run their course—could not

---

[26] Of the five permanent, veto-yielding members of the UN Security Council, the United States, France, and Great Britain supported the resolution for military intervention. Although China and Russia opposed the action, they abstained on the UN vote and effectively allowed the intervention to commence.

be repeated in oil-rich Libya, which was fully engulfed in military conflict and on the verge of wholesale slaughter. Having ruled out U.S. isolation and full-scale military intervention, Obama chose a third way that "committed the United States, but only from the air and only from afar."[27] In "leading from behind," a term used to describe Obama's military strategy, the Pentagon provided the NATO mission with technical support (command, control, communications, and intelligence) while sharing aerial and offshore military operations with other NATO members and leaving the ground fighting in Libya to antigovernment rebels. This arrangement was telling given the weakened state of U.S. military and economic strength. When Obama declared that "the burden should not be America's alone," he sent a broader signal regarding the limits of American foreign policy and its capacity to dictate the terms of faraway conflicts that did not directly threaten U.S. interests.

Obama predicted that NATO's intervention would resolve the conflict in "days, not weeks." His forecast proved overoptimistic as Qaddafi rallied enough followers—in and out of the military forces—to maintain his hold on power for eight months. By August, however, his demise was virtually ensured when rebels gained control of Tripoli and most of the government ministries in the capital city. Qaddafi was soon found to be hiding in his hometown of Sirte, surrounded by his most loyal security forces. While vowing to fight to the death, they were no match for the vengeful rebel groups that surrounded the city and closed in on the Libyan leader. On October 20, he was discovered hiding in a drainage ditch and confronted his most bitter enemies, who quickly made good on their long-standing pledge to kill the Libyan leader with their own hands. Qaddafi's sudden death ended the NATO mission.

Still, Libyans were left without a clear path toward the creation of a functioning new government. Under Qaddafi's iron rule, there were no civil servants capable of leading this transition. There was also a lack of national unity, meaning that Libya was left in the hands of local and regional militias that capitalized on the power vacuum. "Anyone with a gun could command respect," journalist Forouk Chothia observed. Years after the overthrow, the militias "seem more determined than ever to gain more territory and impose their will."[28] Lacking a vibrant economy, educational system, or civil society, the only resources widely available in Libya were weapons that were either seized from government armories or provided by soldiers of

[27] David E. Sanger, "Letting Others Lead in Libya," *New York Times* (April 23, 2011), WK1.

[28] Forouk Chothia, "Why Is Libya Lawless?" *BBC News* (July 15, 2014), 1.

fortune. Armed groups also succeeded in blocking key oil fields and ports, denying Libya billions of dollars in oil revenue.

The United States suffered a major loss when terrorists bombed the U.S. consulate in Benghazi and killed four Americans, including Ambassador J. Christopher Stevens, a diplomat with expertise in North Africa. The date of this attack, the eleventh anniversary of the 9/11 terrorist attacks, was clearly in the minds of the terrorists. The bombing also coincided with widespread Muslim outrage over an amateur American film, titled *The Innocence of Muslims*, which ridiculed the Prophet Muhammad. The sophisticated nature of the attacks suggested that other terrorists were involved. Meanwhile, U.S. diplomacy would have no chance to succeed in the failed state that Libya became after the fall of Qaddafi. For America and its regional allies, protecting Libya's masses could no longer be ensured in the midst of the utter lawlessness following the NATO mission.

Syria's Civil War

The deadliest and most protracted Middle East uprising occurred in Syria, which held a key to the regional power balance by sharing borders with Turkey, Iraq, Israel, Jordan, and Lebanon. Energized by events in Tunisia early in 2011, pro-democracy activists staged nationwide demonstrations against the Syrian government and its leader, Bashar al-Assad. The protests were met with brutal retaliation by Syrian troops, who killed an estimated five thousand citizens by the end of the year.[29] Assad's defiance was no surprise, given the sectarian divisions within Syria. The Assad dynasty's hold on power depended on mistreating the Sunnis, whose first order of business upon taking power would exact bloody revenge on their former rulers. Political survival for Assad and his cronies was literally a matter of life and death.

Russia had served as a strong ally of Syria after World War II. With the Cold War underway, the Soviet Union needed a counterbalance to the power of the United States and Europe. Millions of Russian weapons were provided to Syria every year. The Kremlin also shared intelligence with their loyal ally. This relationship continued after the USSR's collapse in 1991. With the Arab Spring underway in 2011, Putin's Russia escalated its military buildup and counted on Assad's internal security forces whose loyalty to the government was demanded. Unilateral military action against Syria

---

[29]UN News Center, "As Syrian Death Toll Reaches 5,000, UN Human Rights Chief Warns about Key City" (December 12, 2011).

had limited prospects for success while posing multiple risks, including anti-American reprisals by Islamists across the Arab world. Furthermore, the United States could not rely on support from the UN Security Council after China and Russia vetoed a resolution calling for collective action against Syria in February 2012.

Faced with these constraints on American action, Obama could only provide the antigovernment protesters with encouragement and covert economic aid while otherwise avoiding direct intervention. Meanwhile, Assad laid siege to several cities that were deemed pockets of resistance, adding to the casualties. Syria became a magnet for a dizzying array of Islamist terrorist groups, mercenaries, pro-Assad paramilitaries, secular militias, and militant freedom fighters. Lacking united resolve by major powers, Syria's dictator exercised free rein to crush the democratic aspirations of his people. The UN proved unable to stop the bloodletting, marking another low point in the world body's checkered history.

The Syrian civil war took on a darker turn on August 21, 2013, when reports surfaced of deadly chemical weapons attacks on opposition strongholds in the suburbs of Damascus. An estimated 1,400 civilians, including more than 400 children, were killed by the bombs filled with the chemical agent sarin.[30] Assad initially denied the attacks, but his claims were later proven to be lies. Obama, who had declared the use of weapons of mass destruction (WMDs) a "red line" that would trigger U.S. military action, expected global support for a forceful response. Instead, most governments, including that of Washington's closest ally in London, shied away from Obama's call for action. Nor could Obama gain support from Congress, which worried that the missile strikes would only fan the flames of the civil war. Unilateral action by the United States, therefore, proved out of the question.

Obama was relieved by an unlikely source, Russia's Vladimir Putin, whose government had close ties to the Assad regime. Putin, who feared the spread of chemical weapons to his borders in central Asia, relished the opportunity to demonstrate his influence. An agreement approved in September by Russia, the United States, and Syria led to the dismantling of Assad's remaining chemical weapons, the last of which were turned over on June 23. Obama could not take credit for leading this geopolitical breakthrough.

In February 2017, Russian and Syrian air forces shifted from chemical weapons to the use of lethal chlorine gas. In Aleppo, an estimated

---

[30] The death toll in Syria made this the deadliest chemical attack since Saddam Hussein gassed an estimated four thousand ethnic Kurds in Iraq's northern region.

four hundred civilians were gassed in the war zone.[31] Other violations of human rights occurred in Ukraine, where citizens suffered from random killings, intimidation, arbitrary detentions, and torture. The UN High Commissioner for Human Rights discovered ill-treatment and torture against political opponents and minorities. In the province of Chechnya, gay males were susceptible to arbitrary detention, torture, and murder.[32]

President Obama resisted engagement in the Syrian civil war. In his view, the Middle East countries were better equipped to take on the conflict in their own backyard. Another U.S. incursion would only raise images of the past when Washington's muscle dominated the region. With the war dragging, concerns of chemical weapons, ruined urban areas, and threats from outside militias were beyond any settlement. The Trump administration had little leverage with Russia. Instead, the Russian air force used its firepower to protect Assad and his thirst for power. The Syrian civil war left nearly five million deaths between 2011 and 2017.[33]

Iraq's Collapse and the ISIS Challenge

The Arab Spring and its profound aftershocks caught much of the world by surprise. The seeds of the uprising, however, were deeply sown in the economic privation and political estrangement that plagued most Arab citizens throughout their history. More generally, the unraveling of order in the Arab Spring's wake rekindled old questions about the map of the Middle East, which was secretly drawn halfway through World War I by French and British officials. The Sykes-Picot Agreement of 1916, named after its negotiators, authorized the two European powers to dismember the Ottoman (or Turkish) Empire and replace it with territories to be supervised by Paris and London. While France assumed a mandate over modern-day Lebanon and Syria, Great Britain asserted the same authority in Iraq and Palestine (later Israel and Jordan). Missing from these

---

[31] Daryl Kimball, "Timeline of Syrian Chemical Weapons Activity, 2012–2017" (Washington, D.C.: Arms Control Association, 2017).

[32] United Nations Human Rights, "The Human Rights Committee Considers the Report of Russia" (New York: Office of the High Commissioner, March 17, 2015).

[33] Anne Barnard, "Death Toll from War in Syria Now 470,000, Group Finds" (*New York Times*, February 11, 2017).

negotiations, however, were the residents of these territories, nearly all of whom were Arab Muslims.[34]

These mandates ultimately attained statehood in the decades to come. Their leaders and citizens, however, were stuck with the seemingly random maps drawn by the Europeans, which did not reflect the nations' ethnic, religious, and cultural differences. The citizens' newly found freedom was further hobbled by the coming to power of monarchies and despotic governments whose primary goals were self-preservation and financial gain. By taking to the streets nearly a century after the Sykes-Picot Agreement was signed, the Arab Spring democracy advocates merely followed the international community's calls to advance the cause of democracy from the bottom up. While American leaders preached the gospel of democracy, they sent mixed messages to pro-democracy groups across the region.

Their confusion could be traced to the U.S. government's four vital interests in the Middle East:

- the survival of Israel,

- protection from Islamist terrorism,

- continued access to regional oil supplies, and

- preventing regional nuclear proliferation.

Each of these self-interests reflected the uneasy coexistence of realism and moralism in American foreign policy. Although contradictions between nations' words and deeds are inevitable and routine among major powers, such gaps are more pronounced in the context of American "exceptionalism," leaving the nation open to charges of hypocrisy in the world's most combustible region.

A Government in Shambles

President Obama, an early critic of the Iraq invasion, was determined to follow Bush's timetable for full withdrawal by the end of 2011. More than one million Americans had fought in the nine-year war. Of these, nearly 4,500

---

[34] British and French leaders agreed not to colonize these territories and to ensure that they would be directly managed by "indigenous governments and administrations." See James Barr, *Line in the Sand: Britain, France, and the Struggle That Shaped the Middle East* (New York: Simon and Schuster, 2011).

died, and more than 32,000 were wounded. The casualty count for Iraqi forces and civilians was far larger, and more than two million Iraqis were displaced from their homes. While the future of Iraq was highly uncertain, all parties involved in the war were exhausted by the U.S. presence, which cost American taxpayers more than $800 billion between 2003 and 2011.[35] Thus Obama was openly relieved when he announced on October 21, 2011, that "our troops will definitely be home for the holidays."

The American government had three stated objectives when it invaded Iraq in March 2003: to rid Iraq of WMDs that threatened the United States and its allies, to overthrow Saddam Hussein's authoritarian regime, and to help the Iraqis create a democratic and self-sufficient government. The first of these goals proved null and void after Saddam's presumed WMD arsenal was found to be nonexistent. The second goal was clearly achieved with Saddam's execution on December 30, 2006. The third goal, converting Iraq into a functioning democracy, became a work in progress.

The U.S.-led political reforms provided Iraqi citizens their first-ever opportunity to vote in multiparty elections. Beyond this historic milestone in 2006, Iraq's new government struggled to provide basic services to its people, including adequate police and military protection. The presence of U.S. military troops had suppressed regional tensions, although sectarian violence continued along with sporadic terrorist attacks against U.S. forces. As many feared, insurgents responded to the departure of U.S. troops in 2011 by staging attacks on Baghdad and other cities. The turmoil ruptured what little goodwill existed toward Prime Minister Nouri al-Maliki, whose eight-year run as prime minister from 2006 to 2014 left Iraq in worse straits than it was under the rule of Saddam or the United States.

Like Morsi in Egypt, Maliki had promised to represent his country's entire population, not simply those who shared his religious affiliation. As he concentrated his political power, however, Maliki became more repressive, seeking vengeance against Sunni activists who had supported Saddam's Ba'ath Party. He systematically excluded Sunni officials from government positions and, in 2012, launched armed attacks on Sunni strongholds in Anbar Province. Meanwhile, Maliki adopted the same corrupt practices that were standard in the region. He also proved indifferent to the ongoing economic paralysis in Iraq, relying instead on massive flows of development aid provided by the United States and other Western aid donors—much

---

[35] Amy Belasco, *The Cost of Iraq, Afghanistan, and Other Global War on Terror Operations since 9/11* (Washington, D.C.: Congressional Research Service, March 29, 2011), 17.

of which was used to enrich his political cronies. Iraq became a failed state as Maliki's abuse of power deepened, leaving the nation vulnerable to power plays from within and beyond its borders.

Obama assumed all along that a residual U.S. military force would remain in Iraq after the departure of nearly forty thousand troops in 2011. He could not, however, convince Iraqi leaders to provide American troops the legal immunity they needed to avoid prosecution for their military actions. Such immunity was routinely granted to the United States by other allies that allowed American forces to provide security assistance on their territory. Many Iraqis still resented the U.S. invasion and occupation of their country. In their view, the continuing presence of U.S. forces prolonged Washington's violation of their sovereignty.

Calls for an Islamic Caliphate

The dysfunction in Iraq provided an opening for armed groups and insurgents to advance their widely varying agendas. For many activists in the Arab Spring, removing oppressors from political power was a central objective. For others, rethinking the cartography of the Middle East—with an eye toward wholesale changes of boundaries and political units—was long overdue. While radical change in the region's political boundaries was not foreseen as the Arab Spring unfolded, neither was the seemingly endless civil war in Syria or the collapse of Iraq's failed attempt at democratic government. The resulting breakdown in both countries played directly into a powerful Islamist group known as the Islamic State of Iraq and Syria (ISIS), whose stated goal was the creation of a *caliphate*, or a political and social order based on Islamic law.[36]

The group, considered by the Pentagon a "diffused irregular army," had aligned with al Qaeda during the Iraq War, then joined with other jihadist groups fighting in Syria. Its partnership with al Qaeda ended, however, when members of al Qaeda found the tactics of ISIS, including public beheadings and crucifixions, too extreme for their own brutal standards.[37] For followers of ISIS, their missions were based on the expansion of militant Islam. To author Shad Hamid, "The Muslim world is

---

[36] The territory coveted by ISIS, known as the Levant, consists of other nations in the eastern Mediterranean region, including Cyprus, Jordan, Israel, Lebanon, Kuwait, and southern Turkey.

[37] A predecessor to ISIS, Boko Haram had been spreading a reign of terror across northeastern Nigeria for the past decade. Like ISIS, Boko Haram ("Western education is a sin" in English) vowed to topple the secular government and replace it with a state wedded to a strict version of *Sharia* law. See Mike Smith, *Boko Haram: Inside Nigeria's Unholy War* (London: I. B. Taurus, 2015).

unlikely to witness a replay of the West's journey toward liberalism, which depends on separating the church and states."[38]

With a small core of well-trained insurgents, which was organized in the no-man's-land of Syria's civil war, ISIS forces swept across northern Iraq in June 2014, seizing several major cities, including Mosul, Iraq's second most populous urban area. The juggernaut continued swiftly as the rebels captured Tikrit and then Fallujah, moving ISIS forces ever closer to their ultimate prize, Baghdad. Along the way, ISIS gained new recruits, including many members of the Iraqi army who abandoned their bases and joined the ISIS military campaign. As the violence continued, the UN's High Commissioner for Human Rights, Navi Pillay, declared that ISIS fighters "have been actively seeking out, and in some cases killing, soldiers, police, and others, including civilians, whom they perceive as being associated with the Iraqi government."[39] The group routinely publicized its actions, including the torture of declared enemies, via graphic Internet videos and tweets. Its exploitation of social media served as a recruiting tool for future volunteers, many of whom came from the United States and Europe.[40]

As with the Arab Spring, the U.S. government was blindsided by the unfolding events in Iraq and Syria, and by other aftershocks of the Arab Spring. President Obama, beset by domestic problems and the latest spasm of violence in Israel, resorted to his previous strategy of "leading from behind." Specifically, he ordered his operatives to divide and conquer ISIS by exploiting differences and potential rifts between the group and other Sunni militants. Ba'athists, for example, preferred secular societies based on nationalist, not religious, identities. Gaining support from tribal militias would be more difficult, especially after the United States closed its diplomatic outposts throughout Iraq in 2009. Instead of boots on the ground, Obama deployed two hundred U.S. forces to secure the U.S. embassy in Baghdad and train local forces in effective counterterrorism measures. His

---

[38] Shad Hamid, *Islamic Exceptionalism* (New York: St. Martin's Press, 2016), 143.

[39] Human Rights Watch, "ISIS Advance Threatens Civilians" (New York: Human Rights Watch, June 13, 2014).

[40] Members of ISIS had plenty of funding to advance their quest for an Islamist utopia. Much of their riches came from Iraqi banks, which they looted upon taking control of their communities. An estimated $400 million was stolen from a single bank. Opponents of the Assad regime in Syria freely provided funds to ISIS in order to achieve their overlapping missions. In addition, wealthy oil magnates in the Arabian Peninsula provided untold volumes of cash to ISIS, which also benefited by seizing massive caches of heavy weapons. The group's forces grew to more than twenty thousand as they resorted to kidnappings and smuggling operations that included the illicit export of heroin readily available in the region.

Impact and Influence: Abu Bakr al-Baghdadi

AY-COLLECTION/SIPA

Abu Bakr al-Baghdadi, the leader of the Islamic State in Iraq and Syria (ISIS), came to lead the terrorist group after years in isolation. His appearance in July 2014, making a speech that was released on the Internet, signaled his power as chief architect of the group's swift takeover of cities across eastern Syria and northern Iraq. A Sunni *mullah* who grew up in Iraq, he was educated at the Islamic University of Baghdad (now Iraqi University) and later preached the cause of *jihad*, an armed struggle to uphold Islam's traditions and security in the face of "infidels" in the Middle East, including the United States.

During George W. Bush's "war on terror," Baghdadi served among the insurgents affiliated with al Qaeda in Iraq, a forerunner of ISIS. He was taken captive by U.S. forces in 2004 and was alleged to be fomenting the Sunni insurgency that sought control of Iraq's government, which was dominated by Shiite rather than Sunni politicians. After several months in detention, U.S. officials released him due to a lack of evidence that he was directly responsible for the killing spree undertaken by Islamist militants. A decade later, Baghdadi proclaimed an Islamic caliphate, a government that would follow Islamic law and pursue territorial expansion in Sunni-dominated states throughout the Middle East.

offer, gratefully accepted by Maliki, also came with attack helicopters, intelligence support, and nonlethal aerial drones.

The ISIS offensive, which grew to an estimated twenty thousand fighters by 2015, soon engulfed much of Iraq and Syria—a territory roughly the size of Great Britain. In Washington, senior members of Congress demanded that Obama fight fire with fire. "The threat ISIS poses only grows over time," wrote Sens. John McCain and Lindsey Graham, two members of the Senate Foreign Relations Committee. "It cannot be contained. It must be confronted. This requires a comprehensive strategy, presidential leadership and a far greater sense of urgency."[41] Faced also with growing public fears of ISIS, Obama ordered U.S. forces to conduct aerial attacks on the group's suspected

---

[41] Sens. John McCain and Lindsey Graham, "Stop Dithering, Confront ISIS" (*New York Times*, August 29, 2014).

hideouts and military assets. He also offered to share intelligence with U.S. allies in the region. The president insisted, however, that any counteroffensive on the ground must come from regional armies and militias, not the Pentagon.

According to the United Nations, ISIS forces had already injured or killed an estimated twenty-five thousand Iraqi civilians between July 6 and September 10, 2015.[42] Another two million Iraqis were displaced from their homes and communities. According to the UN Assistance Mission to Iraq, another 18,802 Iraq troops were killed or injured in 2016 alone, not including thousands of civilian casualties unable to be counted.[43] Interviews of Iraqis close to the violence described widespread torture, including executions and amputations of those who did not comply with the group's strict rules. Children as young as twelve years old were enlisted in the security forces, and women were frequently sold into sex slavery.[44]

The scale of ISIS violence continued to grow.[45] Since ISIS considers itself a global mission, it extends well beyond Syria and Iraq. As of early 2017, ISIS affiliates were located in Afghanistan, Algeria, Egypt, Libya, Nigeria, Pakistan, Saudi Arabia, Yemen, and the Caucasus. In 2014 and 2015 alone, 25,000 foreigners from Arab countries had joined ISIS, and 5,000 others engaged from Western states. In August 2017, Americans revealed that ISIS and global warming were the two greatest threats facing national security.[46] James Mattis, the U.S. secretary of defense, called ISIS "a threat to all civilized nations."[47]

By late 2017, ISIS has taken a new direction. Most of Syria have fled from the so called caliphate. The Islamic State remain an enemy of Iraq which maintained large territories. Otherwise, ISIS spread into Europe and the United States. On October 31, 2017 a (loan wolf) crashed into a street in Manhattan killing eight citizens and injuring more than ten.

---

[42]United Nations, *Report on the Protection of Civilians in Armed Conflict in Iraq: July 6–September 10, 2014* (New York: UN Assistance Mission for Iraq, September 17, 2014).

[43]United Nations Assistance Mission to Iraq, United Nations, Paris, France, 2017.

[44]A second UN report, released in November, provided similar evidence of mistreatment in Syria. According to the report, "Corporal punishments are imposed during public events in an effort to deter those who may oppose the group's rule and to spread terror among the civilian population." United Nations, *Rule of Terror: Living under ISIS in Syria* (New York: United Nations, Independent International Commission of Inquiry on the Syrian Arab Republic, November 14, 2014), 5.

[45]Jacob Poushter and Dorothy Manevich, "Globally, People Point to ISIS and Climate Change as Leading Security Threats," Pew Research Center (August 1, 2017).

[46]Daniel Byman, "ISIS Goes Global: Fight the Islamic State by Targeting Its Affiliates," *Foreign Affairs* (March–April 2016), 79.

[47]Kathryn Watson, "Fight against ISIS Has Shifted to 'Annihilation Tactics,' Mattis Says" (*CBS News*, May 28, 2017).

The Afghan Muddle

American war planners also found little relief in Afghanistan. President Obama's primary national security goal was to draw down the armed forces after years of warfare. Along with Iraq, Afghanistan reduced its actions to the training of Afghan armies. Still, the scattered regions were committed to a strict version of *Sharia* Islam where Taliban insurgents captured territories far from their power bases in the south. The Taliban, a quasi-government in Afghanistan, had its own armies along with dozens of splinter factions that ensured constant warfare. As in Iraq, the Afghan insurgents faced little resistance from government troops despite the extensive military training those troops received from the United States.

The NATO mission in Afghanistan, meanwhile, came apart as U.S. allies could not agree on the scope of their respective missions. Some governments, including Germany, Italy, Poland, and Spain, supported the effort to stabilize Afghanistan but refused to send their troops into combat. Facing the likely exodus of other NATO allies, the Pentagon declared in February 2012 that the combat role of the United States in Afghanistan would end in 2014. But this timetable was not good enough for French president Nicolas Sarkozy, who announced in 2012 that his troops would be removed by the end of 2013. Events off the battlefields further poisoned the well. The February 2012 burning by American troops of nearly two thousand Korans, the essential religious text of Islam, incited deadly riots and demands for U.S. withdrawal. The Afghans' outrage intensified in March after a U.S. soldier, Staff Sgt. Robert Bales, massacred sixteen Afghan civilians in a Kandahar village.[48] The United States was not only losing ground to the Taliban, but was self-destructing.

The scale of the insurgency grew in 2013 and 2014 with each drawdown of American forces. The militants pledged to escalate their attacks until their demands were met to remove all foreign troops from the nation and to allow Taliban control of regional governments. The rate of civilian casualties in the first six months of 2014 was the highest since 2009, as nearly five thousand civilians were either killed or injured (see Figure 12-3). Nearly half of these casualties occurred when civilians were caught in the crossfire between militants and government forces. Another one-third of the total were killed or maimed by home-made bombs, many of which

---

[48] In August 2013, a military court convicted Bales on all the murder charges and sentenced him to life in prison. His confession for the attacks may have saved him from the death penalty.

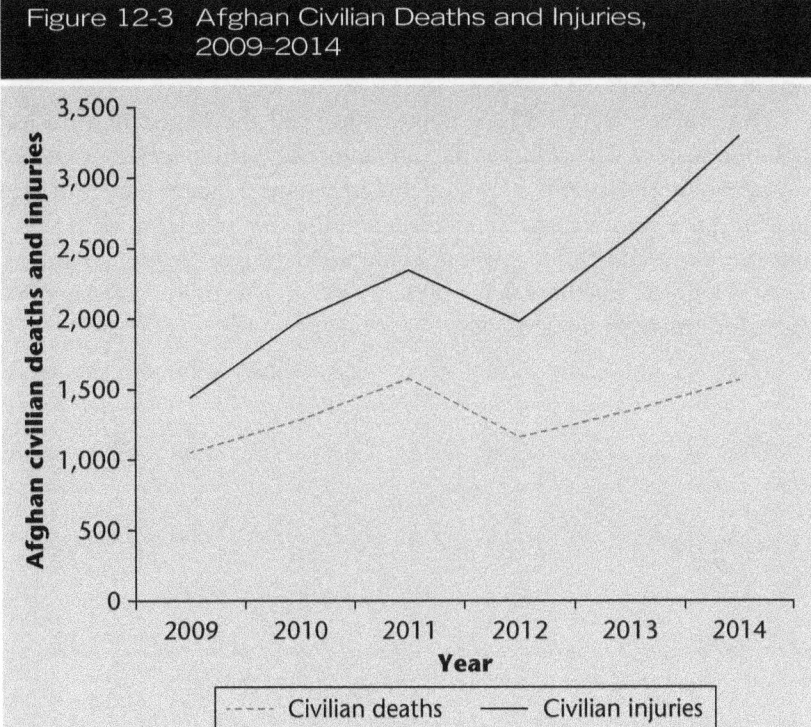

Figure 12-3 Afghan Civilian Deaths and Injuries, 2009-2014

Source: United Nations Assistance Mission in Afghanistan, "UNAMA Report: Number of Afghan Civilian Casualties Rises by 24 per Cent in First Half of 2014," July 9, 2014, http://unama.unmissions.org/Default.aspx?tabid=12254&ctl=Details&mid=15756&ItemI D=38134&language=en-US.

were designed to maim rather than kill civilians.[49] The Taliban's ability to maintain order, however brutally enforced, was not in question.

American and British forces ended their combat operations in Helmand Province, a formerly powerful Taliban stronghold that served as the target of the 2009 surge in allied military forces. The region, home to more than 80 percent of Afghanistan's lucrative (though illegal) opium industry, posted record profits in 2013, much of which financed the nation's endless regional wars. Ashraf Ghani, who succeeded Karzai in September 2014, welcomed twelve thousand U.S. troops for training missions. With fewer U.S. troops on the ground in Afghanistan, the Pentagon turned to targeted

---

[49]United Nations Assistance Mission in Afghanistan, *Mid-year Report on Civilian Protection* (New York: United Nations, July 10, 2014).

killings and the use of aerial drone attacks to reach targets. Still, Gen. John Nicholson informed Congress on February 2, 2017, that the U.S. mission was in a "stalemate."[50]

Two weeks later, the U.S. military dropped the largest non-nuclear bomb in history. The "Mother of All Bombs" (MOAB), targeted at an ISIS cave, was dropped from a cargo plane in remote Afghanistan.[51] An estimated ninety-six militants were killed, and the commander in chief sent a message of how much firepower he could wield deep in the Afghan deserts. Time would tell whether such a presence would constitute a blessing or a curse for American foreign policy.[52]

---

[50] Tom Bowman, "General Requests Thousands More Troops to Break Afghanistan 'Stalemate'" (National Public Radio, February 2, 2017).

[51] Mujib Mashal and Fahim Abed, "U.S. Isn't Saying How Much Damage 'Mother of All Bombs' Did in Afghanistan" (New York Times, April 18, 2017).

[52] Two months later, Obama gained Ghani's support to expand the U.S. mission to include military operations against the Taliban and other militant groups.

The Revival of Power Politics

The U.S. Carrier Carl Vinson is a Nimitz-class super carrier.

The Asahi Shimbun via Getty Images

F or a nation whose foreign policy was shaped by moral distinctions between good and evil, it took little effort for many Americans to understand the violence perpetrated by Islamist groups. Yet the nation's style of foreign policy changed in fundamental ways. Popular notions of this war as an exception to normalcy of peace could no longer be sustained as the fight against terrorism appeared endless.

Americans after Vietnam became more conscious of their nation's own moral deficiencies. Still, such values weakened as growing fears of terrorism preoccupied citizens. In declaring a "war on terror" after the 9/11 attacks, President George W. Bush resorted to torture against enemies in Afghanistan and Iraq. His actions, later considered illegal, contrasted sharply with the nation's "exceptional" self-image. It did not help when, in October 2013, American spies were caught bugging the cell phone of German chancellor

Angela Merkel, an ally of the United States.[1] Nonetheless, it was tempting for Americans to cling to the notion that the United States, for all of its faults, remained a virtuous world leader.

President Obama had hoped to improve America's stature upon coming to power in January 2009. He also hoped to live up to the high expectations of foreign governments and citizens. Instead, the president was immersed in domestic politics, including the repair of the U.S. financial system that nearly collapsed when he arrived at the White House. By the start of his second term, Obama faced an array of regional conflicts and threats from would-be rivals of the United States.

As described in the previous chapter, the Middle East's descent into anarchy could be traced to the Ottoman Empire's demise after World War I and the subsequent remapping of the region in ways that ensured perpetual violence.[2] Iraq's formation in 1932, for example, was bound to be a future powder keg. Previously ruled as a British mandate, the new nation-state included a dominant Shiite majority, a resentful Sunni minority, and an ethnically Kurdish population that sought, above all, their own sovereign state. In these cases, geographic disconnects between nation and state identities created the preconditions for political violence and forceful regime change.

American foreign policymakers, still accustomed to traditional forms of diplomacy and warfare, had difficulty grasping the threats to the interstate system as conceived and codified by the 1648 Treaty of Westphalia. While the treaty created the architecture for this global system, it offered heads of state substantial leeway in managing internal affairs. The Westphalia order's main concern had less to do with governing models than with the maintenance of geopolitical stability, viewed as vital in the rapidly integrating world order of the seventeenth century. Such stability, it was widely assumed, would be maintained naturally by adjustments in power balances and by the honoring of national sovereignty. Meeting this final condition, however, could not be assured by aspiring theocrats who rejected secular governance, traditional diplomacy, and the sanctity of borders.

Despite its frequent ruptures the Westphalian system weathered centuries of turbulence and remains intact today. Most wars in recent years have

---

[1] Ian Traynor, Philip Olterman, and Paul Lewis, "Angela Merkel's Call to Obama: Are You Bugging My Phone?" *The Guardian* (October 24, 2013).

[2] Scott Anderson, *Lawrence in India: War, Deceit, and the Folly of Building the Middle East* (New York: Doubleday, 2013). This casual approach to postimperial cartography had even more devastating effects across Africa, whose demographic and cultural differences were far more complex.

been fought within, not between, countries, and the balance of power continues to serve as the fulcrum of great-power stability. Regional hegemons maintain the physical as well as latent power to suppress internal threats. While networks of "global governance" may provide needed venues for problem solving and mediation, they cannot overcome the pull of contesting national identities, interests, and human impulses of distrust and greed. As Edward Hallett Carr, a respected British historian and diplomat, observed more than a century ago, "Politics are in one sense always power politics. While politics cannot be satisfactorily defined exclusively in terms of power, it is safe to say that power is always an essential element of politics."[3]

The new era of power politics coincided with the Arab Spring in 2011. New dictators took over much of the Middle East region. Russian and Chinese leaders found common cause to bring down America in the balance of power. Their intentions, declared in state visits, reflected a "sense among foreign policy elites . . . that the global order is mutating quite rapidly away from the unipolar moment of the 1990s and the beginning of the last decade."[4]

The USSR kept pace with the United States during the Cold War largely by reaching nuclear "parity" with the West. China (PRC) detonated a nuclear bomb in 1964. Although the two communist powers severed their Cold War Treaty of Friendship by 1960, they later collaborated on global security issues on which they had common interests. China abolished its Maoist economic system in favor of capitalism, which propelled the PRC into the top ranks of global economies.[5] Their partnership continued after the Cold War, and in 1997 the two governments formally issued a United Nations resolution that called for the end of U.S. hegemony.[6]

The two governments also used their veto powers in the UN Security Council to stifle Western initiatives. From the onset of the Arab Spring, they repeatedly rejected UN condemnations of Syria for killing thousands of

---

[3] Edward Hallett Carr, *The Twenty Years' Crisis, 1919–1939* (New York: Harper, 1946), 102.

[4] European Parliament, Directorate-General for External Policies, *The Positions of Russia and China at the UN Security Council in the Light of Recent Crises* (March 2013), 9.

[5] Deng Xiaoping, China's premier from 1978 to 1992 who opened the PRC to global commerce, anticipated his country's gradual emergence as a great power. According to his 24-Character Strategy, proclaimed in 1990, "observe calmly, secure our position, cope with affairs calmly, hide our capabilities and bide our time, be good at managing a low profile, and never claim leadership." Global Security, "Deng Xiaoping's 24-Character Strategy," http://www.globalsecurity.org/military/world/china/24-character.htm.

[6] United Nations, General Assembly, Fifty-Second Session, "China-Russia Joint Declaration on a Multipolar World and the Establishment of a New International Order" (May 20, 1997).

citizens in its ongoing civil war, a position supported elsewhere in the Security Council. The PRC also defended Russian aggression in Ukraine, described below, arguing that the UN had no legal right to meddle in the internal affairs of member states. These coordinated actions by Moscow and Beijing marked "an important shift in the foreign policy thinking of Russia and China."[7]

Cold War II with Russia

As described in the first section, American foreign policy after World War II was driven by Cold War concerns that centered on the Soviet Union, whose communist government offered an alternative to the political and economic institutions of the West. As the largest country in the world, the Soviet Union also created a geopolitical headache for American military planners, whose containment strategy covered a landmass encompassing nearly nine million square miles and eleven of the world's twenty-four time zones. The sheer mass of the Soviet Union prompted the Pentagon's formation of regional alliances and the creation of global military commands. These actions remained vital after the Cold War, when the Soviet Union collapsed and was replaced by a new Russia with fifteen new countries on Russia's border.

Most citizens welcomed a democratic system that would secure political and social rights, observe multiparty elections, and protect a free news media. Once Putin became president in 2000, however, these rights were dismissed and Russia rapidly became an authoritarian state. According to Freedom House, a U.S.-based organization that evaluates all countries, Russia in 2017 had "a subservient judiciary, a legislature dominated by his United Russia party, and a president able to manipulate elections and inhibit formal opposition."[8] With most of the country ruled by oligarchs, the vast number of Russian citizens had little or no rights. The news media was controlled by Putin, and civil society was held with a tight grip. The most obvious sign of tyranny came on February 25, 2015, when Boris Nemtsov, a statesman and rival to the United Russia Party, was assassinated a block away from the Kremlin, home of the Russian government.

Prior to Obama's arrival, ties between the United States and Russia were cordial but clouded by lingering distrust. Putin, citing threats to his own government, supported Bush's war on terror after the 9/11 attacks. He also provided tactical assistance to the United States in the Afghan conflict

---

[7] European Parliament, op. cit., p. 6.

[8] Freedom House, "Freedom in the World 2017" (Washington, D.C.: Freedom House, 2017).

and joined the United States, the European Union, and the United Nations in a diplomatic "quartet" that attempted to resolve Israeli-Palestinian disputes. On the other hand, Putin frequently complained about NATO's eastward expansion, which he claimed was motivated by unfounded fears of future Russian expansion. He also objected to U.S. plans to build nuclear missile defenses in Poland despite American claims they were meant to ward off attacks from Iran and other adversaries, not Russia. Putin's decision to invade neighboring Georgia in 2008, a show of force meant to demonstrate the Kremlin's regional hegemony, was harshly criticized by the United States and most other nations.

Rather than an assault on a remote province, Putin oversaw hack attacks that targeted the United States. As detailed in Chapter 14, Russia was also found to be interfering in the 2016 U.S. presidential elections. Other hackers infiltrated federal, state, and local offices along with school systems. Individuals such as former secretary of state Colin Powell found their personal files made public. His attacks struck a variety of targets, including the headquarters of the Democratic and Republican headquarters. Other targets included Kazakhstan (2009), Germany (2015), Ukraine (2016), and other countries.[9]

Ukraine on the Brink

The sovereign state of Ukraine, formerly a province of the Soviet Union, has immense strategic importance given its location. The borders stretch from Eastern Europe across Poland, Slovakia, Hungary, and Moldova to the west; Belarus to the north; and the Black Sea to the south. A vast common border extends across Russia more than a thousand miles. With fertile croplands encompassing much of the western region, Ukraine has long been known as the "bread basket" of the Soviet Union. This vast terrain further served as a valued trading partner with Russia.

As a newly created nation-state, however, Ukraine was unprepared in the early 1990s for statehood. During the Soviet era, its government engaged in the corruption and public mismanagement that were standard fare across the Soviet Union. These practices continued after the Cold War, as political operatives in Kiev were more concerned with their personal gains than their obligations to create a functional and stable democracy. In another throwback to the past, Ukraine's wealth was concentrated among a

---

[9] Robert Windrem, "Timeline: Ten Years of Russian Cyber Attacks on Other Nations," *NBC News* (December 18, 2016).

Ukrainians attempt to prevent Russians from capturing territory.

small number of oligarchs who controlled the economy and neglected the poverty confronting most of the population.[10]

Ukraine after the Cold War was also separated between western Ukraine, whose citizens looked to Europe as political and economic role models, and the eastern region that looked to Russia for inspiration, guidance, and material support. This schism became problematic in November 2013 when Ukraine's elected leader, Viktor Yanukovych, made a fateful decision. Having agreed previously to an economic partnership with the European Union, Yanukovych cancelled the agreement and chose instead to join Russia as his ally and primary trade partner. His decision, celebrated by ethnic Russians in the east, was condemned by Ukrainians in the west who demanded the president's removal.

As the protests swelled, the police and army ordered riot police to fire upon the protesters. Dozens of undefended citizens were killed by the snipers, which merely stiffened the protesters' resolve to reclaim their government. Facing his own imminent capture, Yanukovych fled from the capital, leaving Ukraine in a political void. Putin showed his support for the separatists by ordering military exercises along the nation's shared border. At the same time, swarms of ethnic Russians in eastern Ukraine

---

[10]See Steven Woehrel, *Ukraine: Current Issues and U.S. Policy* (Washington, D.C.: Congressional Research Service, July 8, 2014), 7.

formed armed militias demanding independence from Kiev. The scale of the Ukrainian crisis grew more ghastly on July 17, when armed forces shot down a Malaysian jetliner as it flew high above the battle zone in eastern Ukraine. The attack killed 298 passengers and crew members and left remnants scattered across hundreds of acres.[11]

Putin's aggression also centered on Crimea, a former Soviet stronghold and, since the Cold War, a valued part of the newly independent Ukraine. The territory had changed hands repeatedly for centuries, beginning with the Greek and Roman Empires. While the foreign powers ruling Crimea took many forms, they had one thing in common: a keen interest in Crimea's location on the Black Sea, which provided an entryway to the Mediterranean Sea through Turkey's Bosporus Strait.

The Russian military unleashed Russia's armed forces to seize control of the Crimean Peninsula's government, military headquarters, media outlets, and other key institutions. Russian troops forced the Ukrainian navy to abandon its base in Sevastopol and took over the Kerch Strait ferry that connected Crimea and Russia, a critical step allowing Russian troops with advanced weapons to pour into the territory.[12] A hastily organized referendum, considered illegal by most other governments, found 96 percent of the voters favoring Russia's annexation of Crimea. Putin rejected a March 27 UN resolution that declared the referendum illegal.

Powers and Calculations

For Putin, well aware that ethnic Russians constituted more than half of Crimea's population, the allure of recapturing Crimea was irresistible.[13] The fact that most Crimeans also spoke Russian as their native language provided them a distinct advantage in keeping up with developments in Moscow. Putin, having just hosted the Winter Olympics in mid-February, and anticipating a surge in his global stature, chose this moment to arouse the nationalistic fervor of ethnic Russians in Ukraine who identified with "mother Russia."

---

[11] "Ukraine Plane Crash, What We Know" (BBC, September 28, 2016).

[12] Observers from the Organization for Security and Co-operation in Europe (OSCE) warned that "relations between ethnic groups on the peninsula are characterized by a growing climate of fear." OSCE, "Developing Situation in Crimea Alarming" (Vienna: OSCE, March 6, 2014), http://www.osce.org/hcnm/116180.

[13] In 2001, the year of the most recent demographic survey in Crimea, 58 percent of the population were ethnic Russian. The other major ethnic groups included Ukrainian (24 percent) and Crimean Tatars (12 percent), who were ethnically Turkic. Government of Ukraine, "All Ukrainian Consensus 2001" (Kiev: State Statistics Committee of Ukraine, 2001).

Map 13-1 Crimean Peninsula

The crisis in Ukraine posed the greatest threat to East-West relations since the Cold War. President Obama, preoccupied with domestic problems and the unraveling Arab Spring, had few sources of leverage beyond repeated appeals to Putin for an easing of tensions. A counteroffensive by NATO was out of the question. As for Obama, the crisis reinforced popular perceptions that he was a weak leader whose lack of resolve merely invited further challenges to the world order. Exasperated, Obama wondered aloud, "Why is it that everybody is so eager to use military force after we've just gone through a decade of war at enormous cost to our troops and to our budget? And what is it exactly that these critics think would be accomplished?"[14] Obama ratcheted up economic sanctions by placing restrictions on Western trade relations in vital sectors of Russia's economy, including its energy and military industries.[15]

Why did Russia's president choose to trigger this power play at this time? Putin's challenge was not only driven by perceived changes in the balance of power. Putin was also inspired by a personal sense of Russian nationalism and its ambition to revive his homeland's stature after years of humiliation. "Putin was forming a more coherent view of history and his place within it," observed journalist David Remnick, an expert on Russian politics. "More and more, he identified personally with the destiny of Russia."[16] Putin, who sought respect from other major powers, expected his provocations would gain the world stature he sought. Instead, the global response left Putin isolated, although his public approval at home climbed to 83 percent.[17]

The financial numbers told the story of Russia. Its gross domestic product (GDP) in 2013 was $2 trillion; the U.S. total stood at $17 trillion.[18] Russia also suffered a mortality crisis reflected in worsening health conditions and higher death rates.[19] Russia's economy shrunk by 4 percent between 2014

---

[14]Mark Landler, "Ending Asia Trip, Obama Defends His Foreign Policy," *New York Times* (April 28, 2014), A1.

[15]Ukraine's faltering economy received a boost from the International Monetary Fund, which approved a $17 billion loan to the government. The European Union also offered Ukraine $16 billion in financial aid, and the U.S. Congress approved a $1 billion loan guarantee and millions of dollars in humanitarian aid and nonlethal military supplies.

[16]David Remnick, "Watching the Eclipse," *New Yorker* (August 11 and 18, 2014), 58.

[17]Moscow, Russia: Levada Center, http://www.levada.ru/eng/ (last accessed July 30, 2014).

[18]Russia's per capita income was less than $14,000 in 2013, about one-quarter the U.S. level of $53,670. World Bank, *World Development Report, 2014* (Washington, D.C.: World Bank, 2014), http://data.worldbank.org/data-catalog/world-development-report-2014.

[19]Nicholas Eberstadt, "The Dying Bear," *Foreign Affairs* (November–December 2011), 97.

Impact and Influence:
Vladimir Putin and Xi Jinping

Two dominating world leaders, Russian president Vladimir Putin and Chinese president Xi Jinping, typify the resurgence of *power politics*, a term that suggests foreign relations based on the law of the jungle rather than cooperative global governance. Late in 1999, Putin succeeded President Boris Yeltsin, who had led the newly re-created Russia after the Soviet Union's collapse in 1991. Putin later became prime minister and, in March 2012, was again elected president despite widespread allegations of voter fraud. Putin, who once declared the Soviet Union's collapse "the greatest geopolitical catastrophe of the century," became more nationalistic in recent years. This devotion led Putin in 2014 to reclaim control over Crimea and incite a revolt among ethnic Russians in Ukraine designed to restore Moscow's control over the region.

In November 2012, meanwhile, the Chinese government turned to Xi Jinping, a lifelong official of the Chinese Communist Party, to lead the population of more than 1.3 billion citizens. Xi, the son of a founding leader of the People's Republic of China (PRC), rose quickly up the party ranks before taking office. His efforts to expand Chinese control of offshore territorial waters and to accelerate the PRC's military spending angered his regional neighbors and raised concerns about possible military clashes in East Asia. Xi expressed interest in peaceful relations with the United States, whose close ties to the Chinese economy had proven beneficial to both countries. At the same time, Xi established much closer relations with Putin, who shared the PRC's autocratic approach to rule along with a desire for a long period of American decline.

and 2017. This slump was due to three factors: (1) a drop of oil revenues by 60 percent, (2) the growing control of corrupt oligarchs, and (3) the financial burden to Russia under $40 billion in economic sanctions imposed by the West. Russia's problems were worse when sanctions from the European Union were taken into account.[20]

China's Pacific Challenge

The primary challenge to U.S. allies in East Asia concerned China, whose economic surge since the 1980s transformed the nation into a significant

---

[20] Cory Welt, *Russia: Background and U.S. Interests* (Washington D.C.: Congressional Research Service), March 1, 2017.

Russian president Vladimir Putin and Chinese president Xi Jinping,

world power. By 2013, the PRC had become the world's largest trading nation, surpassing the United States. Three years later, China led the world's economy with $21.4 trillion in gross domestic production.[21] Much of the PRC's economic growth came at America's expense. In 1980, Washington maintained a small trade surplus with the PRC. By 2010, however, this surplus had turned into a $273 billion deficit, nearly one-half of the nation's trade deficit.

These economic statistics revealed a love-and-hate relationship between Beijing and Washington, D.C. On the positive side, China's export market produces goods that are affordable to American consumers. At the same time, accelerated military technology and growing expansions beyond Chinese borders have threatened the United States and its allies across the Far East. Adding to American vulnerabilities, the Chinese government subsidizes America's soaring national debt through massive purchases of U.S. Treasury bills. By cashing in even a small portion of these bonds, the value of which approached $1.8 trillion by 2016, Chinese leaders could paralyze the United States.[22]

---

[21] Central Intelligence Agency, *The World Factbook*, 2017.

[22] Brad W. Setser, "How Many Treasurers Does China Still Own?" (New York: Council on Foreign Relations, 2016).

Like Russia, China aspires to be a great power after many years of hegemony controlled by the United States. To the Russians, however, American moves to preserve its regional hegemony in the area were too little, too late. "You are pivoting to Asia," Russia's ambassador recently observed. "But we're already there."[23]

The Pivot to Asia

China's economic and military growth, combined with chronic human rights violations, led observers two decades ago to predict the "coming conflict with China."[24] According to this view, as China became stronger and as its leaders appealed to nationalism as a substitute for communism, they would reassert China's rightful place as Asia's dominant power. In the 1990s, President Bill Clinton maintained the more optimistic view that *engagement* with China would yield better results than Cold War–style *containment*. Clinton persuaded Congress in 2000 to normalize Sino-American trade relations, a move widely supported by U.S. firms that sought greater access to China's massive domestic market. Despite this breakthrough in bilateral trade ties, Beijing continued its repressive domestic policies and resistance to U.S. primacy. When George W. Bush entered the White House in January 2001, he declared China to be a strategic competitor rather than a partner, a position he maintained throughout his presidency.[25]

The PRC embraced an economic model of "state capitalism," which combined political repression and engagement in global export markets that improved standards of living among the large populations. The PRC still maintained its communist government, though it came to govern a capitalist economy. President Deng Xiaoping began this transition at the end of the Cold War by embracing private enterprise and export-led growth in the 1980s. His successor, Jiang Zemin, followed the same economic model while crushing political dissent.

President Obama concluded that global trends required a geopolitical "pivot" in American foreign policy. "After a decade in which we fought two wars that cost us dearly," Obama stated, "the United States is turning our attention to the vast potential of the Asia-Pacific region."[26]

---

[23] Peter Baker, "As Russia Draws Closer to China, U.S. Faces a New Challenge," *New York Times* (November 8, 2014), A10.

[24] Richard Bernstein and Ross H. Munro, *The Coming Conflict with China* (New York: Viking, 1997).

[25] Richard Bush, *America's Alliances and Security Partnerships in East Asia* (Washington, D.C.: Brookings, 2016).

[26] "Remarks by President Obama to the Australian Parliament" (Washington, D.C.: Office of the Press Secretary, November 17, 2011).

Figure 13-1 The Hub and Spoke Stratagey

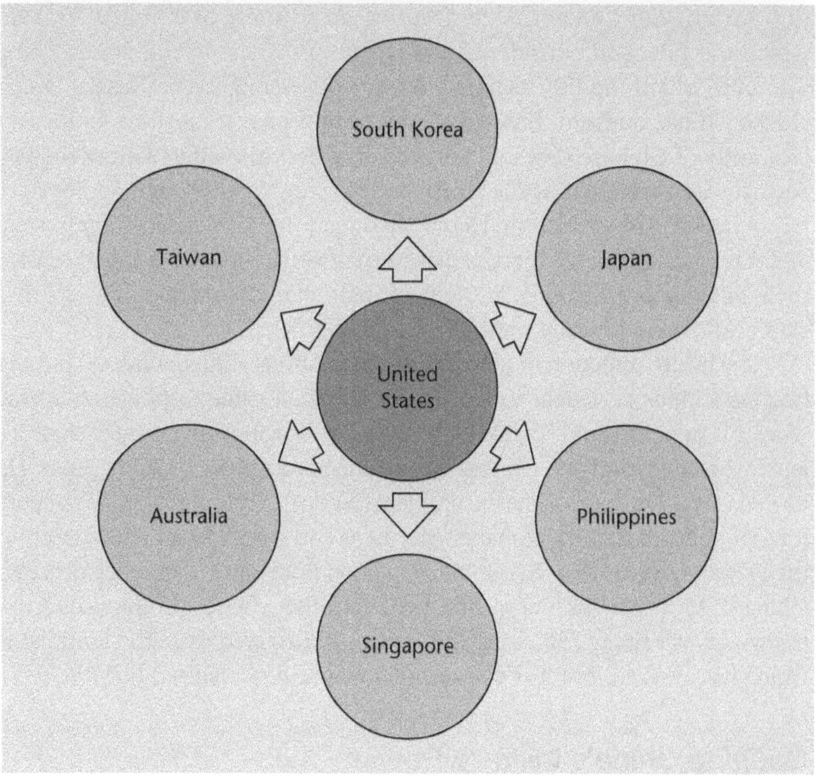

This "rebalancing," as the policy became known, required careful management by Washington. In contrast to U.S. allies in Europe, which were long connected by the multilateral NATO alliance, America's East Asian allies established separate, bilateral ties to Washington. For East Asia, the United States adopted a "hub-and-spoke" strategy in which it established close relations and security agreements with six separate allies (Australia, Japan, Philippines, Singapore, South Korea, and Taiwan). The Pentagon's challenge was to ease these internal tensions while protecting member states against outside threats. To Secretary of State Hillary Clinton, "We are the only power with a network of strong alliances in the region, no territorial ambitions, and a long record of providing for the common good."[27]

---

[27]Hillary Clinton, "America's Pacific Century," *Foreign Policy* (November 2011), 57.

History provides few examples in which rising and declining powers intersect without conflict. With this in mind, "China pessimists" foresaw growing Sino-American competition on a variety of fronts: in Taiwan, which the PRC still considered a renegade province; in the South China Sea, over which the PRC claimed expanded sovereignty; in Russia, which shared China's quest for the end of American primacy; in Africa, home to a vast array of Chinese development projects; and in matters before the UN Security Council such as the treatment of Iran, North Korea, and Syria.[28] "China optimists," including Henry Kissinger, the former secretary of state and a longtime China expert, believed the two superpowers could resolve their differences peacefully in light of their shared strategic interests in a stable, and economically productive, world order.[29]

The future direction of Sino-American relations shifted when Xi Jinping became China's president in November 2012. Xi came to power at a time when his nation's rapid economic growth was slowing, environmental problems worsened, and the Chinese government was beset by corruption. He vowed to resolve these domestic problems while continuing his government's foreign policy based on global engagement and trade. In a 2014 speech to the French government, Xi quoted Napoleon Bonaparte, who once declared China to be "a sleeping lion" and predicted that, "when China wakes up, the world will shake." Revising this vision, Xi declared that "the lion that is China has awoken, but it is a peaceful, amiable, and civilized lion."[30]

Gauging China's Military Power

Xi oversaw the world's largest army and navy, along with a defense budget that grew rapidly to nearly $200 billion after he entered office. Like the United States, the PRC modernized the military so that it was capable of managing an expanded navy—a proven nuclear deterrent—more advanced fighter jets, and widening cyber targets. Still, in 2016, the estimated volume of Chinese military spending ($215 billion) was nearly more less

---

[28] See, for example, Aaron Friedberg, *A Quest for Supremacy: China, America, and the Struggle for Mastery in Asia* (New York: Norton, 2011), and Martin Jacques, *When China Rules the World: The End of the Western World and the Birth of a New Global Order* (New York: Penguin, 2009).

[29] Henry Kissinger, *On China* (New York: Penguin, 2011).

[30] Xi Jinping, "Xi Addresses 50 Years of China-France Ties" (March 28, 2014), www.china.org.cn. Office of the Secretary of Defense, Annual Report, "Military and Security Developments Involving the People's Republic of China 2016" (Washington, D.C.: Department of Defense, 2016). Prashanth Parameswaran, "The Truth about China's New Military Aid to the Philippines," *The Diplomat* (June 30, 2017).

	Military Strength, 2017		
	USA	China	Russia
Military personnel (million)	2.4	2.3	3.4
Total aircraft	13,762	2,955	3,794
Armed fighting vehicles	41,062	4,788	31,298
Aircraft carriers	19	1	1
Submarines	70	68	63
Destroyers	63	35	15
PPT ($ trillions)	18,560	21,270	3,745
Power index (smaller better)	.0857	.0945	.0929

Source: GlobalFirepower.com; McLean, VA. Data gathered June 2017.

than 30 percent of the U.S. volume ($611 billion). Furthermore, U.S. defense spending did not factor in that of France ($56 billion), Great Britain ($54 billion), Japan ($42 billion), and other American allies whose modern military forces further reinforced U.S. power.

Beyond national patriotism, sound government, modern technology, and a healthy economy have led to greater military strength in many major categories of military power. In 2017, for example, China had the most military personnel. Russia had the most intercontinental nuclear missiles. And the U.S. led in armored fighting vehicles, submarines, and naval destroyers. While China and Russia had one aircraft carrier each, the United States had nineteen. Only the U.S. Navy patrolled with a "blue-water navy" that spanned the world.[31]

The Chinese government has moved rapidly to establish regional conflicts at greater distance from the Chinese mainland.[32] Chinese officials flexed their power in East Asia, a region with the same economic, security, and national interests that made the South China Sea a potential for cooperation or conflict. Along with China, Japan and South Korea engage in robust trade and finance. Despite their political conflicts, these wealthy states pursued a strategy of "offshore balancing." In this strategy, the major powers along the East China Sea have not adopted a threatening approach to shift

---

[31] GlobalFirepower.com (McLean, VA: Knoema).

[32] Stockholm International Peace Research Institute, "Trends in World Military Expenditure" (Stockholm, Sweden: SIPRI, 2016–2017).

the balance of power. Instead, the United States maintained strong forces while urging regional powers to "uphold the balance."[33]

Under Xi, China established a security agreement in 2017 with the Philippines, led by new president Rodrigo Duterte. This new alliance was significant, given that the Philippines was a close ally with the United States since the end of World War II. To the new president, who disliked U.S. foreign policy, it was time to "diversify" his country's military. Chinese strategists established security ties with Malaysia and Djibouti on the horn of Africa. The PRC used soft power in southern Africa, providing massive amounts of development aid to poor governments in return for oil and other underground assets. In this context, the "Middle Kingdom" is likely to gain its long-sought stature as a major power in world politics. According to *The Economist* (April 22, 2017),

> Today, after a century and a half that encompassed Western imperial occupation, republican turmoil, the plunder of warlords, Japanese invasion, civil war, revolutionary upheaval and, more recently, phenomenal economic growth, China has resumed its own sense of being a great power. It has done so in a very different world: one led by America. For three-quarters of a century, America has been the hegemon in East Asia, China's historical backyard. But now China is indisputably back.

Clashing over Water Rights

When President Xi Jinping took over in 2012, he pledged to have cordial relations with his neighboring leaders. This changed, however, when Xi extended China's territorial claims beyond its lengthy seacoast, angering China's maritime neighbors who depended on the coastal waters' rich fishing grounds and potential gas and oil deposits. In the South China Sea alone, the governments of Brunei, Malaysia, the Philippines, and Vietnam alleged violations of their freedom of the seas. China's defense minister, Chang Wanquan, dismissed the claims, insisting that the PRC would "make no compromise, no concession, no treaty" regarding the offshore islands.[34] "The Chinese military can assemble as soon as

---

[33] Hal Brands and Peter Feaver, and John Mearsheimer and Stephen Walt, "Should America Retrench? The Battle over Offshore Balancing," *Foreign Affairs* (November–December 2016), 164–171.

[34] Helene Cooper, "Hagel Spars with Chinese over Islands and Security," *New York Times* (April 8, 2014), A6.

summoned, fight any battle and win." Tensions escalated further in May when a Chinese fishing vessel rammed and sank a Vietnamese fishing boat near an oil rig hastily constructed by the PRC off Vietnam's coast.

China's actions were tested in July 2016, when the UN's Permanent Court of Arbitration ruled that Beijing was violating the Philippines' maritime claims. This was the first time the Convention of the Law of the Sea was formally upheld against China's aggressive actions. The UN ruling was ignored by the Chinese government, which continued to build military outposts in Philippine areas.[35] The United States, meanwhile, supported Japan, Malaysia, Vietnam, and other countries that had stakes in China's welfare.

In 2017, Secretary of State Rex Tillerson was critical of China's man-made islands in the South China Sea, multibillion-dollar islands rich in oil and gas, which he considered "illegal." He said the project was "akin to Russia's taking the Crimean Sea. . . . Your access to these islands is not going to be allowed."[36] Many governments urged Beijing to abide by the United Nations Convention on the Law of the Sea, which sets maritime zones of control based on coastlines. Just in case, the U.S. Navy made plans to expand the Pacific Fleet by approximately 30 percent by 2021.

For all of its strengths, the Chinese government faced at least five limitations that worked against its ambitions to become a strategic peer of the United States. Four factors in particular counter the claims made by those who predicted an imminent changing of the guard:

- the state's historical focus on internal concerns, primarily the care and feeding of its massive population;

- its lack of alliances, with its nervous neighbors seeking closer ties to the United States;

- a lack of "soft power" due to its repressive government and suppressed civil society; and

- a workforce based primarily on the assembly of consumer goods rather than new technologies and world-class educational institutions.

---

[35] See Mira Rapp-Hooper, "Parting the South China Sea: How to Uphold the Rule of Law," *Foreign Affairs* 95 (September–October, 2016), 76–82.

[36] David Brunnstrom and Matt Stetalnick, "Trump's Secretary of State Pick Says China Should Be Barred from South China Sea Islands," Reuters (January 11, 2017).

Israel's Shadow in the Middle East

Lurking beyond all the turmoil associated with the Arab Spring was the ongoing struggle between Israel and its Arab neighbors. While many Israelis celebrated the overthrow of Mubarak in Egypt, they feared the new regime would nullify the 1978 Camp David Accords and deprive Israel of a diplomatic partner south of the border. The escalating violence in Syria, meanwhile, threatened to spill across Israel's northern border and unleash a new round of bloodshed. To Israel's prime minister, Benjamin Netanyahu, the democratic uprisings had become an "Islamic, anti-Western, anti-liberal, and anti-Israeli wave." His concerns were reinforced by Iran's nuclear ambitions and growing defiance of outside pressure. To Netanyahu, if the United States was not willing or able to destroy Iran's nuclear program, Israel was ready to do so.

Israel's primary problem remained its relationship with the nearly two million Palestinians who lived within its borders. Some relief had come in 1993 with the Oslo Accords that created a provisional Palestinian government on the West Bank and Gaza Strip. The leader of the Palestinian Authority, Mahmoud Abbas, hoped the agreement would lead to a two-state solution that would finally affirm the political rights of his people. The democratic process, however, moved in another direction with the electoral victories in 2006 of Hamas, an Islamist party based in the Gaza Strip with a long history of terrorism and impassioned calls for Israel's destruction. Far from seeking reconciliation and peace, the leaders of Hamas consolidated their power by expelling their political rivals and taking control of the Palestinian Authority's paramilitary forces. Subsequent cross-border attacks by Hamas led to punishing Israeli air strikes and a ground offensive in December 2008 that left more than 1,400 Palestinians dead.

The United States, preoccupied with the wars in Iraq and Afghanistan, did little to prevent Israeli assaults on Gaza and southern Lebanon, where Hezbollah militants staged periodic attacks on the Jewish state. Nor could the United States stop Netanyahu from building more in the West Bank. Although Abbas reached an agreement among his rival factions to form a unity government early in 2012, there was little hope that the accord would produce reconciliation with Israel. His efforts to gain the UN's recognition of Palestine as a sovereign state, meanwhile, were frustrated by Washington's veto power in the world body.

Nearly two million Palestinians lived in Gaza in 2014, a narrow, twenty-five-mile strip of land surrounded by Israel to the north and east, Egypt to the south, and the Mediterranean Sea to the west. Described by some as an "open-air prison," Gaza had few resources to provide its congested population, who were prevented from leaving the territory. Israel's control of Gaza began with the 1967 Six-Day War, and since then, the government in Tel Aviv assumed control of the enclave's borders, air space, and access to the sea. Hamas defenders had little relief to offer beyond moral support and occasional reprisals against their enemies.

Escalating tensions in 2014 brought even more suffering to the region. After Palestinians kidnapped and killed three Israeli teenagers in July, Israel commenced a bombing campaign that left more than two hundred people dead and nearly one thousand injured. In a dramatic show of force, the Israel Defense Forces launched a ground invasion of Gaza, targeting enemy strongholds and destroying dozens of tunnels that were used to stage missile attacks in Israel. By early August, the two sides were exhausted by the violence and withdrew to their previous positions. Nearly two thousand Palestinians were killed in the latest spasm of Arab-Israeli violence. The death toll among Israelis was less than one hundred.

Both Israel and Egypt maintained their 1979 treaty with both sides facing territorial disputes, terrorist attacks, and violations of human rights on a daily basis. The Israeli and Egyptian forces operated in overlapping and conflicted territories from the Sinai Peninsula through the Gaza Strip and the northern reaches of the Golan Heights. Ever since Egypt's president, Abdel Fattah al-Sisi, took over in 2013 the former general resorted to authoritarian rule that left citizens few democratic rights, including restrictions of speech, assembly, press, and religion. In his first full year, the general approved 7,400 military tribunals that left thousands of prisoners in overcrowded cells.

Gaza's plight continued in the absence of leadership or any semblance of trust. In 2017, the seven hundred thousand Palestinians were cramped within seventeen square miles. They suffered in various ways. Sixty percent of youth were unemployed. The citizens had four hours of electricity on a typical day. Whereas 98 percent of the people had safe drinking water in 2000, just 10 percent of the residents of Gaza could drink the water safely in 2017. After the latest hostilities ended, more than five hundred schools were damaged or destroyed.[37] "In short, Gaza is on the brink of a humanitarian and political point of no return," wrote author Benedetta Berti.[38] Despite this

---

[37] United Nations, *Gaza Ten Years Late* (New York: UN County Team in the Occupied Palestinian Territory, 2017).

[38] Benedetta Berti, "How to Forestall Another Conflict between Hamas and Israel," *Foreign Affairs* (June 27, 2017).

mistreatment, Washington continued to provide Egypt its annual payoff $1.3 billion for military security.[39]

Prime Minister Netanyahu won the 2015 elections and then rejected any prospect for the two-state solution. He then called for more Israeli settlements in territories also claimed by Palestinians. The United States gathered in a "quartet" that included Russia, the European Union, and the UN Secretary-General. Among their findings, the group found in July 2016 that the "continuing policy of settlement construction and expansion, designation of land for exclusive Israeli use, and denial of Palestinian development is steadily eroding the viability of the two-state solution." For his part, President Trump had cordial relations with Netanyahu. He argued, however, that "every time you take for settlements, there is less land left. . . . I am not somebody that believes that going forward with these settlements is a good thing for peace."[40]

In the case of Israel and Egypt, a dilemma arises—for Americans still see the United States as the "city on the hill," "the first new nation," the "special providence," or other visions of national virtue. Citizens, however, saw how the United States stood by while Gaza City, where thousands of people suffered each day, found no way out of their plight. Many Americans also learned how Egypt's strongman left thousands of citizens in foul prisons while refusing his people basic political or social rights. Finally, citizens realized how world leaders praised Iran's president regarding the nuclear agreements while facing charges from the United Nations for ignoring human rights. According to the UN, "Members of religious and ethnic minorities have continued to endure abuse and discrimination and face persecution, including arrest and imprisonment, expulsion from educational institutions, denial of economic opportunities, deprivation of the right to work, the closure of businesses and the destruction of religious sites, such as cemeteries and prayer centers."[41] As in the past, U.S. efforts to resolve problems in the Middle East fail to move the region toward peace.

---

[39] Jim Zanotti, "Israel: Background and U.S. Relations in Brief" (Washington D.C.: Congressional Research Service, February 24, 2017).

[40] Boaz Bizmuth, "I Won't Condemn Israel, Its Been Through Enough," *Israel Hayom* (February 10, 2017).

[41] United Nations, Human Rights Council, Twenty-Eighth Session, "Situation of Human Rights in the Islamic Republic of Iran" (February 20, 2015).

Ongoing Threats of Nuclear Proliferation

Struggling against global terrorists and great-power challengers were not the only security concern of American leaders. They simply deflected other threats, including the potential spread of nuclear weapons to other governments for which nuclear "statehood" would increase leverage over their adversaries, including the United States. India and Pakistan made this leap in 1998, joining the nuclear club that for many years included only the United States, Russia, China, France, Great Britain, and Israel. Their inclusion not only complicated regional stability in South Asia but also raised doubts about the Nuclear Non-Proliferation Treaty (NPT) that was adopted in 1970 and had 190 adherents by the turn of the century. For the United States, Iran and North Korea posed the most serious dangers as potential nuclear proliferators.

A treaty adopted on July 7, 2017, called for all countries to renounce the creation and use of nuclear weapons. The treaty was named "The United Nations Conference to Negotiate a Legally Binding Instrument to Prohibit Nuclear Weapons, Leading toward Their Total Elimination." More than 120 countries announced their support for the treaty; none of the world's nine nuclear-armed countries approved the treaty. To Nikki R. Haley, the U.S. ambassador to the UN, "We have to be realistic. Is there anyone who thinks that North Korea would ban nuclear weapons?"[42]

Iran's Quest for "Nuclear Rights"

Given the centrality of the Middle East in American foreign policy, the question of nuclear proliferation preoccupied the White House. The U.S. withdrawal from Iraq in December 2011 was celebrated in neighboring Iran. With much of Sunni Iraq in shatters, Iran had an opportunity to transform into an Iranian sphere of influence. For the United States, such a move would leave the region more vulnerable to the Islamic State and other groups that were openly hostile to American interests in the Middle East. The prospects for Iranian hegemony increased daily as Iraq succumbed to political disarray.

American relations with Iran had reached new depths in June 2005 with the election of Mahmoud Ahmadinejad, a favorite of Iranian clerics known for his intense hatred of Israel and calls to make Iran a major power.

---

[42] Rick Gladstone, "A Treaty Is Reached to Ban Nuclear Weapons Arms. Now Comes the Hard Part," *New York Times* (July 7, 2017).

Upon taking office, Ahmadinejad pledged to diversify Iran's energy sources by developing nuclear power. His plan was peculiar for such an oil-rich nation, but it excited Iranians for whom "nuclear rights" had become a rallying cry. Thus, Iran began the process of uranium enrichment, the key step in producing nuclear fuel. In February 2006, the International Atomic Energy Agency (IAEA) declared that any efforts to restrain Iran's nuclear ambitions were futile. By April, Iran had enriched uranium to produce a modest stockpile of "deliverable" nuclear warheads by 2015. Meanwhile, Iranian scientists developed long-range ballistic missiles that could strike targets across the Near East and southern Europe.

Although Iran's ascension to the nuclear club would not produce the first "Islamic bomb"—Pakistan had already claimed that honor—a nuclear Iran would further complicate the global strategic balance and inflame tensions in the Middle East. Other Islamic states in the region, including Egypt and Saudi Arabia, would be tempted to follow suit in order to protect their own security. A nuclear Iran would also directly threaten Israel, its sworn enemy, which for years had been plagued by Iran-backed terrorist groups. The United States found itself in a bind as its nuclear showdown with Iran unfolded. Economic sanctions had failed to gain concessions from Tehran. Gaining the required unanimous vote for a critical resolution against Iran in the UN Security Council was out of the question since China and Russia were certain to object. With no better choices, the White House stuck to its policy to isolate Iran globally while supporting domestic groups that sought a democratic and more pro-American government.

Iran had emerged as a vital power broker in the region, at once exerting leverage in the Syrian civil war and fomenting sectarian violence in Iraq. In many regional conflicts, Iran had become more influential than the permanent members of the UN Security Council. President Obama sensed a potential break in the Iranian talks when Hassan Rouhani, a former head of Iran's Supreme National Security Council, was elected president in June 2013. Rouhani adopted a moderate stance toward the West and expressed support for a resolution of the nuclear controversy. When Obama had a face-to-face talk with Rouhani on September 28, 2013, he marked the first conversation between Iranian and American leaders since 1979.

On July 14, 2015, six major powers approved a Joint Comprehensive Plan of Action that offered Iran a way out of its financial crisis and a potential door into the global economy.[43] The agreement required that Tehran

---

[43] The "5 + 1" powers included the United States, Russia, China, Great Britain, and France (all permanent member of the UN Security Council), along with Germany.

suspend most of its nuclear enrichment programs that were capable of creating and launching a nuclear weapon. In addition to the Comprehensive Plan, the International Atomic Energy Agency demanded frequent and sudden inspections. Compliance by Iran triggered a suspension of the sanctions that crippled the nation's economy. By January 2016, nearly all of the U.S. and European Union sanctions were lifted. President Trump, angry over an Iranian missile test in January 2017, threatened to reject the agreement. Under pressure from other governments, Trump supported the agreement, although he let Iranian leaders know he had little patience with their government.

Nuclear Brinkmanship in North Korea

Power politics was also evident on the Korean Peninsula, as three generations of totalitarian rulers pursued the means to build and deliver nuclear bombs on targets as close as South Korea and as far away as the United States. The problem first confronted President Clinton in the early 1990s, when North Korea's long-standing dictator, Kim Il Sung, threatened to build nuclear weapons in defiance of the government's earlier pledge to respect the terms of the Treaty on the Non-Proliferation of Nuclear Weapons (NPT). The prospect of nuclear weapons in North Korea was disturbing to the United States for several reasons. A sudden crisis in the region or miscalculations by government officials could produce untold carnage and a wider war.

The fact that North Korea's thirteen thousand artillery launchers could quickly decimate Seoul, South Korea's capital, was not lost on anyone involved in the conflict. A nuclear North Korea would also threaten an arms race in East Asia, as South Korea and Japan would be unlikely to ignore such a threat to their security. More broadly, North Korea's nuclear arsenal, however small, would embolden other anti-American regimes that sought to upend the existing balance of power.

In 1994, Clinton dispatched former president Jimmy Carter to Pyongyang, the nation's capital, to negotiate an end to the nuclear threat. All Carter could do, however, was gain Kim's agreement to freeze North Korea's ongoing nuclear program. The ransom paid for this deal was incredible: $4 billion for the construction of two light-water nuclear power generators that would not yield weapons-grade plutonium, a free supply of oil for eight to ten years, and diplomatic relations with the United States and Japan. What did the United States receive in return? Only promises that North Korea would allow weapons inspections and shut down the reprocessing plant—a promise it also had made years earlier and then violated.

Kim Il Sung's success with nuclear brinkmanship served his domestic interests in North Korea, where a protracted famine had left more than two million dead and spurred a worldwide relief effort.[44] The nation's Stalinist regime, like that of the defunct Soviet Union, was adept at building military hardware for export even as its civilian economy floundered. North Korean engineers had developed and launched a three-stage missile over Japan in 1998. Gaining nuclear technology and know-how from a variety of unsavory arms dealers became a top priority for North Korean leaders. Kim Jong Il, who came to power following the death of his father, renounced the agreement with Washington in 2002, ejected international weapons inspectors, and vowed to withdraw from the NPT. Kim raised the stakes further in 2006 by conducting an underground atomic bomb test that officially brought North Korea into the nuclear club.

Obama became the third American president to confront North Korea's nuclear ambitions.[45] His prospects, though, steadily worsened in 2010 as Kim Jong Il ordered a series of provocative actions that included the sinking of a South Korean naval vessel and the bombing of a South Korean island that produced an exchange of artillery fire between the two rivals. In December 2011, the heightened tensions coincided with Kim Jong Il's death and the coming to power of his son, Kim Jong Un. Although little else was known about the "great successor," as he was known, North Korean military leaders pledged their allegiance to him and dutifully applauded his stated intention to maintain the country's "military-first" approach to South Korea.

Amid each of these power transitions, North Korea maintained its status as one of the world's most impoverished and repressive states. A 2011 report by the World Food Program found one in three North Korean children to be malnourished. Meanwhile, the human rights group Freedom House aptly summarized the government's mistreatment of its people: "Corruption is believed to be endemic at every level of the state. . . . All media outlets are run by the state. . . . Freedom of assembly is not recognized and there are no known associations or organizations other than those created by the state. . . . There is no freedom of movement, and forced resettlement is routine. . . . The economy remains both centrally controlled and grossly mismanaged."[46]

---

[44]For more on the causes of this crisis and faltering relief efforts, see Andrew W. Natsios, *The Great North Korean Famine* (Washington, D.C.: U.S. Institute of Peace, 2001).

[45]See Mike Chenoy, *Meltdown: The Inside Story of North Korea's Nuclear Crisis* (New York: St. Martin's, 2009).

[46]Freedom House, "Freedom in the World, 2011: North Korea," https://freedomhouse.org.

Kim Jong Un continued his nuclear provocations by testing yet another nuclear explosive in February 2013, a move that triggered new UN condemnations and sanctions. Even the Chinese government grew weary of its ally's nuclear brinkmanship. Xi Jinping signaled his dismay by visiting South Korea in July 2014 before making his government's customary stop in Pyongyang. Still, Kim accelerated his pace by testing two underground nuclear tests in 2016. Above the ground, North Korea launched a missile in May 2017, the Hwasong-12, that reached 1,300 miles. This advance made it clear that North Korea had the capacity to create and deliver a nuclear weapon that could reach the United States.

Geopolitics could not be ignored at a time when foreign policy was overshadowed by domestic politics. This favored China and other major powers, leaving North Korea a free path to further its nuclear threats. History shows that once nuclear weapons are produced, countries don't reverse their programs. Pyongyang knows that its weaponry elevated the country to a higher status in global meetings. Two questions were posed in 2017. First, will Chinese leaders prohibit their communist neighbor from moving further? Second, will the United States use its nuclear firepower to deter any first-strike attack on America and its friends in the Far East?

CHAPTER 14

The End of the American Century?

America's moralistic style of foreign policy takes place in an *amoral* context of clashing national interests, power struggles, and competition for finite resources. Lacking world government, leaders are wary of other nation-states and seek dominance in regional and global conflicts. Anarchic "state of nature" leaders pursue cooperative and self-sacrificing foreign policies at great risk to their own sovereignty.[1]

World War II provided the most devastating example of how humans are capable of mass killings for any reasons they devise. Henry Luce, the publisher of *Life* magazine, still found reasons in 1941 for optimism in the midst of the war. Luce declared that the "American Century" had come.[2] In his view, only the United States could be the vessel that spreads democracy worldwide. Yet the author also observed a pessimistic strain in the public:

> We Americans are not happy about America. We are not happy about ourselves in relation to America. We are nervous—or gloomy—or apathetic. As we look out at the rest of the world we are confused; we don't know what to do. . . . There is a striking contrast between our state of mind and that of the British people. On Sept. 3, 1939, the first day of the war in England, Winston Churchill had this to say: "Outside the storms of war may blow and the land may be lashed with the fury of its gales, but in our hearts this Sunday morning there is Peace."

As noted earlier, the United States remained neutral, having deployed millions of troops in the First World War. Presidents, generals, and most citizens expressed little interest when Italy invaded Ethiopia (1935), when the Spanish Civil War broke out (1936–1939), and when Japan invaded China (1937). The United States became a powerful source for weapons, tanks, and advanced fighter jets. Luce watched these developments closely

---

[1] Kenneth Waltz, *Man, the State, and War* (New York: Columbia University Press, 1959).

[2] Henry Luce, "The American Century," *Life* magazine (February 17, 1941).

in 1941 and made his case for the "American Century" even as the imminent attack of Pearl Harbor approached:

> There is one fundamental issue that faces America as it faces no
> other nation. It is an issue peculiar to America and peculiar to
> America in the twentieth century. It is deeper even than the imme-
> diate issue of War. If America meets it correctly, then, despite hosts
> of dangers and difficulties, we can look forward and move forward
> to a future worthy of men, with peace in our hearts. If we dodge
> the issue, we shall flounder for 10 or 20 or 30 bitter years in a
> chartless and meaningless series of disasters.[3]

In this book, we examined how this "American Century" proceeded
during and after the Cold War. The challenge of Soviet power, with the
first detonation of its nuclear weapon in 1949, led to a race for nuclear
supremacy that ultimately had little relevance. Instead, most of the U.S.
government was engaged with the burgeoning postwar economy, the
growth of secondary education, and the emergence of global governance,
including the newly created United Nations and the Bretton Woods
System. The Soviet Union, with the many flaws of its communist system,
was limited to proxy wars from the Koreas to Vietnam and Cuba. The
growth of emerging democracies fortified Luce's image of a benevolent
American hegemon. As we examined earlier, this image was shattered following the 9/11 terrorist attack, the 2003 Iraq War, and the 2007–2008
financial crisis when investors worldwide lost faith in American markets.
Constant wars in the Middle East engaged U.S. fighters through the
Obama and Trump years.

Today's world politics is as turbulent as it has been since World War II.
To author Richard Haass, "the fundamental elements of world order that has
served the world well since World War II have run their course."[4] Cyber-
techs make weapons that destroy grids of power. Democracy has given
way to nationalism and populism across much of the European Union.
Similar changes swept in rural areas of the United States. Their voters were
more worried about their failing futures at home rather than foreign policy
debates at home. As the scholar Walter Russell Mead declared in 2017,
"The American people have elected a president who disparages the policies, ideas, and institutions at the heart of postwar U.S. foreign policy."

---

[3] Ibid.

[4] Richard Haass, *A World in Disarray* (New York: Basic Books, 2013).

As we described earlier, profound shifts in world politics altered the balance of power. Historically, such a change has profound alterations for the economics, political priorities, and grand strategies of all countries. The economic growth of China, for example, has allowed military planners to modernize and expand their weaponry. These actions, in turn, allowed President Xi to infringe on the territorial borders of nations across the South China Sea. Russia, another country seeking great-power status, manipulated the 2016 presidential election through encroaching cyber-hackers and sophisticated spies.

The current balance of power resembles *weakened unipolarity*, or a period when the unipolar maintains a lead in most categories but is weakening relative to other powers. Analysts debate whether the future will feature a *bipolar* balance, with the United States and China prevailing, or whether a period of *complex multipolarity* will emerge that includes China, Russia, the European Union, and nonstate aggressors such as ISIS and other Islamist movements. Recent conflicts resembled wars of the fifth century when Thucydides, a Greek historian, provided evidence that changes in balances of power are most likely to provoke major wars.[5]

Internal Threats to Democracy

As described earlier, President George W. Bush declared after the 9/11 attacks that only an open-ended war on terror would rid the United States of the threat posed by terrorist groups. In such an "existential" war, national survival trumped democratic freedoms that were affordable luxuries in a more benign setting.[6] Still, many Americans became concerned that such actions threatened the nation's moral stature. These controversies struck at the heart of America's righteous self-image, a vital source of its world power. The internal threats to democracy in America took three forms:

- the overreach of presidential war powers,
- restrictions on personal freedoms and privacy rights, and
- the treatment of prisoners in the war on terror.

---

[5] Graham Allison, *Destined for War* (New York: Houghton Mifflin, 2017).

[6] All governments face this dilemma in times of war. In some cases, such as Israel, restrictions on individual liberties are a semipermanent feature of everyday life. Germany's government is currently engaged in a controversial effort to curb freedoms in the name of national security.

First, Bush's war began inside the U.S. government, with an aggressive push to strengthen presidential powers at the expense of Congress. Vice President Cheney claimed that "unwise compromises" over the Vietnam War caused "an erosion of the powers and the ability of the president of the United States to do his job."[7] In his view, Congress had granted Bush unlimited war powers in the joint resolution it passed just after the September 11 attacks. The resolution authorized presidents to "use all necessary and appropriate force against those nations, organizations, and persons who they determined planned, authorized, committed, or aided in the New York City attacks."[8] These presidential powers remained stronger in the Trump administration. In such war zones as Libya, Somalia, Syria, and Yemen, U.S. forces engaged against suspected terrorists without knowledge from Congress or information provided to most American citizens. An approval in 2017 allowed commanders to fight in war zones up to 180 days without gaining approval from Congress.[9]

Second, White House curbs on personal freedoms were embodied in the USA PATRIOT Act, approved by Congress and signed by Bush within weeks of the 9/11 attacks. The act eased government restrictions on domestic surveillance. It also allowed federal agents to gain access to citizens' phone and medical records, business transactions, e-mail messages, and the use of libraries. The act allowed "sneak-and-peek" searches of private property without owners' knowledge. Although defended as an essential step toward national protection, the USA PATRIOT Act alarmed many citizens and groups. Seven state legislatures and 396 local governments, including those of New York City, Los Angeles, and Chicago, passed resolutions declaring the act a violation of civil liberties. The act also made it easier for federal agents to detain and deport foreign citizens suspected of either being or supporting terrorists. These practices continued under President Trump, who resorted to multiple deportations, almost entirely from the Middle East.

Other breaches of personal freedom came to light in December 2005 when the National Security Agency (NSA) was found to be secretly collecting the telephone records of millions of Verizon customers.[10] In 2013, former intelligence agent Edward Snowden exposed further evidence of domestic surveillance. This time, the federal government gained access

---

[7] Quoted in Charlie Savage, *Takeover: The Return of the Imperial Presidency and the Subversion of American Democracy* (New York: Little, Brown, 2007), 75.

[8] U.S. Congress, "Resolution on the Use of Military Force" (September 18, 2001).

[9] Bonnie Kristian, "Trump's Dangerous Expansion of Executive War Powers," *Politico* (April 3, 2017).

[10] James Risen and Eric Lichtblau, "Bush Secretly Lifted Some Limits on Spying in U.S. after 9/11, Officials Say," *New York Times* (December 15, 2005), A1.

to Google, Facebook, and other social media sources under a secret program called Prism.[11] Snowden's leaks of classified documents led to charges of espionage by the U.S. government. By the time the arrest warrant was issued, Snowden had been granted asylum in Russia.[12]

In 2016, President Obama signed legislation that ended the mass collection of citizens' private communications. The NSA, meanwhile, retained its broad authorities to oversee the private information of foreign citizens.[13]

Third, U.S. policy toward war prisoners raised further concerns about the nation's values. In George W. Bush's "war on terror," captured terrorists would lose the protections reserved for war prisoners under the 1949 Geneva Conventions.[14] A year later, the Pentagon opened a detention center at Guantánamo Bay, Cuba. "High-value" detainees were hooded, chained to their seats, and transported eight thousand miles from Afghanistan to Cuba.[15] The whereabouts of other detention centers were less clear. American officials later confirmed that several secret prisons, or "black sites," operated in Eastern Europe along with Afghanistan and Thailand. The extent of coercive "interrogations" were unknown. Military officers acknowledged that they used techniques such as waterboarding, sleep deprivation, and placing detainees in stress positions.[16]

In February 2006, the UN Commission on Human Rights found that the evidence of abuse at Guantánamo Bay warranted closing the facility. Bush later signed the Military Commissions Act of 2006, which suspended the right of *habeas corpus* to suspected terrorists held at the prison, most of whom were held indefinitely without a hearing or trial. By 2017, the Detainee Treatment Act of 2005 had banned the military from engaging

---

[11] Glenn Greenwald, Ewen MacAskill, and Laura Poitras, "Edward Snowden: The Whistleblower behind the NSA Surveillance Revelations" (*Guardian*, June 11, 2013).

[12] The Russian government extended Edward Snowden a stay to 2019, a decision that prevented him from a likely extradition to the United States.

[13] Still, a report by the Inspector General found that the agency "did not fully meet the intent of decreasing the risk of insider threats to NSA operations." Department of Defense, Inspector General, *The National Security Agency Should Take Additional Steps to Effectively Implement Its Privileged Access-Related Secure-the-Net Initiatives* (Department of Defense, August 29, 2016).

[14] The United States had also ratified the International Covenant on Civil and Political Rights. It was a founding signatory of the Universal Declaration of Human Rights, which declared in Article 5, "No one shall be subjected to torture, or to cruel, inhuman, or degrading treatment or punishment."

[15] Dana Priest, "CIA Holds Terror Suspects in Secret Prisons," *Washington Post* (November 2, 2005), A1. In other cases, the U.S. government turned over suspected terrorists to allied governments that had more lenient restrictions on the interrogation of prisoners.

[16] U.S. Congress, "Inquiry into the Treatment of Detainees in U.S. Custody" (Senate Armed Services Committee, December 11, 2008).

in torture and required that the Red Cross have access to prisoners being held by the U.S. government. Barack Obama announced a ban on torture when he took office in 2009. His successor, President Trump, claimed that torture "absolutely works" when he took power.[17] His advisers in the Pentagon, however, followed the laws that were already established.

Trump and Turmoil

President Trump had little knowledge in foreign policy, but he had strong views of how the United States would approach world politics. According to the White House, "The Trump Administration is committed to a foreign policy focused on American interests and American national security."[18] What was missing in the declaration were references to U.S. allies, global poverty and population growth, nuclear proliferation, global warming, and the United Nations. The new president was prone to using Tweets to announce his positions. On April 11, 2017, for example, Trump threatened North Korea: "North Korea is looking for trouble. If China decides to help, that would be great. If not, we will solve the problem without them! U.S.A.!"[19]

The early period of Trump's presidency included many controversial policies regarding American foreign policy. His actions at home and overseas surprised most citizens. These policies included the environment, the State Department, immigration, global trade, and the White House's legal problems with Russia and at home.

Environment

As noted in Chapter 1, President Trump angered nearly all heads of state by rejecting U.S. membership in the Paris Agreement, a global treaty that bonded nearly two hundred countries to reduce greenhouse gas emissions. Specifically, the treaty called for global temperatures to fall by 2 degrees Celsius in pre-industrial levels. Emmanuel Macron, the newly elected French president, told his people that Trump had "committed an error for the interests

---

[17] Barney Henderson and Chris Graham, "Donald Trump: Torture 'Absolutely Works' Says US President in Interview with ABC News: Thursday Morning Briefing'" (January 26, 2017).

[18] "America First Foreign Policy," *whitehouse.gov*, accessed November 11, 2017. https://www.white house.gov/america-first-foreign-policy

[19] Trump, Donald J. Twitter Post. April 11, 2017, 5:03 AM. https://twitter.com/realdonaldtrump/status/851767718248361986?lang=en

of his country, his people, and a mistake for the future of our planet." The Vatican viewed the U.S. decision a "huge slap in the face" for the Pope and a "disaster for everyone." At home, the Trump administration called for steep cuts in budgets and staff in the Environmental Protection Agency (EPA), the primary government program designed to reduce pollution across the United States. The president, whose major concern was saving jobs, highlighted his efforts to restore coal, a highly toxic source of energy.[20] Scott Pruitt, the head of EPA under Trump, served as a critic rather than an advocate of cleaner air.

A detailed study of the environment concluded that "this period is now the warmest in the history of modern civilization. . . . these trends are expected to continue over climate timescales."[21] Among other threats: Extreme storms, large scale climate variability, rise in sea levels, record wild fires and droughts, and loss of arctic territory and livelihood. The department of defense has concluded that climate change poses the greatest threat to the future.[22]

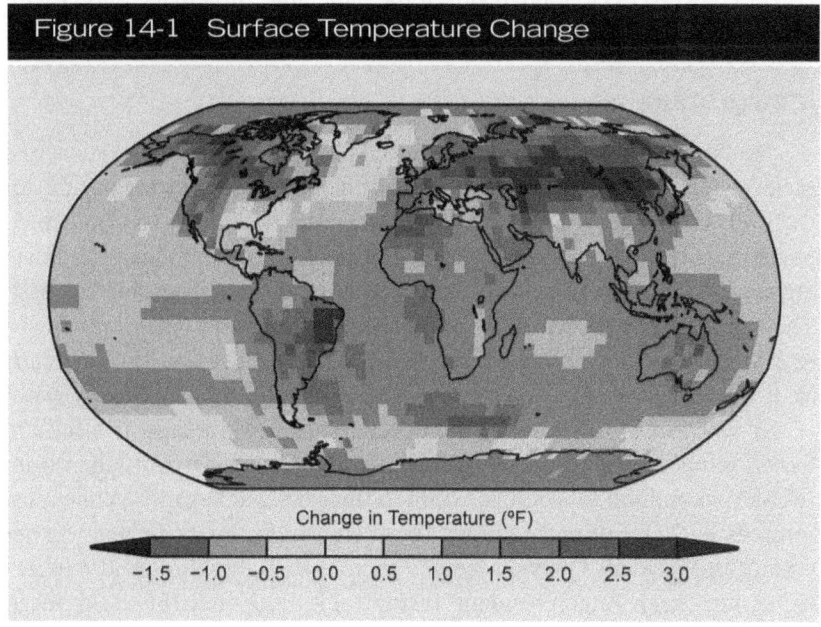

Figure 14-1   Surface Temperature Change

Change in Temperature (°F)

-1.5 -1.0 -0.5 0.0 0.5 1.0 1.5 2.0 2.5 3.0

---

[20] Annie Sneed, "Trump Wants Deep Cuts in Environmental Monitoring," *Scientific American* (March 24, 2017).

[21] Climate Science Special Report(CSSR), *Fourth National Climate Assessment.* (US Global Change Research Program, Washington D.C. November 2017).

[22] Oliver Milman, "Military experts say climate change poses 'no significant risk' to security" (*Guardian*, September 14, 2016).

State Department

The same pattern appeared in American foreign policy, as the president called for deep cutbacks in the State Department. Of the seventy thousand workers engaged worldwide, half faced job loss. A mid-level State Department officer said that the new officials "really want to blow this place up. . . . I don't think this administration thinks the State Department needs to exist."[23] Gen. Jim Mattis, who oversaw the Central Command in the Middle East, called for more rather than fewer Foreign Service officers. "If you don't fund the State Department fully, then I need to buy more ammunition."[24] Meanwhile, hundreds of ambassadorial positions were vacant long after Trump took office. As a result, conflicts in many areas received little attention, making entire regions more violent and unpredictable. The U.S. Agency for International Development (USAID), part of the State Department and a long-standing program that reduced chronic poverty in the poorest countries in the world, also faced deep cuts in foreign aid. At the same time, diplomats found themselves less important as military solutions were sought.

Immigration

Among his goals, President Trump pledged to build a wall across Mexico. He also claimed that the Mexican people would be paying for the wall. In his view, too many illegal Mexicans were entering the United States and creating problems over the border. As the Republican candidate argued, "When Mexico is sending its people, they're not sending the best. They are bringing in drugs. They are bringing in crime. They are rapists. And some, I assume, are good people."[25] Mexican president Enrique Peña said, "I have said it over and over again: Mexico will not pay for any wall."

A different problem faced the new president. More than five million Syrian refugees fled from the country whose population had fallen from twenty-two million to seventeen million since the war began.[26] While most refugees left for Europe, millions of others sought safety in many other countries. President Obama accepted more than eighty thousand refugees in his final year. After President Trump took office in 2017, he reduced

---

[23] Julia Ioffe, "The State of Trump's State Department," *The Atlantic* (March 1, 2017).

[24] David E. Sanger, "Tillerson Leads from State Dept. Shadows as White House Steps In," *New York Times* (March 11, 2017).

[25] Katie Reilly, "Here Are All the Times Donald Trump Insulted Mexico" (August 31, 2016). http://time.com/4473972/donald-trump-mexico-meeting-insult/

[26] Syria Regional Refugee Response, *3RP Regional Refugee and Resilience Plan 2017–18*, Damascus, Syria.

the flow of refugees to fifty thousand. He also signed an executive order that banned six Islamic countries—Iran, Libya, Somalia, Sudan, Syria, and Yemen—from entering the United States. Two federal judges blocked the president from limiting refugees to remain in the United States no more than 120 days. As of this publication, the case is before the Supreme Court.

Global Trade

As noted earlier, Donald Trump campaigned aggressively against global trade, arguing that other rivals were gaining markets not offered to American firms. The president rejected membership of the Trans-Pacific Partnership. To an analyst, Trump "demonstrated that he would not follow old rules, effectively discarding longstanding Republican orthodoxy that expanding global trade was good for the world and America, and that the United States should help write the rules of international commerce."[27] The president was most concerned with China (PRC), whose exports had outgrown the United States by manipulating the PRC's currency. Smaller countries such as Malaysia and Vietnam were accused of making profits by exploiting the low wages of workers. The president also fought with members of the World Trade Organization, who argued that the United States harmed world trade by favoring bilateral rather than multilateral negotiations. For Sebastian Dullien, a fellow at the European Council on Foreign Relations, "Contrary to what Donald Trump is saying, it is not just other countries screwing the US, but sometimes it's the United States screwing other countries."

Russia

President Trump faced a crisis when it became clear that expert hackers in Russia infiltrated the U.S. government.[28] The Director of National Intelligence announced with high confidence that Vladimir Putin "ordered an influence campaign in 2016 aimed at the U.S. presidential election. Russia's goals were to undermine public faith in the U.S. democratic process, denigrate Secretary Clinton, and harm her electability and potential presidency. We further assess Putin and the Russian Government developed

---

[27] Peter Baker, "Trump Abandons Trans-Pacific Partnership, Obama's Signature Trade Deal," *New York Times* (January 23, 2017); Walter Russell Mead. "American Populism and the Liberal Order," *Foreign Affairs* 96 (March–April, 2017).

[28] Intelligence Community Assessment, *Assessing Russian Activities and Intentions in Recent U.S. Elections* (Washington, D.C.: Director of National Intelligence, January 6, 2017)

a clear preference for President-elect Trump." In January 2017, the Senate and House of Representatives began investigations into the incursions. The Federal Bureau of Investigation (FBI) also gathered information regarding Russia's actions. President Trump, who remained friendly with the Russian government, became a suspect due to potential ties between Trump campaign and Russian officials. These problems raised questions about the legitimacy of the 2016 election.[29] As of publication, a special counsel, former FBI director Robert Mueller, is investigating the issue.

Rethinking American Power

As we have seen, American foreign policy continues to reveal the persistence of a distinctive national style. Shaped by the rationalist thought of the Enlightenment era and its possibilities for democratic political order, the "first new nation" viewed the world through a distinct lens. From its perspective, the anarchic nation-state system need not be forever plagued by power politics and the daily prospect of violent conflict. American values, in short, were universal values; it was America's destiny to remake the world order in its own image.

This American identity came by ideas as well as material concerns. Early leaders constructed a national character and image of American citizens as purveyors of a harmonious world order. This *weltanschauung*, or worldview, proved remarkably resilient as the United States grew from a remote North American outpost to a regional and global superpower. This display of "manifest destiny" encouraged Americans to see their adversaries as morally deficient, not simply as rational competitors seeking scarce resources. It was not surprising that American victories in World War I and World War II were attributed to the immorality of its enemies. The same could be said during the Cold War and the Soviet Union's "godless communism." While George W. Bush limited the proclaimed "axis of evil" to Iran, Iraq, and North Korea, he attributed the same moral deficiencies to the al Qaeda terrorists who attacked the United States on September 11, 2001.

Recent developments revealed the underlying realism that coexists uneasily with the idealism of American foreign policy. Three historic shifts in governance typify this revival of realism.

---

[29]Reuters, "Highlights—US Intelligence Report: Russian Cyber Attacks in 2016 Election," January 6, 2007; Freedom House, *Populists and Autocrats: The Dual Threat to Global Democracy* (Washington, D.C.: Freedom House, 2017).

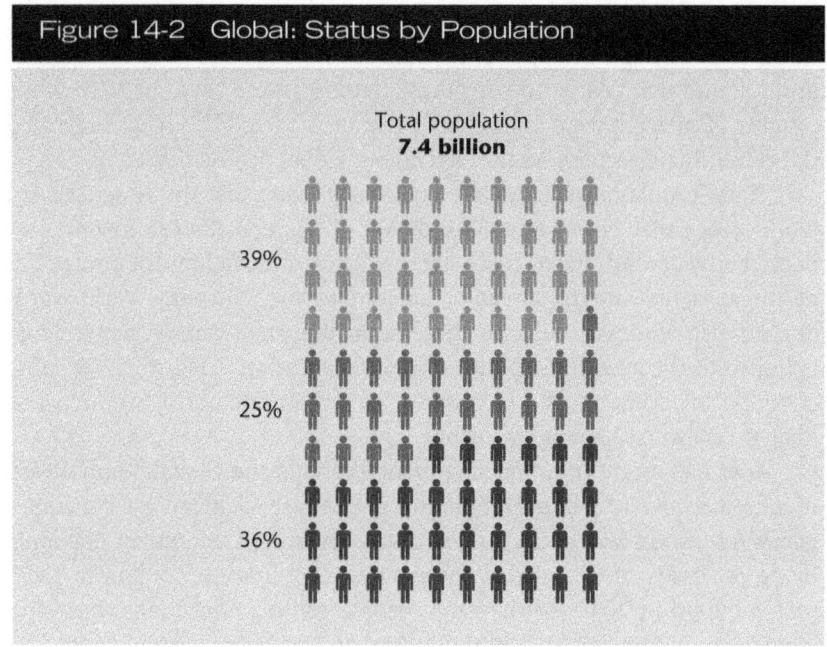

Figure 14-2 Global: Status by Population

Total population
7.4 billion

39%

25%

36%

First, the executive branch has amassed unprecedented war powers as members of Congress waived their constitutional authority to declare war. The second shift relates to the U.S. government's acceptance of war as a semipermanent condition in American life. In this daunting new world, the United States no longer had the luxury of swinging between periods of global detachment and immersion in foreign affairs. From now on, America was all in, all the time. Finally, the U.S. government expanded the scope of domestic intelligence to such an extent that Americans could assume their telephones and other communications were being stored in data-mining sweeps. Each of these shifts in wartime governance became an entrenched fixture of American foreign policy.

Further troubling, fewer democracies were established or maintained in recent years.[30] "Populist and nationalist political forces made astonishing gains in democratic states, while authoritarian powers engaged in brazen acts of aggression, and grave atrocities went unanswered in war zones across two continents," according to Freedom House, a Washington-based think

---

[30] Freedom House, *Populists and Autocrats: The Dual Threat to Global Democracy* (Washington, D.C.: Freedom House, 2017).

tank. The findings demonstrated that the United States was not immune to the kind of populist appeals that had resonated across the Atlantic. The group found that nearly 40 percent of countries were "free" in 2016 while roughly 60 percent were either partly free or not free. This record revealed the eleventh consecutive year of decline in global democracy.[31]

These problems aside, it is worth recognizing that the American-led world order that began after World War II has contributed to unprecedented advances in global trade, technological innovation, the protection of human rights, and the spread of democratic rule. The post–World War II era has also witnessed a rapid decrease in interstate wars, a pattern that is linked to the accelerating pace of democratization. Civil wars, far more common in recent years, are ruinous in concentrated areas, though less likely to spawn systemwide violence.

After half a century of development efforts in the Global South, levels of extreme poverty fell as commodity prices rose, demand for consumer goods rose, and fewer droughts led to less poverty.[32] The number of people living on less than $2 per day, for example, fell from 2.3 billion in 1990 to 1.3 billion in 2010. With young people gaining educations, men and women are more likely to find thoughtful and prosperous employment.[33]

Only by taking stock of the gaps between American's values and foreign policy actions, and only by learning from the past can today's leaders gain the wisdom to secure its citizens while enriching the wider world. Informed students and practitioners can, and will, shape the future course of American foreign policy.

---

[31] Brazil, Denmark, France, Hungary, Poland, Serbia, South Africa, Spain, and Turkey went backward in their concern for democracy. As in past years, the Middle East and North Africa had the poorest levels of freedom.

[32] World Bank, *Global Economic Prospects* (Washington, D.C.: World Bank), 109.

[33] Steven Pinker, The Better Angels of Our Nature: Why Violence Has Declined (New York: Penguin, 2012).

Appendix A

U.S. Administrations since World War II

President	Secretary of State	Secretary of Defense	National Security Adviser
Harry Truman 1945–1953	Edward Stettinius James Byrnes George Marshall Dean Acheson	James Forrestal Louis Johnson George Marshall Robert Lovett	
Dwight Eisenhower 1953–1961	John Dulles Christian Herter	Charles Wilson Neil McElroy Thomas Gates	Robert Cutler Dillon Anderson Robert Cutler Gordon Gray
John Kennedy 1961–1963	Dean Rusk	Robert McNamara	McGeorge Bundy
Lyndon Johnson 1963–1969	Dean Rusk	Robert McNamara Clark Clifford	McGeorge Bundy Walt Rostow
Richard Nixon 1969–1974	William Rogers Henry Kissinger	Melvin Laird Elliot Richardson James Schlesinger	Henry Kissinger
Gerald Ford 1974–1977	Henry Kissinger	James Schlesinger Donald Rumsfeld	Henry Kissinger Brent Scowcroft
Jimmy Carter 1977–1981	Cyrus Vance Edmund Muskie	Harold Brown	Zbigniew Brzezinski
Ronald Reagan 1981–1989	Alexander Haig George Shultz	Caspar Weinberger Frank Carlucci	Richard Allen William Clark Robert McFarlane John Poindexter Frank Carlucci Colin Powell

(Continued)

(Continued)

President	Secretary of State	Secretary of Defense	National Security Adviser
George H. W. Bush 1989–1993	James Baker Lawrence Eagleburger	Richard B. Cheney	Brent Scowcroft
Bill Clinton 1993–2001	Warren Christopher Madeleine Albright	Les Aspin William Perry William Cohen	Anthony Lake Samuel Berger
George W. Bush 2001–2009	Colin Powell Condoleezza Rice	Donald Rumsfeld Robert Gates	Condoleezza Rice Stephen Hadley
Barack Obama 2009–2017	Hillary Clinton John Kerry	Robert Gates Leon Panetta Chuck Hagel	James Jones Thomas Donilon Susan Rice
Donald Trump 2009–	Rex Tillerson	James N. Mattis	Michael Flynn H. R. McMaster

Appendix B

Chronology of Significant Events, 1945–2017

1945   Yalta Conference seeks to organize postwar world.

World War II with Germany ends.

World War II with Japan ends after two atomic bombs are dropped on Japan.

President Franklin D. Roosevelt dies; Vice President Harry S. Truman succeeds him.

United Nations is established.

Soviet military forces occupy Poland, Romania, Bulgaria, Hungary, and Czechoslovakia.

1946   United States confronts the Soviet Union over Iran; Moscow withdraws its troops.

Winston Churchill, Britain's wartime prime minister, delivers "iron curtain" speech at Fulton, Missouri, warning of Soviet threat.

George F. Kennan, a U.S. Foreign Service officer, submits "long telegram" that becomes the basis of the containment policy of the Soviet Union.

1947   Truman Doctrine commits the United States to assisting Greece and Turkey.

Secretary of State George Marshall, formerly U.S. Army chief of staff and architect of victory during World War II, devises plan for the economic recovery of Western Europe.

India becomes independent from British colonial rule.

1948   Soviet coup d'état takes place in Czechoslovakia.

Soviets blockade all ground traffic from West Germany to West Berlin; the Berlin airlift starts.

Vandenberg resolution in U.S. Senate commits American support to the Brussels Pact of self-defense.

U.S. Congress passes Marshall Plan.

North and South Korea are established.

State of Israel is established and receives immediate U.S. recognition.

Truman wins upset election.

Stalin expels Yugoslavia's Josip Tito from communist bloc.

1949   North Atlantic Treaty Organization (NATO) is formed.

Soviet Union ends Berlin blockade.

East and West Germany are established.

Soviet Union explodes atomic bomb.

Nationalist China collapses and People's Republic of China (PRC) is established.

U.S. troops are withdrawn from South Korea.

Truman announces Point Four foreign aid program for developing countries.

1950   Soviet Union and communist China sign treaty of mutual assistance.

North Korea crosses the thirty-eighth parallel and attacks South Korea.

United States intervenes on behalf of South Korea.

Communist China intervenes after U.S. forces advance into North Korea toward China's frontier.

Sen. Joseph McCarthy begins his attacks on the government for treason and "coddling communists."

1951   U.S.-Japanese mutual security pact is signed.

Truman fires Gen. Douglas MacArthur in Korea for proposing that the United States attack communist China.

European Coal and Steel Community (ECSC) is formed.

1952   Dwight D. Eisenhower is elected president.

Greece and Turkey join NATO.

Britain tests its first atomic weapon.

1953   Joseph Stalin dies.

Armistice negotiated along thirty-eighth parallel in Korea.

Soviet Union intervenes in East Germany to quell revolt.

United States backs overthrow of democratically elected government in Iran.

1954   United States explodes first hydrogen bomb.

France is defeated at Dien Bien Phu in Indochina. United States intervenes.

Vietnam is partitioned at the seventeenth parallel.

Southeast Asia Treaty Organization (SEATO) is formed.

U.S.-Korea pact is signed to prevent a renewal of the war.

U.S.–Nationalist China defense treaty is signed.

U.S. Central Intelligence Agency (CIA) overthrows Guatemala's left-wing government.

1955   Communist China shells the Nationalist Chinese (Taiwanese) islands of Quemoy and Matsu.

Formosa resolution authorizes Eisenhower to use force, if necessary, to protect Taiwan against a possible communist Chinese invasion.

Middle East Treaty Organization (Baghdad Pact) is formed.

West Germany joins NATO; Soviets establish "their NATO," called the Warsaw Treaty Organization.

1956   United States withdraws offer to help finance Egypt's Aswan High Dam.

Egypt nationalizes the Suez Canal.

Suez War breaks out after Israel attacks Egypt; France and Britain intervene.

UN forces are sent to Egypt to keep the peace between Israel and Egypt.

Soviets suppress Hungarian revolt and almost intervene in Poland.

Soviet leader Nikita Khrushchev attacks Stalin at twentieth Communist Party Congress.

Eisenhower is reelected president.

1957   Soviet Union tests intercontinental ballistic missile (ICBM).

Soviets launch two Sputniks, or satellites, into space.

British test hydrogen bomb.

Eisenhower Doctrine commits United States to protect Middle East countries that resist communist aggression.

1958　　United States lands Marines in Lebanon.

Soviet Union declares it will end four-power occupation of Berlin and turn West Berlin into a "free city."

European Economic Community (Common Market) is established.

Communist China shells Quemoy and Matsu again.

1959　　Khrushchev and Eisenhower meet at Camp David over Berlin issue.

Fidel Castro seizes power in Cuba.

Central Treaty Organization (CENTO) replaces the Baghdad Pact.

1960　　Soviets shoot down U.S. U-2 spy plane over the Soviet Union. Paris summit conference collapses over the incident.

The Congo becomes independent from Belgium, causing first superpower crisis in sub-Saharan Africa.

UN forces sent to the Congo to help resolve the crisis.

France becomes an atomic power.

John F. Kennedy wins presidential election.

1961　　Kennedy launches abortive Bay of Pigs invasion of Cuba.

Kennedy proposes Alliance for Progress for Latin America.

Soviets send Yuri Gagarin into orbital spaceflight.

Khrushchev holds summit conference with Kennedy in Vienna.

Kennedy sends first military advisers to South Vietnam.

Soviets build Berlin Wall.

1962　　United States sends John Glenn into orbital spaceflight.

In the Cuban missile crisis, U.S. blockades Cuba to compel Soviets to withdraw nuclear missiles.

Chinese-Indian frontier conflict erupts.

1963　　French president Charles de Gaulle vetoes Britain's entry into the Common Market.

"Hotline" established between the White House and the Kremlin for direct emergency communications.

Atomic test ban treaty is signed.

President Kennedy is assassinated; Vice President Lyndon B. Johnson succeeds him.

1964   Congress passes Gulf of Tonkin Resolution, raising the U.S. commitment to the defense of South Vietnam.

Khrushchev falls from power and is replaced by Prime Minister Aleksey Kosygin and Communist Party Secretary Leonid Brezhnev.

Lyndon Johnson is elected president.

1965   United States starts bombing North Vietnam and sends American land forces into South Vietnam.

Antiwar protests start.

United States intervenes in the Dominican Republic.

War erupts between Pakistan and India.

1966   People's Republic of China becomes a nuclear power.

France withdraws its forces from NATO's integrated command structure but remains a member of the alliance.

1967   Six-Day War takes place between Israel and its Arab neighbors.

Greek colonels seize power in Greece.

1968   Tet Offensive in South Vietnam escalates demand for U.S. withdrawal from Vietnam.

Johnson withdraws from presidential race.

Richard Nixon is elected president.

Vietnamese peace talks begin in Paris.

Nuclear Non-Proliferation Treaty (NPT) is negotiated.

Soviet Union intervenes in Czechoslovakia to quell revolt.

1969   Brezhnev Doctrine asserts right of Soviet Union to intervene in Soviet sphere of influence.

U.S. Senate approves antiballistic missile (ABM) deployment.

United States tests multiple independently targeted reentry vehicle (MIRV).

Strategic Arms Limitation Talks (SALT) begin.

"Vietnamization" program begins U.S. troop withdrawals from South Vietnam.

North Vietnamese leader Ho Chi Minh dies.

United States lands men on the moon.

Lt. William Calley Jr. stands trial for My Lai massacre of civilians in South Vietnam by U.S. troops.

1970   West Germany, East Germany, the Soviet Union, and Poland conclude treaties recognizing Poland's western border and acknowledging Germany's division into East and West Germany.

Senate repeals Gulf of Tonkin Resolution.

Invasion of Cambodia causes widespread student protests, which escalate after National Guard kills four students at Kent State University.

1971   India and Pakistan go to war over the Bangladesh (East Pakistan) secession effort.

People's Republic of China joins UN.

Four-power Berlin settlement is reached, ensuring Western access to Berlin.

1972   Nixon visits communist China, beginning a process of normalizing relations after two decades of hostility.

North Vietnam invades South Vietnam.

Nixon visits Moscow for summit conference with Soviet leaders; he signs SALT I and ABM Treaty.

Watergate affair starts with a break-in within Democratic Party headquarters.

Paris peace talks break down; the United States bombs North Vietnam; Nixon is reelected president in a landslide.

1973   Henry Kissinger is appointed secretary of state while remaining national security adviser.

Vietnamese peace agreement is signed.

United States and China establish liaison offices, or informal embassies, in Washington and Beijing.

Yom Kippur War breaks out in Middle East.

Arab members of the Organization of the Petroleum Exporting Countries (OPEC) embargo oil to the United States because of U.S. support for Israel.

OPEC quadruples oil prices.

U.S.-Soviet Mutual and Balanced Force Reductions talks start in Europe.

East and West Germany exchange ambassadors, acknowledging division into two countries.

U.S. Congress passes the War Powers Resolution over Nixon's veto.

United States backs overthrow of Salvador Allende, the elected leader of Chile.

1974   India detonates "peaceful" nuclear device.

Kissinger negotiates first agreements between Israel and Egypt and Syria as part of his "step-by-step" diplomacy intended to achieve a comprehensive regional peace.

Nixon, upon threat of impeachment, resigns, and Vice President Gerald Ford becomes unelected president.

1975   Soviet Union rejects U.S.-Soviet trade agreement because of the Jackson-Vanik amendment.

South Vietnam collapses; a unified communist Vietnam is established.

Cambodia falls to communist insurgents.

Helsinki agreements, including Western recognition of Europe's division (and Soviet domination in Eastern Europe), issued by Western and Eastern states.

1976   Soviet-Cuban forces in Angola win victory for Marxist-led faction over pro-Western factions.

Communist Chinese leader Mao Zedong dies.

Jimmy Carter is elected president.

1977   Soviets denounce Carter's human rights campaign as a violation of Soviet sovereignty.

Carter submits new SALT II plan to Soviet Union, which quickly rejects it because it is not based on Vladivostok guidelines.

United States and Panama sign Panama Canal treaties.

Menachem Begin is elected prime minister of Israel.

Egyptian president Anwar Sadat pays historic visit to Israel, offering peace and friendship.

1978   Soviet and Cuban military forces intervene in war between Ethiopia and Somalia.

Soviet-inspired coup occurs in Afghanistan.

At Camp David, representatives of the United States, Israel, and Egypt arrive at "framework for peace" between Israel and Egypt.

U.S. Senate approves Panama Canal treaties.

1979   Mohammad Reza Shah Pahlavi leaves Iran.

United States officially recognizes the People's Republic of China.

China invades Vietnam in response to its invasion of Cambodia.

Shah's regime in Iran is replaced by Islamic republic led by Ayatollah Ruhollah Khomeini.

U.S. embassy in Tehran is seized as employees are held hostage by militant Islamic students.

Oil prices shoot upward as Iranian oil production drops and world supplies tighten.

SALT II treaty signed by Brezhnev and Carter at Vienna summit conference.

Soviets deploy eighty thousand troops into Afghanistan to ensure survival of pro-Soviet regime.

1980   U.S. mission to rescue hostages in Tehran ends in disaster before it reaches embassy.

SALT II temporarily withdrawn from Senate after Soviet invasion of Afghanistan.

Carter embargoes shipments of feed grain and high technology to Soviet Union; declares United States will boycott Summer Olympic Games in Moscow.

Carter Doctrine commits United States to security of Persian Gulf oil-producing states if they are externally threatened.

Iraq attacks Iran, sparking an eight-year war of attrition.

Ronald Reagan is elected president.

1981   U.S. hostages released moments after Reagan assumes presidency.

Menachem Begin is reelected in Israel.

Anwar Sadat assassinated in Egypt.

Reagan decides on large program to rebuild U.S. military power.

Poland's communist government imposes martial law.

United States imposes economic sanctions on Poland and Soviet Union.

1982   Reagan supports El Salvador's government against rebel forces.

Israel invades Lebanon, attempting to destroy the Palestine Liberation Organization (PLO).

U.S. Marines are sent into Beirut as part of a peacekeeping force to supervise the PLO's departure.

China and the United States sign agreement on the reduction of U.S. arms sales to Taiwan.

Brezhnev dies and is succeeded by Yuri Andropov, former head of the Soviet secret police.

Argentina invades the British Falkland Islands, long claimed by Argentina. Britain reconquers the islands.

1983   Reagan denounces the Soviet Union as an "evil empire."

In pastoral letter, Catholic bishops condemn immorality of nuclear deterrence.

More than 240 U.S. Marines are killed in truck-bomb suicide attack on their barracks in Lebanon.

Soviet Union accidentally shoots down Korean jetliner with 269 passengers aboard after it strays into Soviet airspace.

U.S. forces invade the island of Grenada and depose its Marxist government.

United States deploys Pershing II and ground-launched cruise missiles in Europe. Soviet Union responds by breaking off arms control talks.

1984   Bipartisan commission calls for foreign aid to Central America to combat poverty.

Yuri Andropov dies; Konstantin Chernenko succeeds him.

Congress cuts off all military assistance to the contras in Nicaragua.

Reagan is reelected president.

United States declares Iran a supporter of international terrorism.

1985   Konstantin Chernenko dies and is succeeded by Mikhail Gorbachev.

Africa—especially Ethiopia, which is engaged in a civil war—suffers from widespread starvation.

Reagan orders economic sanctions against South Africa; Congress imposes harsher sanctions in 1986.

Reagan and Gorbachev hold their first summit conference in Geneva, Switzerland.

1986   Ferdinand Marcos in the Philippines and Jean-Claude Duvalier in Haiti flee their respective countries.

United States bombs targets in Libya in response to terrorist acts.

Catastrophic nuclear accident takes place at Chernobyl in Ukraine.

Reagan and Gorbachev meet in Iceland.

Iran-contra scandal damages Reagan's public approval.

1987   Congressional hearings are held regarding Iran-contra scandal.

United States and Soviet Union agree to a worldwide ban on short- and intermediate-range missiles.

United States reflags Kuwaiti oil tankers in the Persian Gulf and escorts them with U.S. warships to protect them from Iranian attacks.

Five Central American presidents devise a plan for peace in their region.

Palestinians begin the *intifada*, or uprising, protesting Israeli opposition to a Palestinian state.

Gorbachev denounces Stalin's historical legacy and defends his own program of *perestroika* at the seventieth-anniversary celebration of the Bolshevik revolution.

1988   George H. W. Bush is elected president.

Gorbachev proposes democratic reforms of Soviet government.

U.S. Navy shoots down Iranian commercial jetliner with 290 people aboard over Persian Gulf.

Iran and Iraq agree to a cease-fire in their eight-year war.

Panama's leader, Gen. Manuel Noriega, is indicted for trafficking narcotics in United States.

A new Palestinian state in the West Bank and Gaza Strip leads to recognition of Israel.

Soviet Baltic republics assert their desire for autonomy, if not independence.

Gorbachev announces unilateral military reductions.

1989   Gorbachev is elected president of the Soviet Union.

Free elections in Poland repudiate the Polish Communist Party.

Hungary allows emigration to the West.

Czechoslovakia and Bulgaria follow the reformist path of Poland, Hungary, and East Germany.

Soviet Union withdraws its troops from Afghanistan.

Gorbachev states Soviet Union has no moral or political right to interfere in the affairs of its neighbors.

Ayatollah Khomeini dies in Iran.

Large pro-democracy demonstrations in Beijing are suppressed by the communist leadership.

Berlin Wall is opened, beginning process of German reunification.

United States overthrows Panama's Manuel Noriega and is arrested on drug-trafficking charges.

1990 Lithuanian Communist Party breaks from the Soviet party and speaks for independent Lithuania.

Gorbachev renounces the communist monopoly of power in the Soviet Union.

Eastern European free elections in the spring produce noncommunist governments.

Iraqi troops invade neighboring Kuwait.

East and West Germany reunify. New government remains in NATO.

Soviet Union's largest republics, Russia and Ukraine, declare their sovereignty. Other republics follow.

The Nicaraguan contras disband after government agrees to free election.

1991 Iraq, refusing to withdraw from Kuwait, is forced out in forty-three days by a U.S.-led UN coalition.

United States and Soviet Union sign Strategic Arms Reduction Talks (START) agreement, reducing strategic weapons by 30 percent.

Warsaw Treaty Organization is formally dissolved. Soviet troops leave Hungary and Czechoslovakia.

Boris Yeltsin becomes the first elected leader of the thousand-year-old Russian republic.

Gorbachev's political opponents launch coup. Yeltsin defies the coup attempt and it fails.

Estonia, Latvia, and Lithuania are granted independence. After efforts to establish a confederation fail, Russia, Belarus, and Ukraine declare the Soviet Union dead and form the Commonwealth of Independent States.

Soviet Union dissolves. Gorbachev resigns and cedes the Kremlin to Yeltsin.

Slovenia and Croatia secede from Yugoslavia.

1992   Government of El Salvador reaches accord ending decade of civil war.

U.S. government begins forcible repatriation of Haitian refugees.

UN peacekeeping troops intervene in Balkans. European Commission (EC) and United States recognize Bosnia and Herzegovina along with independent Croatia and Slovenia. Yugoslavia expelled by General Assembly.

United States and Russia ratify new START agreement.

U.S. and German governments agree to provide Russia with $24 billion in economic aid.

Asia-Pacific Economic Cooperation (APEC) sets rules for liberal trading cooperation.

Bill Clinton is elected president.

1993   European Union (EU) initiates single market.

United States and Russia approve new START treaty calling for deeper cuts in strategic arms.

Terrorist bomb damages World Trade Center, killing six people.

North Korean government announces withdrawal from the NPT.

UN Security Council imposes economic sanctions against Haitian military regime.

Twelve American soldiers are killed in Mogadishu, Somalia.

U.S. Congress ratifies North American Free Trade Agreement (NAFTA).

South African government abolishes apartheid and sets agenda for national elections.

1994   United States suspends linkage between bilateral trade and China's behavior in human rights.

Assassination of Rwandan president sparks genocide that kills nearly one million Tutsi citizens.

North Korea agrees to freeze its nuclear weapons program in exchange for economic and technological assistance from the United States and other countries.

Uruguay Round of the General Agreement on Tariffs and Trade (GATT) yields multilateral trade pact.

Iraqi armed forces amass along Kuwaiti border. U.S. forces deployed to Persian Gulf to deter invasion.

UN announces plans to withdraw from Somalia by March 1995.

1995   Russian troops reclaim control of Grozny, Chechnya's capital, after secession attempt.

United States provides $10 billion in loan guarantees to prevent collapse of Mexican economy.

NATO launches air strikes against Serbian forces after Serbs seize "safe havens" in Srebenica and Žepa and attack civilians in Sarajevo.

Massacre of Israeli citizens by Islamic terrorists undermine peace accord between Israel and PLO. Israeli prime minister Yitzhak Rabin is assassinated and is succeeded by Benjamin Netanyahu.

Muslim and Croatian forces launch successful offensive against Serbs, changing balance of power in region. All sides agree to cease-fire and form of new Bosnian government.

1996   U.S. Congress ratifies START II accord with Russia.

United States deploys naval forces in response to Chinese military provocations in Taiwan Strait.

Control over peacekeeping mission in Haiti is transferred from United States to UN.

United States deploys naval forces to free foreign nationals trapped in Liberia.

Boris Yeltsin is reelected president of Russia.

Clinton signs Comprehensive Nuclear Test-Ban Treaty, which prevents nuclear testing.

Ethnic violence spreads from Rwanda and Burundi to other parts of Central Africa.

Clinton is elected to second term.

1997   Chinese leader Deng Xiaoping dies.

Clinton and Boris Yeltsin meet in Helsinki, Finland, and agree to new round of nuclear weapons reductions, labeled START III.

Israel plans new Jewish settlements in East Jerusalem, setting off protests by Palestinians.

British Labour Party leader Tony Blair replaces Conservative John Major as prime minister.

Congress ratifies Chemical Weapons Convention.

Czech Republic, Hungary, and Poland are invited to join NATO.

1998   President Clinton visits six African countries and denounces past U.S. support for dictatorships.

Eleven Western European countries agree to adopt a common currency, the euro.

Underground nuclear tests conducted by India and Pakistan provoke worldwide condemnation.

Iraqi leaders suspend cooperation with UN weapons inspectors.

U.S. embassies in Kenya and Tanzania are bombed in terrorist attacks. United States retaliates by bombing suspected terrorist bases in Sudan and Afghanistan.

North Korea fires a three-stage ballistic missile over Japan.

1999   On its fiftieth anniversary, NATO expands to include the Czech Republic, Hungary, and Poland.

NATO bombers conduct aerial assaults against hundreds of targets in Serbia.

Residents of East Timor vote to secede from Indonesia. Attempt by Indonesian government to prevent secession prompts UN to deploy peacekeepers to region.

Russian troops escalate their crackdown against separatists in Chechnya.

U.S. Senate rejects the Comprehensive Nuclear Test-Ban Treaty signed by Clinton in 1996 and by the leaders of more than 150 foreign governments.

Protesters disrupt annual meetings of the World Trade Organization (WTO) in Seattle.

U.S. troops abandon peacekeeping mission in Haiti.

Yeltsin resigns as Russian president and names Prime Minister Vladimir Putin as his successor.

2000   Leaders of North Korea and South Korea agree to hold the first-ever summit meeting.

Congress pledges $1 billion to support Colombia's efforts to stem its flow of illegal narcotics.

Russia ratifies START II and Comprehensive Nuclear Test-Ban Treaty.

EU endorses Chinese entry into WTO. U.S. Congress approved trade relations with China.

Terrorist attack on USS *Cole* kills seventeen and wounds thirty-nine American sailors.

World leaders at UN Millennium Summit approve measures to reduce global poverty by 2015.

George W. Bush is elected president.

2001   Bush announces he will not seek Senate ratification of the Kyoto Protocol.

U.S. Navy plane makes forced landing after colliding with a Chinese surveillance plane.

United States is denied a seat on UN Human Rights Commission.

Former Yugoslav president Slobodan Milosevic is extradited for charges of war crimes.

On September 11, Islamic terrorists hijack four U.S. passenger jets and use them to destroy the World Trade Center in New York City and to damage the Pentagon near Washington, D.C. The fourth jet crash-lands in Pennsylvania. Bush declares a "war on terror."

Letters laced with anthrax spores are mailed to several federal offices, media outlets, and other locations. Five people die.

Bush signs the USA PATRIOT Act, a wide-ranging measure designed to strengthen domestic security.

United States invades Afghanistan, routing the Taliban regime from power.

2002   Bush declares Iran, Iraq, and North Korea to be part of an "axis of evil."

Venezuelan populist Hugo Chávez resigns amid national uprising.

United States and Russia agree to deeper cuts in nuclear arsenals.

Hamid Karzai is elected president of Afghanistan.

U.S. Congress approves resolution that calls for the disarmament of Iraq, by force if necessary.

UN Security Council demands that Iraq disarm and submit to new weapons inspections.

2003   Space shuttle *Columbia* breaks up while reentering atmosphere. All seven astronauts are killed.

Secretary of State Colin L. Powell makes case to UN Security Council for a war against Iraq.

United States and Britain lead invasion of Iraq and overthrow Saddam Hussein.

First Palestinian prime minister, Mahmoud Abbas, takes office.

Iran is found to be developing materials that could be used for nuclear weapons.

NATO assumes control of peacekeeping force in Afghanistan.

Bush suspends higher tariffs on foreign steel in response to pressure from WTO.

U.S. troops in Iraq capture Saddam Hussein.

2004   Weapons inspectors in Iraq conclude WMDs are not present.

Al Qaeda bomb attacks kill more than two hundred on commuter trains in Madrid, Spain.

NATO admits new members: Bulgaria, Estonia, Latvia, Lithuania, Romania, Slovakia, and Slovenia.

Photographs of U.S. prisoner abuses at Abu Ghraib prison in Iraq provoke anti-American protests.

EU grows to twenty-five member states with addition of Eastern European states.

Palestinian leader Yasir Arafat dies in Paris.

Bush is reelected president.

2005   More than eight million Iraqi citizens vote in parliamentary elections amid widespread violence.

Kyoto Protocol on global warming goes into effect without U.S. participation.

Terrorist attacks in London kill fifty-six commuters and injure more than seven hundred.

United States and India reach agreement on development of India's nuclear energy program.

Grand jury indicts I. Lewis "Scooter" Libby, chief of staff to Vice President Dick Cheney, for leaking identity of undercover CIA agent Valerie Plame to news media.

Voters in Iraq approve constitution and elect permanent National Assembly.

2006   Hamas, a Palestinian political party with a violent history, assumes control of Palestinian Authority.

UN Human Rights Commission calls for closing U.S. detention center at Guantánamo Bay, Cuba.

U.S. National Security Agency (NSA) acknowledges monitoring millions of domestic phone calls while tapping international phone calls by suspected terrorists.

United States fortifies Mexican border to restrict illegal immigration.

North Korea test fires six long-range missiles over the Sea of Japan.

Saddam Hussein is found guilty and executed for crimes against humanity.

UN Security Council approves new economic sanctions on Iran in response to its growing nuclear research program.

2007   Bush announces "surge" of U.S. troops in Iraq.

North Korea agrees to dismantle its nuclear facilities in exchange for $400 million in economic aid from the United States, Japan, South Korea, and several European countries.

Russian president Putin suspends 1990 treaty on conventional armed forces in Europe.

United States expands economic sanctions against Sudan in response to the Muslim government's campaign of genocide against black Africans in Darfur province.

2008   Fidel Castro resigns as president of Cuba after forty-nine years in power.

Russian military invades the republic of Georgia to defend pro-Moscow separatists.

U.S. military death toll in Iraq reaches four thousand.

Bush vetoes congressional bill to prohibit "coercive interrogations" of suspected terrorists.

Iran tests long-range missiles capable of reaching Israel.

International Criminal Court charges Sudanese president Omar Hassan al-Bashir with genocide.

United States and Iraq agree on timetable for withdrawal of U.S. combat forces by end of 2011.

Rampant mortgage foreclosures and bank failures in United States spark economic crisis worldwide.

Barack Obama is elected president.

2009   Obama announces plans to close Guantánamo Bay detention camp in Cuba and to end coercive interrogations of war prisoners.

Federal court affirms domestic wiretapping for purposes of national security.

Federal security forces are sent to Mexican border to combat violence among rival drug smugglers.

North Korea launches intercontinental ballistic missile over Japan.

Navy SEALs rescue captain of ship near Somalia and kills pirates who held the captain hostage.

Obama announces limits on automotive fuel consumption in effort to curb global warming.

North Korea detonates second underground nuclear device.

Obama lifts travel restrictions to visit relatives in Cuba and send remittances.

2010   An earthquake in Haiti kills hundreds of thousands of people, prompting a global relief effort.

U.S. and coalition forces launch their largest offensive in Afghanistan since the war began in 2011.

The collapse of a drilling rig in the Gulf of Mexico creates an oil spill that lasts nearly three months.

The United States, Russia, and other major powers approve new sanctions on Iran amid heightened strains over its alleged nuclear weapons program.

The European Union and International Monetary Fund (IMF) provide Ireland a bailout of $114 billion to prevent the bankruptcy of its government.

The public suicide of a disgruntled street vendor in Tunisia sparks nationwide protests and the start of the "Arab Spring."

2011   Mounting opposition to Tunisia's government leads its president to resign, paving the way for multiparty elections and the establishment of political freedoms.

Egyptian president Hosni Mubarak is forced out of power after decades of repressive rule.

U.S. and NATO forces strike military targets in Libya in support of a mass uprising. Muammar al-Qaddafi is later captured, tortured, and killed by Libyan rebels.

American commandos raid Osama bin Laden's compound in Pakistan, executing the leader of al Qaeda and burying his body at sea.

Last U.S. troops withdraw from Iraq.

North Korean leader Kim Jong Il dies; his son, Kim Jong Un, is named as the "great successor."

2012   Russian prime minister Vladimir Putin is elected to six-year term as president of Russia.

Obama and Hamid Karzai agree on U.S. withdrawal from Afghanistan by end of 2014.

Mohamed Morsi is elected president of Egypt in first election since the ouster of Hosni Mubarak.

Number of U.S. military deaths in Afghanistan exceeds two thousand.

Russia becomes member of WTO.

U.S. ambassador J. Christopher Stevens and three American officials killed in bombing raid in Libya.

President Obama is reelected to second term.

2013   France deploys troops to Mali in struggle against Islamic extremists.

Israeli prime minister Benjamin Netanyahu is elected to third term in office.

Syrian forces attack citizens in a suburb of Damascus with chemical weapons. United States and Russia broker deal that requires Syria to dismantle its chemical stockpiles.

Xi Jinping is elected president of China.

Edward Snowden, a U.S. intelligence agent, reveals campaign of U.S. domestic surveillance.

NATO grants Afghanistan full responsibility for national security.

Hassan Rouhani, considered a moderate, is elected president of Iran.

2014   Ukrainian president Viktor Yanukovych cancels financial partnership with EU and turns to Russia.

Russia forcefully annexes Crimea and incites rebellions in ethnic Russian territories in eastern Ukraine.

Boko Haram, an Islamist terrorist group, kidnaps and kills hundreds of female students.

Malaysian passenger jet shot down over eastern Ukraine. Russia was found to be complicit.

Chinese fishing vessel sinks a Vietnamese fishing boat in disputed territory in South China Sea.

ISIS (Islamic State of Iraq and Syria) overruns key cities and government armies in both countries.

Israel invades Gaza following rocket attacks on Israeli neighborhoods.

Death toll in Syrian civil war climbs to four hundred thousand.

Sudden Ebola epidemic in northwest Africa leaves more than eight thousand dead.

2015   ISIS attacks kill civilians in Paris, Kenya, and Turkey.

Russia enters conflict in Syria on behalf of the Assad regime.

Syria's civil war creates a refugee crisis across Europe and other locations.

President Obama visits Cuba, the first meeting of the governments in more than fifty years.

Iran agrees to suspend its nuclear weapons program in return for lifting the nation's economic sanctions.

The Trans-Pacific Partnership, a global trade agreement, is signed with eleven members. The United States rejects membership.

Justin Trudeau wins elections and becomes prime minister of Canada.

2016   Coup in Turkey fails to oust President Recep Tayyip Erdoğan.

Rodrigo Duterte wins Philippine elections and unleashes violence against drug dealers.

Civil war in South Sudan intensifies.

Syria's civil war rages in Syria. City of Aleppo suffers immense damage and casualties.

Great Britain votes to leave European Union. "Brexit" becomes a reality.

Hurricane Matthew devastates large parts of Haiti.

Rise of populism in Eastern Europe leads to rise of antidemocratic parties.

Donald Trump is elected president.

2017   U.S. elections are fraught with allegations of Russian interference. Congress tightens economic sanctions against Russia.

With Syria's acceptance, The United States became the only country to reject the Paris Climate Accord.

Mexican president Peña refuses to pay for President Trump's wall across the border.

Saudi Arabia and other regional allies accuse Qatar of harboring terrorist groups.

North Korea threatens long-range nuclear attacks toward the United States.

A vicious hurricane virtually destroys Puerto Rico, a territory of the United States.

An ISIS attack leaves eight dead and others injured in New York City.

The death toll in Syria approached five hundred thousand by 2018.

Appendix C

Select Bibliography

The following bibliographic entries are books. Readers who wish to keep up with the journal literature on American foreign policy will find the articles in the following useful: *Foreign Affairs*, *Foreign Policy*, *Foreign Policy Analysis*, *World Politics*, *International Organization*, *International Security*, and *International Studies Quarterly*. Among primary sources, foreign policy reports published by the Congressional Research Service and compiled by the Federation of American Scientists are essential (www.fas.org/sgp/crs/index.html).

American Society and Style in Foreign Policy

Almond, Gabriel A. *The American People and Foreign Policy*. New York: Praeger, 1960.

Boorstin, Daniel J. *The Genius of American Politics*. Chicago: Phoenix Books, 1953.

Dallek, Robert. *The American Style of Foreign Policy*. New York: Knopf, 1983.

Ekbladh, David. *The Great American Mission: Modernization and the Construction of an American World Order*. Princeton, N.J.: Princeton University Press, 2010.

Go, Julian. *Patterns of Empire: The British and American Empires, 1688 to the Present*. New York: Cambridge University Press, 2012.

Goodman, Melvin. *National Insecurity: The Cost of American Militarism*. San Francisco: City Lights Books, 2013.

Haass, Richard. *Foreign Policy Begins at Home: The Case for Putting America's House in Order*. New York: Basic Books, 2013.

Hartz, Louis. *The Liberal Tradition in America*. New York: Harvest Books, 1955.

Hofstadter, Richard. *The Paranoid Style in American Politics*. New York: Vintage Books, 1967.

Hunt, Michael H. *Ideology and U.S. Foreign Policy*. New Haven, Conn.: Yale University Press, 1987.

Ikenberry, G. John. *Liberal Leviathan: The Origins, Crisis, and Transformation of the American World Order*. Princeton, N.J.: Princeton University Press, 2011.

Kagan, Robert. *The World America Made*. New York: Knopf, 2012.

Kane, John. *Between Virtue and Power: The Persistent Moral Dilemma of U.S. Foreign Policy.* New Haven, Conn.: Yale University Press, 2008.

Kennan, George F. *American Diplomacy, 1900–1950.* Chicago: University of Chicago Press, 1951.

Kohut, Andrew, and Bruce Stokes. *America against the World: How We Are Different and Why We Are Disliked.* New York: Times Books, 2006.

Lieber, Robert J. *Power and Willpower in the American Future: Why the United States Is Not Destined to Decline.* New York: Cambridge University Press, 2012.

Lippmann, Walter. *U.S. Foreign Policy: Shield of the Republic.* Boston: Little, Brown, 1943.

Lipset, Seymour Martin. *American Exceptionalism.* New York: Norton, 1996.

Mabee, Bryan. *Understanding American Power: The Changing World of U.S. Foreign Policy.* New York: Palgrave Macmillan, 2013.

McDougall, Walter A. *Promised Land, Crusader State.* Boston: Houghton Mifflin, 1997.

Mead, Walter Russell. *Special Providence.* New York: Knopf, 2001.

Morgenthau, Hans J. *In Defense of the National Interest.* New York: Knopf, 1951.

Osgood, Robert. *Ideals and Self-interest in America's Foreign Relations.* Chicago: University of Chicago Press, 1953.

Potter, David M. *The People of Plenty.* Chicago: Phoenix Books, 1954.

Smith, Tony. *America's Mission.* Princeton, N.J.: Princeton University Press, 1994.

Weber, Steven, and Bruce W. Jentleson. *The End of Arrogance: America in the Global Competition of Ideas.* Cambridge, Mass.: Harvard University Press, 2010.

American Foreign Policy during the Cold War

Applebaum, Anne. *Iron Curtain: The Crushing of Eastern Europe, 1944–1956.* New York, Doubleday, 2012.

Bosterdoff, Denise M. *Proclaiming the Truman Doctrine: The Cold War Call to Arms.* College Station: Texas A&M University Press, 2008.

Craig, Campbell, and Sergey Radchenko. *The Atomic Bomb and the Origins of the Cold War.* New Haven, Conn.: Yale University Press, 2008.

Fulbright, J. William. *The Crippled Giant.* New York: Vintage Books, 1972.

_____. *The Arrogance of Power.* New York: Vintage Books, 1967.

Gaddis, John Lewis. *We Now Know: Rethinking Cold War History.* New York: Oxford University Press, 1997.

_____. *Strategies of Containment.* New York: Oxford University Press, 1982.

_____. *Russia, the Soviet Union, and the United States*. New York: Wiley, 1978.

_____. *The United States and the Origins of the Cold War, 1941–1947*. New York: Columbia University Press, 1972.

Gordin, Michael D. *Red Cloud at Dawn: Truman, Stalin, and the End of the Atomic Monopoly*. New York: Farrar, Straus, and Giroux, 2009.

Halle, Louis J. *The Cold War as History*. New York: Harper and Row, 1967.

Hoffmann, Stanley. *Gulliver's Troubles, or the Setting of American Foreign Policy*. New York: McGraw-Hill, 1968.

Larson, Deborah Welch. *Origins of Containment*. Princeton, N.J.: Princeton University Press, 1985.

Leffler, Melvyn P. *A Preponderance of Power*. Stanford, Calif.: Stanford University Press, 1992.

Logevall, Fredrik. *Embers of War: The Fall of an Empire and the Making of America's Vietnam*. New York: Random House, 2012.

Matlock, Jack F., Jr. *Reagan and Gorbachev: How the Cold War Ended*. New York: Random House, 2004.

Mikoyan, Sergo. *The Soviet Cuban Missile Crisis: Castro, Mikoyan, Kennedy, Khrushchev, and the Missiles of November*. Stanford, Calif.: Stanford University Press, 2012.

Schulzinger, Robert D. *The Wise Men of Foreign Affairs*. New York: Columbia University Press, 1985.

Steel, Ronald. *Pax Americana*. New York: Viking Press, 1967.

Stuckey, Mary E. *Jimmy Carter, Human Rights, and the National Agenda*. College Station: Texas A&M University Press, 2008.

Yergin, Daniel. *Shattered Peace*. Boston: Houghton Mifflin, 1977.

Zelizer, Julian E. *Arsenal of Democracy*. New York: Basic Books, 2010.

American Foreign Policy after the Cold War

Allman, T. D. *Rogue State: America at War with the World*. New York: Nation Books, 2004.

Bergen, Peter L. *The Longest War: Inside the Enduring Conflict between America and al-Qaeda since 9/11*. New York: Free Press, 2011.

Brooks, Stephen G., and William C. Wohlforth. *World Out of Balance: International Relations and the Challenge of American Primacy*. Princeton, N.J.: Princeton University Press, 2008.

Brzezinski, Zbigniew. *Strategic Vision: America and the Crisis of Global Power*. New York: Basic Books, 2012.

Brzezinski, Zbigniew, and Brent Scowcroft. *America and the World: Conversations on the Future of American Foreign Policy*. New York: Basic Books, 2008.

Daalder, Ivo H., and James M. Lindsay. *America Unbound*. Washington, D.C.: Brookings, 2003.

Ferguson, Niall. *Colossus: The Price of America's Empire*. New York: Penguin, 2004.

Gaddis, John Lewis. *The United States and the End of the Cold War*. New York: Oxford University Press, 1992.

Gray, Colin. *War, Peace, and Victory*. New York: Simon and Schuster, 1990.

Halberstam, David. *War in a Time of Peace*. New York: Scribner, 2001.

Hogan, Michael J., ed. *The End of the Cold War*. New York: Cambridge University Press, 1992.

Hyland, William G. *Clinton's World*. Westport, Conn.: Praeger, 1999.

Ikenberry, G. John, ed. *America Unrivaled*. Ithaca, N.Y.: Cornell University Press, 2002.

Kagan, Robert. *The World America Made*. New York: Knopf, 2012.

Kapstein, Ethan B., and Michael Mastanduno, eds. *Unipolar Politics: Realism and State Strategies after the Cold War*. New York: Columbia University Press, 1999.

Katzenstein, Peter J., and Robert O. Keohane. *Anti-Americanisms in World Politics*. Ithaca, N.Y.: Cornell University Press, 2007.

Kupchan, Charles A. *No One's World: The West, the Rising Rest, and the Coming Global Turn*. New York: Oxford University Press, 2012.

Luce, Edward. *Time to Start Thinking: America in the Age of Descent*. New York: Atlantic Monthly Press, 2012.

Lynch, Timothy J., and Robert S. Singh. *After Bush: The Case for Continuity in American Foreign Policy*. New York: Cambridge University Press, 2008.

Mandelbaum, Michael. *The Case for Goliath*. New York: Public Affairs, 2005.

McFaul, Michael. *Advancing Democracy Abroad: Why We Should and How We Can*. Lanham, Md.: Rowman and Littlefield, 2010.

Mead, Walter Russell. *Power, Terror, Peace, and War: America's Grand Strategy in a World at Risk*. New York: Knopf, 2004.

Muravchik, Joshua. *The Imperative of American Leadership: A Challenge to Neo-isolationism*. Washington, D.C.: American Enterprise Institute, 1996.

Oberdorfer, Don. *From the Cold War to a New Era*. Baltimore: Johns Hopkins University Press, 1998.

Prestowitz, Clyde. *Rogue Nation*. New York: Basic Books, 2003.

Ralph, Jason. *America's War on Terror: The State of the 9/11 Exception from Bush to Obama*. New York: Oxford University Press, 2013.

Ripley, Randall B., and James M. Lindsay, eds. *U.S. Foreign Policy after the Cold War*. Pittsburgh, Pa.: University of Pittsburgh Press, 1997.

Steel, Ronald. *Temptations of a Superpower*. Cambridge, Mass.: Harvard University Press, 1995.

Walt, Stephen M. *Taming American Power*. New York: Norton, 2005.

Zakaria, Fareed. *The Post-American World: Release 2.0*. New York: Norton, 2011.

Diplomatic Histories

Ambrose, Stephen E. *Rise to Globalism: American Foreign Policy since 1938.* 7th rev. ed. New York: Penguin, 1993.

Anderson, Fred, and Andrew Cayton. *The Dominion of War.* New York: Viking, 2005.

Bailey, Thomas. *A Diplomatic History of the American People.* 10th ed. Englewood Cliffs, N.J.: Prentice Hall, 1980.

Clarfield, Gerard. *U.S. Diplomatic History.* 2 vols. Englewood Cliffs, N.J.: Prentice Hall, 1992.

Cohen, Warren. *The New Cambridge History of American Foreign Relations: Volume 4. Challenges to American Primacy, 1945 to the Present.* New York: Cambridge University Press, 2014.

Combs, Jerald A. *The History of American Foreign Policy.* 3rd ed. Armonk, N.Y.: M. E. Sharpe, 2008.

Fleming, D. F. *The Cold War and Its Origins, 1917–1960.* 2 vols. Garden City, N.Y.: Doubleday, 1961.

Gaddis, John Lewis. *The Cold War: A New History.* New York: Penguin, 2005.

Herring, George C. *From Colony to Superpower: U.S. Foreign Relations since 1776.* New York: Oxford University Press, 2008.

Jentleson, Bruce W., and Thomas G. Paterson, eds. *The Encyclopedia of U.S. Foreign Relations.* 4 vols. New York: Oxford University Press, 1997.

Kissinger, Henry. *Diplomacy.* New York: Simon and Schuster, 1994.

McCormick, Thomas J. *America's Half-Century.* 2nd ed. Baltimore: Johns Hopkins University Press, 1995.

McMahon, Robert J. *The Cold War: A Very Short Introduction.* New York: Oxford University Press, 2003.

Melanson, Richard A. *American Foreign Policy since the Vietnam War.* 3rd ed. Armonk, N.Y.: M. E. Sharpe, 2000.

Merry, Robert W. *A Century of Vast Designs: James K. Polk, the Mexican War, and the Conquest of the American Continent.* New York: Simon and Schuster, 2010.

Nau, Henry R. *Conservative Internationalism: Armed Diplomacy under Jefferson, Polk, Truman, and Reagan.* Princeton, N.J.: Princeton University Press, 2013.

Schulzinger, Robert D. *U.S. Diplomacy since 1900.* 5th ed. New York: Oxford University Press, 2002.

Winkler, Allan A. *The Cold War: A History in Documents.* 2nd ed. New York: Oxford University Press, 2003.

Wood, Gordon S. *Empire of Liberty: A History of the Early Republic, 1789–1815.* New York: Oxford University Press, 2009.

Revisionist Interpretations and Debates

Alperovitz, Gar. *Atomic Diplomacy*. New York: Vintage Books, 1967.

Bacevich, Andrew J. *Washington Rules: America's Path to Permanent War*. New York: Metropolitan Books, 2010.

Barnet, Richard. *Roots of War*. New York: Atheneum, 1972.

Campbell, David. *Writing Security*. Rev. ed. Minneapolis: University of Minnesota Press, 1998.

_____. *United States Foreign Policy and the Politics of Identity*. Minneapolis: University of Minnesota Press, 1992.

Chomsky, Noam. *9-11*. New York: Seven Stories Press, 2002.

Gardner, Lloyd. *Architects of Illusion*. Chicago: Quadrangle Books, 1970.

Hixson, Walter. *The Myth of American Diplomacy: National Identity and U.S. Foreign Policy*. New Haven, Conn.: Yale University Press, 2008.

Hodgson, Godfrey. *The Myth of American Exceptionalism*. New Haven, Conn.: Yale University Press, 2009.

Hopf, Ted. *Reconstructing the Cold War: The Early Years, 1945–1958*. New York: Oxford University Press, 2012.

Immerman, Richard H. *Empire for Liberty: A History of American Imperialism from Benjamin Franklin to Paul Wolfowitz*. Princeton, N.J.: Princeton University Press, 2010.

Johnson, Chalmers A. *The Sorrows of Empire: Militarism, Secrecy, and the End of the Republic*. New York: Metropolitan, 2004.

_____. *Blowback: The Costs and Consequences of American Empire*. New York: Metropolitan, 2000.

Kagan, Robert. *Dangerous Nation: America's Place in the World, from Its Earliest Days to the Dawn of the 20th Century*. New York: Knopf, 2006.

Kolko, Gabriel. *The Roots of American Foreign Policy*. Boston: Beacon Press, 1969.

Kwitny, Jonathan. *Endless Enemies*. New York: Penguin, 1984.

LaFeber, Walter. *The New Empire*. Ithaca, N.Y.: Cornell University Press, 1963.

Margulies, Joseph. *What Changed When Everything Changed: 9/11 and the Making of National Identity*. New Haven, Conn.: Yale University Press, 2013.

McMahon, Robert J. *The Cold War on the Periphery*. New York: Columbia University Press, 1994.

Melanson, Richard A. *Writing History and Making Policy*. Lanham, Md.: University Press of America, 1983.

Mertus, Julie. *Bait and Switch: Human Rights and U.S. Foreign Policy*. 2nd ed. New York: Routledge, 2008.

Michaels, Jeffrey. *The Discourse Trap and the US Military: From the War on Terror to the Surge.* New York: Palgrave Macmillan, 2013.

Parenti, Michael. *Against Empire.* San Francisco: City Lights Books, 1995.

Peck, James. *Ideal Illusions: How the U.S. Government Co-opted Human Rights.* New York: Metropolitan, 2010.

Rohde, David. *Beyond War: Reimagining American Influence in a New Middle East.* New York: Viking, 2013.

Sanders, Jerry W. *Peddlers of Crisis.* Boston: South End Press, 1983.

Smith, Tony. *A Pact with the Devil: Washington's Bid for World Supremacy and the Betrayal of the American Promise.* New York: Routledge, 2007.

Thrall, Trevor A., and Jane K. Cramer, eds. *American Foreign Policy and the Politics of Fear: Threat Inflation since 9/11.* New York: Routledge, 2009.

Wallerstein, Immanuel. *The Decline of American Power: The U.S. in a Chaotic World.* New York: New Press, 2003.

Weldes, Jutta. *Constructing National Interests.* Minneapolis: University of Minnesota Press, 1999.

Williams, William Appleman. *The Tragedy of American Diplomacy.* New York: Norton, 1988.

American Military Strategy

Art, Robert J. *America's Grand Strategy and World Politics.* New York: Routledge, 2009.

Bacevich, Andrew J. *The Limits of Power: The End of American Exceptionalism.* New York: Metropolitan Books, 2008.

Bellamy, Alex J. *Security and the War on Terror.* New York: Routledge, 2008.

Benjamin, Daniel, and Steven Simon. *The Age of Sacred Terror.* New York: Random House, 2002.

Betts, Richard K. *American Force: Dangers, Delusions, and Dilemmas in National Security.* New York: Columbia University Press, 2011.

Burk, James, ed. *How 9/11 Changed Our Ways of War.* Stanford, Calif.: Stanford University Press, 2013.

Coffee, Patrick. *American Arsenal: A Century of Waging War.* New York: Oxford University Press, 2014.

Doyle, Michael W. *Striking First: Preemption and Prevention in International Conflict.* Princeton, N.J.: Princeton University Press, 2008.

Echevarria, Antulio Joseph. *Reconsidering the American Way of War: U.S. Military Practice from the Revolution to Afghanistan.* Washington, D.C.: Georgetown University Press, 2014.

English, Richard. *Terrorism: How to Respond.* New York: Oxford University Press, 2009.

Futter, Andrew. *Ballistic Missile Defense and U.S. National Security Policy: Normalization and Acceptance after the Cold War.* New York: Routledge, 2013.

Gaddis, John Lewis, Philip H. Gordon, Ernest R. May, and Jonathan Rosenberg, eds. *Cold War Statesmen Confront the Bomb: Nuclear Diplomacy since 1945.* New York: Oxford University Press, 1999.

Gavin, Francis J. *Nuclear Statecraft: History and Strategy in America's Atomic Age.* Ithaca, N.Y.: Cornell University Press, 2012.

George, Alexander L., and Richard Smoke. *Deterrence in American Foreign Policy.* New York: Columbia University Press, 1974.

Gordon, Michael R., and General Bernard E. Trainor. *Cobra II: The Inside Story of the Invasion and Occupation of Iraq.* New York: Pantheon, 2006.

Hersh, Seymour M. *Chain of Command: The Road from 9/11 to Abu Ghraib.* New York: HarperCollins, 2004.

Jordan, Amos A., William J. Taylor Jr., Michael J. Meese, and Suzanne C. Nielsen. *American National Security.* 6th ed. Baltimore: Johns Hopkins University Press, 2009.

Kaplan, Fred. *The Insurgents: David Petraeus and the Plot to Change the American Way of War.* New York: Simon and Schuster, 2013.

_____. *The Wizards of Armageddon.* New York: Simon and Schuster, 1983.

Kissinger, Henry A. *Nuclear Weapons and Foreign Policy.* New York: Harper and Brothers, 1957.

Nichols, Thomas M. *Eve of Destruction: The Coming Age of Preventive War.* Philadelphia: University of Pennsylvania Press, 2008.

Power, Samantha. *"A Problem from Hell": America and the Age of Genocide.* New York: Basic Books, 2002.

Ricks, Thomas E. *The Generals: American Military Command from World War II to Today.* New York: Penguin, 2012.

_____. *Fiasco: The American Military Adventure in Iraq.* New York: Penguin, 2006.

Talbott, Strobe. *Deadly Gambits.* New York: Knopf, 1984.

Viotti, Paul R. *American Foreign Policy and National Security: A Documentary Record.* Upper Saddle River, N.J.: Pearson/Prentice Hall, 2005.

Warren, Aiden. *The Obama Administration's Nuclear Weapon Strategy: The Promises of Prague.* New York: Routledge, 2013.

Wirls, Daniel. *Irrational Security: The Politics of Defense from Reagan to Obama.* Baltimore: Johns Hopkins University Press, 2010.

Woodward, Bob. *The War Within: A Secret White House History, 2006–2008.* New York: Simon and Schuster, 2008.

_____. *State of Denial: Bush at War, Part III*. New York: Simon and Schuster, 2006.

_____. *Plan of Attack*. New York: Simon and Schuster, 2004.

_____. *Bush at War*. New York: Simon and Schuster, 2002.

_____. *The Commanders*. New York: Simon and Schuster, 1991.

American Policy in Europe and the Former Soviet Union

Allison, Roy. *Russia, the West, and Military Intervention*. New York: Oxford University Press, 2013.

Aybet, Gülnur, and Rebecca R. Moore. *NATO: In Search of a Vision*. Washington, D.C.: Georgetown University Press, 2010.

Benjamin, Daniel. *Europe 2030*. Washington, D.C.: Brookings, 2010.

Dunlop, John B. *The Rise of Russia and the Fall of the Soviet Empire*. Princeton, N.J.: Princeton University Press, 1993.

Foglesong, David. *The American Mission and the "Evil Empire": The Crusade for a Free Russia since 1881*. New York: Cambridge University Press, 2007.

Hill, Fiona, and Clifford G. Gaddy. *Mr. Putin: Operative in the Kremlin*. Washington, D.C.: Brookings, 2013.

Judah, Tim. *Kosovo: War and Revenge*. New Haven, Conn.: Yale University Press, 2000.

Kaplan, Lawrence S. *The Long Entanglement: NATO's First Fifty Years*. Westport, Conn.: Praeger, 1999.

Kaplan, Robert D. *Balkan Ghosts*. New York: St. Martin's Press, 1993.

Majone, Giandomenico. *Europe as the Would-Be World Power: The EU at Fifty*. New York: Cambridge University Press, 2009.

Marquand, David. *The End of the West: The Once and Future Europe*. Princeton, N.J.: Princeton University Press, 2011.

Stent, Angela E. *The Limits of Partnership: U.S.-Russian Relations in the Twenty-first Century*. Princeton, N.J.: Princeton University Press, 2014.

Thies, Wallace J. *Why NATO Endures*. New York: Cambridge University Press, 2009.

Vladislov, M. Zubok. *A Failed Empire: The Soviet Union in the Cold War from Stalin to Gorbachev*. Chapel Hill: University of North Carolina Press, 2007.

Wilson, Andrew. *Virtual Politics: Faking Democracy in the Post-Soviet World*. New Haven, Conn.: Yale University Press, 2005.

Zimmerman, William. *Ruling Russia: Authoritarianism from the Revolution to Putin*. Princeton, N.J.: Princeton University Press, 2014.

American Policy in East Asia

Bernstein, Richard, and Ross H. Munro. *The Coming Conflict with China*. New York: Knopf, 1997.

Bush, Richard C. *Uncharted Strait: The Future of China-Taiwan Relations*. Washington, D.C.: Brookings, 2012.

Calder, Kent E. *Pacific Alliance: Reviving U.S.-Japan Relations*. New Haven, Conn.: Yale University Press, 2009.

Chan, Steve. *Looking for Balance: China, the United States, and Power Balancing in East Asia*. Stanford, Calif.: Stanford University Press, 2012.

Chinoy, Mike. *Meltdown: The Inside Story of the North Korean Nuclear Crisis*. New York: St. Martin's Press, 2008.

Cole, Bernard D. *Asian Maritime Strategies: Navigating Troubled Waters*. Annapolis, Md.: Naval Institute Press, 2013.

Elliott, David W. P. *Changing Worlds: Vietnam's Transition from Cold War to Globalization*. New York: Oxford University Press, 2012.

Foot, Rosemary, and Andrew Walter. *China, the United States, and Global Order*. New York: Cambridge University Press, 2010.

Friedberg, Aaron. *A Contest for Supremacy: China, America, and the Struggle for Mastery in Asia*. New York: Norton, 2011.

Gelb, Leslie, et al. *The Pentagon Papers*. New York: Bantam Books, 1971.

Halberstam, David. *The Best and the Brightest*. New York: Random House, 1969.

Hess, Gary R. *Vietnam: Explaining America's Lost War*. Malden, Mass.: Blackwell, 2009.

Hunt, Michael H. *Lyndon Johnson's War*. New York: Hill and Wang, 1996.

Karnow, Stanley C. *Vietnam*. New York: Viking Press, 1983.

Kimball, Jeffrey P. *The Vietnam War Files*. Lawrence: University Press of Kansas, 2004.

Kissinger, Henry. *On China*. New York: Penguin, 2011.

Lieberthal, Kenneth, and Peter W. Singer. *Cybersecurity and U.S.-China Relations*. Washington, D.C.: Brookings, 2012.

Luttwak, Edward N. *The Rise of China vs. the Logic of Strategy*. Cambridge, Mass.: Belknap Press, 2012.

McFarland, Keith. *The Korean War: An Annotated Bibliography*. 2nd ed. New York: Routledge, 2009.

McMahon, Robert J., ed. *Major Problems in the History of the Vietnam War: Documents and Essays*. 3rd ed. Boston: Houghton Mifflin, 2003.

Prados, John. *Vietnam: The History of an Unwinnable War, 1945–1975*. Lawrence: University of Kansas Press, 2009.

Rapkin, David P., and William R. Thompson. *Transition Scenarios: China and the United States in the Twenty-first Century.* Chicago: University of Chicago Press, 2013.

Rosencrance, Richard, and Gu Guoliang. *Power and Restraint: A Shared Vision for the U.S.-China Relationship.* New York: Public Affairs, 2009.

Sheehan, Neil. *A Bright Shining Lie.* New York: Random House, 1988.

Swaine, Michael D. *America's Challenge: Engaging a Rising China in the Twenty-first Century.* Washington, D.C.: Carnegie Endowment for International Peace, 2011.

Tucker, Nancy B. *Strait Talk: United States–Taiwan Relations and the Crisis with China.* Cambridge, Mass.: Harvard University Press, 2009.

American Policy in the Middle East and South Asia

Akbar, Ahmed. *The Thistle and the Drone: How America's War on Terror Became a Global War on Tribal Islam.* Washington, D.C.: Brookings, 2013.

Al-Ali, Zaid. *The Struggle for Iraq's Future: How Corruption, Incompetence, and Sectarianism Have Undermined Democracy.* New Haven, Conn.: Yale University Press, 2014.

Allawi, Ali A. *The Occupation of Iraq: Winning the War, Losing the Peace.* New Haven, Conn.: Yale University Press, 2007.

Auserwald, David P., and Stephen M. Saideman. *NATO in Afghanistan: Fighting Together, Fighting Alone.* Princeton, N.J.: Princeton University Press, 2013.

Baxter, Kylie. *United States Foreign Policy in the Middle East: The Roots of Anti-Americanism.* New York: Routledge, 2008.

Bergen, Peter. *Manhunt: The Ten-Year Search for bin Laden from 9/11 to Abbottabad.* New York: Crown, 2012.

Chandrasekaran, Rajiv. *Imperial Life in the Emerald City: Inside Iraq's Green Zone.* New York: Knopf, 2006.

Chivvis, Christopher. *Toppling Qaddafi: Libya and the Limits of Liberal Intervention.* New York: Cambridge University Press, 2013.

Cole, Juan. *Engaging the Muslim World.* New York: Palgrave Macmillan, 2009.

Coll, Steve. *Ghost Wars.* New York: Penguin, 2004.

Davidson, Christopher M. *After the Sheikhs: The Coming Collapse of the Gulf Monarchies.* New York: Oxford University Press, 2013.

Duffield, John S., and Peter J. Dombrowski. *Balance Sheet: The Iraq War and U.S. National Security.* Stanford, Calif.: Stanford University Press, 2009.

Friedman, Thomas L. *From Beirut to Jerusalem.* New York: Anchor Books, 1989.

Ganguly, Sumit, and S. Paul Kapur. *India, Pakistan, and the Bomb*. New York: Columbia University Press, 2010.

Haqqani, Hussein. *Magnificent Delusions: Pakistan, the United States, and an Epic History of Misunderstanding*. New York: Public Affairs, 2013.

Hashemi, Nadr, and Danny Postel, eds. *The Syria Dilemma*. Cambridge, Mass.: MIT Press, 2013.

Jentleson, Bruce W. *With Friends Like These*. New York: Norton, 1994.

Jones, Seth. *Hunting in the Shadows: The Pursuit of al Qa'ida Since 9/11*. New York: Norton, 2012.

Kroenig, Matthew. *A Time to Attack: The Looming Iranian Nuclear Threat*. New York: Palgrave, 2014.

Lieven, Anatol. *Pakistan: A Hard Country*. New York: Public Affairs, 2011.

Lynch, Mark. *The Arab Uprising: The Unfinished Revolutions of the New Middle East*. New York: Public Affairs, 2012.

Markey, Daniel S. *No Exit from Pakistan: America's Tortured Relationship with Islamabad*. New York: Cambridge University Press, 2013.

Migdal, Joel S. *Shifting Sands: The United States in the Middle East*. New York: Columbia University Press, 2014.

Packer, George. *The Assassins' Gate: America in Iraq*. New York: Farrar, Straus, and Giroux, 2005.

Parsi, Trita. *A Single Roll of the Dice: Obama's Diplomacy with Iran*. New Haven, Conn.: Yale University Press, 2012.

Pollack, Kenneth M. *Unthinkable: Iran, the Bomb, and American Strategy*. New York: Simon and Schuster, 2013.

Randal, Jonathan. *Osama: The Making of a Terrorist*. New York: Knopf, 2004.

Riedel, Bruce. *Avoiding Armageddon: America, India, and Pakistan to the Brink and Back*. Washington, D.C.: Brookings, 2013.

Safran, Nadav. *Intifada*. New York: Simon and Schuster, 1989.

Schaffer, Howard B., and Teresita C. Schaffer. *How Pakistan Negotiates with the United States: Riding the Roller Coaster*. Washington, D.C.: Brookings, 2011.

Schaffer, Teresita C. *India and the United States in the Twenty-first Century*. Washington, D.C.: Center for Strategic and International Studies, 2009.

Takeyh, Ray. *Guardians of the Revolution: Iran and the World in the Age of the Ayatollahs*. New York: Oxford University Press, 2009.

Thies, Cameron. *The United States, Israel, and the Search for International Order: Socializing States*. New York: Routledge, 2013.

Wehry, Frederick M. *Sectarian Politics in the Gulf: From the Iraq War to the Arab Uprisings*. New York: Columbia University Press, 2014.

American Policy in Africa

Bowden, Mark. *Black Hawk Down*. New York: Atlantic Monthly Press, 1999.

Brautigam, Deborah. *The Dragon's Gift: The Real Story of China in Africa*. New York: Oxford University Press, 2009.

Clarke, Walter, and Jeffrey Herbst, eds. *Learning from Somalia*. Boulder, Colo.: Westview Press, 1997.

Cockett, Richard. *Sudan: Darfur and the Failure of an African State*. New Haven, Conn.: Yale University Press, 2010.

French, Howard. *China's Second Continent: How a Million Migrants Are Building a New Empire in Africa*. New York: Random House, 2014.

Lyman, Princeton N. *Partner to History: The U.S. Role in South Africa's Transition to Democracy*. Washington, D.C.: U.S. Institute of Peace Press, 2002.

Packenham, Robert A. *Liberal America and the Third World*. Princeton, N.J.: Princeton University Press, 1973.

Reyntjens, Filip. *The Great African War: Congo and Regional Geopolitics, 1996–2006*. New York: Cambridge University Press, 2009.

Rothchild, Donald, and Edmond J. Keller, eds. *Africa-U.S. Relations: Strategic Encounters*. Boulder, Colo.: Lynne Rienner, 2006.

Schmidt, Elizabeth. *Foreign Intervention in Africa: From the Cold War to the War on Terror*. New York: Cambridge University Press, 2013.

Stevenson, Jonathan. *Losing Mogadishu*. Annapolis, Md.: Naval Institute Press, 1995.

American Policy in Latin America

Barshefsky, Charlene, and James T. Hill. *U.S.–Latin American Relations: A New Direction for a New Reality*. New York: Council on Foreign Relations, 2008.

Bowden, Mark. *Killing Pablo*. New York: Atlantic Monthly Press, 2001.

Carpenter, Ted Galen. *Bad Neighbor Policy*. New York: Palgrave Macmillan, 2003.

Corrales, Javier, and Michael Penfold. *Dragon in the Tropics: Hugo Chavez and the Political Economy of Revolution in Venezuela*. Washington, D.C.: Brookings, 2010.

Crandall, Britta H. *Hemispheric Giants: The Misunderstood History of U.S.-Brazilian Relations*. Lanham, Md.: Rowman and Littlefield, 2011.

Crandall, Russell. *The United States and Latin America after the Cold War*. New York: Cambridge University Press, 2008.

Draper, Theodore. *The Dominican Revolt*. New York: Commentary, 1968.

Gutman, Roy. *Banana Diplomacy*. New York: Simon and Schuster, 1988.

Haney, Patrick J., and Walt Vanderbush. *The Cuban Embargo: The Domestic Politics of an American Foreign Policy.* Pittsburgh, Pa.: University of Pittsburgh Press, 2005.

Holden, Robert H., and Eric Zolov. *Latin America and the United States: A Documentary History.* 2nd ed. New York: Oxford University Press, 2010.

Immerman, Robert H. *The CIA in Guatemala.* Austin: University of Texas Press, 1982.

Jones, Howard. *The Bay of Pigs.* New York: Oxford University Press, 2008.

Lake, Anthony. *Somoza Falling.* Boston: Houghton Mifflin, 1989.

LeoGrande, William M., and Peter Kornbluh. *Back Channel to Cuba: The Hidden History of Negotiations between Washington and Havana.* Chapel Hill: University of North Carolina Press, 2014.

McPherson, Alan. *Yankee No! Anti-Americanism in U.S.–Latin American Relations.* Cambridge, Mass.: Harvard University Press, 2003.

O'Neil, Shannon. *Two Nations Indivisible: Mexico, the United States, and the Road Ahead.* New York: Oxford University Press, 2013.

Pastor, Robert A. *Whirlpool.* Princeton, N.J.: Princeton University Press, 1993.

_____. *Condemned to Repetition.* Princeton, N.J.: Princeton University Press, 1987.

Schlesinger, Stephen, and Stephen Kinzer. *Bitter Fruit.* Garden City, N.Y.: Anchor Books, 1982.

Schmidli, William Michael. *The Fate of Freedom Elsewhere: Human Rights and U.S. Cold War Policy toward Argentina.* Ithaca, N.Y.: Cornell University Press, 2013.

Sigmund, Paul. *The Overthrow of Allende and the Politics of Chile.* Pittsburgh, Pa.: University of Pittsburgh Press, 1977.

Smith, Peter H., and Andrew Selee, eds. *Mexico and the United States: The Politics of Partnership.* Boulder, Colo.: Lynne Rienner, 2013.

Teixeira, Carlos Gustavo Poggio. *Brazil, the United States, and the South American Subsystem: Regional Politics and the Absent Empire.* Lanham, Md.: Lexington Books, 2012.

America and the International Political Economy

Ahamed, Liquat. *Lords of Finance: The Bankers Who Broke the World.* New York: Penguin, 2009.

Baldwin, David A. *Economic Statecraft.* Princeton, N.J.: Princeton University Press, 1985.

Eichengreen, Barry. *Exorbitant Privilege: The Rise and Fall of the Dollar and the Future of the International Monetary System.* New York: Oxford University Press, 2011.

Friedman, Thomas, and Michael Mandelbaum. *That Used to Be Us.* New York: Farrar, Strauss, and Giroux, 2011.

Gorton, Gary B. *Misunderstanding Financial Crises: Why We Don't See Them Coming*. New York: Oxford University Press, 2012.

Hubbard, R. Glenn, and William Duggan. *The Aid Trap: About Ending Poverty*. New York: Columbia Business School Publishing, 2009.

Iriye, Akira, ed. *Global Interdependence: The World after 1945*. Cambridge, Mass.: Harvard University Press, 2014.

Krist, William. *Globalization and America's Trade Agreements*. Baltimore: Johns Hopkins University Press, 2014.

Krugman, Paul. *The Return of Depression Economics and the Crisis of 2008*. New York: Norton, 2009.

McKinnon, Ronald I. *The Unloved Dollar Standard: From Bretton Woods to the Rise of China*. New York: Oxford University Press, 2013.

Pettis, Michael. *The Great Rebalancing: Trade, Conflict, and the Perilous Road Ahead for the World Economy*. Princeton, N.J.: Princeton University Press, 2013.

Piketty, Thomas. *Capital in the Twenty-first Century*. Translated by Arthur Goldhammer. Cambridge, Mass.: Belknap Press, 2014.

Reinhart, Carmen M., and Kenneth S. Rogoff. *This Time Is Different: Eight Centuries of Financial Folly*. Princeton, N.J.: Princeton University Press, 2009.

Sachs, Jeffrey. *Common Wealth: Economics for a Crowded Planet*. New York: Penguin, 2008.

Steil, Ben. *The Battle of Bretton Woods: John Maynard Keynes, Harry Dexter White, and the Making of a New World Order*. Princeton, N.J.: Princeton University Press, 2013.

Stiglitz, Joseph E. *Freefall: America, Free Markets, and the Sinking of the World Economy*. New York: Norton, 2010.

Yergin, Daniel. *The Quest: Energy, Security, and the Remaking of the Modern World*. New York: Penguin, 2011.

America and International Organizations

Byers, Michael, and Georg Nolte. *United States Hegemony and the Foundations of International Law*. New York: Cambridge University Press, 2003.

Feinstein, Lee, and Tod Lindberg. *Means to an End: U.S. Interest in the International Criminal Court*. Washington, D.C.: Brookings, 2009.

Held, David, and Charles Roger, eds. *Global Governance at Risk*. Malden, Mass.: Polity Press, 2013.

Iriye, Akira, ed. *Global Interdependence: The World after 1945*. Cambridge, Mass.: Harvard University Press, 2014.

Keck, Margaret, and Kathryn Sikkink. *Activists beyond Borders*. Ithaca, N.Y.: Cornell University Press, 1998.

Ku, Julian, and John Yoo. *Taming Globalization: International Law, the U.S. Constitution, and the New World Order*. New York: Oxford University Press, 2011.

Luck, Edward C. *Mixed Messages: American Politics and International Organization, 1919–1999*. Washington, D.C.: Brookings, 1999.

McCleary, Rachel M. *Global Compassion: Private Voluntary Organizations and U.S. Foreign Policy since 1939*. New York: Oxford University Press, 2009.

Patrick, Stewart. *The Best Laid Plans: The Origins of American Multilateralism and the Dawn of the Cold War*. Lanham, Md.: Rowman and Littlefield, 2009.

Slaughter, Anne-Marie. *A New World Order*. Princeton, N.J.: Princeton University Press, 2004.

Thompson, Alexander. *Channels of Power: The UN Security Council and U.S. Statecraft in Iraq*. New York: Cornell University Press, 2009.

Domestic Politics and American Foreign Policy

Adams, Gordon, and Cindy Williams. *Buying National Security: How America Plans and Pays for Its Global Role and Safety at Home*. New York: Routledge, 2009.

Allison, Graham T., and Philip Zelikow. *Essence of Decision*. 2nd ed. New York: Longman, 1999.

Bamford, James. *A Pretext for War: 9/11, Iraq, and the Abuse of America's Intelligence Agencies*. New York: Doubleday, 2004.

_____. *Body of Secrets: Anatomy of the Ultra-secret National Security Agency*. New York: Doubleday, 2001.

Baum, Matthew A., and Tim J. Groeling. *War Stories: The Causes and Consequences of Public Views of War*. Princeton, N.J.: Princeton University Press, 2009.

Betts, Richard K. *Enemies of Intelligence: Knowledge and Power in American National Security*. New York: Columbia University Press, 2007.

Chatterjee, Pratap. *Halliburton's Army: How a Well-Connected Texas Oil Company Revolutionized the Way America Makes War*. New York: Nation Books, 2009.

Diamond, John. *The CIA and the Culture of Failure: U.S. Intelligence from the End of the Cold War to the Invasion of Iraq*. Stanford, Calif.: Stanford University Press, 2008.

Foyle, Douglas C. *Counting the Public In*. New York: Columbia University Press, 1999.

Friedberg, Aaron L. *In the Shadow of the Garrison State*. Princeton, N.J.: Princeton University Press, 2000.

Goldsmith, Jack. *Power and Constraint: The Accountability President after 9/11*. New York: Norton, 2012.

Haney, Patrick J. *Organizing for Foreign Policy Crises*. Ann Arbor: University of Michigan Press, 1997.

Henkin, Louis. *Foreign Affairs and the U.S. Constitution.* 2nd ed. Oxford: Clarendon Press, 1996.

Herman, Susan E. *Taking Liberties: The War on Terror and the Erosion of American Democracy.* New York: Oxford University Press, 2011.

Hess, Gary R. *Presidential Decisions for War: Korea, Vietnam, the Persian Gulf, and Iraq.* 2nd ed. Baltimore: Johns Hopkins University Press, 2009.

Janis, Irving L. *Groupthink.* 2nd ed. Boston: Houghton Mifflin, 1983.

Mann, James. *Rise of the Vulcans.* New York: Viking, 2004.

Mayer, Jane. *The Dark Side: The Inside Story of How the War on Terror Turned into a War on American Ideals.* New York: Doubleday, 2008.

Mearsheimer, John J., and Stephen Walt. *The Israel Lobby and U.S. Foreign Policy.* New York: Farrar, Straus, and Giroux, 2007.

Pillar, Paul R. *Intelligence and U.S. Foreign Policy: Iraq, 9/11, and Misguided Reform.* New York: Columbia University Press, 2011.

Pious, Richard M. *Why Presidents Fail: White House Decision Making from Eisenhower to Bush II.* Lanham, Md.: Rowman and Littlefield, 2008.

Rathbun, Brian. *Trust in International Cooperation: International Security Institutions, Domestic Politics, and American Multilateralism.* New York: Cambridge University Press, 2012.

Richelson, Jeffrey T. *The U.S. Intelligence Community.* 5th ed. Boulder, Colo.: Westview Press, 2008.

Rothkopf, David J. *Running the World: The Inside Story of the National Security Council and the Architects of American Power.* New York: Public Affairs, 2005.

Rovner, Joshua. *Fixing the Facts: National Security and the Politics of Intelligence.* Ithaca, N.Y.: Cornell University Press, 2011.

Sapolsky, Harvey, Eugene Gholz, and Caitlin Talmadge. *U.S. Defense Politics: The Origins of Security Policy.* New York: Routledge, 2009.

Scahill, Jeremy. *Blackwater: The Rise of the World's Most Powerful Mercenary Army.* New York: Nation Books, 2008.

Schafer, Mark, and Scott Crichlow. *Groupthink vs. High-Quality Decision Making in International Relations.* New York: Columbia University Press, 2010.

Schlesinger, Arthur, Jr. *The Imperial Presidency.* Boston: Houghton-Mifflin, 1973.

Stanger, Allison. *One Nation under Contract: The Outsourcing of American Power and the Future of Foreign Policy.* New Haven, Conn.: Yale University Press, 2009.

Starkman, Dean. *The Watchdog That Didn't Bark: The Financial Crisis and the Disappearance of Investigative Journalism.* New York: Columbia University Press, 2014.

Treverton, Gregory F. *Intelligence for an Age of Terror.* New York: Cambridge University Press, 2009.

Witcover, Jules. *The American Vice Presidency: From Irrelevance to Power*. Washington, D.C.: Smithsonian Books, 2014.

Zegart, Amy B. *Spying Blind: The CIA, the FBI, and the Origins of 9/11*. Princeton, N.J.: Princeton University Press, 2007.

_____. *Flawed by Design: The Evolution of the CIA, JCS, and NSC*. Stanford, Calif.: Stanford University Press, 1999.

Memoirs and Biographies of American Leaders

Acheson, Dean. *Present at the Creation*. New York: Norton, 1969.

Baker, James A., III. *The Politics of Diplomacy*. New York: Putnam, 1995.

Berg, A. Scott. *Wilson*. New York: Allen Lane, 2013.

Blackman, Ann. *Seasons of Her Life: A Biography of Madeleine Korbel Albright*. New York: Scribner, 1998.

Broadwell, Paula. *The Education of General David Petraeus*. New York: Penguin, 2012.

Bumiller, Elisabeth. *Condoleezza Rice: An American Life*. New York: Random House, 2007.

Bundy, McGeorge. *Danger and Survival*. New York: Random House, 1988.

Bush, George H. W., and Brent Scowcroft. *A World Transformed*. New York: Knopf, 1998.

Bush, George W. *Decision Points*. New York: Crown, 2010.

Caro, Robert. *The Passage of Power: The Years of Lyndon Johnson*. New York: Knopf, 2012.

Carter, Jimmy. *Keeping Faith*. New York: Bantam Books, 1982.

Chollet, Derek, and Samantha Power. *The Unquiet American: Richard Holbrooke in the World*. New York: Public Affairs, 2011.

Christopher, Warren. *In the Stream of History*. Stanford, Calif.: Stanford University Press, 1998.

Clarke, Richard A. *Against All Enemies: Inside America's War on Terror*. New York: Free Press, 2004.

Clinton, Hillary R. *Hard Choices*. New York: Simon & Schuster, 2014.

Costigliola, Frank, ed. *The Kennan Diaries*. New York: Norton, 2014.

Eisenhower, Dwight D. *Waging Peace*. New York: Doubleday, 1965.

Gaddis, John Lewis. *George F. Kennan: An American Life*. New York: Penguin, 2011.

Gates, Robert M. *Duty: Memoirs of a Secretary at War*. New York: Knopf, 2014.

Gati, Charles. *Zbig: The Strategy and Statecraft of Zbigniew Brzezinski*. Baltimore: Johns Hopkins University Press, 2013.

Guhin, Michael. *John Foster Dulles*. New York: Columbia University Press, 1972.

Holbrooke, Richard C. *To End a War*. New York: Random House, 1998.

Immerman, Richard H. *John Foster Dulles and the Diplomacy of the Cold War*. Princeton, N.J.: Princeton University Press, 1990.

Isaacson, Walter, and Evan Thomas. *The Wise Men*. New York: Simon and Schuster, 1986.

Johnson, Lyndon B. *The Vantage Point*. New York: Popular Library, 1971.

Kearns, Doris. *Lyndon Johnson and the American Dream*. New York: Harper and Row, 1976.

Kennan, George F. *Memoirs*. Boston: Little, Brown, 1967.

Kennedy, Robert F. *Thirteen Days*. New York: Norton, 1971.

Kinzer, Stephen. *The Brothers: John Foster Dulles, Allen Dulles, and Their Secret World War*. New York: Times Books, 2013.

Kissinger, Henry A. *Years of Upheaval*. Boston: Little, Brown, 1982.

Lukacs, John. *George Kennan: A Study of Character*. New Haven, Conn.: Yale University Press, 2007.

Mann, James. 2009. *The Rebellion of Ronald Reagan: A History of the End of the Cold War*. New York: Viking, 2009.

McCullough, David. *Truman*. New York: Simon and Schuster, 1992.

McNamara, Robert S. *In Retrospect: The Tragedy and Lessons of Vietnam*. New York: Vintage, 1996.

Panetta, Leon. *Worthy Fights: A Memoir of Leadership in War and Peace*. New York: Penguin Press, 2014.

Perry, Mark. *The Most Dangerous Man in America: The Making of Douglas MacArthur*. New York: Basic Books, 2014.

Pogue, Forrest C. *George C. Marshall*. New York: Viking Press, 1987.

Powell, Colin L. *My American Journey*. New York: Random House, 1995.

Rumsfeld, Donald. *Known and Unknown: A Memoir*. New York: Sentinel, 2011.

Sachs, Jeffrey D. *To Move the World: JFK's Quest for Peace*. New York: Random House, 2013.

Smith, Gaddis. *Dean Acheson*. New York: Cooper Square Publishers, 1972.

Sorensen, Theodore C. *Kennedy*. New York: Bantam Books, 1966.

Talbott, Strobe. *The Russia Hand*. New York: Random House, 2002.

Tenet, George. *At the Center of the Storm: My Years at the CIA*. New York: HarperCollins, 2007.

Truman, Harry S. *Memoirs*. 2 vols. New York: New American Library, 1965.

Truman, Harry S., Dean Acheson, and David McCullough. *Affection and Trust: The Personal Correspondence of Harry S. Truman and Dean Acheson, 1953–1971*. New York: Knopf, 2010.

Vance, Cyrus. *Hard Choices*. New York: Simon and Schuster, 1982.

Appendix D

Select Websites

The following websites may be useful to students of American foreign policy—either as supplements to this text or as resources for research projects. This list is by no means exhaustive. It can, however, provide a gateway to related sites and sources of information.

U.S. Government: Executive Branch

White House (www.whitehouse.gov)

Department of Commerce (www.commerce.gov)

Department of Defense (www.defense.gov)

Defense Intelligence Agency (www.dia.mil)

Joint Chiefs of Staff (www.jcs.mil)

North Atlantic Treaty Organization (www.nato.int)

U.S. Air Force (www.af.mil)

U.S. Army (www.army.mil)

U.S. Marine Corps (www.marines.mil)

U.S. Navy (www.navy.mil)

Department of Homeland Security (www.dhs.gov)

Transportation Security Administration (www.tsa.gov)

Department of State (www.state.gov)

U.S. Agency for International Development (www.usaid.gov)

Federal Bureau of Investigation (www.fbi.gov)

Millennium Challenge Corporation (www.mcc.gov)

National Security Agency (www.nsa.gov)

National Security Council (www.whitehouse.gov/nsc)

Office of the Director of National Intelligence (www.dni.gov)

Central Intelligence Agency (www.cia.gov)

U.S. Mission to the United Nations (www.usunnewyork.usmission.gov)

U.S. Trade Representative (www.ustr.gov)

U.S. Government: Legislative Branch

Congressional Budget Office (www.cbo.gov)

Library of Congress (www.loc.gov)

Congressional Research Service (www.loc.gov/crsinfo)

U.S. House of Representatives (www.house.gov)

House Armed Services Committee (http://armedservices.house.gov)

House Committee on Foreign Affairs (http://foreignaffairs.house.gov)

U.S. Senate (www.senate.gov)

Senate Armed Services Committee (www.armed-services.senate.gov)

Senate Foreign Relations Committee (www.foreign.senate.gov)

U.S. Government: Judicial Branch

U.S. Court of International Trade (www.cit.uscourts.gov)

U.S. Federal Courts (www.uscourts.gov)

International Governmental Organizations

Asia-Pacific Economic Cooperation (www.apec.org)

Association of Southeast Asian Nations (www.asean.org)

European Union (www.europa.eu)

International Court of Justice (www.icj-cij.org)

International Criminal Court (www.icc-cpi.int)

International Criminal Police Organization (www.interpol.int)

International Finance Corporation (www.ifc.org)

International Labour Organization (www.ilo.org)

International Monetary Fund (www.imf.org)

Organisation for Economic Co-operation and Development (www.oecd.org)

Organization of American States (www.oas.org)

Organization of the Petroleum Exporting Countries (www.opec.org)

United Nations (www.un.org)

World Bank (www.worldbank.org)

World Trade Organization (www.wto.org)

Major Nongovernmental Organizations

American Israel Public Affairs Committee (www.aipac.org)

Amnesty International (www.amnesty.org)

Corporate Watch (www.corpwatch.org)

Foreign Policy Research Institute (www.fpri.org)

Freedom House (www.freedomhouse.org)

GreenNet (www.gn.apc.org)

Greenpeace (www.greenpeace.org)

Human Rights Watch (www.hrw.org)

International Chamber of Commerce (www.iccwbo.org)

International Committee of the Red Cross (www.icrc.org)

Middle East Research and Information Project (www.merip.org)

Program on International Policy Attitudes (www.pipa.org)

Sierra Club (www.sierraclub.org)

Stockholm International Peace Research Institute (www.sipri.org)

World Wildlife Fund (www.wwf.org)

Think Tanks and Foundations

American Enterprise Institute (www.aei.org)

Atlantic Council (www.atlanticcouncil.org)

Brookings Institution (www.brookings.edu)

Carnegie Endowment for International Peace (http://carnegieendowment .org/about/?lang=en)

Cato Institute (www.cato.org)

Center for a New American Security (www.cnas.org)

Center for Defense Information (www.pogo.org/our-work/straus-military-reform-project)

Center for Security and International Studies (http://csis.org)

Council on Foreign Relations (www.cfr.org)

Economic Policy Institute (www.epi.org)

Federation of American Scientists (www.fas.org)

Foreign Policy in Focus (www.fpif.org)

Global Policy Forum (www.globalpolicy.org)

Heritage Foundation (www.heritage.org)

Hoover Institution (www.hoover.org)

RAND (www.rand.org)

United States Institute of Peace (www.usip.org)

Appendix E

Select Blogs on American Foreign Policy

American Diplomacy (www.unc.edu/depts/diplomat). Commentary by current and past practitioners of American foreign policy as well as leading scholars.

Democracy Arsenal (www.democracyarsenal.org). Analysis and commentary by the National Security Network, whose goal is to bring "cohesion and strategic focus to the progressive national security community."

Foreign Policy Association (www.fpa.org). Experts' daily analysis of a wide variety of policy issues in order to serve the association's goal of public education. A great source for students and researchers.

Foreign Policy Watch (www.fpwatch.blogspot.com). Wide-ranging posts on global issues and American foreign policy to which readers are invited to respond.

Just Foreign Policy (www.justforeignpolicy.org/blog). Foreign policy–related posts hyperlinked to an array of news reports, NGO studies, and government documents.

Passport (blog.foreignpolicy.com). News updates along with commentary by prominent analysts such as Thomas Ricks, Daniel Drezner, and Stephen Walt. Among the most widely read American foreign policy blogs.

Real Clear Defense (http://realcleardefense.com). A good source of information regarding U.S. foreign policy issues and developments in the U.S. security bureaucracy.

Real Clear World (www.realclearworld.com). Provides coverage from U.S. and foreign news sources of major global developments.

UN Dispatch (www.undispatch.com). An essential source of information on global and regional issues. Compiled by staff members of the UN.

The Washington Note (www.thewashingtonnote.com). Compilation of informed commentary and a useful video archive on many aspects of American foreign policy. Sponsored by the New America Foundation.

Whirled View (www.whirledview.typepad.com/whirledview). "A look at world politics and most everything else" that features analysis and a thorough set of links to think tanks, government documents, and other foreign policy blogs.

Index

Page references followed by (figure) indicate an illustrated figure; followed by (map) indicates a map; followed by (table) indicates a map; and followed by (photograph) indicates a photograph.

political collapse and genocide of
Somalia in, 208–209, 243
Soviet Union and U.S. involvement in
decolonialized, 79–83
Tutsi–Hutus violence
(1972–1994), 77, 209
Ahmadinejad, Mahmoud, 355–356
Aidid, Mohammed Farah, 209
Al Qaeda
assassination of Massoud by, 278
connection to terrorism by, 8, 242
(photo), 254 (table), 255,
256–257, 277
forces crossing into Pakistan
(2001–2002), 279–280
ISIS alliance with, 328
Osama bin Laden's leadership of,
256–257, 260, 268
prisoners held in U.S. Guantánamo
Bay, 279
relationship between Taliban and, 278
U.S. counterterrorism campaign
against, 256–272
U.S. war on terror's failure to
break, 272
World Trade Center attacks (2001) by,
8, 242 (photo), 254 (table), 255
See also Bin Laden, Osama; Islamic
militants; Terrorism
Albright, Madeleine, 230 (photo)
Algeria, 93
Allende, Salvador, 90
Alliance for Progress (U.S., 1961), 85
"American Century"
during and after the Cold War,
362–363
Henry Luce's notion of, 361–362
internal threats to democracy and end
of, 363–366
rethinking American power and,
370–372
Trump's controversial policies
threatening notion of, 366–370
See also American hegemony
American containment strategy
analysis as successful factor in ending
the Cold War, 181–182
applied to Asian region, 47

excesses of the, 180–181
focus on rebuilding European
economies part of, 46–47
George Kennan's leadership of the,
35–37, 38 (photo), 47, 178, 284
long-term objectives regarding Soviet
behavior by the, 178
new economic and military structures
supporting the, 47–51
origins and development of the,
45–47
Reagan's return to the, 136–138
revolution in East Asia and
continuation of, 59
Truman Doctrine (1947), 32–33,
40–43
two alternatives to the, 37–40
Vietnam War and the limits of, 74
(photo), 92–103, 105, 194
See also American foreign policies
(Cold War)
American embassies bombings (1998),
156, 254 (table)
American exceptionalism, 13–15, 302
American foreign policies
driven by economics after
World War II, 14–15
exceptionalism and exceptions of,
13–15, 302
four pivotal questions confronting
contemporary, 3
Good Neighbor Policy (1933), 84
hegemony or sphere of
influence of, 9–11
Marshall Plan, 52–54, 55, 56, 58
Monroe Doctrine (1823) of, 10, 12,
56, 83, 126, 213, 271
National Security Council historically
coordinating the, 51,
146–148 (photo), 149–150,
304 (photo), 312
national style of, 4–5
traditionally moralistic approach of,
361, 370
underlying realism coexisting with
idealism of, 370–372
Washington's Farewell Address (1796)
influencing, 6, 213

About the Authors

Steven W. Hook is professor and former chair of political science at Kent State University. He has authored and edited numerous books, including *U.S. Foreign Policy Today: American Renewal?* (2012, with James M. Scott), *Routledge Handbook of American Foreign Policy* (2012, with Christopher Jones), *Democratic Peace in Theory and Practice* (2010), *Comparative Foreign Policy* (2002), and *National Interest and Foreign Aid* (1995). His journal articles have appeared in leading journals, including *World Politics*, *International Studies Quarterly*, and *Foreign Policy Analysis*. Professor Hook is a past president of the Foreign Policy Analysis sections of the American Political Science Association and the International Studies Association.

John Spanier received his PhD from Yale University. He joined the faculty of the University of Florida in 1957 and lectured at the U.S. State Department's Foreign Service Institute, the Naval War College, military service academies, and several universities. Among his many other books is *Games Nations Play*. Professor Spanier passed away in 2016.